30° E
60°
90°
120°
150°
180°
OCEAN
RUSSIA
NORWAY
SWEDEN
FINLAND
EST.
LATVIA
LITH.
DENMARK
BELARUS
POLAND
GERMANY
CZECH REP.
UKRAINE
MOLDOVA
AUST.
HUNG.
ROMANIA
SLOV.
BOSN. & HERZG.
SERB.
ITALY
BULG.
MONTENEGRO
KOSOVO
ALBANIA
MACED.
GREECE
GEORGIA
ARM.
AZERB.
TURKEY
KAZAKHSTAN
UZBEKISTAN
TURKMENISTAN
KYRGYZSTAN
TAJIKISTAN
MONGOLIA
NORTH KOREA
SOUTH KOREA
JAPAN
CHINA
MALTA
TUNISIA
CYPRUS
LEB.
ISRAEL
SYRIA
IRAQ
IRAN
AFGHANISTAN
JORDAN
KUWAIT
PAKISTAN
BHUTAN
NEPAL
LIBYA
EGYPT
BAHRAIN
QATAR
U.A.E.
SAUDI ARABIA
OMAN
INDIA
BANGLADESH
LAOS
MYANMAR
PACIFIC OCEAN
Northern Mariana Islands (U.S.)
NIGER
CHAD
SUDAN
ERITREA
YEMEN
THAILAND
VIETNAM
DJIBOUTI
CAMBODIA
PHILIPPINES
NIGERIA
CAMEROON
CENT. AFRICAN REPUBLIC
ETHIOPIA
SRI LANKA
PALAU
FEDERATED STATES OF MICRONESIA
MARSHALL ISLANDS
SOMALIA
BRUNEI
MALAYSIA
GUINEA
UGANDA
MALDIVES
SINGAPORE
KIRIBATI
NAURU
GABON
CONGO
DEMOCRATIC REPUBLIC OF THE CONGO
KENYA
RWANDA
BURUNDI
INDONESIA
TANZANIA
SEYCHELLES
PAPUA NEW GUINEA
SOLOMON ISLANDS
TUVALU
COMOROS
INDIAN OCEAN
TIMOR-LESTE
ANGOLA
ZAMBIA
MOZAMBIQUE
ZIMBABWE
MADAGASCAR
MAURITIUS
VANUATU
FIJI ISLANDS
NAMIBIA
BOTSWANA
New Caledonia (FR.)
SOUTH AFRICA
SWAZILAND
AUSTRALIA
LESOTHO
NEW ZEALAND
0 2,000 miles
0 2,000 kilometers
SCALE AT THE EQUATOR
Winkel Tripel Projection, Central Meridian 0°
Kerguelen Islands (FR.)

DRIVES *of a* LIFETIME

500 *of the World's Most Spectacular Trips*

DRIVES *of a* LIFETIME

500 *of the World's Most Spectacular Trips*

INTRODUCTION BY KEITH BELLOWS

EDITOR-IN-CHIEF, *NATIONAL GEOGRAPHIC TRAVELER* MAGAZINE

NATIONAL GEOGRAPHIC

WASHINGTON, D.C.

GUEST
LOADING
ZONE

Contents

Previous Page: In southwestern Italy, the gorgeous blue waters of the Mediterranean are your constant companion as you drive the Amalfi coast road, here curving around a headland in Atrani. Opposite: A canary-yellow classic convertible is parked on Ocean Drive in the art deco district of Miami Beach, Florida.

Introduction

I'm on the Eastern Shore of Maryland, hard by the gray swell of the Chesapeake Bay. Trolling along at only 50 mph (80 km/h) in my green 1972 MGB—with the top down—gives me the luxury of really seeing what passes. I'm on the road again. I love the primal feeling of being out, about, and able to take any route I choose. Motoring from here to there has been a part of my life ever since I remember: trips in the old Rambler from Montreal to Cape Cod while counting state license plates and overnighting in gas stations so somebody could minister to the latest breakdown; spontaneous escapes with buddies from my New Hampshire college to nearby Vermont or far, far away Mexico; retreats with my wife to some quiet place to read, restore, and reconnect; cacophonous excursions with my kids to wherever we think they can be happy; or a solo slip-away to rethink my life. Taking to the tarmac is the way to find yourself, explore new places, and connect with others.

Recently, the road has begun to whisper more insistently to me. An old buddy whom I haven't seen in years came to visit in his restored '57 Chevy. Now middle-aged, he was preparing to drive it across America, from his home in Tennessee to places he would choose as he went. I was jealous, because I understood why he was compelled to do this. Any road trip, whether it be for a day, a week, or longer, can uncork our imaginations and rekindle the wanderlust and curiosity that makes true travel—as opposed to vacationing—so intoxicating. You see the passing parade in a way that allows you to experience life as it is lived. This has happened to me so often, and I can readily unspool the memories. I stop at an antique store in Appalachia and am seduced into a world of handmade quilts, locally crafted fiddles, and—if you ask the right question to the right person—down-home moonshine. I lose myself on a roller-coaster road in New Zealand, and the getting lost is its own dividend (I meet a family that hosts me for two days in their oceanside cottage). In India, on the drive from Agra to Jaipur, I am delayed by demonstrations for seven hours; rather than fume as I would in Los Angeles traffic, I experience the Indians' world of sublime patience as I watch delayed drivers cook at the roadside, play backgammon, and tend to their children. In the Scottish Highlands, I stumble upon a pub and meet a man who invites me to dine at his castle, then takes me fly-fishing the next day at his private salmon run. I drive my favorite highway in America, Highway 101 through Big Sur, and I'm alone with stupefying grand views of ocean and headlands, switchbacks and precipitous drops—which remind me that a drive itself has an ability to entertain and astound.

This book showcases many of the world's greatest drives. It is an invitation to get behind the wheel. To embrace the road and discover a way of life that would otherwise exist beyond your knowing. So put your foot to the pedal and head on out.

Keith Bellows
Editor-in-Chief, National Geographic Traveler *magazine*

Opposite: Travelers along Western Australia's Gibb River Road ford the Pentecost River, with the orange ramparts of the Cockburn Range rising in the background.

CHAPTER 1

OVER HILLS & MOUNTAINS

THIS IS WHAT DRIVING WAS MEANT TO BE: vertiginous, soul-stirring journeys where every turn brings fresh rewards—constantly changing vistas, different permutations of light, rolling meadows, eerie rock formations, waterfalls spilling down rockfaces, tantalizing forest tracks, and remote settlements where life moves to its own rhythm. Some journeys wend their way along peaceful byways. Others are for those who like to test their mettle behind the wheel, featuring hairpin bends, hidden dips, ear-popping gradients, and a chance to look down from a great height on birds of prey swooping far below. The Blue Ridge Parkway evokes the spirit of early settlers setting out to fulfill their American dreams, whereas Colorado's San Juan Skyway offers another vision of the past, climbing into a lost world of prehistoric Puebloan settlements and 19th-century mining towns. An ascent into Costa Rica's cloud forest provides the possibility of a close encounter with that dandy of the tropics, the rainbow-feathered quetzal bird. Across the Pacific, the emerald-hued rice terraces of the Philippines, cut by hand into slopes, rise thousands of feet into the sky.

As Fremont Peak looks out over Island Lake in Wyoming's Wind River Range, it's clear why engineers have taken so much effort to build roads through mountains—to open scenes like this to the masses.

Skyline Drive winds through elegant and tranquil Shenandoah National Park.

VIRGINIA

Spectacular Skyline Drive

Motorists treasure this route, which teeters along the spine of northern Virginia's Blue Ridge in Shenandoah National Park, providing wondrous views of the Shenandoah Valley to the west and rolling foothills to the east.

Heading south from Front Royal on U.S. 340, your first view of the valley that Native Americans purportedly called "Daughter of the Stars" is from Shenandoah Valley Overlook, with its sweeping panorama of the meandering Shenandoah River and Massanutten Mountain. The overlook comes at Mile 2.8 of Skyline Drive, which begins at Shenandoah National Park's northern entrance. Continue along forested Dickey Ridge; 6 miles (10 km) past Dickey Ridge Visitor Center, the road runs through Compton Gap and follows the mountain crest. You can view the river's looping course at Hogback Overlook before taking the snaking road down to Thornton Gap and through Mary's Rock Tunnel, where Tunnel Parking Overlook peers into a hollow that was inhabited by 20 families when the park was established in the 1930s. Just beyond, Hazel Mountain Overlook has views of the park's third highest peak (3,815 feet/ 1,163 m); hikes along the streams and forest paths of Hazel Country begin half a mile (800 m) ahead. Keep a lookout for white-tailed deer, skunks, and barred owls as you wind south around The Pinnacle and Stony Man Peak. You have a good view of Old Rag granite on the mountain's upper peaks at Old Rag View Overlook. Two hikes begin within the next 2 miles (3.5 km). The first runs from Upper Hawksbill Parking to the park's highest peak, the 4,050-foot (1,234 m) Hawksbill Mountain; the second, a steep trail, descends to the cascades of Dark Hollow Falls. Big Meadows is a remnant of the ancient plains that once covered the region. Hazeltop Ridge Overlook has views of the Blue Ridge's smoky peaks, and at Bearfence Mountain Parking you can scramble up a trail to one of the few 360-degree vistas in the park. The drive winds on to Swift Run Gap and crosses the park's southern boundary to end at Rockfish Gap, where a bison path once ran.

FROM: Front Royal, Virginia
TO: Rockfish Gap, Virginia
ROAD: U.S. 340, Skyline Drive
DISTANCE: 105 miles (159 km)
DRIVING TIME: 3 hours
WHEN TO GO: Spring and fall
PLANNING:
www.visitshenandoah.com

VIRGINIA/NORTH CAROLINA

Blue Ridge Parkway

One of the most scenic drives in the U.S., the Blue Ridge Parkway follows on from the Skyline Drive, winding across the heights of the southern Appalachians with endless views of forested hills, farmland, river gorges, and distant mountains.

After a brief climb from Rockfish Gap, the Blue Ridge Parkway sweeps along the narrow, forested spine of the Blue Ridge, soaring above foothills to the east and the Shendandoah Valley to the west. At James River, you reach the parkway's lowest point, before climbing sharply back up to the crest to reach Apple Orchard Mountain, the highest point in Virginia, whose northern red oaks resemble apple trees. Once past the three Peaks of Otter, you enter the Roanoke River Basin and cruise below a series of lofty peaks for the next 30 miles (48 km). South of Roanoke, the scenery turns pastoral as you climb onto the Blue Ridge Plateau.

Continuing south into North Carolina, you approach the soaring mountains and deep valleys of Pisgah National Forest. The Northwest Trading Post, with an array of regional crafts, antiques, and homemade pastries, adds local color. Beyond solitary Mount Jefferson, the route dips into rugged Deep Gap and climbs back up, past the mountain resort of Blowing Rock and 5,964-foot (1,818 m) Grandfather Mountain, the highest peak in the Blue Ridge. Beyond Crabtree Meadows Recreation Area, the parkway begins its last climb on the ridge and, after about 15 miles (24 km), leaves it at Ridge Junction, skirts the Black Mountains, and meanders across the Great Craggy Mountains. Farther on, look for views of Glassmine Falls cascading down Horse Range Ridge. After crossing the French Broad River near Asheville, ascend rocky Pisgah Ledge, with views of Mount Pisgah on the right, and then swing through the Great Balsam Mountains on a twisting, undulating road with views of Cold Mountain and Looking Glass Rock. The parkway reaches its highest point (6,047 feet/1,843 m) at Richland Balsam. For the last 10 miles (16 km), it traverses the Appalachian Mountains, part of the Cherokee Indian Reservation.

FROM: Rockfish Gap, Virginia
TO: Great Smoky Mountains National Park, North Carolina
ROAD: Blue Ridge Parkway
DISTANCE: 469 miles (755 km)
DRIVING TIME: 10.5 hours
WHEN TO GO: Spring through fall
PLANNING: There are no gas stations on the parkway. www.blueridgeparkway.org

Hidden History Four miles (6 km) north of the parkway, on U.S. 25 near Asheville, is the monumental **Biltmore House.** Built by George Washington Vanderbilt in the late 19th century as a country retreat, the 250-room mansion is styled on the Renaissance chateaus of the Loire Valley in France. Allow a day to see the house, farm, and estate winery.

Fall colors along the parkway create a magical drive.

SOUTH CAROLINA

Cherokee Foothills

The Cherokee Foothills Scenic Byway in northern South Carolina runs southwest from Gaffney through the Blue Ridge foothills, past peach orchards, clear lakes, streams filled with darting fish, and country meadows.

First stop is Cowpens National Battlefield—9.5 miles (15 km) west of Gaffney along S.C. 11—where a quiet meadow marks the site of a strategic victory for the colonists during the Revolutionary War. From here, the road begins to rise and fall as the mountains ahead grow ever closer. About 9 miles (14 km) beyond the pretty town of Campobello, the road passes Hogback and Glassy Mountains and enters the beautiful Blue Ridge foothills. Crossing the North and Middle Saluda Rivers, the road passes through Cleveland and continues along the South Saluda River, popular with trout anglers. About 12 miles (19 km) along, you'll spot a 1,200-foot (365 m) precipice, known as Caesar's Head, protruding from the mountainside. You can reach it by taking a 7.5-mile (12 km) detour up dizzying U.S. 276, which offers fantastic views of the Blue Ridge and surrounding states. Back on S.C. 11, drive about 7 miles (11 km) to the quirky village of Aunt Sue's Country Corner, full of craft and food shops. Table Rock State Park, 2 miles (3 km) beyond the village, was revered by the Cherokee Nation as the favored dining spot for the Great Spirit. The park's east gate leads to historic Table Rock Lodge, famous for its fantastic views; the west gate leads to Pinnacle Lake, with trails up the slopes of Pinnacle and Table Rock Mountains. Forested ridges close in on the road and Sassafras Mountain, the state's highest peak, towers 3,554 feet (1,083 m) above the hills. Soon the highway soars above Keowee River and continues to the small town of Walhalla. It then veers south, back into a flat, rural landscape. The final stop is at Lake Hartwell State Recreation Area, which has a pretty shoreline, picnic tables, boating, and a nature trail.

Stay a While Shortly after crossing the Keowee River, you can turn onto Rte. 37-25 for 5 miles (8 km) to **Devils Fork State Park** on the shores of mountain-ringed Lake Jocassee. The lake is popular for trout fishing and scuba diving, or you can take a boat ride to see the many waterfalls that feed the lake. Hiking and nature trails offer good opportunities to enjoy the park's spring flowers and fall foliage. The park has a campground and holiday cabins.

FROM: Gaffney, South Carolina
TO: Lake Hartwell State Recreation Area, South Carolina
ROADS: S.C 11, U.S. 276
DISTANCE: 112 miles (180 km)
DRIVING TIME: 3 hours
WHEN TO GO: Peach bloom peaks in May, the fall foliage in mid-October.
PLANNING: The byway makes a good alternative to I-85 if you're not in a hurry.
www.discoversouthcarolina.com

A hiking trail skirts the shoreline of one of the lakes at Table Rock State Park.

In spring, colorful blooms along the roadside enhance the extensive views from Newfound Gap Road.

TENNESSEE/NORTH CAROLINA

Newfound Gap Road

From hardwood forests to alpine spruce and fir, finely colored by more than 1,500 different species of flowering plants, this road through a gap in the Appalachian Mountains in eastern Tennessee is a path through a botanical paradise.

Set in Great Smoky Mountains National Park, this beautiful road sets off from the Sugarlands Visitor Center through a forest of red maples, white oaks, tulip trees, and magnolias. Massive Mount LeConte comes into view after about 2 miles (3 km) as the road begins to ascend, bringing the twin peaks of Chimney Tops into sight. The road curves dramatically here, and northern hardwoods dominate the slopes. To negotiate the complex geography of the mountains, the route goes through a tunnel and then loops up, around, and over itself. Anakeesta Ridge, about 8 miles (13 km) farther on, is characterized by rocky outcrops, Fraser fir, and red spruce. From sky-high Morton Overlook, you can peer down into Sugarlands Valley or up at the notch in the State Line Range, where Newfound Gap links Tennessee and North Carolina. Even better views await around the corner, from Newfound Gap Overlook, at 5,048 feet (1,539 m) the road's highest point. You can take a 7-mile (11 km) detour here, along a spur road to Clingmans Dome, the highest peak in the park (this road is closed in winter). From the parking lot at the peak, you can take a short walk to a lookout tower offering 360-degree views of the park's main summits. Otherwise, continue downhill on the Newfound Gap Road, passing the Oconaluftee Valley Overlook on Thomas Divide ridge. The road then switches back downhill, with breathtaking views of the Smoky Mountains. Once past Webb Overlook, you delve into deciduous forest and follow the Oconaluftee River toward Mingus Mill, a working mill built in 1886. At the Oconaluftee Visitor Center, you can visit Mountain Farm Museum, which explains the life of a pioneer in the early days of the U.S.

FROM: Sugarlands Visitor Center, Tennessee
TO: Oconaluftee Visitor Center, North Carolina
ROAD: Newfound Gap Road
DISTANCE: 40 miles (64 km)
DRIVING TIME: 1 hour
WHEN TO GO: Blooms are best from mid-March through July.
PLANNING: www.gov.nps

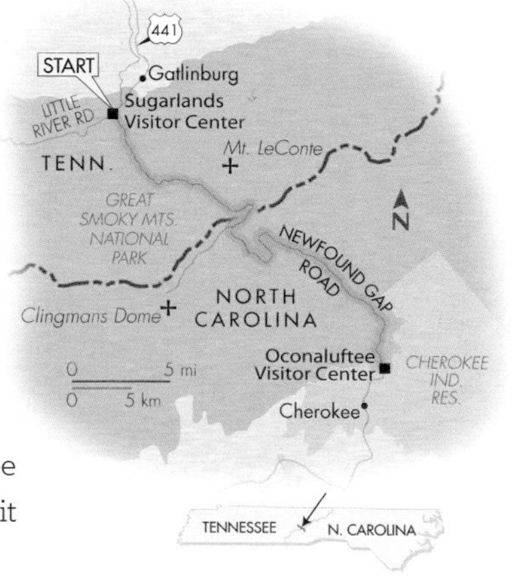

MISSOURI/ARKANSAS

Crowley's Ridge Parkway

Rising more than 150 feet (46 m) above the surrounding plains, this thin strip of upland between the Ohio and Mississippi Rivers is a distinctive landmark. The drive runs from southeastern Missouri to eastern Arkansas along the top of the ridge.

Only 14 miles (23 km) of the parkway lie in Missouri, but during this brief section on U.S. 62 from Malden, you can see the unique geology of Crowley's Ridge. Start by taking a short loop hiking trail through Morris State Park to view some of the area's unusual plants, such as tulip-poplar, American beech, and cucumber trees. After crossing the St. Francis River into Arkansas, on Ark. 141, you soon enter the town of St. Francis, near Chalk Bluff Battlefield Park (see Excursion). Ernest Hemingway visited the small town of Piggott, just along the parkway, several times between 1927 and 1940, and wrote most of *A Farewell to Arms* here at his second wife's family home. Continue along the ridge on Ark. 135, through pastures and croplands and the small city of Paragould to reach Crowley's Ridge State Park, where you can explore the local scenery on a network of hiking trails or take a rest beside one of the pretty lakes. The route rejoins Ark. 141, and 20 miles (32 km) farther on reaches Jonesboro, the largest city on the ridge and home to Arkansas State University, whose museum has exhibits on paleontology and Native American and pioneer history, as well as a fine glassware and ceramics collection. Visit Village Creek State Park, down Ark. 163 and 284, for a tour of the area's natural history and to tackle the hiking and horseriding trails around woodland, streams, and lakes. It was through here, in 1829, that the Creek, Chickasaw, and Cherokee Nations were marched away from their homes in the East to new Indian Territories farther west, along the Arkansas section of what became known as the Trail of Tears (now called the Military Road Trail). The parkway continues south on Ark. 1 to Marianna and Ark. 44 to the old river port of Helena-West-Helena.

Excursion History-lovers can take a short detour to the **Chalk Bluff Battlefield Park,** one of the best-preserved sites in the area, 3 miles (4.8 km) northwest of St. Francis. During the Civil War, Confederate and Union armies fought here repeatedly for control of the strategic St. Francis River crossing, which marks the border between Missouri and Arkansas. The short Chalk Bluff Hiking Trail around the preserved portion of the battlefield has markers and interpretive panels along the way.

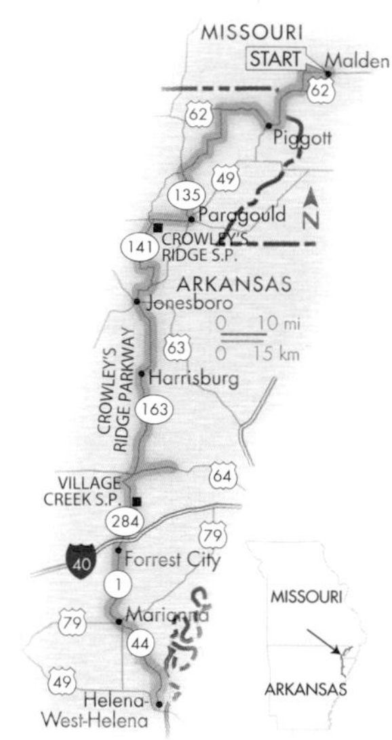

FROM: Malden, Missouri
TO: Helena-West-Helena, Arkansas
ROADS: U.S. 62, Ark. 141, 135, 163, 284, 1, 44, minor connecting roads
DISTANCE: 212 miles (341 km)
DRIVING TIME: 5.5 hours
WHEN TO GO: Year-round
PLANNING: www.mostateparks.com

Piggott's Hemingway-Pfeiffer Museum is the family home of Pauline Pfeiffer, Ernest Hemingway's second wife.

The road swoops through Ouachita National Forest, the largest national forest in the American South.

Highlights

- Just beyond Winding Stair Mountain, you can stop and admire views of the Poteau River Valley, Cedar Lake, and Lake Wister from the **Emerald Vista Overlook.**
- The **Robert S. Kerr Arboretum,** about midway along the drive, has exhibits on forest environments as well as three interpretive trails through pine and hardwood forests.
- **Rich Mountain Fire Tower** was built in 1952 to keep a watchful eye on Ouachita National Forest. The views from the top are among the most spectacular in the park.

OKLAHOMA/ARKANSAS

Talimena Scenic Highway

This short road across the **Oklahoma/Arkansas** border was built in the 1960s to give access to the wonderful views of the **Ouachita Mountains**—a favorite hunting spot of the Choctaw Indians and still full of wildlife.

Ouachita is a Native American word meaning "good hunting grounds," and the Ouachita National Forest still holds plentiful deer, squirrel, and a host of other wildlife. The byway starts at the forest visitor center, 7 miles (11 km) northeast of Talihina on Okla. 1. Just beyond the visitor center is Choctaw Vista, which overlooks the dark blue hills and valleys through which the Choctaw traveled on their way west from the Mississippi on the Trail of Tears following the 1830 Indian Removal Act. The road cuts through a forest of shortleaf pine and scrub oak, with prairie grasses such as little bluestem covering the ground. Panorama Vista, about 5 miles (8 km) into the forest, has sweeping views of mountains and the small farming villages of the Holson Valley. The soaring updrafts here attract hang-gliding enthusiasts as well as golden eagles, vultures, and hawks. Past Horse Thief Springs (Mile 16), the road snakes back and forth down Winding Stair Mountain (see Highlights), providing constantly shifting views, and continues to Robert S. Kerr Arboretum and Nature Center (Mile 23) (see Highlights). The byway now follows the crest of Rich Mountain for several miles through dwarf oaks stunted by ice storms and wind. Entering Arkansas, the road becomes Ark. 88 and leads into Queen Wilhelmina State Park, which has dramatic views of Rich Mountain's crest. Three miles (5 km) east of the park, you reach Rich Mountain Fire Tower (see Highlights), which at 2,681 feet (817 m) is the highest point on the route. The drive ends at the visitor information center in Mena, an old timber, railroad, and cattle town.

FROM: Talihina, Oklahoma
TO: Mena, Arkansas
ROADS: Okla. 1/U.S. 271, Ark. 88
DISTANCE: 54 miles (87 km)
DRIVING TIME: 1 to 2 hours
WHEN TO GO: Spring bloom occurs in April and May; fall foliage peaks from mid-October through early November.
PLANNING: www.arkansasstateparks.com

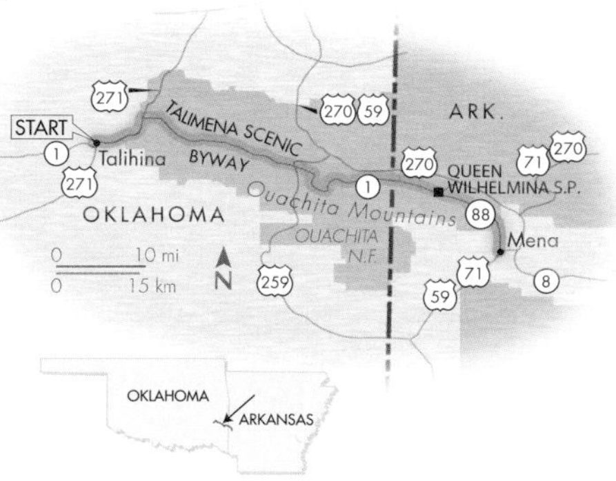

COLORADO

San Juan Skyway

The skyway follows a meandering course across southern Colorado's San Juan Mountains, past old mining towns and through the desert to Mesa Verde National Park, reaching a height of more than 10,000 feet (3,048 m) three times on its journey through the sky.

Ranchers drive cattle along Girl Scout Road near the old railroad and ranching town of Ridgway.

Highlights

- **San Juan County Historical Museum** in Silverton tells the story of the region's railroad and mining past.
- **Mesa Verde National Park** protects the ruins of ancient Puebloan villages. Rangers lead tours of the major buildings. Views from the mesa are extraordinary.
- South of Dolores, make a 10-minute detour west onto Colo. 184 from Colo. 145 for the **Anasazi Heritage Center,** which explains the evolution of the ancient Puebloans. Self-guided trails lead to two ruins.

The Uncompahgre Valley narrows below mountains that rise at least 6,000 feet (1,829 m) above the river as U.S. 550 travels southeast from Ridgway, bouncing from side to side between red-rock cliffs and forested foothills. Look around the historic district of the mountain town of Ouray, which dates from the 1880s gold- and silver-mining boom, before continuing into the mountains. Waterfalls spill from Uncompahgre Gorge to the right of the road as Abrams Mountain looms overhead. After a series of hairpin bends, you are confronted by a group of vivid peaks, Red Mountain Nos. 1, 2, and 3, whose slopes are streaked with red and orange gravel. The road curves around them, alongside a meadow and past old shacks and gravel heaps, remnants of the area's mining past, before ascending to the 11,075-foot (3,375 m) Red Mountain Pass and descending to cross the broad Animas River Valley. At the junction with Colo. 110, turn left to Silverton (see Highlights), where you might come across the Durango & Silverton Narrow Gauge Railroad steaming into view.

Back on U.S. 550, climb Sultan Mountain to Molas Pass for fine views of the West Needle Mountains and Grenadier Range rising over tiny Molas Lake. The road winds for 7 miles (11 km) to Coal Bank Pass before leaving the mountains for plateau and canyon country. Hermosa Cliffs soon appear above a lush canyon of grass and hayfields. From the former mining town of Durango, follow U.S. 160 west through minor canyons and mesas as La Plata Mountains rise to the north over a dark forest. After visiting Mesa Verde National Park (see Highlights), continue along U.S. 160 toward Cortez, then follow Colo. 145 north beside the river to Dolores (see Highlights), back into the San Juan Mountains. After the incredible views of San Juan Crest at 10,222-foot (3,116 m) Lizard Head Pass, glide across a meadow toward Ophir Needles, past Trout Lake and huge, glaciated valleys. Turn right at the T-junction to Telluride, with its magnificent Victorian downtown district and 365-foot (111 m) Bridal Veil Falls. You can take a ride on the gondola that links Telluride with the ski area of Mountain Village to enjoy some outstanding mountain views. From Telluride, Colo. 145 and the San Miguel River head through a sandstone-cliff canyon to Placerville. Turn right on Colo. 62 for 11 miles (18 km) to the Dallas Divide and return to Ridgway.

FROM: Loop route from Ridgway, Colorado
ROADS: U.S. 550, Colo. 110, U.S. 160, Colo. 145, 62
DISTANCE: 233 miles (375 km)
DRIVING TIME: 5 hours
WHEN TO GO: Spring through fall
PLANNING: The section from Silverton to Ouray is also known as the Million Dollar Highway. www.coloradobyways.org

OPPOSITE: At 14,150 feet (4,313 m) high, Mount Sneffels dominates the beautiful scenery around Ridgway.

The surrounding hills are reflected in the still waters of tree-fringed Grand Lake.

COLORADO

Trail Ridge Road

The Trail Ridge Road through Rocky Mountains National Park in northern Colorado climbs well above the treeline, bringing views of high peaks, deep valleys, and alpine plateaus, sometimes against the dramatic backdrop of an approaching thunderstorm.

FROM: Estes Park, Colorado
TO: Granby, Colorado
ROAD: U.S. 34/Trail Ridge Road
DISTANCE: 63 miles (101 km)
DRIVING TIME: 2 hours
WHEN TO GO: Open from late May to mid-October (weather permitting)
PLANNING: Be prepared for crowds between mid-June and mid-August. www.nps.gov/romo

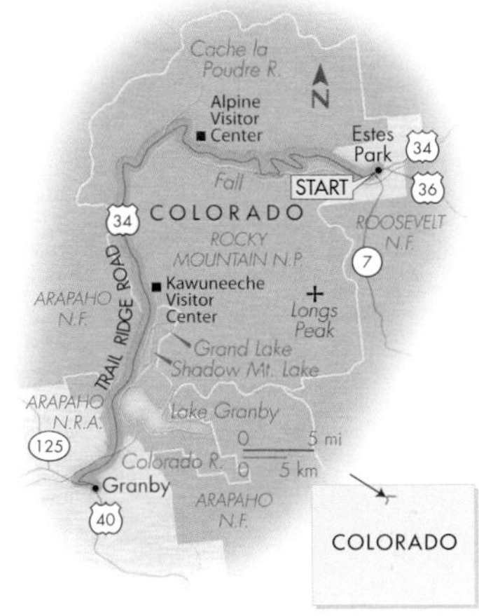

Beneath the summit of Longs Peak in Estes Park, Trail Ridge Road winds west along the Fall River, past wooded ridges and granite domes, toward Sheep Lakes in Horseshoe Park, where bighorn sheep, mule deer, and, especially in fall, elk come to graze. Follow the road through Horseshoe Park, up the slope to Deer Ridge Junction, and turn right, quickly ascending into a forest of Engelmann spruce, subalpine fir, and limber pine. At the peak of Many Parks Curve, a boardwalk offers expansive views of the long, glaciated basins of Moraine Park and Horseshoe Park. Back on the road, continue skyward past trees struggling to survive on the rocky ground. Beyond Rainbow Curve, the road passes a knife-edged ridgeline and enters wide, rolling alpine tundra. Stop at Forest Canyon Overlook and take the footpath down to the viewing platform, which identifies the peaks that stretch away from you for more than 20 miles (32 km). The road reaches its highest point between Lava Cliffs and Gore Range Overlook, before descending quickly to the hairpin bend at Medicine Bow Curve, which overlooks the rocky Medicine Bow Mountains, 20 miles (32 km) in the distance, and the silvery headwaters of the Cache la Poudre River below.

As you twist down through forest, you approach pine-ringed Poudre Lake. Two miles (3 km) farther on is Fairview Curve, with views of the Never Summer Mountains and the wide Kawuneeche Valley, with the Colorado River in the distance. Follow the switchbacks to the valley floor, which is carpeted with meadows. At the mountain-ringed Grand Lake, the largest natural lake in Colorado, you can enjoy a drink or meal at the historic Grand Lake Lodge. Continue south to Shadow Mountain Lake and Lake Granby, which has picnic areas, campgrounds, and boating ramps. The road continues for another 5 miles (8 km) to Granby, a former logging community, now popular with outdoor-loving vacationers.

NEBRASKA

Pine Ridge Country

In this rugged corner of northwestern Nebraska, scenery seems to change from mile to mile as hilly farm and ranch land mingle with prairie, high buttes and ridges, steep gullies, and clear streams.

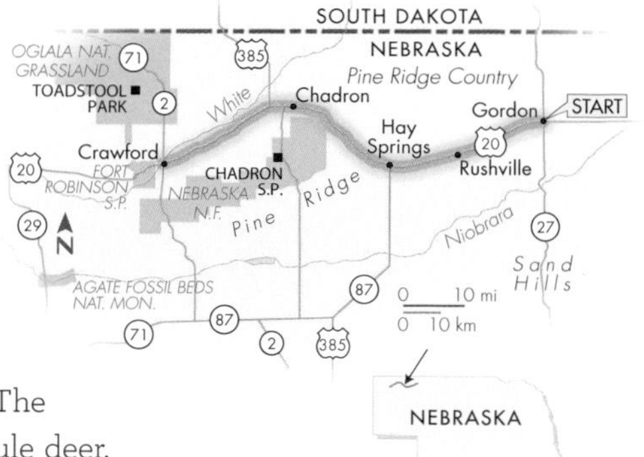

From the old frontier town of Gordon, a small community in Nebraska's rural heart, drive west on U.S. 20 along the western reaches of the desolate grassy desert known as Sand Hills, which lies 10 miles (16 km) to the south and east; ahead are flat plains where trees and cattle are scarce. Drive through the isolated towns of Rushville and Hay Springs, and on to the furrowed uplands of Pine Ridge, a narrow, 100-mile (160 km) long escarpment that defines the edge of Nebraska's High Plains. The forested hills of ponderosa pine and deciduous trees are home to bighorn sheep, elk, mule deer, and wild turkeys. Across the ridge, the old fur-trading town of Chadron has a row of handsome, two-story, Western-style buildings along Main Street. A 10-mile (16 km) detour to the south of town on U.S. 385 takes you to Chadron State Park, an excellent stop for horseback riding, swimming, and hiking. Back on U.S. 20, continue west along the White River—to the north you can see rolling hills, to the south the first buttes of the Badlands. Crawford (see Excursion), 24 miles (39 km) farther on, was an important town in the old West and is now known chiefly for Fort Robinson State Park. The fort itself dates from the Indian Wars of the 1870s—Chief Crazy Horse, of Little Bighorn fame, was killed here. During World War II, the fort housed German prisoners. Fifteen miles (24 km) north of Crawford on Nebr. 2, you can visit Oglala National Grassland, a popular haunt for camping and hunting, as well as Toadstool Park, named for its strange, mushroom-shaped rocky outcrops.

FROM: Gordon, Nebraska
TO: Crawford, Nebraska
ROAD: U.S. 20, 385, Nebr. 2
DISTANCE: 67 miles (108 km)
DRIVING TIME: 1.5 hours
WHEN TO GO: Spring through fall
PLANNING: www.nebraskahighcountry.com

Excursion Twenty-three miles (37 km) southwest of Crawford is **Agate Fossil Beds National Monument,** where you can follow a 2-mile (3 km) walk around the fossilized remains of mammals that lived between 13 and 25 million years ago. The site is best known for the surviving evidence of species such as the Moropus—part horse, part giraffe, and part tapir—and the Menoceras, a pony-sized rhinoceros. The Cook Collection in the museum includes more than 500 unique Native American artifacts collected by Captain James Cook, owner of the Agate Springs Cattle Ranch in the late 19th century.

Around Chadron, prairie grasslands have been turned into hayfields that extend to the horizon.

WYOMING

Centennial Scenic Byway

The long, undulating, doglegging Centennial Scenic Byway winds through the mountains and river valleys of the Rockies in northwestern Wyoming, passing the Tetons, the Snake River, and the Wind River Range along the way.

Fremont Peak and Island Lake, in the Wind River Range, can be reached via hiking trails north of Pinedale.

Highlights

- The **Wind River Historical Center** in Dubois has displays on the pioneer, archaeological, and natural history of the region.
- The **National Elk Refuge** in the town of Jackson is home to some 10,000 elk every winter, viewable by a sleigh ride from the refuge headquarters.
- The **National Museum of Wildlife Art**, situated 2.5 miles (4 km) north of Jackson, has fine wildlife and nature displays.
- Pinedale's **Museum of the Mountain Man** explores the history of the fur-trappers who roamed this region.

Rise with the cowboys of Dubois (see Highlights) to catch a glimpse of the morning sun on the Teton Mountains. Climb from the town past the eastern flank of the Wind River Range on U.S. 26, with the Wind River meandering alongside you. After around 20 miles (32 km), Breccia Cliffs and Pinnacle Buttes burst into view above the tree line. Stop at Falls Campground to explore the waterfall before continuing on U.S. 26 up a steep incline forested with Engelmann spruce, silvery-barked subalpine fir, and lodgepoll pine. Moose, elk, and bears visit the meadows. After crossing Togwotee Pass, descend to Teton Range Overlook to gaze at Wyoming's best-known mountains. U.S 26 now slopes down to the floodplain of Buffalo Fork River, soon entering Grand Teton National Park. At Moran Junction turn south through wetlands inhabited by moose, elk, and bison and across gentle terrain toward Snake River Overlook, which provides a classic view of 13,770-foot (4,197 m) high Grand Teton and its neighboring peaks. Pass through the valley of Jackson Hole and in another 10 miles (16 km) you reach the tourist mecca of Jackson (see Highlights), with its galleries, restaurants, bars, and famous ski resorts. Seven miles (11 km) on, follow the Snake River to Hoback Junction, where the Hoback River joins the Snake to rush into the the Snake River Canyon. Drive up Hoback Canyon on U.S. 189/191, dropping out of the mountains past Bondurant and onto the flatlands of Green River Valley, with the ancient Wind River Range coming into view. Take a short detour north to watch the sun set at Fremont Lake, stretched out below the Winds. U.S. 189/191 continues into nearby Pinedale and the Museum of the Mountain Man (see Highlights).

Excursion At Moran Junction you can take the **Teton Park Drive,** which runs for 25 miles (40 km) through the heart of the magnificent Teton Mountains. Oxbow Bend Turnout has classic views of Mount Moran and the Snake River. At Jackson Lake Junction, you can turn onto Signal Mountain Road and drive to the summit of Signal Mountain, with grand views of the Tetons. When you reach North Jenny Lake Junction, follow the loop road to Cathedral Group Turnout, with close-up views of Mount Owen, Teewinot Mountain, and Grand Teton. The drive rejoins the Centennial Scenic Byway at Moose Junction.

OPPOSITE: A moose feeds on vegetation in the Snake River, with Mount Moran in the distance.

FROM: Dubois, Wyoming
TO: Pinedale, Wyoming
ROADS: U.S. 26/Colo. 287, U.S. 189/191
DISTANCE: 162 miles (261 km)
DRIVING TIME: 4 hours
WHEN TO GO: Spring through fall
PLANNING: Grand Teton National Park has almost 200 miles (320 km) of hiking trails. www.wyomingtourism.org

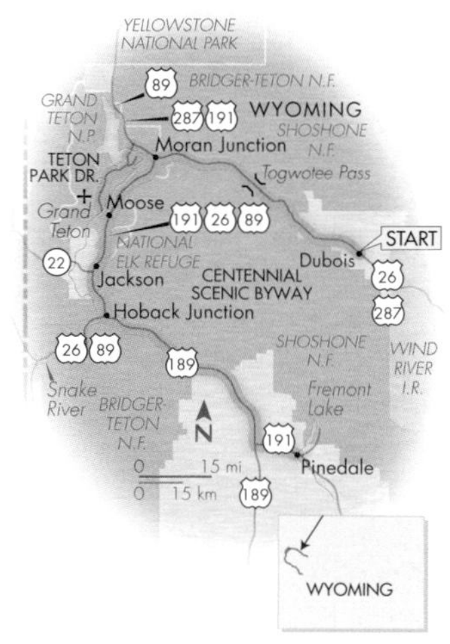

MONTANA/WYOMING

Beartooth Highway

Southern Montana's foothills cower beneath the black mass of the Beartooth Plateau, whose sharpened peaks prick the sky. The drive meanders across the plateau and through the varied Yellowstone region.

Following Rock Creek from Montana's ranching and mining town of Red Lodge, the Beartooth All-American Road passes grassy hills that soon develop into forested mountains and climbs toward the 1,800-foot (550 m) cliffs that enclose the valley head. The next 5 miles (8 km) include dramatic switchbacks that culminate at Vista Point (9,200 feet/2,804 m), where you can take a short path to a promontory with views across Rock Creek Canyon and Hellroaring Plateau. Back on the road, trees gradually give way to alpine tundra. The route cuts back to the rim of the canyon, and narrow turnouts provide views of glacial lakes, including Twin Lakes 1,000 feet (305 m) below. In the Beartooth Pass ski area, you can see the jagged peaks of the Absaroka Range breaking the southwest horizon. Continue through wildflower meadows to the 10,947-foot (3,337 m) high Beartooth Pass, where only marmots, squirrels, and mountain goats survive year-round. From here, the road descends through scattered islands of pine and spruce, wildflowers, and hundreds of small lakes. As you approach the turnoff to Island Lake campground, the Absaroka's 11,708-foot (3,569 m) Pilot Peak and 11,313-foot (3,448 m) Index Peak swing into view. Continuing your descent through a forest of lodgepole and whitebark pines toward Beartooth Butte, you pass a great picnic spot at Beartooth Lake, and as the road breaks out of the trees, look across the canyon to your left to see the cascading Beartooth Falls. The road follows the flank of the plateau to a bridge over silvery Lake Creek. From Crazy Creek Campground the road picks up Clarks Fork River and passes through the old mining camp of Cooke City to reach the northeast entrance to outstanding Yellowstone National Park.

Excursion The **Chief Joseph Scenic Highway** follows part of the route taken by the Nez Perce on their journey from Oregon under Chief Joseph. The 46-mile (74 km) drive follows Wyo. 296 along the northeastern edge of Yellowstone National Park between Cooke City and Cody, Wyoming, with stunning views of Beartooth Peak and the Yellowstone River. A few miles north of Cody, the road crosses Sunlight Creek Bridge, which spans the sheer cliffs of Sunlight Gorge.

FROM: Red Lodge, Montana
TO: Yellowstone National Park northeast entrance, Wyoming
ROAD: U.S. 212/ Beartooth All-American Road
DISTANCE: 69 miles (111 km)
DRIVING TIME: 2 to 3 hours
WHEN TO GO: The route is open from Memorial Day weekend to October—the exact opening and closing dates depend on the weather. Aspens are glorious in late September.
PLANNING: www.beartoothhighway.com

Granite outcrops, clumps of firs, and small pools near Island Lake in the Absaroka Range

The Boise Basin Museum in Idaho City tells the history of this gold rush town.

IDAHO

Sawtooth & Ponderosa Pine

This spectacular drive, a combination of two scenic byways through central Idaho's wilderness area, ascends from the desert floor around Boise, the state capital, into the heights of the Sawtooth Range, before winding back down to the volcanic plain below.

FROM: Boise, Idaho
TO: Shoshone, Idaho
ROADS: Idaho 21/Ponderosa Pine Scenic Byway, Idaho 75/ Sawtooth Drive
DISTANCE: 246 miles (396 km)
DRIVING TIME: 6 hours
WHEN TO GO: Year-round
PLANNING: Winter weather can be severe. www.idahobyways.gov

Climbing into the brown hills above Boise, the Ponderosa Pine Scenic Byway (Idaho 21) follows the Boise River through a twisting canyon and into thick forest. As the road approaches the old mining town of Idaho City, you can see heaps of cobblestones, leavings from the 1860s goldrush, scattered around. Idaho 21 continues climbing to Mores Creek Summit. Ten miles (16 km) farther on you enter Lowman Burn, where roadside signs chart the impact of the wildfires of 1989—one such sign, a few minutes past Lowman village, overlooks Kirkham Hot Springs, where the South Fork Payette River flows through a granite chasm. After 24 miles (39 km), the road follows the South Fork through a ponderosa pine forest to reach snowcapped Banner Summit, then passes broad meadows—ringed by a forest that is home to elk, deer, and hawks—before the Sawtooth Range bursts into view.

At Stanley, turn right onto Idaho 75, the start of the Sawtooth Drive, and follow the Salmon River through Sawtooth Valley, home to peaks that are more than 10,000 feet (3,048 m) high. Many of them lie within the Sawtooth Wilderness, an enticing landscape for day hikes. The biggest lake in the area, Redfish Lake, is lined with beaches set against pine forests and imposing mountains—follow signs off the main road. Back on Idaho 75, continue past Sawtooth City and Vienna, both old mining towns, and up to Galena Overlook. Soon you top Galena Summit and descend into Big Wood River Valley, with the Boulder Mountains rising to your left. A mile (1.6 km) beyond the sign to Magic Dam are the Shoshone Ice Caves, an ice-filled lava tube, and another 8 miles (13 km) brings you to enormous underground tunnels at Mammoth Cave. The drive ends in the agricultural town of Shoshone.

THE TOP

10 Into the Action

However much you love your car, you'll still want to get into the thrilling world outside. Here are ten of the best action destinations in the U.S.A.

1 Route to Riding, Vermont

Vermont's ski towns are a summer paradise for equestrians. Begin near Rutland and Killington, spending a few days on a Green Mountain riding getaway with cool summer mornings and mountains veiled in fog rather than snow, then drive an hour south on Rte. 7 to watch professional riders at the six-week-long Summer Festival Horse Show in East Dorset.

PLANNING: Vermont also has sightseeing and shopping to offer in its charming New England towns. *www.vt-summerfestival.com*

2 Old Canada Road Scenic Byway, Maine

For 78 scenic miles (126 km) in western Maine, Old Canada Road follows Kennebec River, home to populations of trout and salmon, and ideal for white-water rafting. Follow U.S. 201, go west on Falls Road, and reach a haven for any angler. Here, the fish-filled water flows past the site of Benedict Arnold's 1775 Revolutionary War camp.

PLANNING: For information on angler's permits and fishing spots, visit *www.maine.gov*.

3 Chesapeake Bay, Maryland

Starting from the expansive farmland and small towns of the Eastern Shore, cross the towering Chesapeake Bay Bridge and follow Rte. 50 toward historic Annapolis. Stop to admire the view at Sandy Point State Park just across the bridge, and then continue to exit 24B to reach the Annapolis docks and boating heaven.

PLANNING: Best in summer. You can hire a boat or use one of the public launches listed on *www.visitannapolis.org*.

4 Lake Placid, New York

The five-hour drive along the Adirondack Northway (Rte. 87) moves from New York City's gleaming towers to Lake Placid, a town that has hosted the Winter Olympics twice. Drive through Albany and Saratoga Springs, and stop in Lake George to hike up Black Mountain. At the summit are views of the Hudson River and Lake Champlain.

PLANNING: Lake Placid is a year-round outdoors town with everything from horseback riding to winter ice climbing. *www.lakeplacid.com*

5 Savannah River Scenic Byway, South Carolina

For a full day of fishing and water sports on three different lakes, begin at J. Strom Thurmond Lake with an early-morning cast for largemouth bass. Then, from Clarks Hill, drive 110 miles (177 km) to Oakway through Sumter National Forest, stopping at Richard B. Russell Lake in Calhoun Falls State Recreation Area, and finally Hartwell Lake in Sadler's Creek Recreation Area.

PLANNING: Each park has its own admission fee. *www.southcarolinaparks.com*

6 A1A Scenic and Historic Coastal Byway, Florida

Start at the World Golf Hall of Fame in St. Augustine and travel along the Atlantic Ocean and Intercoastal Waterway. Keep an eye out for wildlife along the route as the area is home to 50 endangered species. Before or after a day of golf, you can also make a stop at the PGA Tour's national headquarters in Ponte Vedra Beach and play the infamous hole 17 at the Stadium course at TPC Sawgrass.

PLANNING: Visit in early May to watch one of the tour's most famous golf events, the Tournament Player's Championship. *www.scenica1a.org*

Opposite: Maine's Kennebec River is a white-water dream for enthusiastic kayakers and rafters.

7 Kettle Moraine Scenic Drive, Wisconsin

The Kettle Moraine Scenic Drive traverses 120 miles (193 km) of glacier-molded rock and swirling geological formations clad in thick woods—a perfect backdrop to outdoor pursuits such as mountain biking. Conclude the drive at Long Lake Recreation Area to swim or canoe in glacial lakes, or take hiking trails through the Moraines.

PLANNING: In winter sections of the drive can be dangerous. *www.dnr.wi.gov*

8 Payette River Scenic Byway, Idaho

From the suburbs of Eagle, Idaho 55 takes you north to Horseshoe Bend, where you begin to wind along 80 miles (130 km) of the Payette River. Rafters and kayakers dot the streams. After 33 miles (53 km), the historic Rainbow Bridge takes you over the Payette and toward excellent fishing at Lake Cascade.

PLANNING: For further adventures, visit nearby Ponderosa State Park. *www.idahobyways.gov*

9 Cascade Lakes Scenic Byway, Oregon

Enjoy volcanoes, streams, forest, and wildflowers as you drive 83 miles (134 km) from Bend to Sunriver, along Oreg. 372 and Country Roads 46 and 42. After Deschutes, drive to Mount Bachelor Ski and Summer Resort and take a chairlift to the summit of the volcano. The road continues past Elk Lake and Hosmer Lake—both excellent for fishing and boating.

PLANNING: Portions of the route are closed in winter. *www.traveloregon.com*

10 Banning Idyllwild Panoramic Highway, California

California's scenic Rte. 243 connects I-10 and Rte. 74 through the peaks of Mount San Jacinto State Park. The park is one of five in California that comprise the Pacific Crest Trail stretching from Mexico to Canada. The granite peaks all along the drive and in Idyllwild are excellent for climbing and hiking.

PLANNING: The drive is 30 miles (48 km) long. If you plan to go climbing, make sure you follow safety advice and take the correct equipment. *www.parks.ca.gov*

NEW MEXICO/TEXAS

Guadalupe Drive

In the deserts of southern New Mexico, beauty and history combine with some of the country's most fascinating spots, such as the old Western outlaw town of Lincoln, set against the dramatic escarpments of the Guadalupe Mountains.

The dunes of White Sands National Monument appear opalescent at sunrise.

Just east of 5,719-foot (1,743 m) San Agustin Pass, and overlooked by the needle-like spires of the Organ Mountains, lies the tranquil Aguirre Springs Recreation Area. The 5.5-mile (8.8 km) entrance road winds around granite pillars and a rock garden to reach this high desert oasis—a perfect picnic spot.

From Aguirre Springs, head northeast on U.S. 70, flanked on the west by what a creative mind might imagine were 60-foot (18 m) waves on a snow-white sea. White Sands National Monument, at around 300 square miles (777 km^2), is the world's largest gypsum dune system, created by crystals blown in from the dry bed of nearby Lake Lucero. Here, in 1945, the world's first atomic bomb was detonated with a huge rumble and an eerie light that inaugurated the nuclear age. The filled-in crater is still off-limits, except for the first Saturdays of April and October. The area around the dunes is now a testing-ground for missiles, and the whole park is occasionally closed to the public. You can take the 16-mile (26 km) Dunes Drive through the desert (see page 151).

Continue northeast on U.S. 70 to Alamogordo (see Highlights), whose Holloman Air Force Base played a crucial role in America's space program. Following U.S. 54 north from Alamogordo, look for an old ranch road heading east to the Three Rivers Petroglyph Site, where more than 500 images of birds, humans, animals, and fish were carved into the rock more than 1,000 years ago by the Jornada Mogollon people.

> "Walk five miles . . . on the Alkali Flat Trail [in White Sands] to find a ready-made moonscape, just you and bleached earless lizards surrounded by miles of pure white gypsum dunes."
>
> -ROBERT EARLE HOWELLS
> NATIONAL GEOGRAPHIC WRITER

Just west of Carrizozo, the Valley of Fires is one of the youngest lava deposits in the lower 48 states. About 1,500 years ago the flow erupted from several volcanoes in the area, solidifying into a 44-mile (71 km) long scar. For a good picnic spot, head east on U.S. 380 to Smokey Bear Historical Park, where the gardens re-create New Mexico's half-dozen biological life zones. Ten miles (16 km) farther along, U.S. 380 brings you to Lincoln State Monument, a town preserved from the gun-toting 1870s, when Billy the Kid participated in an orgy of violence known as the Lincoln County Wars and escaped from the courthouse by killing his two guards. The courthouse is now home to a museum.

Roswell, an old Western town, is best known for alleged alien visitations (see sidebar this page). After visiting the Historic District, centered on Main and Second Street, stop at the Roswell Museum and Art Center, with its reproduction of the workshop of rocket-pioneer Robert Goddard, who tested his prototypes in the city from 1930 to 1941. A short way east of Roswell is Bitter Lake National Wildlife Refuge. More than

Claims of U.F.O. Sightings

In 1947, a top-secret U.S. government air balloon crashed in the desert outside Roswell, according to the U.S. government at least. Some 30 years later, however, U.F.O. researchers claimed to have gathered evidence that the vehicle was in fact a spacecraft, that alien bodies had been recovered from the site, and that the government was engaged in a major cover-up. The incident has become the world's most famous "alien visitation" and put Roswell on the map, with the town holding an annual U.F.O. Festival, at which people dress up in alien costumes, attend conferences, and enjoy a parade.

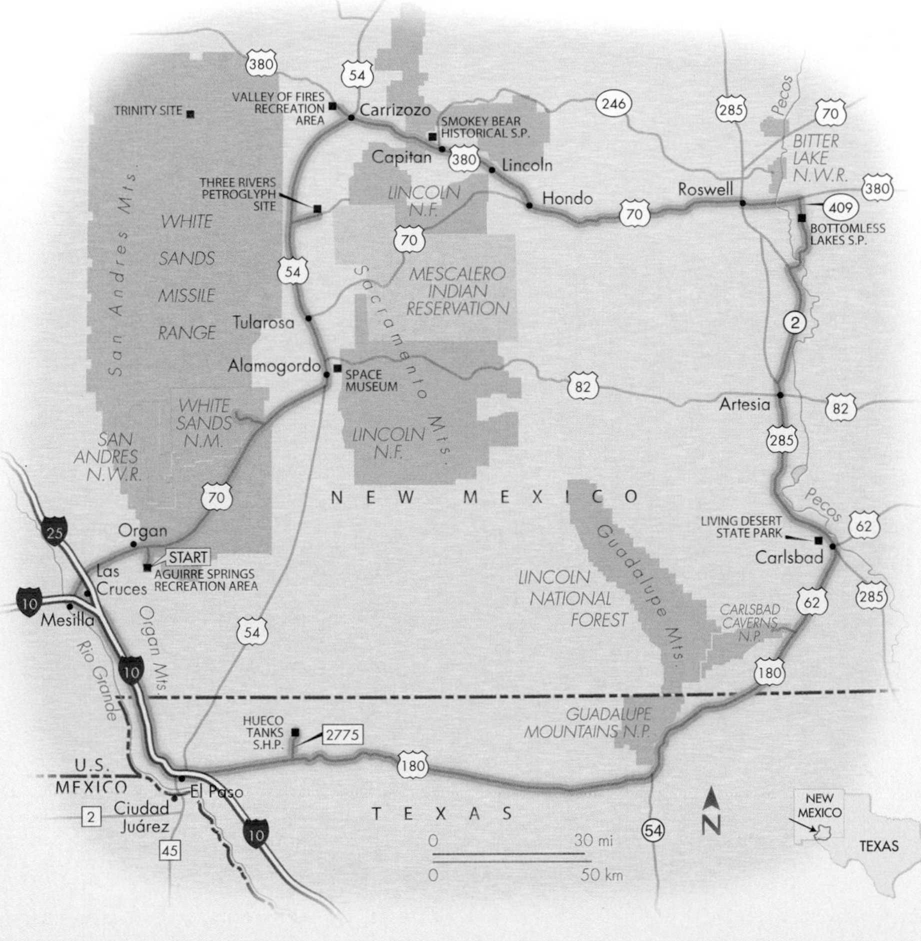

300 species of birds use these wetlands as a refuge in winter, and from October through February, sandhill cranes tread the lake, carefully avoiding the bobcats, foxes, and coyotes prowling the shore.

Turn south on N. Mex. 2 to Living Desert Zoo and Gardens State Park, whose plants include more than 200 kinds of cactuses and succulents. Follow U.S. 285 south through Carlsbad to visit Carlsbad Caverns (see Highlights). Then, continue south on U.S. 62/180, passing the Guadalupe Range to the west. At Guadalupe Mountains National Park, a 2.3-mile (3.7 km) loop trail leads to Smith and Manzanita Springs and glades filled with fern, juniper, oak, and maple.

The road crosses into Texas and continues to El Paso, the largest city on the U.S./Mexican border, with many buildings in the Spanish-American architectural style known as Southwest Territorial. You can see a perfect example at Magoffin Homestead Historic Site, a 19th-century, 19-bedroom house with original furnishings.

Stalagmites and stalactites fill the magnificent chambers of Carlsbad Caverns.

FROM: Aguirre Springs Recreation Area, New Mexico

TO: El Paso, Texas

ROADS: U.S. 70, 54, 380, N.Mex. 2, U.S. 285, 62/180

DISTANCE: 452 miles (727 km)

DRIVING TIME: 8.5 hours

WHEN TO GO: Year-round, but best in spring, when the desert blooms, and in fall

PLANNING: www.nps.gov/gumo

Highlights

- Alamogordo's **New Mexico Museum of Space History** has an excellent collection of early rockets, and documents the postwar research that took place in White Sands as the U.S. took its first step into space.

- South of Carlsbad is **Carlsbad Caverns National Park.** This underground labyrinth, one of the world's most extensive cave systems, has myriad rock formations, stalagmites, and stalactites. Self-guided and ranger-guided tours are available.

Yuccas grow in Humboldt-Toiyabe National Forest, which covers a huge, unforested area.

NEVADA

Jewel of the Ruby Mountains

Drive along Lamoille Canyon in northeastern Nevada and you'll see dozens of small, elegant waterfalls spill from the cliffs above as the gentle, glaciated descent breaks out from subalpine forests onto the high desert plains.

FROM: Elko, Nevada
TO: Road's End, Nevada
ROADS: Nev. 227, FR 660/Lamoille Canyon Byway
DISTANCE: 44 miles (71 km)
DRIVING TIME: 2 hours
WHEN TO GO: Spring through fall
PLANNING: There is a self-guided tour signposted along the way. www.travelnevada.com

The Ruby Mountains seem to burst from the flat valley floor as you approach the well-marked start of the Lamoille Canyon Byway (FR 660), 20 miles (32 km) southeast of the town of Elko on Nev. 227. The byway crosses Lamoille Creek, through a lush corridor of cottonwoods, willows, and aspens, and past waterfalls of melting snow cascading over the canyon's wall, as it enters Humboldt-Toiyabe National Forest. For a quick orientation on the canyon's features, stop at Powerhouse Picnic Area. As you head on to Glacier Overlook, a number of the peaks in front of you top 10,000 feet (3,048 m). An exhibit at the overlook explains the area's glacial history, pointing out the path the ice took as it carved out the valley. Thomas Canyon Campground, 2 miles (3 km) ahead, sits at the mouth of a glacial side canyon. Put on your hiking boots and take the tricky trail up the floor of Thomas Canyon to wildflower meadows and forests of limber and whitebark pine. Another good walk is Changing Canyon Nature Trail, starting 1.5 miles (2.4 km) up the road at the pull-off for Hanging Valley. Farther along the road, Terraces Picnic Area is an off-road spot where you can stop for views of a 1,500-foot (457 m) cliff of metamorphic rock swirled with light-colored granite.

Continue past gently undulating meadows of grasses, sedges, and wildflowers as willow thickets cloak the canyon's meandering course. Within 2 miles (3 km) you'll arrive at Road's End, where a ring of peaks rises from the forest, stopping the byway in its tracks. The 33-mile (53 km) Ruby Crest National Recreation Trail starts from here, leading into 90,000 acres (36,422 ha) of forests, lakes, meadows, and glacial peaks that are home to bighorn sheep, mountain goats, and eagles. You don't have to hike far to see the backcountry: 2 miles (3 km) away from Road's End, in a glacial cirque, is Island Lake, and you can fish for brookies at Lamoille Lake, 2 miles (3 km) up Ruby Crest.

ARIZONA

The Twisting Coronado Trail

Navigate your way around the hundreds of switchbacks that make up U.S. 191. The rewards are great, for this winding route through eastern Arizona is one of the least traveled in the U.S.A., full of fun turns and excellent views.

After exploring the old copper-mining town of Clifton, head north on U.S. 191 and in 10 miles (16 km) you'll have a splendid view of the 3-mile (5 km) wide, 6-mile (10 km) long Phelps Dodge Copper Corporation Morenci Mine, one of the largest man-made holes on the planet. From the observation point, the huge trucks hauling 125,000 tons of copper a day look tiny. Past here, the road runs through narrow and colorful Chase Canyon and then enters forest as it ascends higher into the mountains. Cherry Lodge Picnic Area, about 10 miles (16 km) farther north, is a pleasant place to rest. Farther into the mountains, you can stop at a parking area and take a 1-mile (1.6 km) hike up to the top of 8,786-foot (2,678 m) Rose Peak, where a fire lookout tower provides great views of the surrounding terrain. The highway continues up Mogollon Rim to a 9,184-foot (2,799 m) overlook at Blue Vista (turn left at Milepost 225), from where you can see an endless parade of ridges and mountains to the southeast and west, including Mount Graham, 70 miles (113 km) away. You soon enter an area of spruce, fir, and aspen forests around Hannagan Meadow lodge and store. The road skirts the eastern edge of the White Mountains for the next 22 miles (35 km), passing aspen groves and alpine meadows to reach the mountain town of Alpine, which has places to stay, restaurants, and supplies. Farther north still is 10,912-foot (3,330 km) Escudilla Mountain, an old volcano and Arizona's third highest peak, at the heart of Escudilla Wilderness Area. As U.S. 191 drops down to the volcanic field around Springerville, you pass Nelson Reservoir, which is popular for boating and fishing.

Hidden History **Casa Malpais,** or **House of the Badlands,** is a National Historic Landmark, 2 miles (3 km) north of Springerville, close to the Coronado Trail. The Puebloan settlement, which was inhabited by the Mogollon people during the 13th century, has been preserved to an unusually high level due to its mysterious abandonment around A.D. 1400. You can tour the ruins with a guide, and, with prior booking, it is also possible to join excavations at the site. A visitor center and museum on Main Street in Springerville have artifacts from the complex on display.

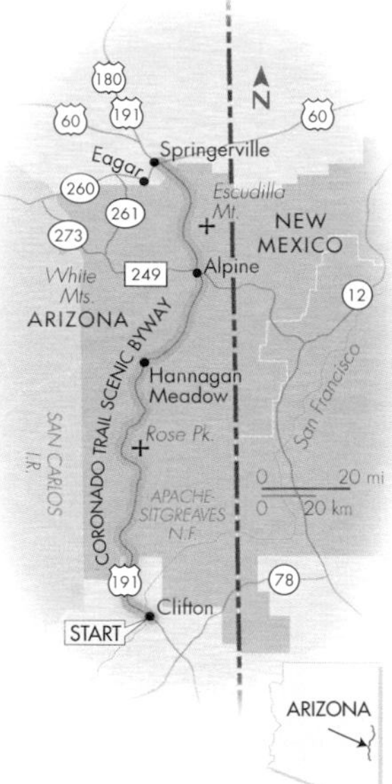

FROM: Clifton, Arizona
TO: Springerville, Arizona
ROAD: U.S. 191
DISTANCE: 123 miles (198 km)
DRIVING TIME: 4 to 5 hours
WHEN TO GO: Spring through fall (the road is often closed in winter)
PLANNING: The length of vehicles on the road is limited to 40 feet (12 m). Watch out for sharp curves and steep drop-offs. www.azdot.gov

The Coronado Trail takes a looping course as it ascends Chase Canyon.

THE TOP

10 Drivers' Drives

From the adrenaline rush of a Formula One track to the sedate pleasures of a quiet Alaskan highway, here's our choice of roads that are fun to drive.

1 Highway 89, Arizona/Utah/Idaho/Wyoming/Montana

From the Sonoran Desert to the Rocky Mountains, this geological field trip of a drive from Flagstaff, Arizona, to the Canadian border traverses cactus-filled desert, a volcanic plateau with lava flows, the red rocks of Sedona, and the Great Salt Lake. Open roads rarely come finer.

PLANNING: Visit the route's national parks, including Yellowstone. *www.untraveledroad.com*

2 Denali Highway, Alaska

Completed in 1957 to give access to Denali National Park, this largely gravel road offers bracing views of untamed wilderness with few signs of human occupation. It was replaced in 1971 by a newer road, now known as the George Parks Highway.

PLANNING: The highway leads from Paxson Junction to Cantwell Junction and is closed in winter. *www.bellsalaska.com*

3 Ruta 40, Argentina

Ruta 40 stretches along the whole country from Cabo Virgenes in the south to La Quiaca in the north, extending more than 3,045 miles (4,900 km). It runs parallel to the Andes, crossing 236 bridges and many rivers, lakes, national parks, and mountain passes. From sea level, it ascends dramatically to 16,404 feet (5,000 m) in the north around Salta.

PLANNING: Ruta 40 is largely paved, but the southern part crosses mostly barren terrain. *www.ruta40.gov.ar*

4 Nürburgring, Nürburg, Germany

Designed to flaunt Germany's automotive prowess, the original mountain ring track emerged between 1925 and 1927 for the country's first Grand Prix. A new track was completed in 1984, but the original 12.9-mile (20.8 km) *Nordschleife* (Northern Loop) regularly opens to the public as a toll road. This is probably the world's most challenging purpose-built racetrack, featuring a relentless series of hairpin or blind bends.

PLANNING: Check opening times. There's no speed limit but German driving laws apply; unlicensed racing is banned. *www.nuerburgring.de*

5 Davos to Stelvio via Bormio, Switzerland/Italy

Implausibly etched through the peaks of the eastern Alps, this dizzying zigzag road built in the early 19th century is a hardcore workout for even the very best of drivers and automobiles. The 60 hairpin turns bring you up the mountains to a height of 9,042 feet (2,756 m). The heady views are mostly yours alone.

PLANNING: The road often closes in winter. Midway along, Bormio offers year-round skiing. *www.davos.ch*

6 E4, Norway

Starting in southern Norway and driving as far north as you can is an excellent way of testing both you and your car's endurance. This rugged 1,499-mile (2,412 km) road leads from Haugesund on the west coast, Norway's oldest settlement, into the Arctic Circle, ending up at the bleak headland of Nordkapp, one of the most northerly points in Europe. Visual highlights along the way include fjords, forests, fishing villages, glaciers, mountains, and tundra, as well as the northern lights. Expect little traffic, but watch out for roaming reindeer.

PLANNING: Allow 36 hours for the drive. In summer expect continual daylight. *www.visitnorway.com*

Opposite: The steep inclines and sharp zigzags of Italy's Alpine Stelvio Pass offer up one of Europe's most thrilling drives.

7 Col de Turini, Alpes-Maritimes, France

With as many hairpin bends as a tightly coiled spring and the skimpiest of barriers, this vertiginous death-trap of a mountain pass looks designed for a James Bond car chase. It's a high point of the Monte Carlo Rally, held every January, when spectators throw snow on the normally ice-clad track for added fun.

PLANNING: Focus on the road and try not to look down. *www.frenchriviera-tourism.com*

8 A18 Snaefell Mountain Road, Isle of Man

The Isle of Man has been a leading motorsport destination since 1904, when racing was legalized on public roads. This 15-mile (25 km) road between Douglas and Ramsey is the motorcycle-race circuit used for the Isle of Man TT and the Manx Grand Prix. The Isle of Man is one of the few British territories with no national speed limit, a key attraction for many.

PLANNING: The TT runs from late May to mid-June; the Manx Grand Prix starts in late August. Both last 14 days. *www.gov.im*

9 B4560, Wales

Crossing some of Britain's loveliest open countryside and frequently used for test-drives, this narrow winding road packs in panoramic views over Brecon Beacons National Park and the Black Mountains—along with plenty of challenging mountain corners and dreamy villages.

PLANNING: The B4560 runs north from Beaufort to Talgarth via Llangynidr, Bwlch, and Llangors, but the prettiest part is between Llangynidr and Bwlch. Ice and snow sometimes close the road. *www.breconbeacons.org*

10 Atlas Mountains, Morocco

From Marrakech, take the N9 southeast toward Ouarzazate across the majestic Atlas Mountains. The road's twists and turns provide a test of skill and nerves for drivers, while the ascent into the Khaki Mountains provides passengers with panoramic pleasures.

PLANNING: Snow may close the road in winter. The 200-mile (322 km) drive takes about four hours. *www.visitmorocco.com*

CANADA

Along Icefields Parkway

Spectacular views of mountains, ridges, waterfalls, lakes, and more than 100 glaciers make the Icefields Parkway (Hwy. 93) between Lake Louise and Jasper in Alberta one of the world's greatest scenic highways. It's also Canada's highest road.

This sensational two-lane highway sweeps through the highest mountains in the Canadian Rockies. Heading north from Lake Louise, the road passes Hector Lake at the foot of the Waputik Range and soon rounds isolated Bow Peak as Crowfoot Glacier comes into view. Bow Lake, 3 miles (5 km) on, is fed by waters from Bow Glacier, one of eight glaciers descending from the Waputik Icefield. A little farther on, a short trail leads to a viewpoint above the blue-green waters of glacier-fed Peyto Lake. The road soon descends into Mistaya Valley and passes Waterfowl Lake, which has awe-inspiring views of the mountains of the Continental Divide. As the Mistaya River drops down to the North Saskatchewan River basin, it carves through the narrow Mistaya Canyon, where you can take a short footpath beneath vertical walls. The town of Saskatchewan River Crossing lies 3 miles (5 km) ahead, and the valley is much narrower by the time the road reaches the gentle waterfalls of the Weeping Wall. The road ascends to Big Bend hairpin, with views of the North Saskatchewan Valley. Parker Ridge, 8 miles (13 km) on, has a steep trail rising 900 feet (275 m) through subalpine forest to an unforgettable view of the Saskatchewan Glacier. At Sunwapta Pass, the road crosses into the wildly beautiful Jasper National Park and soon reaches the glaciers of the 1,000-foot (305 m) deep Columbia Icefield, and farther on, the Sunwapta Falls, where the Sunwapta River crashes into a gorge. Athabasca Valley, north of the falls, is the Rockies' longest and widest valley. Continue on to Goats and Glaciers Viewpoint, with great views of the valley's pine-covered floor. Athabasca Falls, another 3 miles (5 km) on, is a 70-foot (21 m) high spectacle of crashing water. The drive ends at Jasper.

Stay a While The **Columbia Icefield Center,** opposite the Athabasca Glacier just past Sunwapta Pass, has exhibits explaining how glaciers form, grow, and retreat, as well as a natural history museum examining wildlife of the alpine zone. You can take a bus tour of the glaciers from here. You can also hike to the edge of the Athabasca Glacier, but if you want to venture onto the ice itself, be sure to go with a guide as the glacier has deep, dangerous crevasses.

FROM: Lake Louise, Canada
TO: Jasper, Canada
ROAD: Hwy. 93/Icefields Parkway
DISTANCE: 143 miles (232 km)
DRIVING TIME: 3.5 hours
WHEN TO GO: Spring through fall
PLANNING: The only services are at Saskatchewan River Crossing, where gas, food, and lodgings are available, and at the Columbia Icefield Center. www.icefieldsparkway.ca

Two climbers tackle the Columbia Icefield in Jasper National Park.

Forests and wildflower meadows surround Mount Rainier, a heavily glaciated, active volcano.

WASHINGTON

Around Mount Rainier

As you circle the 14,410-foot (4,392 m) Mount Rainier, southeast of Seattle, this great peak is seldom out of view during a drive that takes in old-growth forest, wilderness areas, glacial rivers, and subalpine meadows.

Even at this drive's starting point in Tacoma, 70 miles (133 km) to the northwest, Mount Rainier dominates the horizon. Head southeast on Wash. 167 and 410, following the White River to Mount Rainier's glacial northeastern flank and entering Federation Forest State Park. Fifteen minutes south on Wash. 410 you cross the boundary of Mount Rainier National Park; 5 miles (8 km) on, take the road to Sunrise, which at 6,400 feet (1950 m) is the park's highest point accessible by car. The town has grand views and many hiking trails. Continue on Wash. 410 to Cayuse Pass, take Wash. 123 south for 11 miles (18 km), and turn west along Stevens Canyon Road to arrive at the Grove of the Patriarchs trailhead, where you can take a short, easy walk along the Ohanapecosh River to this grove of old-growth trees. The road next runs through pristine forest, past ridges and creeks, to Box Canyon/Muddy Fork Cowlitz, where you can see a deep, narrow gorge above crashing white water. Reflection Lakes, a few miles on, have rippling views of Mount Rainier. Finally, you reach Paradise. The town was named by early travelers, inspired by the surrounding flower-filled meadows. Many hiking trails through the meadows start in the town; the short Nisqually Vista Trail heads to the rim of the ravine above Nisqually Glacier, while the 6-mile (10 km) Skyline Trail ascends the glacier's eastern flank. From Paradise, Wash. 706 takes you through 10 miles (16 km) of waterfalls, forest, and rock pinnacles to arrive at Longmire, with a park museum, historic lodge, and hiking trails. Leaving the park, follow Wash. 706 west to Wash. 7, turn north, and continue on Wash. 161 and 167 back to Tacoma, with Mount Rainier looking on.

FROM: Loop route from Tacoma, Washington

ROADS: Wash. 167, 410, 123, 706, 7, 161

DISTANCE: 200 miles (322 km)

DRIVING TIME: 5 hours

WHEN TO GO: Cayuse Pass is only accessible in summer.

PLANNING: Stop—or stay—at Paradise's historic Paradise Inn, built in 1917. www.visitrainier.com

CALIFORNIA

Lakes and Mountains

Northern California is blessed with some of the state's most stunning scenery and least crowded parks. Best appreciated at a leisurely pace, this tour along quiet roads offers true natural wonders, wildlife refuges, solitude, and one of California's highest peaks.

Tule Lake is a winter home for several species of migrating birds, including Canada geese.

From the small town of Red Bluff, follow I-5 north through Anderson and Redding, and cross an arm of scenic Shasta Lake to reach Castle Crags State Park (just before Dunsmuir). The dramatic 6,000-foot (1829 m) spires of Castle Crags mark the site of the last battle, in 1855, at which Native Americans exclusively used traditional weapons. To the north, you can see the 14,162-foot (4,316 m), snow-covered peak of Mount Shasta, the second highest peak in the Cascade Range and classified as a dormant volcano, having last erupted 200 years ago. The drive continues north on I-5 to the old lumber town of Weed, then turns northeast on U.S. 97 to cross the Cascade Range, which extends north all the way to British Columbia. Just before you reach the state border, turn onto Calif. 161 across the northernmost reaches of California. Lower Klamath National Wildlife Refuge, part of an 180,000-acre (72,843 hectare) protected wetland, and nearby Tule Lake National Wildlife Refuge (south on Calif. 139) together form a vast basin of marshes and shallow lakes that are a winter home for bald eagles and more than a million migrant ducks, geese, swans, heron, egrets, double-crested cormorants, and cinnamon teal.

After visiting the wetlands, turn off Calif. 139 to Lava Beds National Monument (see Highlights). Just beyond Canby, detour on Calif. 299 east to the small town of Alturas. Nearby, Modoc National Wildlife Refuge is a huge draw for ornithologists. The refuge is an important resting and feeding area for migratory birds on the Pacific flyway, and 246 different bird species, including Canada geese, teal, mallard, and widgeon, have been spotted here. Returning to Canby, take Calif. 299 southwest, and turn north on Calif. 89 to reach McArthur-Burney Falls Memorial State Park. The beautiful and powerful 129-foot (39 m) high waterfall, which was described by Theodore Roosevelt as the "eighth wonder of the world," is easily reached via a footpath. The park has stands of fantastic incense cedar and ponderosa pine and its rich wildlife includes the rare black swift. Back on the road, drive south on Calif. 89 through spectacular Lassen Volcanic National Park, home of Lassen Peak, the largest plug-domed volcano in the world. From Calif. 89, take Calif. 36 west to return to Red Bluff.

OPPOSITE: Hikers climb Cinder Cone, a volcano in Lassen Volcanic National Park.

Highlights

- **William B. Ide Adobe State Historic Park,** about a mile (1.6 km) north of Red Bluff, is the preserved home of Ide, an early settler, entrepreneur, and leader of the 1846 Bear Flag revolt.

- Just to the south of Tule Lake is **Lava Beds National Monument,** where, with the help of a flashlight and a guide, you can explore 30,000-year-old lava tubes, many of which contain brightly colored lichens.

FROM: Loop route from Red Bluff, California
ROADS: I-5, U.S. 97, Calif. 161, 139, 299, 89, 36
DISTANCE: 431 miles (694 km)
DRIVING TIME: 8 hours
WHEN TO GO: Year-round
PLANNING: The old lumber town of McCloud, a few miles east of I-5, is a good place to stay.
www.visitmountshasta.org

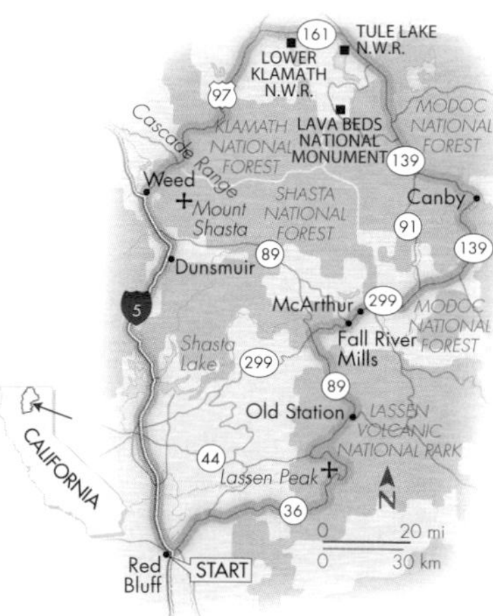

At Agua Azul, crystal-clear water cascades over layers of travertine that have built up to create a network of falls.

MEXICO

Maya Ruins and Waterfalls

This route through the Chiapas highlands of southern Mexico, which includes a section of the Pan-American Highway, climbs from tropical jungle, pleasant rolling hills, and tranquil valleys into the evergreen mountains around San Cristóbal de las Casas.

FROM: Palenque, Mexico
TO: Parque Nacional Lagunas de Montebello, Mexico
ROADS: Hwys. 199, 190
DISTANCE: 200 miles (322 km)
DRIVING TIME: 3 days
WHEN TO GO: Year-round
PLANNING: www.travelchiapas.com

After visiting the ruined Maya city of Palenque, head south along Hwy. 199, stopping at the spectacular 130-foot (40 m) Misol-Ha waterfall, most impressive after late summer and fall rains, and with a cave leading to a subterranean pool. After about 25 miles (40 km), take the dirt road signposted to the falls of Agua Azul, where the river plunges through a rocky gorge over hundreds of frothy falls, surrounded by exuberant vegetation. You can hike along the gorge to bathe in the pools or climb up to a viewpoint above them. Back on the road, Hwy. 199 curves and climbs past fields and farms into the refreshing climate of Ocosingo Valley. At the town of Ocosingo, you can take a 6-mile (10 km) detour to the Maya ruins of Tonina, home to one of the tallest pyramids in the Maya world, standing 230 feet (70 m) above the ancient Grand Plaza. Back on Hwy. 199, turn northwest onto Hwy. 190, the Pan-American Highway, and head west past cattle ranches, farms, and coffee plantations until you reach the city of San Cristóbal de las Casas, with its brightly colored homes, old churches, and architecture with strong Maya influences. Backtrack southeast on Hwy. 190, and after 22 miles (35 km), look for the pottery-making Tzeital village of Amatenango del Valle on the right. Another 25 miles (40 km) southeast brings you to the small city of Comitán de Domínguez, full of narrow streets with pretty colonial architecture. Six miles (10 km) beyond Comitán are the ruins of Tenam Puente, once a major Maya city. Another 8 miles (15 km) down Hwy. 190, go east along a road marked "Lagunas de Montebello" for 3 miles (5 km) to reach the Maya ruins of Chinkultic. Built on top of a bluff, this ruined city has step pyramids and 200 smaller buildings and is famous for its views of the surrounding terrain. Parque Nacional Lagunas de Montebello, with its intensely colored lakes and peaceful atmosphere, marks the journey's end.

CUBA

Escambray Mountain Roads

The elevated roads of this circular route in the Escambray Mountains, with perfect views of the Caribbean Sea and some of Cuba's most pristine mountain scenery, are often virtually deserted—letting you savor the delights of the Cuban countryside in peace and quiet.

The Circuito Sur coast road leaves the remarkably unspoiled colonial city of Trinidad along Calle Pino Guinart. Drive west, and after 3 miles (5 km) follow the sign for the spa resort of Topes de Collantes, driving north across the dips and troughs of the Rio Canas Valley. You soon ascend up a steeply curving road into the lushly forested Sierra del Escambray before arriving at Topes de Collantes (see Stay a While). Two miles (3 km) north of the resort, bear right at the Y-junction. For the next few miles, you drive through pine and eucalyptus forest with breathtaking views of rising mountains to the west and Valle de Caburní to the east. After a short drive, the road corkscrews down the mountains past rows of coffee bushes to the village of Jibacoa. Soon the descent eases and the northern views open up, revealing *bohios* (thatched huts), royal palms, and ox-tilled fields. Ten miles (16 km) beyond Jibacoa, in the center of Manicaragua, turn left onto Rte. 4-206, and 3 miles (5 km) beyond the small community of Ciro Redondo, turn left again for views of the pea-green lake at Embalse-Hanabanilla. Return to the main highway and head west through orange groves to Cumanayagua, turning south at the western end of town. Once beyond Los Cedros, you see the Circuito Sur again—turn left onto it. The landscape changes abruptly as orange groves give way to cattle-grazed grasslands. After about 10 minutes, the road touches the Caribbean coast at the mouth of the Rió La Jutía. A little farther on is Hacienda La Vega, a cattle ranch where you can go horseback riding. The mountains crowd down to the shore as you drive east from here across rivers and deep ravines. Beyond the Rió Cabagán, you enter Sancti Spíritus province and power up the hill back to Trinidad.

FROM: Loop route from Trinidad, Cuba

ROADS: Circuito Sur, Rte. 4-206, local roads

DISTANCE: 96 miles (154 km)

DRIVING TIME: 5 hours

WHEN TO GO: Year-round

PLANNING: www.gocuba.ca

Stay a While **Topes de Collantes** is the name of a resort and a nature reserve in the Escambray Mountains. Hike one of the short trails in the park to explore tropical rain forest filled with banana trees, begonia, jasmine, ginger, West Indian mahogany, and several species of orchids and ferns. You can also see the park's underground river systems, coffee plantations, and waterfalls, and visit the massive 210-room Kurhotel, built in 1954, with its excellent art collection.

The Crocodile House in Trinidad, dating from the 18th century, is a former industrialist's residence.

PUERTO RICO

The Panoramic Route

Zigzagging through some of the most exquisite scenery in Puerto Rico, the Panoramic Route is an extremely narrow road traversing the length of the island from east to west, with endless views of sea and mountains.

From the unspoiled colonial coastal town of Maunabo, Rte. 3 heads inland to Yabucoa, crosses the Rio Guayanés, and climbs into the Puerto Rican foothills. Running along a ridge dotted with small settlements and valleys filled with banana trees, firs, and bamboo on either side for about 6 miles (10 km), the road then begins to climb steeply as small coffee plantations replace the lowland cattle ranches. Rte. 3 next enters the rain forest of the Reserva Forestal Carite, home to 50 species of birds, several waterfalls, and a blue pool known as the Charco Azul. Views of sea and coastal plains soon open up to the south. Continue along the ridgebacks of the Sierra de Cayey and up to the observation tower at the summit of Mirador Piedra Degetau for great views. The once grandiose town of Aibonito, the highest town in Puerto Rico and a former retreat of the wealthy, is just to the north of the main road. Beyond Aibonito is the Cañon San Cristóbal, a deep gorge with a waterfall plunging 700 feet (213 m) to the Río Usabón below. Return to Rte. 3, which twists along the spine of the Cordillera Central giving wonderful views of the whole island and the shimmering Caribbean. Beyond Cerro El Malo, you enter the Reserva Forestal Toro Negro, where a canopy of leafy bamboo shades the road. Six miles (10 km) to the northeast is the Área de Recreo Doña Juana, where you can take a short walk to a huge natural swimming pool in the forest. Beyond the pool, the path heads gently up Cerro Doña Juana, where a small tower has views of the mountains and coastline. The main road descends to the quiet town of Adjuntas before climbing once again through the Cordillera Central, skirting the towering Montañas de Uroyan, to reach Mayagüez on the west coast.

FROM: Maunabo, Puerto Rico
TO: Mayagüez, Puerto Rico
ROADS: Road numbers change constantly. The route is marked with brown R.U.T.A. signs, but not at all junctions.
DISTANCE: 120 miles (193 km)
DRIVING TIME: At least 1 day
WHEN TO GO: Year-round
PLANNING: Mountain inns along the route provide places to stay. www.topuertorico.org

Excursion Just south of Mayagüez lies **Cabo Rojo,** one of Puerto Rico's most popular towns. The local beaches have been dubbed the most scenic on the island, especially Playa Sucia, a slightly rustic yet charming sandy beach with fabulous sunsets. The town's Los Morrillos Lighthouse, built in 1882, is situated on top of 200-foot (60 m) high white-lime cliffs and has some of the island's best views. Cabo Rojo is also known for its fresh fish and seafood restaurants.

The Cordillera Central is Puerto Rico's heart of green wooded mountains.

A male quetzal bird on Cerro de la Muerte—the Mountain of Death—shows off its colors.

Highlights

- At the Km 70 marker, a detour takes you to **Mirador del Quetzales** (also known as Finca Eddie Serrano). Set amid forest-clad mountains, this simple hotel is a superb location for spotting quetzals and exotic hummingbirds. Members of the Serrano family will guide you along the forest trails.
- The **Dantica Cloud Forest Lodge and Gallery,** near San Gerardo de Dota, shows Latin American art from contemporary and indigenous artists, and is a great starting-point for hiking into the **Parque Nacional Los Quetzales.**
- The **Savegre Biological Reserve** in San Gerardo de Dota is another excellent place to find out about the elusive quetzal bird.

COSTA RICA

Quetzal Country

Soaring across some of the highest mountains accessible by road in Costa Rica, through the haunt of the rare quetzal bird, this section of the Pan-American Highway links the valleys of the Meseta Central and El General, offering spectacular views.

The delightful old colonial city of Cartago is home to the ornate 19th-century Basílica de Nuestra Señora de Los Ángeles and many other historic buildings. Two miles (3 km) south of the city, Hwy. 2 begins to climb, rising to the village of Vara de Roble before falling to Santa Maria de Dota. The views become ever more impressive as you ascend to Empalme village, your last gas-stop. Here the road is flanked by orchards, pastures, and slopes forested with pines and oaks. Roadside trout farms offer fishing and horseback rides. Continue to the yellow church of Cañon (at the Km 58 marker), which sits on the crest of the Continental Divide, a perfect spot to admire the views. Settlements begin to thin from here as you continue up through the Río Macho Forest Reserve and the Iyöla Amí Cloud Forest Reserve, which protect 500-year-old cipresillo oaks and *aguacatillos* (avocados), a favorite food for quetzals. Soon you reach a refuge hut once used by traders before a mountain road existed and now a tiny museum. At Km 80, take a right turn onto a side road that spirals westward to the valley of the Río Savegre. The rocky roadway plunges 2,100 feet (640 m) in 5.5 miles (9 km), ending at the valley hamlet of San Gerardo de Dota (see Highlights), with its trout-filled streams, orchards, and (the occasional) strikingly colored quetzal bird. Back on the main highway, continue south to Km 85. Here you can take a short path (by 4WD) to the 11,450-foot (3,490 m) summit of Cerro de la Muerte—the Mountain of Death, named for the many farmworkers who froze to death around its bog- and paramo grass-covered peak before the highway was built. The road continues to a truck stop, Las Torres, before descending steeply into the Valle de El General.

FROM: Cartago, Costa Rica
TO: Las Torres, Costa Rica
ROAD: Hwy. 2
DISTANCE: 45 miles (72 km)
DRIVING TIME: 2 hours
WHEN TO GO: Avoid the rainy season (May–November)
PLANNING: www.costarica.com

PANAMA

Plazas and Pines in Panama

The breathtaking scenery along this drive through the foothills of the Cordillera Central has been described as a series of natural film sets unfolding before you, as green-clad mountains, their peaks often shrouded in cloud, dot the landscape.

Tambo
Cerro Chichibalí
Trinidad Spa & Lodge
Toabré
Miraflores
Caimito
Churuquita Grande
Las Minas
Coclé
La Pintada
Cigarros Joyas de Panamá
N
0 5 mi
0 5 km
PANAMA
START
Cañaveral
Penonomé

After admiring Penonomé's charming colonial main plaza (see Stay a While), set off along the road leading from the plaza's northwest corner and drive through the valley of the Rio Coclé, encircled by gracefully rounded peaks in the distance. La Pintada, 9 miles (14 km) on, is a pretty agricultural town with a gleaming white church—Iglesia de Candelria—that gives it added beauty. A small road runs east from the church to Charco Las Lavanderas, whose natural swimming pools are said to have healing powers. From La Pintada continue northeast toward Las Minas, following the partially paved road as it drills into ever more rugged terrain. Ascending eastward, you can enjoy a spectacular view to the west of the Cerro Orari, a flat-topped, sheer-walled mesa. The next few miles provide stunning vistas of a series of forest-draped valleys and mountains. In the community of Toabré, turn left at the crossroads for Tambo—a small village flanked by citrus groves. Turn right at the church in Tambo, soon passing a charming cemetery against a backdrop of mountain ridges. The Cerro Chichibalí, a volcanic rock tower, dominates the scene, towering over the nearby community of Miraflores, whose church is enfolded by pines. The road continues through conifer forest and past cattle ranches, with views opening up of valleys studded with spectacular limestone formations. At the junction in the small town of Churuquita Grande, take the left turn to Caimito, a village graced by the charming little chapel of Capilla Católica de la Medalla Milagrosa. For the next few miles the ridge road delivers breathtaking views, as the road narrows and steepens, before arriving at Trinidad Spa and Lodge.

FROM: Penonomé, Panama
TO: Trinidad Spa and Lodge, Panama
ROADS: There are no road numbers, but most intersections are signed.
DISTANCE: 32 miles (51 km)
DRIVING TIME: 2 hours
WHEN TO GO: Year-round
PLANNING: www.visitpanama.com

Stay a While The agricultural town of **Penonomé** is known for its *sombreros pintados* (straw hats) and a striking colonial plaza, the Parque 8 de Diciembre. Shaded with flametrees and centered around a bandstand, the plaza has beautiful buildings, such as the Iglesia San Juan Bautista, and a handsome medieval-style police station. The Museo de Penonomé, situated in four blue-and-white 18th-century cottages, has history exhibits, pre-Columbian ceramics, and colonial religious icons.

Churuquita Grande holds its Feria de la Naranja (Orange Festival) at the end of January each year.

The ancient, hand-carved rice fields of Banaue extend up the lower slopes of the Cordillera Mountains, occupying every available patch of land.

PHILIPPINES

Terraces of the Cordillera

The Halsema Highway clings to the mountainsides as it climbs past farms and rice terraces into the Cordillera Mountains, in the northern Luzon region, to reach the highest point in the Philippines' highway system.

Begin in sprawling Baguio City, and head north on Magsaysay Avenue to La Trinidad, 2 miles (3 km) to the north. Catch glimpses of the town's hundreds of strawberry fields before turning right onto La Trinidad Avenue at the Benguet Provincial Capitol building to reach the Halsema Highway. At first, the highway follows the path of lumber vehicles, which now bring in vegetables from farms that sprang up in the old forest. Plenty of trees remain, however, as the road begins its mountain ascent and you get your first view of bright green, terraced rice fields stepping down the mountainsides. The road continues uphill past Sayangan Town to 7,200-foot (2,195 m) Highest Point and then winds downhill past spectacular high ridges and rocky cliffs. The highway enters Mountain Province around 25 miles (40 km) from Sayangan, clinging to the mountainsides as it descends through low valleys of rice farms to the Chico River at Sabangan Town. The river and highway travel together to the provincial capital, Bontoc—don't miss the colorful locally made fabrics at the Pasalubong Center. Head south across the Chico River bridge to the town of Samoki to reach Mount Polis and Banaue, where you can see the area's most spectacular terraced farms (see In Focus).

In Focus The stone-walled **Banaue rice terraces,** one of the world's most awe-inspiring sites, were created around 2,000 years ago and extend thousands of feet up into the mountains. They are irrigated by natural springs and streams that have been channeled into small canals running downhill. It is thought the terraces were built, mainly by hand, by the descendents of Chinese immigrants who fled the mainland around 2100 B.C.

FROM: Baguio City, Philippines
TO: Banaue, Philippines
ROADS: Magsaysay Avenue, La Trinidad Avenue, Halsema Highway, local roads
DISTANCE: 80 miles (130 km)
DRIVING TIME: 5 hours
WHEN TO GO: Avoid the rainy season (June through October)
PLANNING: www.heirloomrice.com

TAIWAN

Driving Taroko Gorge

Following the twisting and turning lip of Taroko Gorge, famous for its sheer marble cliffs and deep gorges, this route showcases spectacular scenery and intriguing rock against the backdrop of the Central Mountain Range in secluded eastern Taiwan.

Bridges and trails along the Taroko Gorge lead deep into Taroko National Park.

Highlights

- **Swallow Grotto** is a pedestrianized section of the original road where traffic has been rerouted to allow visitors to enjoy the view. The lower marble sections on the opposite cliff are pockmarked with hundreds of small grottoes created by underground streams long dried-up. Swallows are common here, especially in spring and summer.

- The **Tunnel of Nine Turns** is a series of short tunnels excavated through the marble cliffs, with tiered waterfalls cascading down to the Liwu River. The far end of the tunnel opens onto extensive vistas, providing a sense of the gorge's true size.

The pristine blue waters of Taiwan's Liwu River have taken millennia to cut through marble cliffs to create this magical deep-sided gorge, now the centerpiece of Taroko National Park. The drive begins at the park's headquarters, south of the small city of Hualien. Just 1.4 miles (2.2 km) from the start, follow signposts to the Eternal Spring (Changchun) Shrine. Set above the multiple streams of a 45-foot (14 m) waterfall weaving down the cliffside, the shrine commemorates the 212 workers who died constructing the road. A steep trail with awe-inspiring views of the Central Mountain Range leads into the mountains from here. From the shrine, the road climbs alongside the gorge's steep walls for 5 miles (8 km) to a turnoff to Buluowan Recreation Area. From here, a steep, short road takes you to a local Atayal community. Set in the foothills and encircled by mountains on three sides, the village's setting is spectacular, and you can see elderly Atayal demonstrating their traditional weaving.

Continue west on the main road for 2.5 miles (4 km) to Swallow Grotto (see Highlights), where the road originally went through a long tunnel blasted through the cliffs. A new road bypasses the tunnel so that people can now walk through and enjoy the dramatic scenery at a leisurely pace. At Jinheng Bridge across the Liwu River, you are greeted on the north bank by the brooding Yindianren, or Indian Head Rock, a huge monolith that has been weathered into the shape of a Native American chief's head and is one of the park's most famous sites. The twisting, pedestrian-only Tunnel of Nine Turns awaits a couple of miles (3.2 km) on (see Highlights). From the viewpoint at Lioufang Bridge, just before the tunnel, you get a good view of the way in which the tunnel was blasted through the mountains. Cross the Bridge of Motherly Devotion, 1.25 miles (2 km) beyond the tunnel, where the riverbed is scattered with huge boulders, and head toward the resort of Tiansiang. Just before you reach the town, a suspension bridge leads across the river to a six-story pagoda perched on a mountain ridge with outstanding views from the top. The pagoda is part of the Xiangde Temple complex. Tiansiang, on the edge of the gorge, is Taroko's largest settlement.

FROM: Taroko National Park Headquarters, Taiwan
TO: Tiansiang (Tianxiang), Taiwan
ROAD: Hwy. 8/Central Cross-Island Highway
DISTANCE: 11.4 miles (19 km)
DRIVING TIME: 40 minutes
WHEN TO GO: Year-round
PLANNING: The park is closed on the second Monday of each month. Traffic along the gorge is very heavy on weekends and holidays. www.taroko.gov.tw

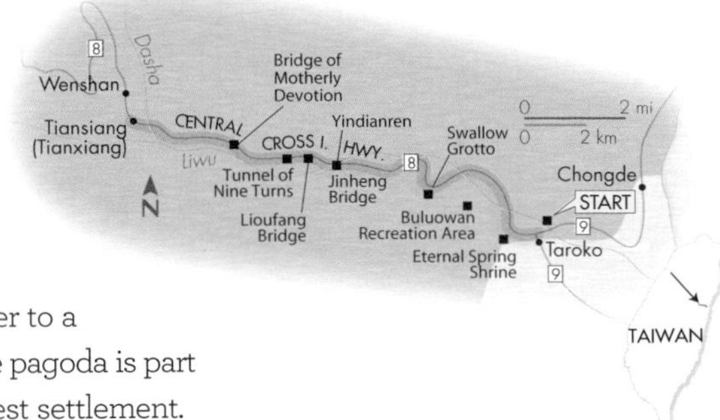

OPPOSITE: Pay your respects at the Eternal Spring (Changchun) Shrine, set above a powerful waterfall.

The buildings of the Tatra Mountains are often constructed in the unique Zakopane style, as seen in this wooden farmhouse.

POLAND/SLOVAKIA

Tatra Mountains

Drive through peaceful rural villages and spa towns, forested valleys, rolling pastoral countryside, and beautiful rocky mountains on this tour through Poland's and Slovakia's Tatra National Parks, linking the gateway towns of Zakopane and Starý Smokovec.

FROM: Zakopane, Poland
TO: Starý Smokovec, Slovakia
ROADS: Rtes 47, 961, 960, 67, 537
DISTANCE: 46.5 miles (75 km)
DRIVING TIME: 1.5 hours
WHEN TO GO: Spring through fall
PLANNING: You will need your passport. www.zakopane-life.com

Poland's skiing capital, Zakopane, originally developed as a mountain health resort, where people flocked to benefit from the mountain air and inspiring vistas. From here, follow Rte. 47 (Ulica Kasprowicza) northeast to the traditional village of Poronin. Cross the bridge and turn right along Rte. 961, before turning right again toward Bukowina Tatrzańska. Settlements begin to thin out, with many buildings in the distinctive local style characterized by high wooden roofs. On the edge of Bukowina Tatrzańska, the region's highest village, turn right along Rte. 960. The narrow road climbs steadily through forest, then descends from Glodówka, steeply in places, to Lysa Polana, a small mountain village. Bear left to cross the border into Slovakia and continue along Rte. 67.

The road slices through a narrow valley then turns right to the village of Tatranská Javorina, clustered around a tight bend in the road. Continue, mostly through forest, to the hamlet of Podspády. Turn right to stay on Rte. 67, which soon descends into open countryside and the skiing village of Ždiar, where a small museum explains the local culture. Next comes a forested valley and, beyond, the small mountain village of Tatranská Kotlina. The large institutional building here is a former sanatorium, where you can enjoy some first-class rest, and you can visit Belianska Cave, with its spectacular stalagmites. Turn right along Rte. 537. The forest flanking the road was devastated by a fierce storm in November 2004 but is recovering strongly. The views of the rugged Tatra peaks, dominated by 8,635-foot (2,632 m) Lomnický Štít, are very impressive. Pass through Tatranské Matliare, another sanatorium village, and you soon reach Tatranská Lomnica, originally a 19th-century spa town. Continue along Rte. 537 to your final destination, the spa town of Starý Smokovec.

CZECH REPUBLIC

The "Swiss" Czech Republic

When visiting in the 1770s, Swiss Romantic artists, with literary flair and a poet's prejudice, described the delightful region as the "Czech Switzerland," since its steep hills, wooded valleys, and well-kept villages reminded them of home.

The pretty village of Hřensko, filled with half-timbered German-style cottages, sits in a gorge edged by overhanging rocks where it joins the Labe Valley. The nearby Pravčická brána, a natural bridge measuring some 85 feet (26 m) across and 68 feet (21 m) high, is the area's most stunning attraction. The only way to reach it is by walking through the woods from Hřensko or Mezní Louka. From Hřensko, head east on a local road to Mezní Louka, where a path leads to another stone bridge, the Malá Pravčická brána, and on to the hamlet of Mezná. This tranquil place, perched on a grassy slope above the forested Kamenice Gorge, is quiet even in summer and has a handful of rustic guesthouses and restaurants. Rejoin the main road east to the town of Jetřichovice, a small village where old farmhouses have been converted into simple guesthouses. Continue southward to Česká Kamenice, which has a fine baroque chapel. Three miles (5 km) to the east is the rock formation of Panksá Skála, where thousands of basalt columns resemble organ pipes. From Česká Kamenice, continue toward Děčin via Benešov nad Ploučnici with its two 16th-century castles. The higher of the two has changing art exhibitions, while the lower has collections of furniture and Oriental art. České Švýcarsko National Park continues to the west of Děčin, so head past town on Rte. 13 to Libouchec, where a road runs north to Tisá, which has footpaths leading to a landscape of sandstone boulders, and on to the tabletop mountain of Děčínský Sněžník. Continue on Rte. 13 to Jilově and turn eastward to Děčin, an inland port on the River Labe with a sprawling, late 18th-century castle (see Hidden History).

FROM: Hřensko, Czech Republic
TO: Děčin, Czech Republic
DISTANCE: 70 miles (112 km)
ROADS: Local roads, Rte. 13
DRIVING TIME: 2 hours
WHEN TO GO: Year-round
PLANNING: www.czechtourism.com

Hidden History Fourteenth-century **Děčin Castle** was built as a fort, then reconstructed as a king's castle, before being used as a fort again. It was rebuilt over many years to its present Renaissance appearance by the Thun-Hohenstine family, who owned it from 1628 to 1932 and added the famous Rose Garden with its beautiful city views. In the 20th century, the castle was used as a barracks by Czech, German, and Soviet troops, who left it in a state of disrepair. After lying derelict for decades, the castle has now been restored to its former glory.

The Pravčická brána sandstone bridge is the largest natural bridge in central Europe.

GERMANY

Alpine Road

Built with pleasure motoring in mind, the 260-mile (450 km) Deutsche Alpenstrasse (German Alpine Road) opens up the Bavarian Alps—with their romantic mountain scenery, picturesque towns, and traditional villages—to the driving adventurer.

The charming wooden maypole in Grassau shows off skilled Bavarian craftsmanship.

The eastern section of the Alpine Road—described here—zigzags its way through stunning scenery in the Chiemgau Mountains (Chiemgauer Alpen). Coming from Munich, leave the Autobahn E52/E60 at exit 106 and follow the B305 south through Bernau to the old health resort town of Grassau, which has a classic example of an onion-domed church and is overlooked by the peak of Hochplatte. Continue south to Marquartstein, a ski resort where Richard Strauss composed his opera *Salome.* Visit the 11th-century castle, then continue on the B305 as it winds its way to Reit im Winkl, a village with Tyrolean-style houses set in a valley surrounded by forested mountains. In Reit im Winkl, turn northeast through the Chiemgau Mountains, part of the Eastern Alps, and past a silvery chain of lakes. Turn left 20 minutes after Reit im Winkl to arrive in the town of Ruhpolding (see Highlights), where Duke Wilhelm V of Bavaria built a hunting lodge in 1597. Visitors come to see the 13th-century wood-carved Ruhpolding Madonna, an exquisite example of Bavarian craftmanship on display in the baroque parish church.

Back on the B305, drive east and detour left onto the B306 to the village of Inzell with an onion-domed church, before the road joins the Alps-to-Baltic Vacation Route and runs southeast along the wooded Schwarzbach Valley. After crossing the watershed at the Schwarzbachwacht-Sattel Pass, the road descends through forest and pastureland with wonderful mountain views all around. Turn right into the village of Ramsau, whose early 16th-century parish church provides an irresistibly perfect Bavarian photo opportunity. After a few minutes' drive, the road comes to a little lake at Hintersee, above which steep slopes rise up to mountain peaks and a glinting glacier. Go back to the B305, and head to your destination, Berchtesgaden, a gorgeous little town sitting on a natural balcony over an idyllic valley (see Highlights).

OPPOSITE: Ramsau's beautiful church often appears on postcards of the area.

Highlights

- The **Woodcutters Museum** in Ruhpolding is devoted to the days when wood was the primary building material. It has a selection of forestry huts and cabins.
- Berchtesgaden's **Nationalparkhaus**, the interpretive center of Berchtesgaden National Park, is a good place to enjoy sublime views of the landscape surrounding the town.
- From 1923–33, Berchtesgaden's **Königliches Schloss** was the home of Crown Prince Ruprecht, head of the former Bavarian royal family, the Wittelsbachs. It contains the Wittelsbach collections of paintings, sculptures, carvings, and furniture.

FROM: Autobahn exit 106 (Prien-Bernau), Germany
TO: Berchtesgaden,Germany
ROADS: B305, B306
DISTANCE: 63 miles (102 km)
DRIVING TIME: 1.5 hours
WHEN TO GO: Year-round
PLANNING: The Biathlon World Cup is held in Ruhpolding every January, so make reservations early.
www.germany-tourism.de

GREECE

A Corner of a Greek Island

The mountain heights of northern Évia, Greece's second largest island, offer spectacular views of the mainland and of the island's green pastures, vineyards, olive groves, and forests, punctuated by delightful villages, old churches, and monasteries.

The long, thin, mountainous island of Évia hugs Greece's eastern Aegean coast and has a unique charm all its own. Start at the seaside town of Halkída, with its excellent Archaeological Musem, leaving on Rte. 44, then turning left onto Rte. 77, marked for Mandoudion. The road passes coastal salt marshes, with glorious vistas back to the Greek mainland. After 7.5 miles (12 km), take the right fork on the local road to the small market town of Psahná, whose main church contains captivating 13th-century frescoes. Head back to Rte. 77 and continue north, passing olive groves and pine forest as mountains impose themselves on the scenery. As you ascend, look back to the mainland for ever more incredible views. You'll also begin to see just how beautifully green Évia is. The road now follows a shimmering river through the deep, wooded Kleisoura Valley, furnished with walnut, plane, and poplar trees. Greek refugees who fled Turkey in 1923 founded Prokópion and brought the mummified body of St. John the Russian, which is now in the church of Agios Ioannis o Rosos. From here, continue along Rte. 77 for 5 miles (8 km) toward Limni, past the enchanting whitewashed houses of the village of Mandoúdion, whose main square is a delightful place to stop. Continue north past vineyards before leaving Rte. 77, following the left-hand fork in Strofylia past more hill villages. Descend to the pretty coastal village of Límni, which has excellent seafood and pleasant pebble beaches. While here, make time to walk to the spectacular seventh-century monastery of Moni Galataki, built on the site of a temple to Poseidon. It has no formal opening hours, but everyone is welcome as long as they are dressed modestly.

FROM: Halkída, Greece
TO: Límni, Greece
ROADS: Rtes. 44, 77
DISTANCE: 52.5 miles (84 km)
DRIVING TIME: 1.5 hours
WHEN TO GO: Year-round
PLANNING: www.aroundevia.com

Excursion Just south of Halkída, along the coastal road, lies **Eretia,** the most important historical site on Evia. Although the modern town has grown up on top of the ancient site, there is still plenty to enjoy here. The Archaeological Museum includes a fearsome Gorgon's head, and the nearby House of Mosaics is a restored fourth-century dwelling with fabulous floor mosaics. The town has other interesting remains, such as the ruins of an acropolis and the foundations of a temple of Apollo.

Farms and olive groves lie at the feet of snowcapped mountains on the island of Evia.

The beautiful Lago di Cecita was created in 1951 to provide hydroelectric power to the area.

ITALY

Calabrian Mountain Roads

Granite plateaus, meadows, mixed forests, pastures, lakes, deep valleys, and the high, snowy peaks of Calabria's Sila Mountains in Sila National Park combine to create a glorious variety of scenery in this deserted corner of southern Italy.

FROM: San Demetrio Corone, Italy
TO: Catanzaro, Italy
ROADS: SS660, SS177, SS282, local roads, Strada delle Vette, SS108bis, SS179, SS109
DISTANCE: 88 miles (141 km)
DRIVING TIME: 2 hours
WHEN TO GO: Year-round
PLANNING: www.turiscalabria.it

The village of San Demetrio Corone lies at the heart of southern Italy's Albanian (Arbëërëësh) population, who arrived over hundreds of years due to military ties between Naples, Venice, and Albania. The people here have a unique dialect and maintain close links to their agrarian traditions. Take the minor, twisting road from the village, following it south through the Arbëërëësh village of Acri, and pick up SS660 east. The road climbs through varied countryside to below Monte Forgiari on the northernmost edge of Sila National Park, which encompasses Calabria's finest wild mountain scenery. Bear right on SS177 to the junction with SS282 at the eastern edge of Lago di Cecita, one of the area's three large artificial lakes. You can take a short detour east here on SS282 to La Fossiata, the starting point of a number of well-organized hiking trails through the park. There is also a trailhead to the top of Serra Ripollata.

Return to the SS177 and continue to the ski trails and summer hiking routes of the resort of Camigliatello Silano. Then pick up the minor road (not the SS107) toward Spezzano, and after 6 miles (10 km) turn south on the Strada delle Vette (Road of the Peaks) toward Lorica and Laga Arvo. This mountain road is spectacular, reaching an altitude of more than 6,000 feet (1,829 m) on the slopes of Monte Botte Donato, the Sila's highest point. Turn right after 17 miles (27 km) at the lakeshore, following SS108bis west, then left onto the SS179 at Bocca di Piazza, toward Taverna. You'll soon pass the modern resort of Villaggio Mancuso, with a visitor center for the Parco Nazionale della Sila. From Taverna, the SS109 winds to Catanzaro, a large city at the heart of the Ionian Coast known for its silk.

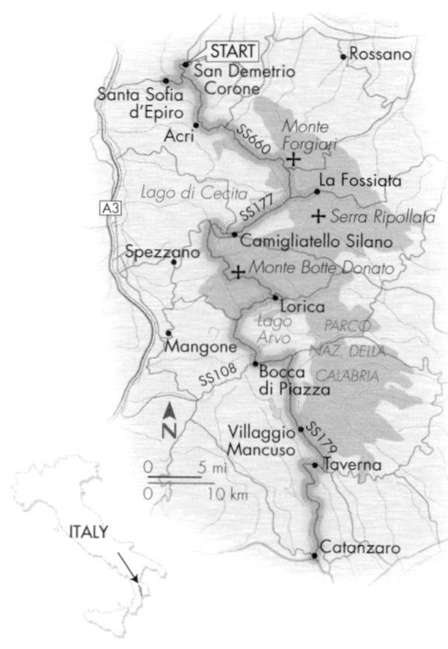

THE TOP 10 Skyscraping Drives

Nothing tests a car and its driver to the limit like taking a twisting, turning road past sheer drops. Here are ten of the world's best mountain roads.

❶ Top of the Rockies Scenic Byway, Colorado

Piercing three national forests, the byway rarely dips below 9,000 feet (2,743 m) as you drive through old gold-rush towns such as Leadville, the highest incorporated community in the U.S.A., with a quaint Victorian-era filmset appeal.

PLANNING: The drive starts at the junction of I-70 and Colo. 91 and runs south along Colo. 90 to Leadville, on U.S. 25 and Colo. 82 to Twin Lakes, and then back north to Minturn on U.S. 24. *www.topoftherockiesbyway.org*

❷ Trans-Andean Highway, Chile/Argentina

This dizzying 220-mile (350 km) drive from Santiago to Mendoza steeply snakes up through Chile to the 2-mile (3 km) long Cristo Redentor tunnel. On a clear day, look out for 22,841-foot (6,962 m) Cerro Aconcagua, the southern hemisphere's highest peak. In contrast, the Argentine side is a gentle descent past an alpine lake and through cactus fields.

PLANNING: Check weather forecasts; fog and clouds can impede mountain views. The road sometimes closes in winter. *www.visit-chile.org, www.turismo.gov.ar*

❸ Osado Skyline Drive, Sado Island, Japan

Sado Island's finest views are from the Osado Skyline Drive, slicing through mountains from Chigusa to the Sado goldmine. The panoramas of the island's verdant mountains are spectacular.

PLANNING: Car ferries to Ryotsu on Sado go from Niigata and Naoetsu on the mainland. The road closes in winter (November through April). *www.jnto.go.jp*

❹ Te Anau-Milford Sound, Fiordland, South Island, New Zealand

The hub of Fiordland National Park is the town of Te Anau, on the shores of the eponymous lake. From here the 73-mile (117 km) drive to the beautiful fjord at Milford Sound is alpine driving nirvana.

PLANNING: In winter, avalanches often close the road; snowchains are compulsory. The road has no gas stations. *www.fiordland.org.nz*

❺ Thunderbolt's Way, Great Dividing Range, Australia

Named for Frederick Ward, alias Captain Thunderbolt, a 19th-century bushranger, who roamed these parts, this 180-mile (290 km) paved road runs between Gloucester and Inverell. Completed in 1961, it slices through national parks and some of Australia's steepest, craggiest, and highest mountains, including the country's loftiest peak, Mount Kosciuszko, 7,310 feet (2,228 m) above sea level.

PLANNING: Allow time to stop at Carson's Lookout between Gloucester and Nowendoc, for delirious valley views, and the picnic area near the Barrington river bridge. *www.thunderboltsway.com.au*

❻ Shimla-Manali, India

A 145-mile (233 km) road runs between the historic hill station of Shimla—once the summer capital of the British Raj with India's second oldest church—and Manali, a trekking trailhead with a more Asian ambience. Along the way you discover lush countryside, fruit orchards, rustic villages, small towns, and hotwater springs of the Kunlun Valley, all backed by snowcapped Himalayan peaks. For southern Indians unused to ice and snow, the region makes an exotic retreat.

PLANNING: Both Shimla and Manali are year-round resorts. *www.hpkullu.nic.in*

Opposite: The Grossglockner High Alpine Road brings the motorist to the sheer, icy world of Austria's highest mountain.

❼ Transfăgărășan Road, Romania

Running north from Arefu to near Cârțişoara across the Făgăraș mountain range, the road rises from 3,392 feet (1,034 m) to 6,673 feet (2,034 m), its highest point, in only 19 miles (30 km). Precipitous switchbacks, viaducts, and tunnels all add to the fun.

PLANNING: The road is driveable from late June through late October only. *www.transfagarasan.net*

❽ Grossglockner-Hochalpenstrasse (High Alpine Road), Austria

On the road between Heiligenblut and Bruck over Austria's highest peak, the Grossglockner, brace yourself for 36 hairpin bends, wildlife including chamoix, marmots, and ibex, and—on a clear day—views of 37 mountains, all higher than 9,842 feet (3,000 m), alongside 19 glaciers.

PLANNING: The road is generally open May through October, but check conditions before traveling. *www.grossglockner.at*

❾ Via Porrettana (SS64), Italy

This quiet 85-mile (138 km) backroad through the Apennine Mountains is positively bucolic. Linking Tuscany and Emilia-Romagna, it leads northwest from Pistoia, just east of Florence, to Ferrara via Bologna. It crosses thick chestnut forests, the ancient spa resort of Porretta Terme, and small, sleepy towns.

PLANNING: Visit the excellent Lamborghini Museum in Sant'Agata Bolognese, near Bologna. *www.intoscana.it*

❿ St.-Jean-Pied-de-Port–Pamplona, France/Spain

The most challenging stretch of the Tour de France is one of the Basque region's most scenic drives. It leads from the cobbled medieval town of St.-Jean-Pied-de-Port over the red-rock Pyrenees southwest through the mountain pass of Roncevaux to the Spanish city of Pamplona.

PLANNING: During the running of the bulls (July 6–14), accommodations in Pamplona are almost unobtainable. Winter snow can block mountain passes. *www.saintjeanpieddeport-paysbasque-tourisme.com*

The city of Catania stands beneath Etna's imposing, and not always benevolent, glare.

ITALY

Around an Active Volcano

This circuit around the slopes of Sicily's Mount Etna—Europe's largest active volcano—offers stunning scenic diversity, including pretty villages, orange groves and vineyards, scars left by recent lava flows, and a range of historical attractions.

After viewing the Greek and Roman remains of Catania, take the S121 west to Paternò, known for its orange groves and restored Norman castle. Continue on the S121 to the village of Adrano, one of Etna's most ancient settlements, whose 11th-century Norman castle houses an archaeological museum. Leave town on the S121 and, after 5 miles (8 km), look for signs to the Ponte dei Saraceni, a graceful multi-arched medieval stone bridge spanning the rocky Simeto River. Drive upstream on minor roads to the beautiful Gola di Simeto, an 8-mile (13 km) gorge formed by lava flows. Return to Adrano and pick up the S284 north to Bronte, the center of Italy's pistachio industry. The gloriously high road between Bronte and Randazzo has some of the best views of Etna. Randazzo, the closest settlement to the volcano's summit (less than 10 miles/16 km away), has so far avoided Etna's wrath, but not World War II bombing, which took a heavy toll. Many of the buildings have now been restored, so the streets retain a medieval atmosphere. The 15th-century church of Santa Maria has some strange, dark lava columns.

From Randazzo the S120 runs eastward through some of the prettiest scenery in the Etna foothills. Just beyond the wine-making village of Passopisciaro you can see the massive lava flows from the 1981 eruption—the fertile volcanic soil now lush with olive trees and other plants. To explore Etna's northern slopes, continue east to the ski resort of Linguaglossa. Next, turn south on a minor road, through the village of Fornazzo, to the resort of Zafferana Etnea, which is surrounded by vineyards and orange groves. From here, you can detour west up a steep, spectacular minor road to the Rifugio Sapienza, a hotel built on the volcano's upper slopes, and return to Catania by minor roads. Otherwise, head east from Zafferana Etnea to the A18 autostrada to return to Catania.

FROM: Loop route from Catania, Italy
ROADS: S121, S284, S120, A18
DISTANCE: 100 miles (160 km)
DRIVING TIME: 3.5 hours
WHEN TO GO: Year-round
PLANNING: Geological tours of Etna are available. www.bestofsicily.com

WALES

Driving through Snowdonia

This drive through the wild, beautiful mountains that are now part of Snowdonia National Park in northwest Wales takes in medieval castles, steam railways, stunning coastline, moorland views, and attractive old towns.

From Dolgellau, take the A496 west and north to Harlech Castle, one of the Iron Ring of fortresses built by Edward I in the 13th century around the perimeter of the northern half of Wales to subdue the territory. The redoubt's great gatehouse, 40-foot (12 m) walls, and corner towers are perched on top of a crag, exuding impregnability. From here, the road crosses the Dwyryd estuary at Maentwrog—turn left here onto the A487, passing the steam trains and stations of the Ffestiniog Railway, built to carry slate from the Blaenau Ffestiniog hills down to the harbor at Porthmadog. The railway closed for business in 1946, but enthusiasts have re-opened it for passengers. From Porthmadog, head north (right) on the A498 over the steep and spectacular pass of Aberglaslyn, and on to Beddgelert. Here, beside the River Glaslyn, is the grave of Gelert, faithful hound of medieval prince Llewelyn the Great, who killed the dog in a rage, mistakenly thinking that it had killed his baby son. The A4085 snakes its way to Caernarfon (see Hidden History), where you rejoin the A487 and skirt Menai Strait, a narrow strip of water separating the Welsh mainland from the Isle of Anglesey. Just across the strait's westerly bridge is Llanfairpwllgwyngyllgogerychwyrndrobwllllantysiliogogogoch, Britain's longest place-name. It means "Church of St. Mary in the hollow of the white hazel near a rapid whirlpool and St. Tysilio near the red cave," and is usually shortened to Llanfair P.G. Make time to visit Beaumaris Castle, the last castle built by Edward I. Back on the mainland, the A55 heads east, skirting Bangor and continuing north to Conwy, a small town ringed with medieval walls and home to another of Edward's castles, crouching over the Conwy estuary with the mountains rising behind.

Hidden History Started in 1283, **Caernarfon Castle's** crenellated walls and octagonal towers still impart a message of strength. Built by Edward I as part of his Iron Ring, it is Wales's most formidable castle. The Eagle Tower, decorated with eagle sculptures, was where Edward II, the first Prince of Wales, was born in 1307; the Queen's Tower houses the Regimental Museum of the Royal Welch Fusiliers, Wales's oldest regiment. Charles, Prince of Wales, was invested here in 1969.

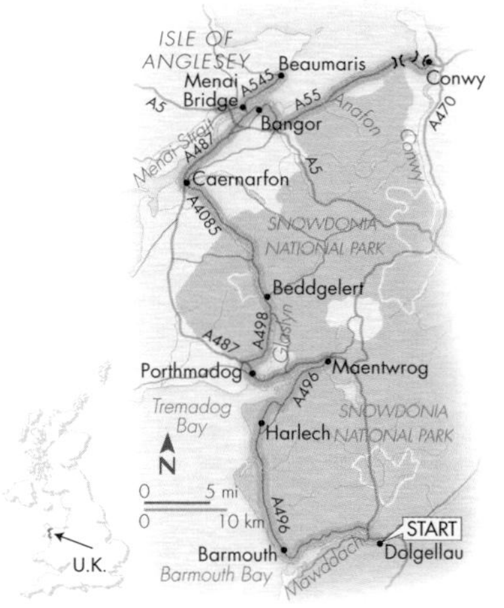

FROM: Dolgellau, Wales
TO: Conwy, Wales
ROADS: A496, A487, A498, A4085, A55
DISTANCE: 85 miles (137 km)
DRIVING TIME: 2.5 hours
WHEN TO GO: Year-round
PLANNING: www.visitwales.co.uk

Perched on top of a rocky outcrop beside the sea, Harlech Castle has breathtaking views inland. In the 15th century, it withstood a seven-year siege.

ENGLAND

The Peak District's High Road

The bleakly beautiful hills, rocky outcrops, and wild moorland of northern England's Peak District—one of Britain's most important national parks—also offer beautiful English villages and winding roads that are a motorist's delight.

The Edwardian Opera House in Buxton was built in 1903 and still presents a variety of shows.

Highlights

- **Haddon Hall** is a country house on the River Wye, with origins in the 11th century. It has a Tudor long gallery and a 14th-century great hall, and has appeared in many TV shows, such as the 2005 adaptation of Jane Austen's *Pride and Prejudice*.
- The Peak District's best known and most impressive house is **Chatsworth House,** the 17th-century Baroque palace of the Dukes of Devonshire with extensive and beautiful grounds. The finely furnished state rooms have ceilings painted by Verrio and Louis Laguerre and paintings by Van Dyck, Van der Vaart, and Rembrandt.

Begin in the Georgian spa town of Buxton, whose elegant central crescent of sandstone houses is modeled on the Royal Crescent in Bath. The Edwardian Opera House is worth visiting for its rich gold-leaf interior. You can also fill your water bottle from the natural mineral stream at St. Ann's Well. Then take the A53 and A54 west for 10 miles (16 km), and pick up the minor road through the village of Wincle to Leek, home to Brindley Mill, a watermill built in 1752. Turn east across the high, lonely moors, passing through the picturesque country villages of Warslow, Alstonefield, and Ilam, to Ashbourne. This beautiful Georgian town is a good base for hiking—the 13-mile (21 km) Tissington Trail and the 17-mile (27 km) High Peak Trail, which both run along disused railway lines, begin here.

From Ashbourne, the B5035 runs through Kniveton to Wirksworth. Turn north here on the A6 to Matlock, a late-Georgian spa town complete with an 1853 hydro health center on the hill above. The B5057 and B5056 run through beautiful upland countryside on the way to Winster and past Haddon Hall (see Highlights). Turn right to Rowsley on the A6, then left on the B6012 to Chatsworth House (see Highlights). You can detour here into Bakewell, a town famous for its eponymous tart, consisting of a pastry filled with ground almond paste and jam.

From Chatsworth House, follow the B6001 north to the pretty village of Hathersage, then the A625 and A6013 to Ladybower Reservoir, and turn left onto the A57 to Snake Pass. The reservoirs to your right are where the Royal Air Force squadron known as the Dambusters trained for their epic bombing raid on German dams in World War II. The ascent to Snake Pass is one of the most exciting roads in the U.K., twisting, turning, and switchbacking across some of the highest points in the Peak District. Descending from the pass, the road offers views of the metropolis of Manchester some 10 miles (16 km) away. And look for Bleaklow, where the remains of a U.S.A.F. Superfortress that crashed in 1948 still lie scattered across the ground. From the former mill town of Glossop, take the A624 and A6 back to Buxton.

FROM: Loop route from Buxton, England
ROADS: A53, A54, B5035, A6, B5057, B5056, B6012, B6001, A625, A6013, A57, A624, local roads
DISTANCE: 120 miles (193 km)
DRIVING TIME: 3.5 hours
WHEN TO GO: Spring through fall
PLANNING: www.visitpeakdistrict.com

OPPOSITE: The green, undulating landscape of the Peak District is a haven for hikers.

FRANCE

Europe's Deepest Canyon

As the Verdon River carved through 16 miles (26 km) of limestone in the Alpes-de-Haute-Provence, in southeast France, it created the deepest and one of the most beautiful canyons in Europe—the Gorges du Verdon.

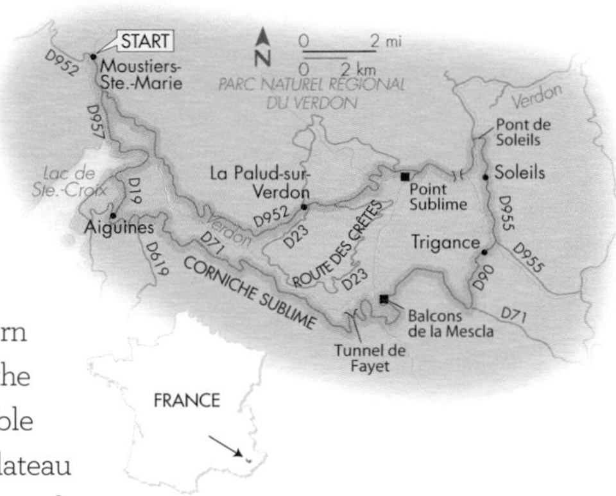

With its narrow medieval streets centered around a 12th-century church and workshops selling the faience pottery for which it is famous, the pretty town of Moustiers-Ste.-Marie has plenty to explore. Leave town along the narrow, twisting D952 as it runs high above the gorge toward the Rive Droite, or northern rim, climbing past views of distant Lac de Ste.-Croix and descending on the edge of a cliff with the Verdon River far below. At the hairpin bend at Bélvèdere de Mayreste, you can stop and scramble 500 feet (152 m) up the rocks for your first view of the canyon. The road then climbs to a plateau filled with lavender fields before descending to La Palud-sur-Verdon, a hub for activities such as rock climbing, rafting, and hiking. Pick up the Route des Crêtes (D23) just outside town. The dizzyingly high 14-mile (23 km) loop road follows the plateau's edge high above the river. Midway around, the Refuge des Malines serves up snacks, drinks, and sublime views. The Martel Trail, the most popular section of the GR4 walking route, runs through here. Back at La Palud, turn east on the D952. After passing woods, valleys, and wildflower fields, the road snakes down to Point Sublime. From here you can hike up the hill to see the view of Samson Corridor, the entrance to the Verdon Gorge.

Drive through the Tunnel du Tusset, cross the river at Pont de Soleils, and take the D955 for the return drive along the Rive Gauche. Beyond tiny Soleils, turn southwest on the D90 to the medieval town of Trigance, with its hilltop castle. Climb through fields and woods, then descend on the D71 through the Balcons de la Mescla, where the Verdon and Artuby Rivers meet. The road reaches Pont de l'Artuby, a 600-foot (183 m) high bridge popular with bungee jumpers. Beyond, you are on the gorge's edge, with pullovers from which to admire the views. After the Tunnel de Fayet, the road turns away from the gorge and follows Cavaliers Cliff. Fill your water bottle from the Source de Vaumale before ascending to the road's highest point, at 2,625 feet (800 m) above the Verdon. The road twists down to Aiguines, with a centuries-old legacy of boules-making, and past Lac de Ste.-Croix, to return to Moustiers on the D957.

FROM: Loop route from Moustiers-Ste.-Marie, France
ROADS: D952, D23/Route des Crêtes, D955, D90, D71, D957
DISTANCE: 50 miles (80 km)
DRIVING TIME: 1.5 hours
WHEN TO GO: Year-round
PLANNING: Lac de Ste.-Croix is popular for watersports—all kinds of equipment can be rented there. www.provenceweb.fr

The steep and rocky Gorges du Verdon is sometimes known as "Europe's Grand Canyon."

The village of Guadalest's clifftop towers can be seen from miles around.

Highlights

- For an antidote to the dry sierra, take a short detour from Callosa down the CV715 toward Bolulla to the rushing springs, environmental exhibits, and small restaurants of **Fonts de l'Algar.**

- The **Casa Orduna**, Guadalest's noble mansion and now the Museo Municipal, was built in 1644 and rebuilt in 1708 after the War of Succession. Inside are the furnishings, paintings (including the anonymous, double-sided *Ecce Homo*), and library of the Orduna family. From the garden, steps lead up to **Sant Josep Castle,** part of which is now a cemetery, with panoramic views.

SPAIN

Hill Villages of Eastern Spain

The terraced hillsides of orange and lemon groves and olive and almond trees settled in the peaceful scenery around the village of Guadalest in eastern Spain have breathtaking views over the surrounding sierra (*serra* in Catalan) and delightful old villages.

From the coastal resort of Altea, take the Valencia road (N332), following the bay. Head northwest toward Callosa d'en Sarrià on the A150 and CV755, as the Serra de Guadalest looms ahead with terraced orange and lemon groves in the foreground. From Callosa d'en Sarrià, an agricultural town with a medieval arch and old walls around its Plaza del Castell, the CV755 runs northwest through rugged limestone hills covered in pine trees and maquis. Granite pinnacles topped by white towers greet your approach to the village of Guadalest, where you can wander the old streets and take tours of the castle (see Highlights) and the ethnological museum, which has displays on the village's history and chocolate-making industry. From Guadalest, the CV70 winds around the flank of the Guadalest Valley, through terraces of almond trees (covered in pink and white blossoms in February), to Confrides at the source of the Guadalest River, where a giant walnut tree graces the village's main square. The road now winds through rocky moorland and over a high pass. Turn left onto the CV770, then right onto the CV781 and stop to look at Penàguila's medieval gateway and noble mansions. Head for Sella on the CV785, through the forested Serra de Aitana where the mountain of Puig Campana keeps watch. Sella has Roman ruins and the remains of a medieval castle, and is a good starting point for hikes. The CV770 and CV758 lead through terraced orchards to Finestrat—walk up to the church and hermitage of the Remedio, built over an old Moorish castle. After enjoying the fine views of the Mediterranean, take the CV758, CV70, and N332 to Albir.

FROM: Altea, Spain
TO: Albir, Spain
ROADS: N332, A150, CV755, CV70, CV770, CV781, CV785, CV758
DISTANCE: 63 miles (102 km)
DRIVING TIME: 2.5 hours
WHEN TO GO: Year-round
PLANNING: In Penàguila, Penya de l'Aguila restaurant serves good local dishes. www.benidorm-info.com

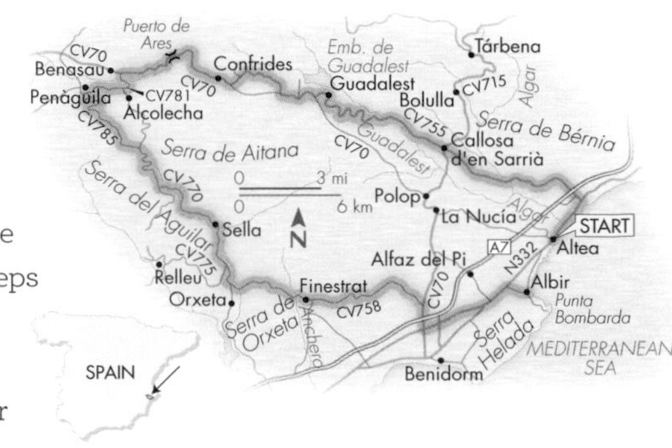

The well-preserved village of Pampaneira hugs the slopes of the Barranco del Poqueira.

Highlights

- Past Pampaneira, take a short detour to the left to the spectacularly sited villages of **Bubión** and **Capileira,** with the Sierra Nevada's highest peaks rising behind them.
- Three miles (5 km) past the Bubión turnoff on the A4312, take a short detour to the villages of **Mecina Fondales,** and **Ferreirola.** They still have unspoiled traditional Alpujarras architecture, with thick stone, whitewashed walls, flat roofs, and Moorish-style covered walkways called *tinaos.*

SPAIN

Las Alpujarras

On this circular route through Las Alpujarras, the foothills of southern Spain's Sierra Nevada, you'll pass quaint old villages and market towns against the backdrop of flower-covered hills and mountains.

FROM: Lanjarón, Spain
TO: Órgiva, Spain
ROADS: A348/C332, A4132/GR4201, A4130, A4127
DISTANCE: 70 miles (113 km)
DRIVING TIME: 3 hours
WHEN TO GO: Year-round
PLANNING: The annual Dragon Festival techno-music rave is held near Órgiva around the end of March, with thousands of people attending. www.lasalpujarras.co.uk

From the spa town of Lanjarón, source of a renowned mineral water and home to a dilapidated Moorish castle, take the A348/C332 toward Órgiva and the dramatic mountain scenery of Las Alpujarras. Órgiva has a popular Thursday market, a twin-towered baroque church, and a Mudéjar mansion. Leaving the town and heading toward Trevélez, switchbacks take you up into the mountains on the A4132/GR4201 past glimmering white villages clinging to the slopes. The road swings north to the Barranco del Poqueira, a deep canyon formed by the Poqueira River. The village of Pampaneira on the slopes of the canyon has a 16th-century church, a pretty square where you can enjoy a drink, and shops filled with handwoven rugs, ceramics, and jewelry. The adjoining Parque Nacional de la Sierra Nevada has its main visitor center here and sells mountain trekking maps. Continue on the A4132 as it climbs to dizzying heights, drive through the villages of Pitres and Pórtugos, and turn north into another gorge. This wild country abounds with goats and free-roaming pigs, some of which are turned into cured ham at the mountain village of Trevélez. The road backtracks on the opposite side of the gorge, curving into the main valley around the peak of Peñabón. Past the village of Juviles, on the A4130 and A4127, drive through moorland dotted with olive trees before crossing the Guadalfeo River and climbing to some vertiginous views. Follow signs to Cádiar, one of the Alpujarras' largest towns, and take the lonely A348 west with continuous scenic views. The road eventually straightens out and brings you to a turnoff back to Órgiva.

Also Recommended

❶ Catskill Mountain Drive, New York

The beautiful scenery of the Catskill Mountains makes for a peaceful drive along N.Y. 28. Following Esopus Creek, enter the radiant mountain range, and hike to the summit of Belleayre Mountain for superb views of peaks and forests.

www.drivers.com/article/794

❷ Peak to Peak Scenic Byway, Colorado

Less than an hour from Denver, this 55-mile (88 km) route from Central City north to Estes Park borders Rocky Mountain National Park, where peaks tower up to a mile (1.6 km) above the road. Detour onto one of the gravel roads off the highway to reach lakes and secluded campgrounds.

www.byways.org

❸ Mount Washington Auto Road, New Hampshire

Leading to the "Top of New England," this road rises steeply above the treeline and climbs to the summit of Mount Washington, the highest peak in the northeastern U.S. The region is famed for its spectacular fall colors, with breathtaking views over White Mountain National Forest and the Presidential Range.

www.mountwashingtonautoroad.com

❹ Richardson Highway, Alaska

Alaska's first major road traces an old gold-rush route from Valdez to Fairbanks, traveling 368 miles (562 km) through lush Alaska scenery. Pass the breathtaking Worthington Glacier, and watch for wildlife, such as the brown bear, crossing the road.

www.travelalaska.com

❺ Munro Trail, Hawaii

The Munro Trail begins in the center of Lanai island and is signposted on the main road from Lanai City. This 7-mile (11 km) dirt track along a razorback ridge brings you to Lanaihale, the highest peak on the island. On a clear day, the views stretch to several of Hawaii's other islands. This drive shouldn't be attempted in bad weather.

www.gohawaii.com

❻ Continental Divide, Panama

Surmounting Panama's serrated spine, Hwy. 4 from Chiriquí snakes sharply as it rises from the Pacific over the Continental Divide and dramatically drops some 5,000 feet (1,524 m) to the town of Punta Peña and the Caribbean coastal plains.

www.visitpanama.com

❼ Ibusuki Skyline Drive, Japan

Close to the shoreline, yet riding high along mountain ridges, this serpentine road along the Satsuma Peninsula is seldom congested. Look out across the sea to catch sight of the active Sakurajima volcano billowing ash as you drive south from Kagoshima around the eponymous bay, relaxing in Ibusuki's warm crater lake before completing this 43-mile (70 km) route to Ei.

www.jnto.go.jp/eng

❽ Flórina to Kastoriá, Greece

From the pretty market town of Flórina, drive east along the E-86 through the mountains of western Macedonia, passing the village of Andartikó. Stop at the Monastery of Panagia Mvriotissa to see Christian art from the 12th century and a nearby tree rumored to be 900 years old. From here, detour one hour to the east to visit Nymfeo, a town set in the heights of 4,429-foot (1,350 m) Mount Visti, or just continue the few remaining miles south to downtown Kastoriá, a city jutting into enormous and beautiful Lake Orestiada.

www.gnto.co.uk

❾ Glossglockner High Alpine Road, Austria

Flower-filled meadows teeming with wildlife bring the Grossglocknerstrasse alpine road alive even on cloudy days. The route begins in the pretty mountain village of Heiligenblut and runs north for 30 miles (48 km), negotiating 36 twisting bends around Grossglockner Mountain and Perenze Glacier. It ends south of the stunning lakeside resort of Zell am See. Many drivers carry on to Salzburg, 25 miles (40 km) farther north.

www.grossglockner.at

❿ Great St. Bernard Pass, Switzerland/Italy

The most famous mountain pass in the Alps, this 45-mile (72 km) route from Martigny, Switzerland, to Aosta, Italy, offers mesmerizing views of glaciers, canyons, and lakes. Traversed by Julius Caesar, Hannibal, and Napoleon, the pass has a special place in history. It is open from the middle of June through October.

www.myswitzerland.com

⓫ Hay-on-Wye, England/Wales

From Hay-on-Wye's bookshops, head south through the tall hedgerows of Forest Road to enter the Black Mountain's rolling hills in Brecon Beacons National Park. Stop at the tiny church of Capel-y-ffin, whose east window, facing the mountains, is engraved with the words, "I shall lift up mine eyes to the hills whence cometh my salvation." Continue to Llanthony to view a ruined medieval priory, before carrying on to the town of Abergavenny.

www.hay-on-wye.co.uk

⓬ Palma to Sa Calobra, Mallorca, Spain

Leave Palma on the MA-20, and exit at 5B for the MA-1130 to Valdemossa to visit the former rooms of composer Frédéric Chopin and pioneering French female novelist George Sand. Ten minutes farther north on the MA-10, you reach Deià set under the mountains of the Serra de Tramuntana. Continue on the MA-10 until it intersects the MA-2141 for a harrowing, wriggling descent into Sa Calobra.

www.spain.info

⓭ Maloti Mountains, South Africa

From Golden Gate Highlands National Park, head west along R712/R711 through the Maloti Mountains, enjoying spectacular sandstone formations that gleam yellow, brown, and pink in the varying light. After 34 miles (54 km) of undulating countryside, passing some of South Africa's finest landscapes, you arrive at the small town of Fouriesburg.

www.southafrica.net

CHAPTER 2

By Sea & Shore

PICTURE A ROMANTIC DRIVE AND THE image most likely to spring to mind is a road that runs along the water's edge, skirting a mountain-fringed lake or curving high above a turquoise sea. Small wonder that these journeys conjure up a powerful sense of freedom and adventure. They take us to places where the worlds of land, sky, and water meet. Some of the roads are legends in their own right. California's Rte. 1, for instance, clings to North America's western edge, swinging out over the Pacific Ocean in a spectacular journey southward through the mountainous landscapes and alluring coves of Big Sur. Italy's famed Amalfi Drive, familiar to lovers of classic European movies, is a veritable thriller of scenic switchbacks and heart-stopping sea views, ideal for drivers with romantic souls and nerves of steel. And for intrepid travelers on a quest for nature, routes lead north to the whale-watching grounds of Nova Scotia and south to Australia's Great Ocean Road for an epic journey of mountainscapes, rain forests, offshore rock formations, and beaches that seem to go on forever.

The coast road along the French Riviera passes through pretty villages and provides stunning views of the Mediterranean, such as this one looking toward St.-Jean-Cap-Ferrat.

A stranded iceberg sits gleaming white and incongruous in the busy little fishing port of Old Bonaventure on the Bonavista Peninsula.

CANADA

Along Newfoundland's Shores

Passing some of the oldest European settlements in North America, this drive around Newfoundland's Avalon and Bonavista peninsulas encompasses desolate land and seascapes, and showcases wildlife from kittiwakes and razorbills to caribou and the odd roadside moose.

St. John's, a steep-alleyed port on the Avalon peninsula, has fortifications at Signal Hill dating from the Napoleonic Wars. From here, head south on Pitts Memorial Drive and Hwy. 10. At Bay Bulls, take a boat to the four islands of Witless Bay Ecological Reserve, a summer breeding ground for more than 2 million seabirds, including kittiwakes, razorbills, and guillemots. Back on the mainland, continue south to Ferryland. Established in the 17th century, this town is one of the earliest British settlements in Canada. From here, the vistas expand and the landscape becomes more barren. The sense of being swallowed by the vastness of the sprawling topography intensifies as you round the peninsula. Watch out for some of the world's largest caribou as the fog rolls in.

From the whale-watching point of St. Vincent's, follow Hwy. 90 toward Holyrood, passing picturesque coves, rocky ridges, and a bevy of fishing villages. Then head north into Brigus, a former sealing port with Protestant churches and a circular plan that reflects its English heritage. Proceed north on Hwy. 70, past the rusting hulk of S.S. *Kyle* beached at Harbour Grace, where Amelia Earhart launched her first solo transatlantic flight in 1932. From windswept Carbonear, take Hwy. 74 northwest across a stark, lunar landscape dotted with stunted spruce trees and shallow ponds. At the eastern shore of Trinity Bay, you pass Heart's Content Cable Station, the western terminal of the first transatlantic cable, laid in 1866. As you turn south on Hwy. 80, you pass the bayside towns of Heart's Desire and Heart's Delight. Drive northwest across expanses of rock-strewn tundra on Trans-Canada 1 until you reach Hwy. 230, which leads up the Bonavista peninsula. Pause in the town of Trinity—a gem not to be missed. An old English fishing and mercantile town, it is now preserved as a national heritage community. Continue to the 500-year-old seaport of Bonavista sprawled across the treeless barrens at the peninsula's tip.

FROM: St. John's, Canada
TO: Bonavista, Canada
ROADS: Pitts Memorial Drive, Hwys. 10, 90, 70, 74, 80, Trans-Canada 1, Hwy. 230, local roads
DISTANCE: 430 miles (692 km)
DRIVING TIME: 7 hours
WHEN TO GO: June through October
PLANNING: www.newfoundlandlabrador.com

CANADA

Cape Breton Island

One of the most memorable drives in North America, the Cabot Trail loops around the northern tip of Nova Scotia, offering sightings of whales offshore, moose inland, and bald eagles overhead, all set against a backdrop of mountains and a rugged coast.

The village of Baddeck was the adopted summer home of Alexander Graham Bell (see Hidden History), who said of the region: "For simple beauty, Cape Breton Island outrivals them all." From Baddeck, head west on Trans-Canada 105 to join the Cabot Trail. Beyond the Margaree River—a great spot for salmon fishing—and the Acadian port of Chéticamp, moody mountains loom ahead as the trail enters Cape Breton Highlands National Park. In the park, a kaleidoscope of views greets you as you follow a rising and falling road past a variety of ecosystems, including lakes, bogs, hardwood forests, mountain ridges, and wild coastline. On the way to Pleasant Bay, stop at one of the designated pull-offs for impressive views of the sea, and at Lone Shieling leave your car and walk to the reconstructed Highland crofter's cottage nearby. Drive inland toward Cape North, keeping an eye out for moose by the road on the way to Neil's Harbour. The road soon hugs the coast again and the pink-colored rocks stretching out to sea at Black Brook Cove come into view, with Ingonish Bay, dominated by the slopes of Cape Smokey, ahead. Park at the Tudor-style Keltic Lodge on the spectacular Middle Head peninsula, which cuts Ingonish Bay in two, and walk the trail to the peninsula's end for views of Cape Smokey and Tern Rock. In summer, whale-watching tours leave from here. After Ingonish, follow the Cabot Trail south over Cape Smokey as it passes a series of Gaelic fishing villages and clings precariously to the steep sides of St. Ann's Bay. At South Gut St. Anns, stop at the Gaelic College of Arts and Crafts, which has been a driving force behind the Gaelic revival in Nova Scotia since 1938.

Hidden History In Baddeck, the **Alexander Graham Bell National Historic Site** presents an interactive walk through Bell's world and a comprehensive collection of his inventions and artifacts, including replicas and models of telephones and the 60-foot (18 m) long hydrofoil HD-4, which was the fastest boat in the world in 1919. The 25-acre (10 ha) site is situated above Baddeck Bay, on Bras d'Or Lake overlooking Bell's summer home, Beinn Bhreagh.

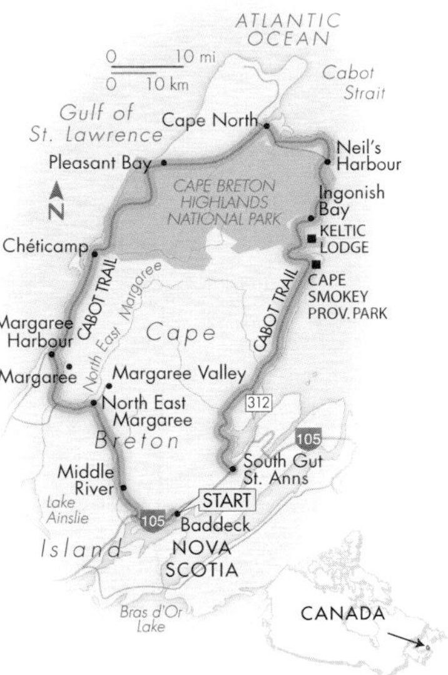

FROM: Baddeck, Canada
TO: South Gut St. Anns, Canada
ROADS: Trans-Canada 105, Cabot Trail
DISTANCE: 186 miles (299 km)
DRIVING TIME: 4 hours
WHEN TO GO: Late June through mid-October
PLANNING: www.cabottrail.com

The Cabot Trail winds along the coast, surrounded by warm, fall colors.

MAINE

Maine's Rugged Coast

An undiscovered gem, this drive is one of the least traveled in the United States. You should be able to watch the surf crashing against Schoodic Point and the "boiling tides" of Cobscook Bay in relative seclusion.

From the small city of Ellsworth, a bustling center in the tourist season, head southeast on U.S. 1, crossing Taunton Bay and past views of Cadillac Mountain and Mount Desert Island. Enjoy coastline scenery for 16 miles (26 km) before turning right on Me. 186 and following the winding road along the shore of Frenchman Bay to Winter Harbor Village, where a turnoff brings you to Acadia National Park's Schoodic Point, a preserve around the windswept granite shores of Schoodic Peninsula. Continue on Me. 186 through Birch Harbor and rejoin U.S. 1 to reach Washington County, once the territory of Passamaquoddy Indians. Drive north through Cherryfield, the "blueberry capital of the world," and on to Columbia Falls on U.S. 1, and stop by the Thomas Ruggles House, built for a rich lumber dealer in 1818. Just past town, take Me. 187 south to the fishing community of Jonesport, where cruises leave to Machias Seal Island or Petit Manan Island. Once back on U.S. 1, look for the turnoff to the sandy beaches and freshwater swimming pond of Roque Bluffs State Park. Continue through the shire town (county seat) of Machias, where you can turn right for a look at the twice-ruined fort at Fort O'Brien State Historic Site. Soon after Machias, U.S. 1 enters Moosehorn National Wildlife Refuge—a breeding ground for migratory birds, including the elusive American woodcock—bordering Cobscook Bay. Tides here average 24 feet (7.3 m) high—Native Americans called the bay "boiling tides." Continue north past the 45th parallel picnic area, through the small town of Perry, and then past the granite cliffs of St. Croix River to Calais, one of the busiest ports of entry on the U.S.-Canada border.

FROM: Ellsworth, Maine
TO: Calais, Maine
ROADS: U.S. 1, Me. 186, 187
DISTANCE: 197 miles (317 km)
DRIVING TIME: 4 hours
WHEN TO GO: Spring through fall
PLANNING: The loop road around Schoodic Point is one way. www.nationalparkacadia.com

Excursion Around 16 miles (26 km) beyond Machias, turn right onto Me. 189 for **Quoddy Head State Park,** the easternmost point in the U.S., with views of the Bay of Fundy, which has tides of up to 40 feet (12 m)—some of the highest tides in the world—and Campobello Island, the Canadian vacation home of Franklin D. Roosevelt. Today, the 2,800-acre (1,133 ha) Roosevelt Campobello International Park preserves the grand, 34-room summer home of the former president.

Sunlight glints on the rocks around the rugged coastline of Schoodic Peninsula.

Among the many attractions of Key West is the house of Ernest Hemingway, now a museum.

FLORIDA

Miami and the Keys

Between Miami's glitzy, high-rise glamor and Key West's bohemian eccentricities, this drive—one of the most scenic in the U.S.—takes in jungle gardens, the wildlife-filled backwaters of Everglades National Park, and the reefs of the Florida Keys.

FROM: Miami Beach, Florida
TO: Key West, Florida
ROADS: U.S. 41/Fla. A1A, Fla. 9336, U.S. 1, Overseas Highway, local roads
DISTANCE: 240 miles (386 km)
DRIVING TIME: 5 hours
WHEN TO GO: Year-round
PLANNING: Traffic is heavy on the Overseas Highway in peak season (winter through spring).
www.fla-keys.com

After enjoying the urban delights of Miami, head out of town on U.S. 41/Fla. A1A from Miami Beach across Biscayne Bay, where you'll get a good view of the city's towering skyline. Drive through the plush suburb of Coconut Grove and take Old Cutler Road to Fairchild Tropical Garden, a botanical wonderland of ferns, shrubs, and lily pools. Continue on U.S. 1 to Biscayne National Park, which is almost entirely submerged in water and inhabited by fish and other marine animals. Farther south, take Fla. 9336 west through fields of strawberries, sugarcane, and tropical plants to reach Everglades National Park, a 1.5-million-acre (607,028 ha) subtropical wilderness that is home to delicate mangrove swamps, crocodiles, alligators, turtles, and many species of birds.

Backtrack to U.S. 1 and head south, crossing over the first of 42 bridges that span the sun-warmed Florida Keys. Snorkel with vibrantly colored tropical fish at the National Marine Sanctuary on Key Largo, the longest island in the Keys, before continuing south on the Overseas Highway. The road is lined with hibiscus and palms, with views of emerald water stretching away on either side. Stop at Long Key State Recreation Area to take the 1.25-mile (2 km) Golden Orb Trail along the lagoon and beach. Back on U.S. 1, cross Seven Mile Bridge—one of the world's longest—and proceed to Bahia Honda State Park, which has exotic West Indian plants and one of the few natural sand beaches in the Keys. Continue across Big Pine Key to the rowdy bars and posh boutiques of Key West, one of the state's most distinctive and endearing cities.

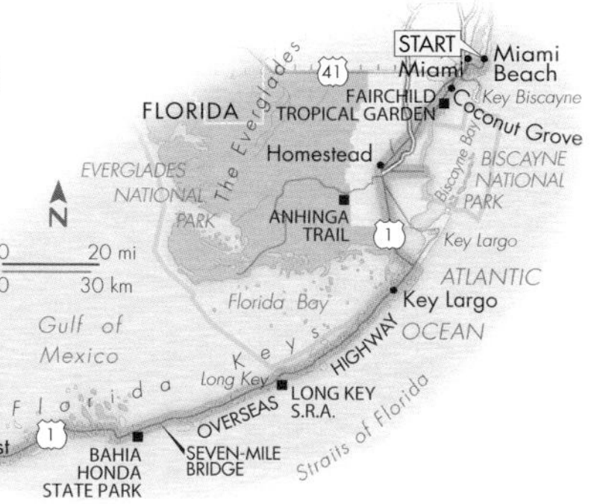

The prow of a skipjack sailboat moored in sunny Dogwood Harbor, Chesapeake Bay

MARYLAND

Chesapeake Country

Wooden skipjacks sail on the Chesapeake Bay, broad tidal rivers drain tranquil farmlands, and Georgian and Victorian architecture lines old town streets in this relaxed part of Maryland, halfway between Philadelphia and Washington, D.C.

FROM: Chesapeake City, Maryland
TO: Tilghman Island, Maryland
ROADS: Md. 213, 662, 322, 33, local roads
DISTANCE: 100 miles (160 km)
DRIVING TIME: 3 hours
WHEN TO GO: Spring and fall
PLANNING: www.chesapeakebyway.org

Chesapeake City, a handsomely restored 19th-century town dotted with inns, cafés, and marinas, is your starting point. The first half of the route follows the Chesapeake Country Scenic Byway (Md. 213 south), past fields of corn and soybeans. You soon cross the Bohemia and Sassafras Rivers—the latter thought to have been explored by the early settler Captain John Smith in 1608. Continue to Chestertown and look around the Colonial House Museum and the 18th-century White Swann Tavern B&B. Continue through Centreville, whose architecture ranges from Federal to Late Victorian. A detour from Queenstown follows the Chesapeake Country Scenic Drive America's Byway toward the Chesapeake Bay Environmental Center, a preserve with trails, exhibits, and ecology-oriented programs. Back on Md. 213, head south to reach the picturesque, 19th-century Wye Grist Mill. To find your way to the old harbor town of St. Michaels for a lunch of boiled crabs at one of the town's dock-side eateries, head south on Md. 662 toward Easton, turning onto Md. 322, then west onto Md. 33. Follow Md. 33 across the bridge over Knapps Narrows to leave the mainland and arrive at Tilghman Island, traditionally home to the hardy individuals who make their living fishing for oysters. At the fork 2.5 miles (4 km) farther on, bear right onto Black Walnut Point road. The drive ends at the Black Walnut Point Inn, perhaps the most secluded and rustic B&B on the entire eastern shore.

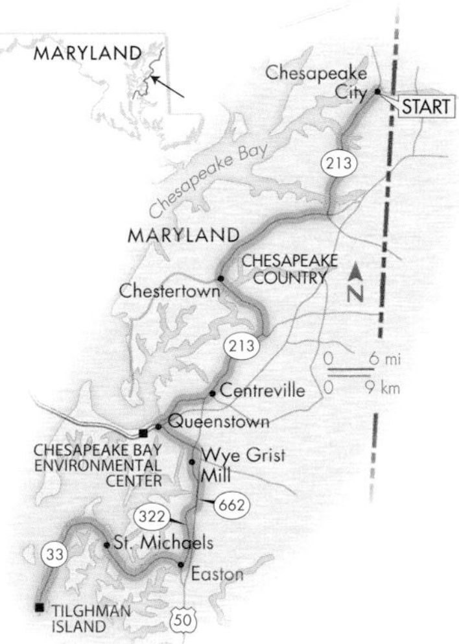

Wildlife Encounter Past Chestertown is **Eastern Neck National Wildlife Refuge,** a short side trip down Md. 20 and 445 west and south. This island refuge is known for its migrant bird populations, which include more than 100,000 ducks, swans, and geese, along with song- and shore birds. You may also spot bald eagles. Recreational activities include boating, fishing, crabbing, and hiking along the more than 6 miles (10 km) of roads, trails, and boardwalks.

MICHIGAN

Around Whitefish Bay

An idyllic journey around Lake Superior's Whitefish Bay reveals pristine hardwood forests, mountains and beaches, wildflowers, shimmering views, and an abundance of wildlife—from black bears, deer, and moose, to hawks, waterfowl, and songbirds.

Keep an eye out for black bears and white-tailed deer as you leave the fishing community of Brimley and head west on Lakeshore Drive through forests of birch, maple, and oak scattered with pine. The drive passes through the Bay Mills Indian Reservation, arcing around South Pond. Tower Road, a 1-mile (1.6 km) detour on the left, leads to Spectacle Lake Overlook with views of the glimmering lake, St. Marys River, and the Canadian shore in the distance. Back on the main road, Lake Shore Drive becomes Curley Lewis Highway after you enter Hiawatha National Forest—a short detour down a shady side road brings you to secluded Monocle Lake. The drive meanders through woods filled with wildflowers from spring through fall. Soon you pass through the town of Dollar Settlement and the Big Pines Picnic Area on Whitefish Bay's 19 miles (31 km) of sandy beach. The road dips between the bay and the forest, and winds along the base of Naomikong Point. Drive north on Mich. 123 before crossing the Tahquamenon River back to the bay's western shore. After the resort town of Paradise, head north along the narrow Whitefish Point Road, which twists as you approach Whitefish Point Lighthouse and the nearby Whitefish Point Bird Observatory—a good place to view migrating hawks, waterfowl, and songbirds. Only a few miles from the Canadian shore, you may spot a moose along the lonely road. Beyond Grand Portage Indian Reservation you will find spectacular mountains, ridges, and peninsulas. The road climbs to a crest near 1,348-foot (411 m) Mount Josephine, which juts into Lake Superior. From the escarpment, Lake Superior, Wauswaugoning Bay, the Susie Islands and, on a clear day, Michigan's Isle Royale, are all in view.

FROM: Brimley, Michigan
TO: Whitefish Point, Michigan
ROADS: Lakeshore Drive, Curley Lewis Highway, Mich. 123/Whitefish Road, Whitefish Point Road
DISTANCE: 54 miles (87 km)
DRIVING TIME: 2 hours
WHEN TO GO: Spring through fall
PLANNING: National forest campgrounds are located at Monocle Lake and Bay View. www.michigan.gov/drive

Excursion Once a camping, fishing, and hunting ground of the Chippewa Indians, **Tahquamenon Falls State Park** is a 10-mile (16 km) detour west on Mich. 123 from Paradise. The upper falls, at 200 feet (61 m) wide and with a 50-foot (15 m) drop, are the largest falls east of the Mississippi, and the lower falls are equally magnificent. There are also opportunities to hike, camp, fish, canoe, spot wildlife, and hunt. The falls have been known to freeze over in Michigan's frigid winters.

At Point Iroquois Lighthouse near Monocle Lake, you can tour the small museum and climb the tower for views of Lake Superior.

WASHINGTON

Island Hopping in Washington

Washington State's coast overflows with maritime culture and history. On this drive, visit decommissioned warships, national parks, and woodlands, and marvel at the plentiful marine life dwelling close to the beaches, coves, and bays of the San Juan Islands.

An orca leaps out of the water in one of the many channels between the San Juan Islands.

Highlights

- Visit the decommissioned destroyer, **USS *Turner Joy,*** at Bremerton. The 1959 vessel is still in its original condition, from the bridge to the closet-sized barber shop.
- The **San Juan Islands** are a great place to spot whales and orcas. A whale boat tour in May or June gives you a 90-percent chance of a sighting.
- **San Juan Island National Historic Park,** known for its splendid vistas and quiet woodlands, is the site where Britain and the U.S.A. almost went to war over a dead pig in a border dispute in 1859.

After exploring the handsome and vibrant city of Seattle, take a ferry across Puget Sound to Bremerton. A tour boat takes you around Puget Sound Naval Shipyard, where you can see dozens of active warships and the decommissioned Mothball Fleet—including some old aircraft carriers (see Highlights). Back on land, Bremerton Naval Museum has artifacts, photos, and models illustrating the history of the U.S. Navy. Continue north through Keyport, another naval town on Wash. 303, before driving around Liberty Bay on Wash. 3 to Poulsbo, known for its Norwegian heritage. The old town teems with shops, cafés, and galleries, and at the Marine Science Center, you can handle sea cucumbers and sea anemones. Farther north, Port Gamble is home to the Of Sea and Shore Museum, which has a large collection of seashells and marine life on display. Cross Hood Canal on Wash. 104, then take U.S. 101 north before turning right onto Wash. 20, on your way passing the 19th-century coastal gun-emplacements of Fort Worden State Park, the Coast Artillery Museum, and the Port Townsend Marine Science Center. Soon you'll reach the waterfront town of Port Townsend, which has one of the best preserved and most extensive historic districts in the northwest, brimming with elaborate 19th-century buildings and pretty, pastel-colored Victorian homes.

Take a ferry across the bay to Whidbey Island, where you'll dock below more historic gun-emplacements at Fort Casey State Park, before continuing on Wash. 20 to the small, but perfectly preserved, 19th-century town of Coupeville, with more than 50 structures on the National Register of Historic Places. Stop off to explore Ebey's Landing National Historic Reserve, which preserves small farms, woodlands, and beaches in a state that is relatively unchanged since the 19th century. Head north on Wash. 20, past Deception Pass State Park, Washington's most popular state park with 4,600 acres (1,862 ha) of trails, beaches, and lakes. Continue across Fidalgo Island to the Anacortes Ferry, which takes you to Friday Harbor on the hilly, forested San Juan Islands. From here, you can book a whale-watching tour to see the orcas, seabirds, Steller sea lions, harbor porpoises, gray whales, and other marine life or visit San Juan Island National Historic Park (see Highlights).

FROM: Seattle, Washington
TO: Friday Harbor, Washington
ROADS: Wash. 303, 3, 104, U.S. 101, Wash. 20, local roads
DISTANCE: 88 miles (141 km)
DRIVING TIME: 3.5 hours
WHEN TO GO: Year-round
PLANNING: Orca-watching is best from May through June. www.travelsanjuan.com

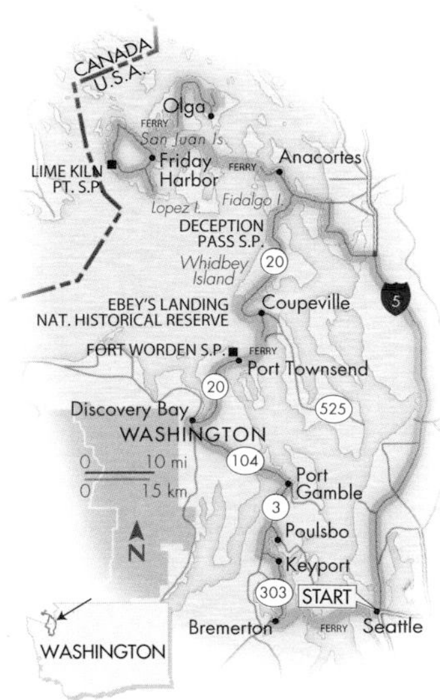

OPPOSITE: Gnarled driftwood by the peaceful waters of Sharpe Bay in Deception Bay State Park

Purple lupines stand tall near Fossil Beach, the perfect place to while away some time hunting for fossils.

Highlights

- **Fort Abercrombie State Historical Park,** near Kodiak, is the remains of a World War II defense installation set in beautiful surroundings with steep, surf-pounded cliffs, spruce forests, and wildflower meadows.
- **Whales** are commonly sighted from the coast of Kodiak from April through November. Look out for fin, minke, sei, humpback, and gray whales from the cliffs along Chiniak Highway.
- The **Alutiiq Museum** in Kodiak houses about 150,000 historical and archaeological artifacts—including weapons, jewelry, and fertility dolls—and is a great starting point for exploring the 7,500-year history of the native people of the island.

ALASKA

Tour Kodiak Island

Zigzagging along the coast of Kodiak Island, this drive shows off deep bays, temperate rain forest, alpine meadows, rolling tundra, wildlife—including emperor geese, silver salmon, and bald eagles—and a dramatic shoreline pounded by waves and turbulent tides.

From Kodiak, the former capital of Russian Alaska, head southwest on Rezanof Drive, which soon turns into Chiniak Highway. At Deadman's Curve, enjoy the panorama of Kodiak Harbor, Chiniak Bay, and some of the archipelago's many islands. Turn left into Buskin River State Recreation Site to enjoy the most popular fishing spot on the island's road network, with big runs of sockeye and silver salmon, and bald eagles soaring overhead. A little farther on, take the turnoff for Anton Larsen Bay Road, a spur leading past the island's golf course and along the western shore of the bay—a pretty fjord with an island at its mouth. Back on the highway, you soon pass America's largest Coast Guard facility, with more than 1,000 employees. After this, the road skirts Womens Bay, which was once favored by Alutiiq women as a place to hunt, fish, and gather food. At the head of the bay, the highway crosses Sargent Creek, where emperor geese spend their winters, and the Russian River, where salmon gather to spawn in August and September. There is an abundance of wildlife here, and you may even see an eagle's nest among the cottonwood trees along Middle Bay. Around Mile 30, take the right fork, Pasagshak Bay Road, heading south, passing the Kodiak Launch Complex (not open to the public), a state-of-the-art aerospace facility that launches commercial and military rockets. At the end of the road you come to Fossil Beach, where fossilized seashells are nestled among the rocks. Retrace your route north to the junction. This time head east along the shore of Chiniak Bay, watching for commercial fishing vessels coming and going from Kodiak, before the road terminates, appropriately enough, at Road's End, a traditional Alaska roadhouse.

FROM: Kodiak, Alaska
TO: Fossil Beach, Alaska
ROADS: Rezanof Drive, Chiniak Highway, Anton Larsen Bay Road, Pasagshak Bay Road
DISTANCE: 85.6 miles (138 km)
DRIVING TIME: 2.5 hours
WHEN TO GO: Spring through fall
PLANNING: www.kodiak.org

OREGON

The Pacific Coast Scenic Byway

Drive past a lighthouse hailed as one of the most beautiful in the U.S., see the tumbling waves of Devils Churn, visit the incomparable Oregon dunes, and stop at waterfront cafés and restaurants where you can sample delicious local clam chowder.

Fishing, crabbing, and clamming are popular pastimes in Pacific City, an oceanside village looking out over Chief Kiawanda Rock, while the dunes and beaches of nearby Bob Straub State Park offer solitude and beauty. From Pacific City, drive south and join U.S. 101, passing state parks with head-turning scenery and wildlife, including brown pelicans near Siletz Bay and gray whales off Yaquina Head. Climb the 93-foot (28 m) high lighthouse at Yaquina Head for some splendid views. Farther on is the coastal city of Newport, home to the Oregon Coast Aquarium and the Hatfield Marine Science Center. After crossing the Yachats River, stop at Cape Perpetua Scenic Area to see waves surging up the narrow channel and exploding against the rocks at Devils Churn. From here, U.S. 101 passes rocky shores and sandy beaches that are home to harbor seals. A mile (1.6 km) on from Heceta Head Lighthouse State Scenic Viewpoint is Sea Lion Caves, where a vast cavern houses a colony of raucous Steller sea lions. The road levels out as it enters Florence, with its waterfront of galleries, cafés, and shops. After you cross the Siuslaw River, you enter Oregon Dunes National Recreation Area (see In Focus), stretching for 40 miles (64 km) along the coast. Soon after, you reach Siltcoos Recreation Corridor, an area with a broad, sandy beach and a trail following the wildlife-rich estuary of the Siltcoos River. The Oregon Dunes Overlook offers a striking vantage point. The road continues south to Gardiner, on the Umpqua River. From the larger town of Reedsport, across the river, continue down to Winchester Bay, where a detour brings you to the Umpqua Lighthouse, whose rotating beam flashes red and white. The drive continues through the coastal towns of North Bend and Coos Bay to picture-perfect Bandon.

In Focus Covering some 31,500 acres (12,748 ha), **Oregon Dunes National Recreation Area** is the largest expanse of coastal dunes in North America. Stretching from Florence to Coos Bay, it is a favorite destination for off-road driving, with ATVs racing up and down the sometimes 500-foot (152 m) high dunes. The area is a mix of small, forested islands, wetlands, forests, lakes, and open dunes, good for hiking, photography, camping, and horseback riding.

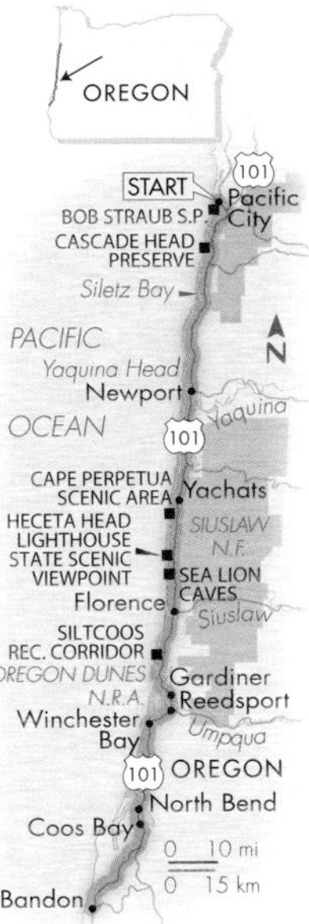

FROM: Pacific City, Oregon

TO: Bandon, Oregon

ROAD: U.S. 101

DISTANCE: 168 miles (270 km)

DRIVING TIME: 4 hours

WHEN TO GO: Year-round

PLANNING: Oregon Dunes Headquarters in Reedsport has lots of information about the dunes. www.visittheoregoncoast.com

Yaquina Head Lighthouse stands sentry before a calm sea and a cloud-strewn sky—it has been a working lighthouse since 1873.

CALIFORNIA

Driving Big Sur

An abundance of state parks, rugged coastlines lined with sandy beaches, majestic redwood forests, soaring waterfalls, and wildlife such as sea otters, grey foxes, and peregrine falcons await you on this drive through the sparsely populated Big Sur region of central California.

An opulent guest bedroom at Hearst Castle, San Simeon

Climbing 1,000 feet (305 m) above the sea, California's Big Sur coastal road passes some of the Golden State's most beautiful state parks. To reach the upscale village of Carmel-by-the-Sea, join Calif. 1 from Monterey (see Highlights) and drive 3 miles (5 km) south. The town is home to quaint, colorful cottages, restaurants, inns, shops, and art galleries set behind a broad, pine-tree-lined beach. Continue to the coves, headlands, meadows, and tide pools that make up Point Lobos State Reserve. More than 250 different animal species have been seen at the park, including black-tailed deer, gray foxes, and sea lions. After Carmel Highlands, with its impressive houses perched on granite cliffs, you reach the start of Big Sur—90 miles (145 km) of fabled coastline road to San Simeon. Redwood groves tower above as the Santa Lucia Range drops away until the jagged rocks meet the waves of the Pacific. One of the few easy-to-reach beaches on the drive is farther on at Garrapata State Park. Cross the photographed Bixby Creek Bridge to reach Hurricane Point, where powerful winds swirl above the Little Sur River. Soon after, you arrive at the 1889 Point Sur Light Station, a state historic park.

Drive on to Andrew Molera State Park, whose oak and redwood forests are only accessible by foot. Pass through the settlement of Big Sur to reach Pfeiffer Big Sur State Park, where the Big Sur River runs through 964 acres (390 ha) of forested park. The sands and arched rocks of Pfeiffer Beach are about 1.5 miles (2.4 km) south, and a little farther on, the Henry Miller Memorial Library displays books and memorabilia of the novelist, who spent 18 years in Big Sur. Visit Julia Pfeiffer Burns State Park, 8 miles (13 km) on, for an underwater preserve—perfect for scuba-diving enthusiasts—as well as the 80-foot (24 m) McWay Falls and 3,000-foot (914 m) high ridges. The road clings to the precipitous coastline from here. After San Simeon—where you can catch a bus to the grand Hearst Castle (see Highlights)—continue to Cambria, where Monterey pines thrive on the hills. Head through the artists' colony of Harmony and past Estero Bay to reach Morro Bay, home to peregrine falcons. The easily identifiable Morro Rock towers over the bay.

OPPOSITE: A spring evening at McWay Falls in Julia Pfeiffer Burns State Park

Highlights

- **Monterey Bay Aquarium** is well worth the pricey entrance fee—it houses a diverse range of marine life, including sea otters, sharks, penguins, numerous fish species, jellyfish, turtles, and octopuses.

- Keep an eye out for **wild sea otters** feeding in kelp forests just off shore—they are protected along this stretch of coast. A good place to see them is at Soberanes Point near Garrapata State Park.

- **Hearst Castle** in San Simeon is a 165-room mansion mixing classical and Mediterranean styles. Perched on a 127-acre (51 ha) estate in the Santa Lucia Range, it has striking views of Big Sur and the Pacific.

FROM: Monterey, California
TO: Morro Bay, California
ROAD: Calif. 1
DISTANCE: 123 miles (198 km)
DRIVING TIME: 3 hours
WHEN TO GO: Year-round
PLANNING: Check in advance for bad weather, as heavy rain may make the narrow road dangerous.

Boulders stud the California coastline near Point Arena.

CALIFORNIA

California's Mist-Covered Coast

This trip along the jagged Pacific coast near Mendocino offers a window on American popular culture, as well as nature at its best: Beautiful state parks, delightful seaside communities, beaches, ferns, grasslands, and cypress groves all lie ahead.

Before you leave sprawling Santa Rosa, pay a visit to the Charles M. Schulz Museum that celebrates the Peanuts cartoonist. From here, drive west through the apple orchards of Sebastopol on Calif. 12, then join Calif. 1 and head north to the fishing village of Bodega Bay—the setting for Alfred Hitchcock's dark movie *The Birds*. Heading north, you soon pass the sands of Sonoma Coast State Beach, an excellent stop for exploring tide pools or sunbathing. At the mouth of the Russian River, you'll see dramatic Goat Rock, looming on a beach where seals raise their cubs in spring, before the road climbs to nearly 1,000 feet (305 m) above the ocean. Continue north to Salt Point State Park, with easy-to-reach tide pools, a harbor seal colony, coastal hiking trails, and an underwater preserve at Gerstle Cove. The park has tan oaks, towering redwoods, and a pygmy tree forest. The northern edge is Kruse Rhododendron State Reserve, where wild pink rhododendrons flower in late April and May. Beyond Gualala (pronounced wa-la-la) is Point Arena, a tiny settlement shared by fishermen and tie-dye-clad hippies. Continue to Van Damme State Park, where sea stars, anemones, and crabs occupy the tide pools. You can walk through a fern-edged river canyon and a forest of stunted pines and cypresses.

Back on the road, you soon come to Mendocino, a coastal village whose clapboard houses give it the look of a New England town. The former lumber town is now an artists' colony and the Mendocino Art Center has collections of local paintings, weavings, ceramics, and photography. Surrounding the town is Mendocino Headlands State Park, which preserves sandstone bluffs, wave tunnels, tide pools, beaches, and grasslands. Farther north are the redwoods, ferns, and wild ginger of Russian Gulch State Park, in the midst of which is a 36-foot (11 m) high waterfall. After sampling the fresh seafood in the harbor town of Noyo, continue to Fort Bragg, a military post, to ride the Skunk Train along the scenic Redwood Route.

FROM: Santa Rosa, California

TO: Fort Bragg, California

ROADS: Calif. 12, 1

DISTANCE: 130 miles (209 km)

DRIVING TIME: 3 hours

WHEN TO GO: Year-round

PLANNING: www.visitmendocino.com

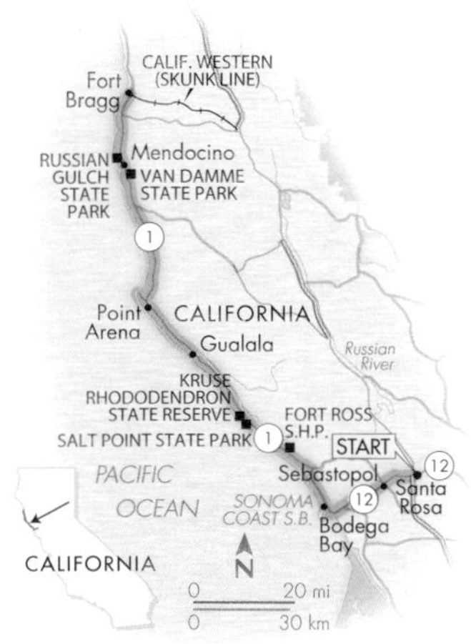

HAWAII

The Winding Road to Hana

This zigzagging highway, which leads to the isolated settlement of Hana, passes cascading waterfalls, dense rain forest, and rugged lava coastlines. Along the way, you'll cross 56 bridges and go around 617 twists and turns.

The road leaving Kahului Airport is deceptively flat as you head east on Hana Highway, passing sugarcane fields and the sandy sweep of Baldwin Beach Park. Paia, a former plantation, is the only major town on the drive to Hana. Windsurfers and surfers congregate here, just 2 miles (3 km) from Hookipa Beach Park, a pilgrimage site for both sports. After about 20 minutes of driving, the twists, turns, and bridges begin. Each bridge has been given a name, such as Kolea, which means "Happiness that comes on the wind." Look out for rainbow eucalyptus (trees with colorfully streaked bark) and stop to pick up roadside guava, mountain apples, and mangoes between the tiny towns of Huelo and Kailua. Soon the road reaches Waikamoi, one of several waterfalls along the route. Scenes from *Jurassic Park* were shot at the nearby Garden of Eden Arboretum & Botanical Garden, which is home to Puohokamoa Falls and more than 500 species of plants. Beyond is the Kaumahina State Wayside Park, with breathtaking coastline views. After stopping at Haipuaena Falls, you come to the Hawaiian ethnobotanical gardens at the Keanae Arboretum, a good place to picnic and swim. From here, drive down to the Keanae Peninsula to see meadows of taro—a widely cultivated tropical plant and Hawaii's traditional food crop. Back on Hana Highway, continue past overlooks with splendid photo opportunities, and pause at Waikani Falls, a sequence of three pretty cascades. The next stop is Waianapanapa State Park, which showcases a fine lava shoreline with black craggy cliffs, sea stacks, lava caves and tubes, and a gleaming black sand beach. From here, the road winds down to Hana.

FROM: Kahului Airport, Hawaii
TO: Hana, Hawaii
ROAD: Hana Highway
DISTANCE: 53 miles (85 km)
DRIVING TIME: 2 hours
WHEN TO GO: Year-round
PLANNING: Paia is the last opportunity to buy gas before Hana. www.hanamaui.com

Excursion To reach the old whaling town of **Lahaina** from Kahului Airport, drive southwest on Hwy. 380, then west on Hwy. 30. The historical museum offers details about those who have made their mark on the island, including Christian missionaries, whalers, and Chinese and Japanese migrants. The town is a center for whale-watching, and organized tours run from the harbor. In addition to galleries, the town's banyan tree is a must-see as it's the largest tree in the U.S.A.

A surfer rides a mighty wave at Hookipa Beach Park, near Paia.

THE TOP

10 Spectacular Bridges

As well as providing unrivaled views, these impressive feats of engineering across the world link places that once seemed irrevocably separate.

1 Confederation Bridge, New Brunswick–Prince Edward Island, Canada

Snaking out from Cape Jourimain, New Brunswick, this 8-mile (13 km) concrete leash has ended the isolation of Prince Edward Island. From December through April, Northumberland Strait is frozen over, making this the longest bridge over ice in the world. The road is a part of the Trans-Canada Highway.

PLANNING: The toll is $42.50 for a round trip. Pedestrians can take a shuttle service. *www.confederationbridge.com*

2 The Lake Pontchartrain Causeway, Louisiana

Driving onto this languorous double causeway on I-10 as it reaches out across Lake Pontchartrain, you could be forgiven for thinking you're heading out to sea. In fact, the lake is a saltwater estuary on the Gulf of Mexico, and sea-going ships pass beneath. The two parallel causeways stretch for almost 24 miles (39 km). Look out for pelicans and other birdlife.

PLANNING: A toll of $3 is taken at the northern terminus, Mandeville. *www.thecauseway.us*

3 Sunshine Sky Bridge, Florida

You may have seen this bridge in a movie or on TV, its cable stays rising like majestic sails above Tampa Bay. Taking I-275 from St. Petersburg in Pinellas County to Terra Ceia in Manatee County, the 5.5-mile (9 km) bridge gives you a lofty view of the sea-going traffic and the Pinellas National Wildlife Reserve.

PLANNING: There's a $1 toll, and you can fish from the bridge. *www.interstate275florida.com/ssb.htm*

4 Rio–Niterói Bridge, Rio de Janeiro, Brazil

The north and south sides of the great Guanabara Bay are now linked by this box-girder bridge, with three lanes of the federal highway BR-101 traveling in each direction. Just over 8 miles (13 km) long, it climbs to 236 feet (72 m) in the middle to allow shipping access—giving you a great view of the bay and, farther south, of Rio de Janeiro.

PLANNING: There are 18 feeder roads onto the bridge, and a small toll must be paid at the Niterói end. *www.braziltourism.org*

5 Akashi Kaikyo Bridge, Kobe–Awaji Island, Japan

Akashi Kaikyo Bridge, the world's longest suspension bridge, has cables that would go seven times around the world. It carries the Honshu-Shikoku highway linking Kobe to Awaji island. The bridge was built in part as a response to a ferry disaster, and crosses the perilous Akashi Strait, withstanding strong currents and high winds, not to mention earthquakes.

PLANNING: At night, the bridge's lights change color every 15 minutes. The Maiko Marine Promenade on the Kobe side of the bridge has an observation lounge and information about the bridge. *www.jnto.go.jp*

6 Hangzhou Bay Bridge, Shanghai–Ningbo, China

This is China's most impressive bridge, a 22-mile (35 km) elongated S shape that whips across the water with six lanes in each direction. The expansive inlet of the South China Sea is a fascinating phenomenon, with enormous waves and tides that can race in at speeds of up to 20 miles (32 km) an hour. There are plans to construct a man-made island halfway across the bridge, which will include a service station and a viewing tower.

PLANNING: Don't slow down or stop to admire the view, or you will face a fine. The toll is 80 Yuan. *www.hangzhoubaybridge.com*

Opposite: The 10.7-mile (17.2 km) Vasco da Gama Bridge over the Tejo River near Lisbon, Portugal, is one of the longest bridges in Europe.

7 The Rion–Antirion Bridge, Gulf of Corinth, Greece

With four distinctive cable stays, this suspension bridge—first crossed by the torchbearers of the Athens Olympics in 2004—stands sentinel at the western end of the Gulf of Corinth, connecting mainland Greece with the Peloponnese. There are two lanes each way, as well as a cycle path and pedestrian walkway.

PLANNING: There is an exhibition and information center about the bridge near the Toll Plaza at Antirion. *www.gefyra.gr*

8 The Great Belt Fixed Link, Funen–Zealand, Denmark

The Great Belt—a major water channel between the North Sea and the Baltic—cuts Denmark in two. This bridge unites the country, allowing you to drive from the European continent to Copenhagen and on across the Øresond Bridge to Sweden. The bridge is in two parts: the western section runs alongside a railway, the eastern section is a majestic suspension bridge.

PLANNING: Paying the 35-euro toll gets you discounts on thousands of goods and services in Denmark. *www.storebaelt.dk*

9 Le Viaduc de Millau, Tarn Valley, France

This bridge is such a vision of grace and beauty that people come from far and wide just for the pleasure of driving over it. But you need a head for heights: It's the tallest bridge in the world. Sailing high above the Tarn valley between two limestone plateaus, it takes the A75 from Paris through the Massif Central to southern France and Spain.

PLANNING: There is a viaduct information center at Aire des Cazalous on the RD92 toward Albi. *www.leviaducdemillau.com*

10 Vasco da Gama Bridge, Lisbon, Portugal

The bridge opened in 1998 in time for the celebrations of the 500th anniversary of Vasco Da Gama's discovery of the trade route to India. The suspended section near the Lisbon shore allows modern-day ships somewhat larger than his to pass through.

PLANNING: The bridge connects the north Lisbon suburb of Sacavém to Montijo on the southern shore. *www.portaldasnacoes.pt*

GUADELOUPE

Northern Basse-Terre

Tracing the northern half of one of Guadeloupe's butterfly-wing-shaped coasts, this route passes through a spectacular rain forest of hardwood and fern, winds between mountain peaks, dips down to fine beaches, and takes in regional museums along the way.

The cobalt-blue bay of Deshaies is framed by hills covered in tropical vegetation and flowers.

Highlights

- Stop near Pointe-Noire, north of Mahaut, to visit the **Maison du Bois** (House of Wood), which has boat-building and furniture-making displays. The museum has built up an impressive collection of antique wooden tools and utensils, including hand whisks, coffee grinders, and cassava -root crushers.

- The **Musée du Rhum** in Sainte-Rose is devoted to a private rum-making enterprise and has historic artifacts such as an enormous cane-juice vat hewn from a single tree trunk. After watching the short film (some English showings), take a tour of the adjacent Distillerie Reimonenq to taste and buy the fiery liquor.

The busy main city of Grande-Terre, Pointe-à-Pitre is the starting point for a delightful tour of one of the Caribbean's lushest forests. Follow signs for Basse-Terre west across the Rivière Salée, and go south on Rte. N1 to the exit for the Route de la Traversée (Rte. D23). The road heads west through cane fields before ascending into the rain forest of giant mahogany, bamboo, and gum trees that populates the Parc National de la Guadeloupe. On the way, you can stop for a two-minute walk to the Cascade aux Écrevisses, a popular waterfall edged by dripping mosses and creepers. The nearby Maison de la Forêt provides an excellent introduction to the 74,000-acre (30,000-ha) park, with exhibits (in French only) explaining the area's flora, fauna, and geology. Hiking maps lay out the 190 miles (306 km) of well-maintained trekking routes, including the challenging Trace des Crêtes, which follows the mountain ridge above the west coast.

The road then traverses the Col des Mamelles, a high pass between two volcano peaks. From its highest point—1,922 feet (586 m)—the road offers great views of the park (when it is not obscured by frequent rain) and then makes a hairpin descent to the coast at Mahaut. Take a short detour south to Plage de Malendure, where glass-bottomed boats depart for trips around the tiny Îlets Pigeon. Named for the French naturalist Jacques Cousteau, the Reserve du Commandant Cousteau is on these islets and harbors a marine world of coral and brilliant fish. Continue north on Rte. N2 to the Maison du Cacao, which explains the history, cultivation, and manufacture of cocoa and sells pure blocks of the rich treat. The drive continues past the attractive fishing village of Deshaies, with its pretty botanical garden. Just over a mile (2 km) farther on, through a screen of glossy mangrove trees, you'll catch your first glimpse of the broad bay at Grande Anse, lined by Guadeloupe's finest beaches. Here, the sweep of the forest meets the curving golden sands, shaded by palm trees and edged with volcanic rock. The road now rounds the tip of the island and continues on to Sainte-Rose (see Highlights). On the main road once more, it's a quick run back to Pointe-à-Pitre.

FROM: Loop route from Pointe-à-Pitre, Guadeloupe
ROADS: Rtes. N1, D23, N2
DISTANCE: 93 miles (149 km)
DRIVING TIME: 3 hours
WHEN TO GO: Year-round
PLANNING: Expect rainfall at any time of year, but especially in the wet season, July through November. www.guadeloupe-info.com

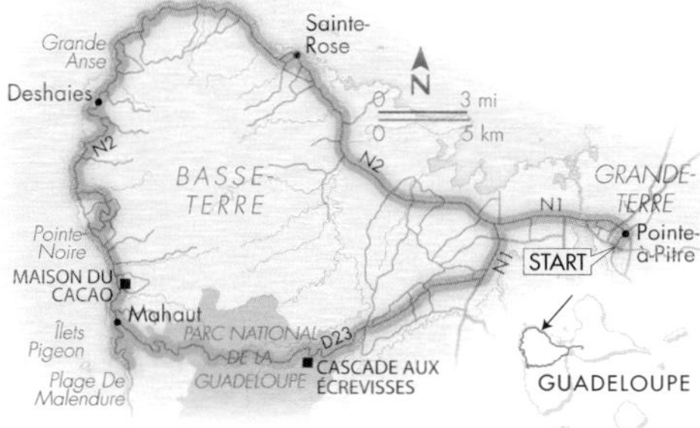

OPPOSITE: A fisherman at Sainte-Rose displays a catch of crayfish, one of many local seafood specialties.

CUBA

Cuban Coasts and Mountains

This lonely yet scenic road threads along the edge of the stark, low-desert coastal strip beneath the towering Sierra Maestra mountains. As you travel westward, the sweeping vistas become even more dramatic.

Sierra Maestra
To Cruce de los Baños
A1
START
Santiago de Cuba
Pico Turquino
Río Seco
20
Las Cuevas
Uvero
Chivirico
Aserradero
PLAYA MAR VERDE
Marea del Portillo
Mar Caribe (Caribbean Sea)
0 10 mi
0 10 km
N
CUBA

From historic Santiago de Cuba, make your way westward to the coastal Playa mar Verde—a popular beach with locals—by following Hwy. 20. Aserradero, where the guns of the Spanish warship *Viscaya* still poke above the surf, is 13 miles (21 km) beyond. It was sunk by U.S. warships in 1898 in a fateful attempt by the Spanish fleet to break out of Santiago harbor during the Spanish American War. Mountains to the north rise prominently above the broad coastal plain. A turnoff to the right, about 8 miles (12 km) west of Aserradero, will lead you up into the mountains to Cruce de los Baños, although a 4WD is recommended for this rugged detour. Return to the main road, which begins to rise and fall between headlands that widen with the miles and which passes beaches of variegated colors. The scenery becomes more stupendous as copper-colored cliffs loom over the sea and the mountains fall away to the shore. Uvero, one of the few rustic communities along the way, is the site of an early battle won by Fidel Castro's revolutionaries in 1957. Cuba's highest point, the 6,477-foot (1,974 m) Pico Turquino, seems almost within reach, while other lushly forested peaks ahead belie the fact that it rains little here. At Las Cuevas, you pass the trailhead to Pico Turquino. Goats and buzzards are your only company as you navigate sharp curves and steep changes in elevation that seem to leave you suspended in the air for a moment before falling steeply into a valley. At last you arrive at Marea del Portillo, known for its beaches of dark sand and excellent diving.

FROM: Santiago de Cuba, Cuba
TO: Marea del Portillo, Cuba
ROAD: Hwy. 20
DISTANCE: 100 miles (160 km)
DRIVING TIME: 4 hours
WHEN TO GO: Year-round
PLANNING: The road is subject to closure due to periodic landslides. If you intend to stay in Marea del Portillo, bring cash as there are no banks in the area. www.cubatravelusa.com

Hidden History Around 105 miles (170 km) from Santiago de Cuba on the island's north coast is **Baracoa.** The isolated settlement of narrow streets, surrounded by mountains and rain forests, clings to a traditional lifestyle. Founded in 1512, it is the oldest colonial city in the Americas, and its historic buildings include the Fuerte Matachin, a preserved fort now home to the Museo Municipal de Historia, which traces the region's history from pre-Columbian days.

Palm trees dominate the landscape near Pico Turquino, in Cuba's Sierra Maestra.

A pleasure boat glides over Hakone Lake's still waters in front of snowcapped Mount Fuji, framed by the lake's forested shore.

JAPAN

In the Shadow of Mount Fuji

A drive through Fuji-Hakone-Izu National Park brings shifting views of Japan's most famous peak, an exhilarating landscape of flower-clad mountains, lakes, and shoreline, and the chance to dip into relaxing and healthful hot springs.

From the unabashedly touristy resort of Hakone, whose art museum is noted for its ceramics, head south on Rte. 1. Pause at the historic Hakone Checkpoint, built in 1619 to monitor travelers between Tokyo and Kyoto. The old Edo structures at the checkpoint have been beautifully restored. Catch glimpses of graceful Mount Fuji, Japan's highest mountain, as you follow Rte. 1 for about 5 miles (8 km), and then hop off the highway at Hakone Lake, known as Ashi-no-ko, and see the peak reflected in its calm waters. Continue on Rte. 1 and head to the top of Mount Katsugari. Its cable car ascends the mountainside in five minutes, and in May azaleas cover the slopes. An additional 7.5 miles (12 km) to the south, just past the city of Mishima, take the turnoff to Rte. 136—the Shimoda Highway—which continues through the Izu Peninsula's rolling hills and ocean views. It connects with Rte. 414, passing through Izu City with its lovely seaside location, before meeting up with Rte. 136 again. Farther south, on the tip of the Izu Peninsula, sits the quiet little town of Minami-Izu, known for its hot springs and beautiful beaches. The Ikona Ryokan and Spa is a perfect place to end the journey, with a soak in an outdoor bath and a full-course Japanese meal.

In Focus Begin the drive a little farther north to visit the **Hakone Open-Air Museum** on Rte. 732. Built in 1969 to integrate art and nature, its 120-piece collection includes a star-shaped maze you can get lost in, a rotating display of works by British sculptor Henry Moore, who fittingly said, "Sculpture is an art of the open air," and more than 300 pottery pieces, paintings, prints, and objects by Pablo Picasso.

FROM: Hakone, Japan
TO: Izu Peninsula, Japan
ROADS: Rtes. 1, 136, 414
DISTANCE: 65 miles (104 km)
DRIVING TIME: 2 hours
WHEN TO GO: Spring through fall
PLANNING: www.jnto.go.jp

A pair of fur seals snuggle up on the shore near Otara, South Island.

NEW ZEALAND

Drive through the Catlins

New Zealand's first touring route, in the southeast corner of South Island, leads through the Catlins, a region of stunning coastlines and abundant forests. Along the way, there are excellent wildlife-spotting opportunities, as well as beaches, caves, and waterfalls to visit.

Leaving behind picturesque Invercargill, take Gorge Road Invercargill Hwy. east to the old port of Fortrose, and turn off to Otara and the coastal road to Waipapa Point—with a golden beach overlooked by a working Victorian lighthouse. Continue to Slope Point, where a walk across private farmland (closed in lambing season) brings you to the mainland's southernmost point, with a sign for the South Pole. Next along the route is Curio Bay, where low tide exposes a 180-million-year-old petrified forest with imprints of fern visible in the rocks. In adjoining Porpoise Bay, Hector's dolphins can be seen in summer. Pass through Waikawa, home to a small museum telling the story of local whaling and goldmining. Farther on, stop for a walk through the forest to McLean Falls, which tumble 72 feet (22 m) in a series of cascades. Back on the road, you will soon find a right turn for the soaring Cathedral Caves, a 100-foot (30 m) long cavern carved by the sea, accessible only at low tide. Leave your car once more to walk to Matai and Horseshoe Falls, two magnificent falls situated minutes from each other. Continue on to Owaka, then turn right to Cannibal Bay, where Hooker's sea lions lumber ashore to sleep in the sun and, in nearby Roaring Bay, you can watch rare yellow-eyed penguins. After Kaka Point beach resort, you end up at the peaceful river town of Balclutha.

FROM: Invercargill, New Zealand
TO: Balclutha, New Zealand
ROADS: Gorge Road Invercargill Hwy., coast road, and local roads
DISTANCE: 99 miles (158 km)
DRIVING TIME: 2.5 hours
WHEN TO GO: Year-round
PLANNING: www.catlins-nz.com

Hidden History Scottish-founded **Dunedin** (1.5 hours from Balclutha along SH1) is one of New Zealand's oldest cities. Gold was discovered nearby in the 19th century and many fine buildings sprang up, including a magnificent cathedral and Olveston, a 35-room mansion furnished with treasures from around the world. Tours include the Taieri Gorge Railway, which travels through exceptional scenery, and the Monarch Wildlife Cruise around the Otago Peninsula to see albatross, penguins, dolphins, and whales.

NEW ZEALAND

Coast Road

Rudyard Kipling described New Zealand as "last, loneliest, loveliest, exquisite, apart," a fitting description of this 336-mile (540 km) long drive hedged-in by sea and mountains, where subtropical rain forests grow at the feet of glistening glaciers.

From the South Island town of Karamea, surrounded by the high plateaus and coastal forests of Kahurangi National Park, head south on the Karamea Highway (Hwy. 67), which winds lazily through peaceful green hills. After crossing the Mokihinui River, the road hugs the coast to the small town of Waimangaroa, where signs lead up the hill to Denniston, an abandoned mining town famous for its old steep railroad that shipped coal down the hill. Back on the main road, continue south to Westport and take a short detour to Cape Foul Wind (named by Captain Cook in 1770), along Hwy. 67A, to see the seal colony and lighthouse. Return to the main road and turn west onto Hwy. 6, which cuts inland briefly as it meanders for 63 miles (102 km) to Greymouth, the largest city on the coast. On the way, visit the spectacular rocks and blowholes at Punakaiki. Greymouth has a long gold-mining history, commemorated in Shantytown, a reconstructed 1880s gold-rush town, just 6 miles (10 km) south of the city. Hokitika, 40 minutes away on Hwy. 6, is in greenstone country, with galleries selling fine jewelry made from local nephrite jade.

Continue south past a series of lakes that offer conservation sanctuaries and sightings of native birds, in particular keas (alpine parrots), wekas, the great white heron, and even the shy kiwi. The road cuts through more green hills as it approaches the town of Franz Josef, with its good range of restaurants and places to stay. A walk to the terminal of the Franz Josef Glacier takes about 10 minutes from the parking area, while Fox Glacier is a short drive south. Both glaciers have walking tours and tracks, but a helicopter flight is the most spectacular way to see these relics of the ice age. Continue under the gaze of Mount Cook and Mount Tasman, two of New Zealand's highest peaks. South of Fox River there are more coastal views before the road turns inland to pass Lakes Moeraki and Paringa, both outstanding for their natural beauty and wildlife. At the coast are colonies of fur seal and the yellow-crested Fiordland penguin, which can be viewed by tours from Lake Moeraki Lodge. The long, one-lane bridge over the Haast River leads into Haast, a frontier town at the center of a pristine wilderness.

FROM: Karamea, New Zealand
TO: Haast, New Zealand
ROADS: Hwys. 67, 67A, 6
DISTANCE: 336 miles (540 km)
DRIVING TIME: 6 to 7 hours
WHEN TO GO: Spring and summer
PLANNING: Be prepared for rain year-round.
www.west-coast.co.nz

The heavily eroded Pancake Rocks at Punakaiki, where the water bursts through a number of blowholes

AUSTRALIA

Great Ocean Road

Built in memory of those who served in World War I, the Great Ocean Road in Victoria remains Australia's finest coastal drive, skirting endless sandy beaches, rugged cliffs, and pretty fishing ports, all set against the forested Otway Ranges.

Limestone stacks, called the Twelve Apostles, punctuate the rocky headlands of Victoria's coast.

From Melbourne's twinkling towers, two routes take you to the Great Ocean Road (B100), which officially starts from the old vacation town of Torquay. The quick, but less scenic, route leads via the Princes Freeway (M1) southwest to Geelong. You can stop off at the National Wool Museum and at Narana Creations, an Aboriginal cultural and tourism center displaying arts and crafts. From Geelong, follow the Surfcoast Highway (B100) to Torquay. The alternative is to take the Nepean Highway (A3) south from Melbourne along the busy flank of Port Phillip Bay. The pleasant, leafy town of Mount Eliza marks the end of suburbanization as you enter a favorite vacation area for Melburnians, with bayside beaches overlooked by leafy peaks. Dromana is a popular town, and there are some great views from the nearby 1,000-foot (305 m) granite outcrop in Arthur's Seat State Park. Cape Schanck features some of the best beach walks, including an 18-mile (29 km) trail through Mornington Peninsula National Park toward delightful Portsea, in the toe of the peninsula. Be aware, however: Although the beaches here are beautiful, the sea's strong currents make swimming dangerous. From Portsea, take the ferry across the mouth of Port Phillip Bay to the old maritime town of Queenscliff. This pretty bayside settlement used to be a naval garrison, but after the arrival of the railway in 1879, it became popular for its yachting and sea breezes.

> "The Great Ocean Road winds past stunning coastal scenery. Don't miss the Twelve Apostles, where the sea crashes with amazing force against the gigantic rock formations."
>
> -ANNIE GRIFFITHS
> NATIONAL GEOGRAPHIC PHOTOGRAPHER

Torquay is a short drive from here, via Ocean Grove and Barwon Heads along C121 and the Surfcoast Highway.

Surf conditions are almost perfect along this part of the coast—Bells Beach is a prime example—and Torquay's Surfworld displays many exhibits and artifacts including old and rare surfboards. The road briefly heads inland, meeting the sea again at Anglesea, where you can go horseback riding along the beach. Farther along, you pass through Lorne, long popular with surfers and bushwalkers, and from here you can scramble up the ranges to see the Erskine Falls and spectacular views of the coast. A most dramatic section of the route lies up ahead, twisting for 25 miles (40 km) to Apollo Bay, winding around steep cliffs and narrow inlets. There are plenty of lookouts so you can keep your eyes on this extremely curvy road but not miss out on the scenery. The Great Ocean Walk, a 57-mile (92 km) trail along the coastline, begins from here.

After Apollo Bay, the road climbs inland again, entering the Otway Ranges. These steep mountains, clad in rain forest,

Surfing on Bells Beach

Bells Beach near **Torquay** is one of the world's most renowned surfing beaches, loved for its reliable waves that regularly swell up to 12-foot (3.7 m) high. Although people had long known about the great surf, they could not manage the scramble down to the isolated beach carrying heavy boards; the introduction of lightweight boards in the 1950s made reaching the beach easier. The accessibility problem was finally rectified when surfer Joe Sweeny bulldozed a road. Since then, the beach has taken its place in surfing history, hosting an international event every easter. The beach has also helped inspire two global surfing brands—Quicksilver and Rip Curl.

offer views of the ocean and the rolling green hills behind. About 12 miles (19 km) on from the bay, take a left on a winding dirt track to Cape Otway lighthouse. It was built from local sandstone by convicts in 1848, and the light has never broken down. Back on the road, you run past the small but lovely Melba Gully State Park, with its luxuriant ferns, dense rain forests, and eerie evening displays of glowworms, and on through the old timber town of Lavers Hill before returning to the ocean at Princetown. The highway traverses Port Campbell National Park, which has the most spectacular coastline of the whole trip. A series of rock pillars, known as the Twelve Apostles, rises more than 200 feet (60 m) out of the sea. Frequent pull-offs enable you to enjoy views of these striking formations from several angles.

The Great Ocean Road ends where it joins the Princes Highway (A1), east of the old whaling town of Warrnambool (see Highlights). Southern right whales, which use the shallows here as a nursery in winter months, are a popular attraction. From Warrnambool, the Princes Highway takes you back to Melbourne.

Brightly colored beach huts line the shore of Port Phillip Bay, with Melbourne's skyline not far away.

FROM: Melbourne, Australia
TO: Warrnambool, Australia
ROADS: Princes Fwy. (M1), Nepean Hwy. (A3), C121, Surfcoast Hwy. (B100), Great Ocean Road (B100), Princes Hwy. (A1)
DISTANCE: 260 miles (418 km)
DRIVING TIME: 12 hours
WHEN TO GO: Year-round
PLANNING: The Rip Curl Pro, one of the world's premier surfing events, is held on Bells Beach near Torquay each year, and Lorne can get extremely busy. Be sure to book places to stay well in advance.
www.greatoceanrd.org.au

Highlights

- Warrnambool's days as a whaling station are remembered at **Flagstaff Hill Maritime Museum,** based around the lighthouse-keeper's cottage, the lighthouse, and the fortifications built in 1887 to thwart Russian invaders. It includes a stunning sound and laser show called "Shipwrecked," about the wreck of the clipper *Loch Ard* in 1878.

- Just outside Winchelsea on the way back to Melbourne on the Princes Highway, stop at **Barwon Park** (open Sundays and Wednesdays), one of Australia's grandest mansions. Its 42 rooms have their original Victorian interiors, including an exquisite cedar staircase.

Tall mountain gum trees are a distinctive feature of the plateau landscape of Barrington Tops National Park.

AUSTRALIA

Pacific Highway

The Pacific Highway in New South Wales runs north from the regional capital of Sydney to the tropical resort of Byron Bay, bringing an eclectic mix of seaside adventure, with rain forest, mountains, organic farms, tourist kitsch, and empty beaches.

Cross the iconic Sydney Harbour Bridge on Rte. 1, and the first big settlement you reach, after about 100 miles (160 km), is the industrial city of Newcastle. Despite the smokestacks on the outskirts, this is a breezy surfing town with wide, leafy streets and some fine art deco architecture. Follow the road inland and make a detour to Barrington Tops National Park (left onto Rte. 15 after Newcastle, and turn north at Maitland to Dungog), through temperate rain forest and mile-high plateaus dotted with snow gums and covered with alpine bogs. Head back onto Rte. 1, and in the bushland around Port Stephens you just might spot a wild koala bear (see Highlights). The next stop is Port Macquerie, popular for its plethora of watersports, wineries, theme parks, and many fine, convict-built, historic buildings. Travel on 90 miles (145 km) and turn off for the laid-back village of Bellingen, 7 miles (11 km) up Rte. 78. At the base of a 1,000-foot (305 m) escarpment and surrounded by rain forest, the village is home to writers, craftspeople, and artists, who have flocked here to escape the city. Another more hair-raising 20 miles (32 km) along Rte. 78 to Dorrigo brings you to the eponymous national park—one of Australia's finest. Return to Rte. 1 via Bellingen or Coramba. You will begin to feel the warmer climate as you reach Coffs Harbour and see the banana plantations clinging to mountainsides that plunge down to the coast (see Highlights). The highway drifts inland now before reaching the genteel country town of Grafton, known for the colors produced by its jacaranda and flametrees in spring (November). Finally, at Byron Bay, you find the most popular resort town on the Pacific coast, with organic markets, galleries, and folk music, and whale watching in June and July.

Highlights

- Should you miss out on glimpsing a koala in the wild, visit **Port Macquarie Koala Hospital.** On the grounds of a historic homestead, around 200 sick and injured animals are regularly treated. Visitors are welcome all day, and a "feed, walk, and talk" tour starts at 3 p.m., during which a staff member explains the history of each injured koala while others are fed.

- The **Big Banana** in Coffs Harbour is a theme park dedicated to the area's most prolific crop. You can tour a banana plantation, buy a smoothie, or learn about the fruit's history in the World of Bananas. Alternatively, just enjoy the attractions offered, including a waterpark, tobogganing, and ice skating.

FROM: Sydney, Australia
TO: Byron Bay, Australia
ROADS: Rtes. 1, 15, 78
DISTANCE: 520 miles (837 km)
DRIVING TIME: 11 hours
WHEN TO GO: Year-round
PLANNING: Take great care driving—stretches of road are not divided and head-on collisions do occur. The back road through Barrington Tops National Park is not paved. www.australia.com

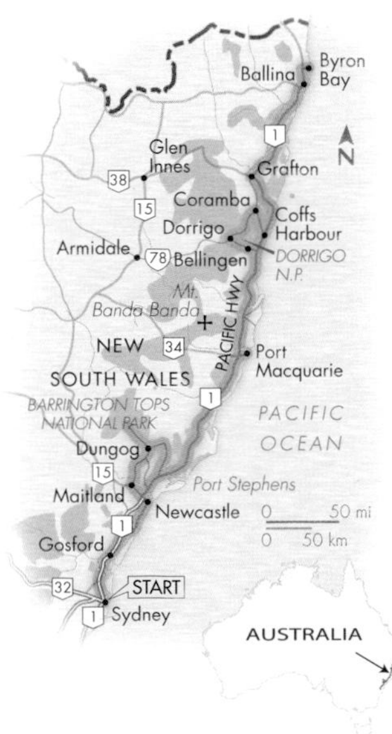

TAIWAN

Hengchun Peninsula

Reach Taiwan's southernmost point, and view the mighty expanse of the Pacific Ocean from the edge of the island's most scenic park, pausing to see intriguing rock formations and ecological curiosities, and to walk along low, sweeping cliffs of coral.

Start at Kenting National Park Headquarters and Visitor Center, with its displays on local topography, corals, flora, and fauna. Head southeast along Provincial Hwy. 26, through the town of Kenting, passing the prominent Frog Rock, and on to Kenting Beach. This golden-sand beach, popular with jet-skiers, sits at the bottom of a small bluff, and you can hire snorkeling gear to explore the corals off shore. Continue along the highway for half a mile (800 m) and you will pass 60-foot (18 m) Sail Rock, which marks the start of the Tropical Coastal Forest—one mile (1.6 km) of woodland with more than 180 plant species growing from coral beds. Several miles farther along lies Shadao, Taiwan's prettiest beach, its sparkling sands made up of seashell and coral fragments and protected from human activity. A little farther south leads to Eluanbi Park at the tip of the Hengchun Peninsula, where the Bashih Channel meets the Pacific. Here monsoon forest combines with shrubs and vines growing atop walls of coral, and superb coastline views appear. You can walk down to the southernmost tip of Taiwan, where one of the world's few fortified lighthouses stands. Nicknamed "The Light of East Asia," it is one of the most powerful lighthouses in the region.

The road begins climbing north through grasslands, leading to Longpan Park. Stop here and head for the coral cliffs for more sweeping views of the Pacific. The road dips inland through pastureland before veering back to the coast a bit farther on at Fongchueisha, noted for its phenomenal shifting sands, swept down to the coast by summer rains. The highway reveals splendid ocean panoramas as it follows the coastline, occasionally dipping down to sea level, before crossing the Gangkou River. Turn right at the T-junction and drive 1.4 miles (2.2 km) to reach Jialeshuei Scenic Area, with wind-and-wave-sculpted honeycomb rocks running along the coast. Follow the path past these weird formations to reach Shanhaipu, or Mountain-Sea Falls, where water tumbles over a cliff into the Pacific. From Jialeshuei, backtrack along the coast or head inland along Country Rte. 200 from Gangkou. This second route passes through rice fields and palm groves to Hengchun, the main town on the peninsula.

FROM: Kenting National Park Headquarters, Taiwan
TO: Jialeshuei or Hengchun, Taiwan
ROADS: Provincial Hwy. 26, Country Rte. 200
DISTANCE: 17.5 miles (28 km)
TIME: 1 hour
WHEN TO GO: Year-round
PLANNING: Take care near cliffs during the monsoon season (June–October), when winds and seas are high. Keep to designated trails, and beware of poisonous snakes. www.taiwan.net.tw

Sail Rock on the Hengchun Peninsula is also called Nixon Rock, as it's said to resemble the profile of the late U.S. president.

THE TOP 10 Asian Coast Drives

The deliciously scenic coasts of Asia provide some of the world's greatest beaches, bays, islands, and coves—all perfect for driving adventures.

❶ Ilju Road, Jeju, South Korea

The volcanic island of Jeju is one of South Korea's finest vacation destinations. Drive along the coastal Ilju Road, with the echoing waves on one side and volcanic cones and curious laval structures on the other. If time allows, head inland on one of the many connecting highways.

PLANNING: There are many observation platforms along the highway. Best in spring. *www.knto.or.kr/enu/index.kto*

❷ Rueigang Road, Taiwan

This 14-mile (22.5 km) highway on Taiwan's east coast snakes along the Siouguluan River and through spectacular green hills. The starting point, Rueisuei, is a popular base for white-water rafting. Just south of Dagangkou, at the road's terminus, a sundial-shaped monolith indicates the Tropic of Cancer.

PLANNING: The summer solstice (June 20 or 21) is the best time to view the Tropic of Cancer marker. *www.eastcoast-nsa.gov.tw*

❸ Patapat Viaduct, Luzon, Philippines

The scenic mountain road winding from the surfers' resort of Pagudpud northeast toward Cagayan is flanked by lush vegetation. A highlight is the elevated Patapat Viaduct, which affords splendid vistas of the Pasaleng Bay on one side and waterfalls on the other.

PLANNING: Driving conditions often unnerve novices, and many prefer hiring a driver. *www.visitmyphilippines.com*

❹ Nha Trang-Quy Nhon, Vietnam

Fringed on three sides by mountains, and on the fourth by a most captivating sandy bay with its own island, Nha Trang is deservedly an up-and-coming star of Vietnam's tourism industry, luring surfers, yachtsmen, and cruise passengers alike. Slicing between the beach-backed ocean and the mountains, this lightly trafficked 134-mile (215 km) drive is truly a coastal drive of a lifetime.

PLANNING: The seven-day Nha Trang Sea Festival falls in June in odd-numbered years. *www.vietnamtourism.com*

❺ Bintulu-Miri Coastal Highway, Malaysia

Of as much environmental as scenic interest, this drive passes dense rain forest sheltering clusters of longhouses on stilts, but also cleared land given over to undulating oil-palm plantations. Ownership and exploitation rights of this prime logging territory are vexed topics in Malaysia and beyond. In Miri, be sure to visit the Tamu Muhibbah market, where indigenous people bring their produce to sell alongside the island's fresh fruit and vegetables, such as durian and limes.

PLANNING: You can choose between the 143-mile (230 km) old road, which has light traffic but is in worse condition, and the less scenic but faster 113-mile (182 km) new road, which opened in 2006. *www.sarawaktourism.com*

❻ East Coast Peninsular Trunk Road, Malaysia

Penetrating luxuriant forests, Hwy. 3 links a string of small towns and photogenic fishing villages. It leads from Johor Bahru, on the border with Singapore, inland to the developed fishing village of Mersing. It then follows the east coast north to Kuantan, the peninsula's largest city, via the quiet beach resorts of Kuala Rompin and Lanjut.

PLANNING: Hwy. 3 is part of the older of the two main roads between Singapore and Kuala Lumpur. *www.tourism.gov.my*

Opposite: Grandfather statues, such as this one, are carved out of lava rock and can be seen all across South Korea's Jeju Island.

❼ Bondalem-Ujung, Bali, Indonesia

Almost untouched by tourism, this coastal route traverses parts of southeast Bali, where fishing remains the breadwinner. The road's most dramatic stretch is the narrow and twisting final leg from Amed to Ujung, overshadowed by the twin peaks of Seraya and the temple-topped Lempuyang.

PLANNING: The marine reserve around Tulamben has a diverse underwater ecosystem and the wreck of the U.S.S. *Liberty*. *www.balitourismboard.org*

❽ A15, Sri Lanka

Opened in 2010, this 82-mile (132 km) highway between Trincomalee and Batticaloa on Sri Lanka's glorious east coast is bliss to drive. Rebuilt with international aid after the 2004 tsunami, a technical and scenic highlight is the 820-foot (250 m) long, 34-foot (10.5 m) wide bridge across the Oddamavadi lagoon.

PLANNING: The May–September dry season is the best time to visit the east coast. *www.srilankatourism.org*

❾ Northeast Loop Drive, Phuket, Thailand

Passing small fishing villages and awash with intoxicating viewpoints over the islands of Phang Nga Bay, this little-known loop road is among Thailand's finest drives.

PLANNING: The usual access route runs north-northeast from the Heroines' Monument just south of Tha Lang. *www.phukettourist.com*

❿ Beirut-Lattakia, Lebanon/Syria

This 115-mile (184 km) Mediterranean coast drive is as much history lesson as visual treat. Starting in Beirut, it heads north through the seaside resort of Jounieh, then Byblos, which probably dates back to around 5000 B.C. Other highlights are the Crusader-era castle and old town of Tripoli and the fortified 12th-century cathedral at Tartus. The road winds up in Lattakia, Syria's cosmopolitan main port, famed for its effervescent café society.

PLANNING: If you need a Syrian visa, it's best to apply for one in your country of residence. *www.syriatourism.org, www.lebanon-tourism.gov.lb*

The islands off Sai Kung Peninsula, seen from the coast, seem to hover on the horizon.

Highlights

- The **Sai Kung Country Park Visitor Centre** has a small but entertaining museum that describes the park's geography, flora, and fauna, as well as traditional village and rural life.
- Both Sai Kung West and Sai Kung East Country Parks are ideal for camping, hiking, and enjoying nature. Seasoned hikers can sample the scenic **Maclehose Trail** that runs through the parks.
- Take a taxi or the 94 bus along the steep, forested road that leads to **Wong Shek Pier.** The top deck of the bus gives the best views of the peaks that dominate the park. At the pier, you can rent sailboards and dinghies, jump on a ferry to view the shoreline, walk along the waterfront, or just relax at the water's edge.

CHINA

Hong Kong's Country Park

This short drive to delightful Sai Kung Country Park takes you along the jagged coast of the New Territories in Hong Kong. En route lies the fishing town of Sai Kung, where you can savor the views of its sheltered, island-dotted bay, as tranquil as a Chinese painting.

The green, looming peak of Ma On Shan dominates the view as you leave Kowloon behind and turn left from Clear Water Bay Road onto Hiram's Highway. The road winds its way to Marina Cove, where hundreds of villas are wrapped around the marina. The road opens up to views of Pak Sha Wan, also called Hebe Haven, 1.2 miles (2 km) farther on. Dozens of small pleasure craft shelter in the scenic bay, which is almost completely enclosed by a narrow, curved peninsula. The highway meanders past villages, wooded areas, and garden nurseries for another 1.8 miles (3 km) to reach Sai Kung. The old fishing town is known for its fine seafood, and a popular local pastime is to hire a sampan and catch your own cuttlefish. The road name briefly changes to Po Tung Road, before becoming Tai Mong Tsai Road and heading past the town to a small beach with waterside restaurants. From here, it hugs the contours of Inner Port Shelter, offering sea glimpses through the eucalyptus trees and grassy picnic areas lining the bay. You can see numerous small islets and the larger Sharp Island and Kau Sai Chau as the road undulates along the most scenic part of the route. Along this stretch, an obelisk—the Sai Kung Memorial—stands as tribute to the villagers and guerrillas who died under Japanese occupation from 1941 to 1945. Leave your car at the entrance to Sai Kung Country Park, and continue by taxi or bus for a 20-minute drive to Wong Shek Pier (see Highlights). To return to Kowloon, either retrace your steps or take Sai Sha Road, with occasional sweeping panoramas of Three Fathoms Cove and Tolo Harbour, before coming to the new town of Ma On Shan with its excellent shopping.

FROM: Kowloon, China
TO: Wong Shek, China
ROADS: Hiram's Highway, Po Tung, Tai Mong Tsai, Sai Sha roads
DISTANCE: 10.5 miles (17 km)
DRIVING TIME: 45 minutes
WHEN TO GO: Year-round
PLANNING: Sai Kung's beaches can get crowded on weekends. Avoid driving in the typhoon season, roughly May–November, when the roads are often flooded.
www.travelinsaikung.org.hk

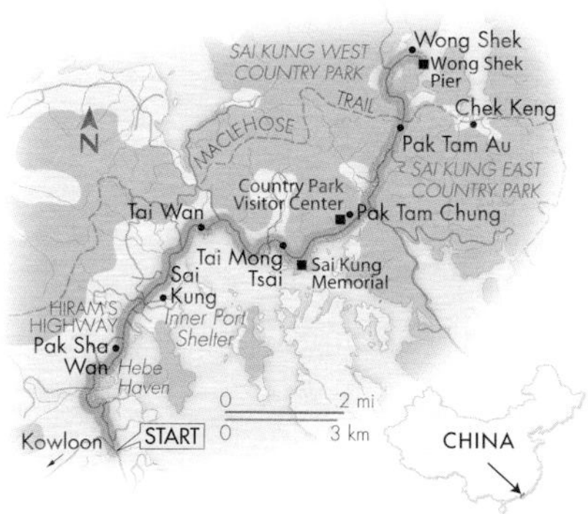

OMAN

Gulf of Oman

The Arabian Sea coastline of the starkly beautiful Sultanate of Oman mixes white sand beaches, desert landscapes, mountains, historical monuments, and scenic canyons that have been visited only by a fortunate few, until now.

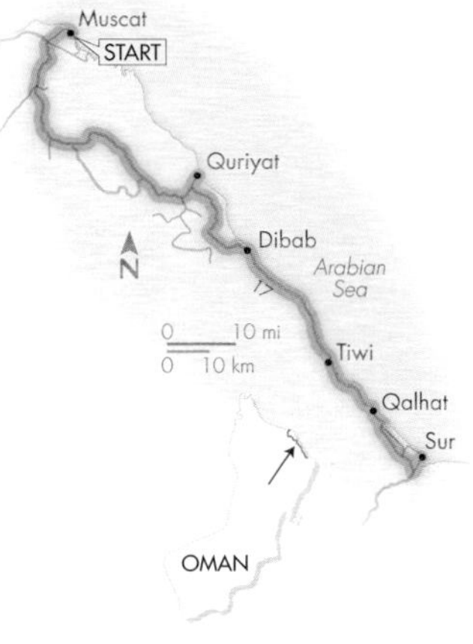

Begin in Muscat, Oman's capital and its most diverse city. Along with the Sultan Qaboos Grand Mosque and numerous smaller mosques, it has two Hindu temples and a number of churches. There are many attractions here, including the Museum of Omani Heritage, charting the country's long history, and the old Mutrah Souk, considered one of the best markets in the Gulf. From Muscat, you reach the brand-new coastal highway, Rte. 17, which begins at Quriyat, by crossing the colorful Hajar Mountains on the Al-Amirate Road, a 58-mile (94 km) drive that passes whitewashed villages, camels, goat-herders, and unusual rock formations. The descent into the harbor town of Quriyat provides spectacular views of the coastal plain below. Pick up Rte. 17 heading south, passing through the tranquil village of Dibab. You can visit the sinkhole in Dibab Lake Park, where the roof of an underground river collapsed, creating a deep hole of clear blue water. Steps lead down to the water, so you can swim there. Continue for 24 miles (39 km) along the peaceful coast to the village of Tiwi. Nearby lies Wadi Shab set among palm trees, where you can swim, scramble up a waterfall, and explore a cave. The ancient city of Qalhat lies another 12.5 miles (20 km) ahead. Its Bibi Maram mausoleum is thought to be a remnant of a mosque proclaimed the most beautiful in the world by the 12th-century explorer Ibn Battuta. While Sur marks the end of the journey, it is an ideal base from which to explore the isolated coves, coral-strewn beaches, and craggy mountains of the Ras al Hadd Peninsula. Sur's tradition of building dhow trading ships is the focus of the Maritime Museum.

In Focus Hundreds of people a night come to the **Ras al Hadd Turtle Reserve,** lured by the appeal of watching giant green turtles lay their eggs on the beach. The reserve, just east of Sur, is a modern facility that has organized evening tours, where visitors can watch the turtles bury their eggs in the sand without disturbing them. A second tour takes place as day breaks, when hatchlings from earlier eggs emerge and crawl to the water. Guides take you to the beach, using their flashlights to show the turtles without disturbing them. Flash photography is not allowed, but photos can be taken after sunrise.

FROM: Muscat, Oman
TO: Sur, Oman
ROADS: Al-Amirate Road, Rte. 17 (Sur Highway)
DISTANCE: 149 miles (239 km)
DRIVING TIME: 3 hours
WHEN TO GO: Year-round
PLANNING: It is illegal to have a dirty car. Dress conservatively: keep shoulders and knees covered in public places; swimwear is only for the beach and hotel pools. www.omantourism.gov.om

Sultan Qaboos Grand Mosque in Muscat is one of the world's largest mosques, with space for 20,000 worshipers.

The pretty harbor at Sochi, one of Russia's most popular summer destinations

RUSSIA

Black Sea Coast

A drive along the Caucasian Riviera—the northeast coast of the Black Sea—features Sochi as its centerpiece. Western Russia's "summer capital" claims the title of the world's longest city, its 90 miles (145 km) set against a landscape of pristine mountains and woodland.

FROM: Dzhubga, Russia
TO: Krasnaya Polyana, Russia
ROADS: M27, A148
DISTANCE: 130 miles (210 km)
DRIVING TIME: 4 to 5 hours
WHEN TO GO: May through September
PLANNING: Sochi hosts Russia's largest annual film festival in June, when accommodations can be difficult to find.
www.sochi-international.ru

From the seaside town of Dzhubga, head south on the M27 past the port of Tuapse and Magri, where "Greater Sochi," a string of coastal settlements running southeast, begins. On your right, the Black Sea stretches out to the horizon from wood-fringed bays and inlets, dotted by resorts such as Lazarevskoye and Loo; on your left rise the Caucasus Mountains. After Dagomys, which has a tea plantation dating back to 1896, you enter Central Sochi, a city of palm-lined avenues, parks, and gardens, and a sea promenade thronged with holidaymakers in the summer. Here you find stately Stalinist buildings designed in the neoclassical style, such as the Sochi Art Museum and the Winter and Summer theaters, along with the more whimsical Maritime Terminal and Railway Station. There is a modernist summer residence set aside for the Russian president, and the lavish homes of oligarchs can be glimpsed through security fences in the upper part of town. Downtown, where the coast is lined with bars, restaurants, and clubs, the atmosphere is more laid-back. Continue south to Adler, where the A148 branches left to the 2,000-foot (600 m) ski resort of Krasnaya Polyana, providing coastal views before it follows the Mzymta River and weaves around its numerous lakes. At the resort, take a ski lift for a bird's-eye view of extensive preparations for the 2014 Winter Olympics.

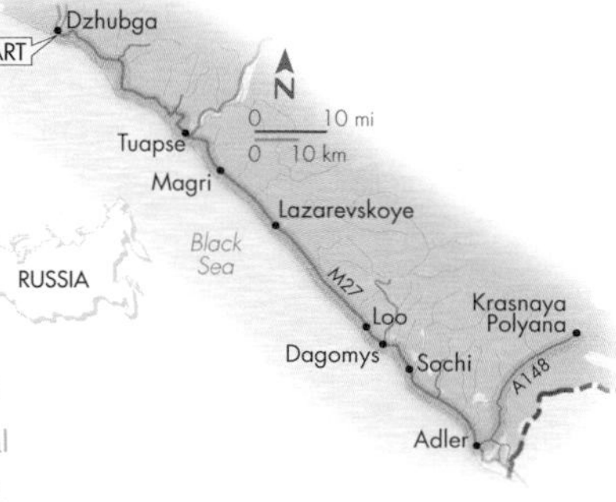

Stay a While Around 15 miles (25 km) northeast of Sochi lies the **Caucasian State Biosphere Reserve,** covering the western end of the Greater Caucasus Mountains, a region that has remained virtually untouched by human impact and includes Sochi National Park. Among its animal species are wolf, lynx, and brown bear; among its tree specimens are several Nordmann fir, which, rising to some 275 feet (84 m), are believed to be the tallest in Europe. Southeast of Central Sochi, Khosta's ancient woodland recalls a primeval environment of some 30 million years past.

FINLAND

Turku Archipelago Trail

Twelve bridges and nine ferries are part of the fun on a drive through the Turku Archipelago, with thousands of wooded islands and rocky islets lying between Finland and Sweden. Most local folk here are bilingual, speaking Finnish and Swedish.

Starting at Turku Cathedral, whose chimes ring out on Finnish national radio every day at noon, leave the small city—Finland's oldest—on Rte. 110 to Kaarina. This is a section of the ancient King's Road along which kings, bishops, merchants, and pilgrims traveled between Norway and Russia. Turn south onto Rte. 180 via Parainen (Pargas), the gateway to the archipelago, whose isles were sculpted round and smooth in the last ice age. Take the Parainen–Nauvo (Nagu) and Nauvo–Korppoo (Korpo) cable ferries, and guided by the brown trail signs, follow Rte. 180 through a forested island landscape. You may spot deer or moose swimming from one island to the next. After passing the village of Korpo, with its 13th-century church, continue to Galtby, with its bustling market and pottery and art shops, before turning right to the inlet at Galtby Brygga. Take the bright yellow ferry past rocky islets lined with cormorants and other seabirds to Houtskari (Houtskär), which has a local museum. Continue on Rte. 1800, heading north to the Roslax–Kivimo ferry. Follow the main road east, then north to the Björkö–Mossala ferry, and across the next island to the Mossala–Dalen ferry, the longest crossing on the route. Look for white-tailed eagles, the iconic bird of the archipelago, and bobbing seal heads.

Cross the small island of Iniö, dominated by the imposing Sophia Wilhelmina Church, and take the cable ferry to Jumo, where Vikings once set sail on trading voyages to Sweden, then the Kannvik–Heponiemi ferry. Follow Rte. 1922 northward, and at Parattula turn left onto Viherlahdentie. At the next major junction, turn right onto Rte. 192 and head east to Taivassalo, with an archipelago visitors center near the harbor. Turn south onto Rte. 1961 to the Hakkenpää–Teersalo ferry. Follow Rte. 1931 to Rauduinen, and turn right onto Rte. 1930 and continue to the junction with Rte. 189. Turn left to the harbor town of Naantali, with its Moominworld island—a theme park based on the books of Finnish artist and storyteller Tove Jansson. Kultaranta, the granite manor house on Luonnonmaa island, is the summer residence of the president of Finland. Open to the public, its formal gardens include a celebrated rose garden with more than 3,500 rose bushes. Finally, follow Rte. 40/E18 via Raisio back to Turku.

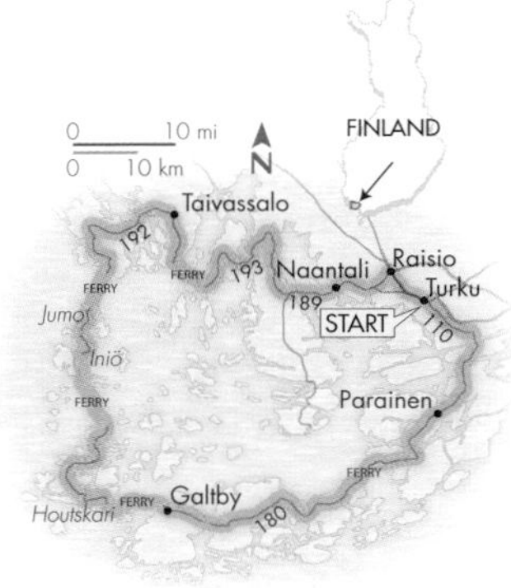

FROM: Loop route from Turku, Finland

ROADS: Rtes. 110, 180, 1800, 1922, 192, 1961, 1931, 1930, 189, 40/E18

DISTANCE: 155 miles (250 km)

DRIVING TIME: 8 hours

WHEN TO GO: June through August. The last Saturday in August is the Night of Ancient Fires, when fireworks fill the sky

PLANNING: Obtain ferry schedules in advance. www.saaristo.org

A signpost helps you to decide between Naantali's multitude of popular tourist attractions.

10 Lakeside Drives

Discover the finest of Europe's lakes, from the Balkans' deepest and the Swedish freshwater archipelago to England's evocative Lake District.

❶ Lake Ohrid, Macedonia/Albania

With cool breezes, clear waters, and a mountainous backdrop, Lake Ohrid is the deepest Balkan lake. The 56-mile (90 km) loop from Ohrid, the main town on the eastern, Macedonian side, lets you drive around the lake, crossing the border twice.

PLANNING: The most striking leg of the drive is the southeast shore between Peštani and the Mausoleum of St. Naum near Macedonia's border. *www.ohrid.com*

❷ Lake Balaton, Hungary

While tacky resorts largely mar its southern shore, the northern coastline of Europe's largest freshwater lake rewards drivers with vineyards, decaying villas, thermal spas, and historic villages fringed by woodlands and reed-beds. From Balatonvilágos, allow four hours to circumnavigate the lake via the town of Siófok on the south coast.

PLANNING: Balaton offers pleasant swimming May–October, but avoid the high season (July–August). Genteel Keszthely makes a fine base. *www.gotohungary.com*

❸ Neusiedlersee/Ferto tó, Austria/Hungary

Central Europe's second largest steppe lake, shallow and windswept, has had dramatic fluctuations in water levels, now minimized by a sluice. From Neusiedl am See on the lake's northern shore, head south via Sopron in Hungary past tall reeds that shelter migratory birds, vineyards, and ancient villages.

PLANNING: The weather is best from late spring through early fall, although winter brings ice-skating. *www.neusiedlersee.com*

❹ Lake Constance, Germany/Switzerland/Austria

Near the Alps, Lake Constance is actually a giant swelling of the River Rhine. Drive clockwise around the lake from Konstanz, taking time to enjoy water sports, swimming, cruising, hiking, and lazing on beaches, as well as medieval towns, nature reserves, and vineyards.

PLANNING: Lake Constance is an hour's drive from Zurich. It is busiest in summer; fall is a good time to visit, with the grape harvest and wine festivals to enjoy. *www.bodensee.eu*

❺ Lake Maggiore, Italy/Switzerland

Renowned for its romantic beauty, this long, narrow lake is surrounded by hills to the north and mountains to the south. The 112-mile (179 km) long road passes abundant attractions, including historic Ascona, the botanical gardens on the Isole di Brissago and in the town of Verbania, the hiking paradise of Centovalli, the glorious Borromean Islands, the Borromeo and Cannero castles, and its main resort, the sedate town of Stresa.

PLANNING: The western shore is the prettier. A car ferry plies between Intra (Verbania) and Laveno on the eastern shore. *www.italiantourism.com*

❻ Lake Garda, Italy

Italy's largest and most scenically diverse lake is a motorist's joy. Start on its south side in Peschiera del Garda, and head west for the main resort town, ancient Sirmione, then Desenzano del Garda, and Salò, Mussolini's capital from 1943 to 1945. Farther northeast, Gardona Riviera heralds the start of more spectacular upland scenery. En route lie several pretty villages, including Riva del Garda, popular with windsurfers.

PLANNING: It's possible to drive around the lake in four hours but better to allow two days to explore the attractions, many just off the main road. Allow time for traffic jams, especially in August. *www.lago-di-garda-tourism.com*

Opposite: Ireland's Lough Corrib has an abundance of wildlife, such as hawks, otters, frogs, bats, mink, and stoats.

❼ Mecklenburg Lake District, Germany

Moorland, marsh, woodland, and countless waterways make up Germany's largest lake network. Boats are the obvious means of transportation and recreation. But motorists, cyclists, and wildlife-spotters also frequent its irregular shoreline roads.

PLANNING: The town of Waren, on the north shore of Müritz, the largest lake, is a useful starting point for the many meandering roads around the district. *www.m-vp.de*

❽ Lake Vänern, Sweden

Sweden's greatest lake is the world's largest freshwater archipelago, where more than 20,000 islands, islets, and rocks await exploration. From Trollhättan, head clockwise via Vanersborg for a 254-mile (408 km) loop. You can fish for oversize salmon and trout, explore Viking boat-graves, or simply imbibe the splendid Scandinavian scenery.

PLANNING: Midsummer and Christmas are joyous times to visit. In summer, near-daylong sunshine encourages alfresco nightlife along Vänern's shores. *www.visitsweden.com*

❾ Lake District, England

A fine drive through this national park starts at Windermere, running south along Lake Windermere to the Lakeside & Haverthwaite Steam Railway, then heading north along the lake's forested western shore to Hill Top, Beatrix Potter's home. The road to Keswick from Hawkswood via the 70-foot (21 m) waterfall of Aira Force delivers breathtaking fell views.

PLANNING: Avoid Lake Windermere in oppressively crowded high summer. *www.cumbria-the-lake-district.co.uk*

❿ Lough Corrib, Ireland

The road around Lough Corrib mainly runs some distance from its shores—reachable by certain access roads—but takes you through dramatic moorland and mountain landscape. The lough reputedly has an island for every day of the year, but for many, its prime appeal is world-class fly-fishing for salmon and trout.

PLANNING: Start at Oughterard, a market town with places to stay, angling shops, and fishing-tour operators. *www.discoverireland.ie*

GERMANY

Along the Baltic Coast

Sandy beaches, lush landscapes, fishing villages, and historic harbors are attractions in this drive along Germany's Baltic shore. Here, you can enjoy the pleasures of smart seaside hotels and the wildness of saltwater lagoons, where migrating birds stop off in spring and fall.

The vivid yellow of rapeseed blossom complements the bright colors of thatched cottages in Ahrenshoop.

Highlights

- **Bad Doberan** bears the imprint of Duke **Friedrich Franz I** of Mecklenburg, who made the town his summer capital. His palace is now a hotel, and one of the charming Chinese-style pavilions in the middle of the Kamp, a park-like village green, is a café.
- Ribnitz-Damgarten's **Bernstein Museum,** housed in a monastery building, has a fascinating collection of amber, including specimens containing immaculately preserved fossilized insects.
- The region's seafaring heritage is in evidence at **Prerow**'s red-brick church, adorned inside with suspended boat models and colorful carvings reminiscent of ships' figureheads.

Leave the ancient port city of Wismar on the old B105 road toward Rostock, ignoring the Autobahn Rostock signs and taking the old road. Turn north before Kröpelin, passing through wooded hills to reach Kühlungsborn, the biggest resort on the Baltic coast, with 2.5 miles (4 km) of sandy beach and many opulent hotels and villas. Even if you don't swim, surf, or sunbathe, do stroll along the pier to enjoy the sea air. Continue along the coast to Heiligendamm, dating from the 1790s, with fine neoclassical buildings. Rejoin the B105 at Bad Doberan (see Highlights), stopping at the town's Gothic minster, with its gilded high altar and a tabernacle carved in oak. Outside, look for the ossuary *(Bienhaus),* where the monks' bones were preserved.

Continue on the B105 through Rostock, turning north at the town of Ribnitz-Damgarten (see Highlights) onto a minor road toward Dierhagen. You are now entering the Fischland-Darss-Zingst peninsula, much of which is preserved as the Nationalpark Vorpommersche Boddenlandschaft. This popular vacation area has woods, meadows, boglands, dunes, and saltwater lagoons. Its old fishing villages have kept much of their original character—there are no swanky villas and plenty of thatched cottages. A good place to get the feel of the Fischland is the village of Ahrenshoop, whose harbor is often filled with traditional fishing boats, known as *Zeesenboote*. Even the village church is built in the shape of an upturned boat. Farther along the peninsula, the Darss region is dominated by woodland and the resort of Prerow (see Highlights). Follow the sea wall for 2.5 miles (4 km), after which the road turns back toward the mainland. The final stop is the little harbor town of Barth, founded in the 13th century. Wander along the quayside, once bustling with the activity of a port, now a peaceful haven for yachts.

FROM: Wismar, Germany
TO: Barth, Germany
ROADS: B105, local roads
DISTANCE: 93 miles (150 km)
DRIVING TIME: 3.5 hours
WHEN TO GO: Year-round
PLANNING: Kühlungsborn is a good place to stop overnight, but book places to stay well in advance. www.germany-tourism.co.uk

NATIONALPARK VORPOMMERSCHE BODDENLANDSCHAFT
Prerow
Darss
GERMANY
Ahrenshoop
Barth
Mecklenburger Bucht
Dierhagen
E22
Kühlungsborn
Warnemünde
105
Ribnitz-Damgarten
N
Heiligendamm
Bad Doberan
Rostock
0 10 mi
0 10 km
105
START
Wismar
A20
Warnow

Excursion From Ribnitz-Damgarten, drive east on the B105 to **Stralsund,** one of the Baltic's best preserved old harbor cities. Almost completely surrounded by water, this compact city has a skyline dominated by three great churches, and its streets are lined with houses that predate the Thirty Years War (1618–48).

OPPOSITE: A pool reflects the elegant lines of Bad Doberan's 14th-century red-brick minster church.

The Svartisen glacier inches its way toward the emerald waters of Holandsfjord, south of Bodø.

NORWAY

Norway's Coastal Route

Cross the Arctic Circle as you follow one of Europe's most mesmerizing drives—the spectacular Kystriksveien (literally, coastal route) in northern Norway, where every bend in the road opens up wondrous new vistas of sea, fjord, and mountain.

Steinkjer lies nearly 40 miles (64 km) inland, yet like much of Norway it is connected to the sea by a fjord. You'll drive through hilly agricultural land around the small town of Namdalseid as you head north on Rte. 17. Soon you reach Namsos, an old lumber town on the shores of a small bay at the mouth of the Namsen, famous as a salmon-fishing river. Hike (or drive) up the Klompen mountain for a superb view of Namsenfjord before heading northwest along Rte. 769 through beautiful coastal scenery. After the Lund–Hoffles ferry, continue to Rørvik, home of a coastal museum, before taking a slight backtrack on Rte. 770 to rejoin Rte. 17. Head north to Holm, after which another ferry ride beckons, crossing a wide fjord to Vennesund. Stop at the textile and ceramic workshop just past the hamlet of Berg before carrying on to Brønnøysund. Running through the center of the nearby Torghatten mountain is a unique, naturally formed tunnel, carved during the last ice age. Continue north, board a ferry from Horn to Anndalsvåg, and drive to Forvik. After the pretty town of Alstahaug, you cross the Helgeland Bridge north of Sandnessjøen, then take the ferry from Levang to Nesna. Sjonfjellet mountain brings some of the route's most spectacular views, and just north of Stokkvågen, you can explore a German World War II fortress. The 60-minute ferry ride from Kilboghamn takes you across the Arctic Circle. You then drive to Ågskardet to take the final ferry to Forøy. From the road to Glomfjord, you can see Svartisen, one of Norway's largest glaciers. North of Reipå, a memorial to a submarine sunk offshore during World War II has a spectacular coastal viewpoint. Continue on Rte. 17, then head west on Rte. 80 to the large city of Bodø.

FROM: Steinkjer, Norway
TO: Bodø, Norway
ROADS: Rtes. 17, 769, 770, 80
DISTANCE: 446 miles (718 km)
DRIVING TIME: 14 hours
WHEN TO GO: Spring through fall
PLANNING: www.rv17.no

CROATIA/MONTENEGRO

Down by the Adriatic

The wars of the early 1990s forced Montenegro to drop from the tourist map for a time, yet it possesses one of Europe's most beautiful coastlines, with mountains rising inland, sparkling beaches, and enticing historic towns and cities.

From the walls of Dubrovnik (see In Focus), near Croatia's southern tip, take the E65 south for the 25-mile (40 km) journey to the Montenegrin border. Soon you arrive at the mountain-shrouded waters of the Bay of Kotor and the medieval town of Herceg Novi, famed for its healing mud. Sitting under the gaze of Mount Orjen, Herceg Novi, like the rest of Montenegro, has been marked by numerous occupying powers, including the Ottoman Turks and the Austrians, who left a diverse blend of architectural styles and a number of impressive fortresses. The road hugs the bay as you approach the town of Perast, with magnificent baroque palaces and churches. In the walled town of Kotor, be sure to visit the 12th-century Cathedral of St. Tryphon, whose altar is a masterpiece of Romanesque craftsmanship, and the Maritime Museum housed in a baroque palace. Leave town on the E65 as it winds around the bay, driving through the hamlet of Pracanj and on to Tivat, a former naval base currently being converted into a port for super-yachts. The road briefly cuts inland through verdant hills before arriving at Budva. Dating from the 5th century B.C., this is one of the oldest towns on the Adriatic, graced with fine Venetian architecture and cliff-backed beaches, while its vibrant nightlife makes it Montenegro's most popular seaside destination. A little farther along is the beach resort of Bečići. The walled village of Sveti Stefan, a near-island connected to the mainland by a narrow isthmus, bewitches visitors with its picturesque streets watched over by green mountains sloping to the sea. After that, the coast road (now the E851) winds on for another 36 miles (58 km) past the beaches of Petrovac, through the historic port town of Bar—home to a collection of centuries-old buildings—to your final destination, Ulcinj, where Montenegro's longest sandy beach awaits you.

FROM: Dubrovnik, Croatia
TO: Ulcinj, Montenegro
ROADS: E65, E851
DISTANCE: 112 miles (180 km)
DRIVING TIME: 4 hours
WHEN TO GO: Year-round
PLANNING: Remember your passport as you may be asked for it. If you want to use public transportation, there is a bus most mornings from Dubrovnik to Budva, where you may have to change to carry on to Ulcinj. www.montenegro.travel

In Focus Medieval walls up to 18 feet (5.5 m) thick and 80 feet (24 m) high surround **Dubrovnik's** ancient center, loved for its architectural treasures and sublime setting between the mountains and the sea. Attractions include Europe's oldest pharmacy still in operation, dating from 1317. Boat tours allow you to explore offshore islands, such as the beautiful Elafiti archipelago.

Perast is a baroque treasure house, dating from its years as an important trading hub under Venetian rule.

ITALY

Along the Amalfi Coast

With numerous switchbacks and plunging drops to the sea, the drive along the Amalfi coast is as hair-raising as it is stunning, with sublime views of towns and villages perched on top of rugged mountains, and tiny inlets and harbors where fishing boats bob at anchor.

Positano's tiled dome and cascade of pastel-colored houses make it one of the jewels of the Amalfi coast.

Starting in genteel Sorrento, take the minor coastal road leading to Massa Lubrense, where you can pick up the little road with spurs that provide access to the Sorrento Peninsula's rugged western tip, Punta Campanella. Compared with much of the coast, this area is beautifully undeveloped—all lemon trees, olive groves, sea views, and coastal trails. From Massa Lubrense, continue on the coast road past the hamlets of Marciano and Termini, and eastward to Sant'Agata sui due Golfi, named for its sweeping views over the Gulf of Naples to the north and Gulf of Salerno to the south. At Sant'Agata, take the proper coast road (SS145), built in 1853, that brings views of the islands of Li Galli, and then the SS163 past Positano, a village of pastel-colored houses set against cliffs and lemon trees. Farther along the coast, the road becomes busier as it heads through Vettica and Praiano, which marks the start of the most rugged part of the trip. At the Vallone di Furore, a dramatic gorge opens to the sea, a little beyond Marina di Praia. Continue to Amalfi (see Highlights) and Atrani, and make a small detour into the hills to the alluring little town of Ravello (see Highlights), a cool retreat in summer. Looping back to the coast road, you pass Maiori, with its large, developed beach, and the Capo d'Orso. The cape is a protected reserve and one of the coast's loveliest features, with trails to the lighthouse and the Abbazia di Santa Maria Olearia, a rock-cut abbey from the 10th century. The road then passes Cetara, known for its tuna industry, to reach Vietri sul Mare, with its famed ceramics on display all over the town.

Stay a While A short boat trip from several points on the coast takes you to **Capri,** a chic island and first-rate luxury playground. Since Roman times, visitors have come for the balmy climate, rugged coastline, whitewashed villages, and subtropical lushness of the hilly interior. A funicular climbs from the harbor to the main village of Capri, which has an impressive array of cafés and designer boutiques. To the east is Villa Jovis, the remains of Emperor Tiberius's hideaway. At the village of Anacapri stands the Villa San Michele with magnificent views.

OPPOSITE: The Mediterranean shimmers in the summer heat—as seen from the gardens of Villa Rufolo, Ravello.

Highlights

- The **Grotta dello Smeraldo,** a little beyond the Vallone di Furore, is a marine cave of luminous emerald waters reached by either an elevator or rock-carved steps from the main road, and then a short boat ride.
- Amalfi's cathedral, the **Duomo di Sant'Andrea,** has an intricate 12th-century facade and wonderful 11th-century Byzantine bronze doors.
- Open to all, the romantic gardens of the **Villa Cimbrone** in Ravello provide a justly celebrated view of the coast framed by a line of statues: the Belvedere Cimbrone. The gardens of Villa Rufolo are the venue for the **Festival di Ravello,** a series of classical concerts held March–November.

FROM: Sorrento, Italy
TO: Vietri sul Mare, Italy
ROADS: Local roads, SS145, SS163
DISTANCE: 50 miles (80 km)
DRIVING TIME: 2 hours
WHEN TO GO: Year-round; the high summer season is the busiest, especially on tiny Capri, where hotels and restaurants should be booked well in advance.
PLANNING: www.sorrentotourism.com

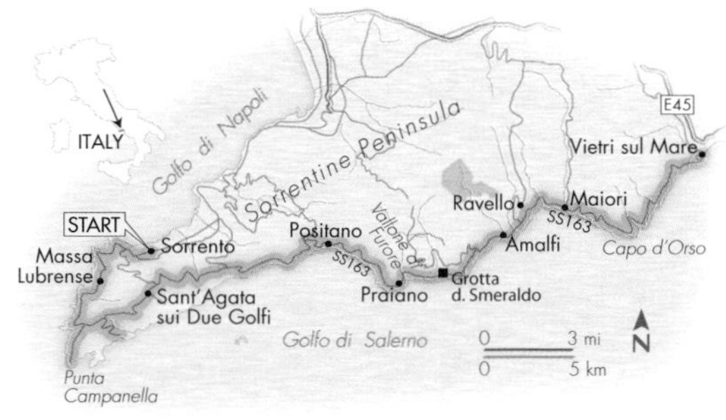

FRANCE/MONACO

The Riviera

The Corniche Inférieure (Low Coast Road) linking Nice and Monaco was built in the 1860s to bring gamblers to the new Monte-Carlo casino. It offers classic views of the Mediterranean, bougainvillea-draped villages, and lavish, belle-époque estates.

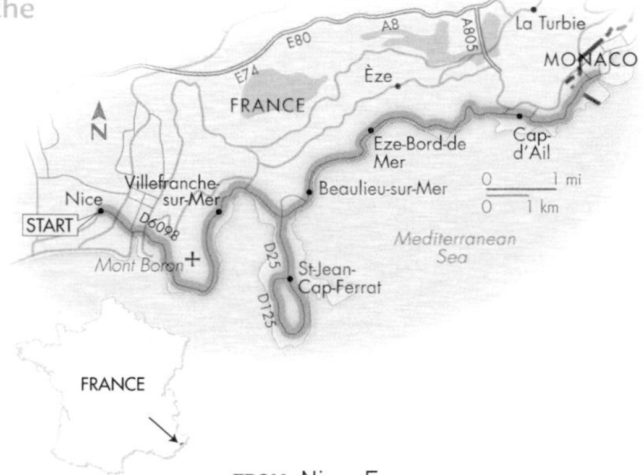

Leaving the elegant town of Nice eastward on Boulevard Carnot (D6098), you follow the sinuous road along the base of Mont Boron, soon coming in view of a striking panorama over Villefranche bay to St.-Jean-Cap-Ferrat, the flowery peninsula where princes, millionaires, and movie stars luxuriate. Almost immediately you come to Villefranche-sur-Mer, its rose- and cream-colored dwellings stacked on the hillside. This splendid little town features the Citadelle St.-Elme, a historic fortress now housing a modern art museum, and the Chapelle de St.-Pierre, its thick walls and barrel vaults decorated in 1957 by the avant-garde artist Jean Cocteau. Farther east, take a quick tour of Cap-Ferrat by dipping south onto the peninsula via the D25 and the D125. Watch for glitterati as you stretch your legs on the path edging the peninsula, and visit the powder-pink Villa Ephrussi de Rothschild, full of paintings and objets d'art. The nine gardens, watered by fountains, are astonishingly beautiful. Back on the road, another upmarket village, quiet Beaulieu-sur-Mer awaits a few miles farther east—the wide, sandy beach is a gem, graced with a long promenade. At the village of Èze-Bord-de-Mer, peer up the mountain to the 14th-century village of Èze teetering on a rock pillar high above the beach—there are stairs to walk up, but be forewarned: they're steep! Onward, a succession of views over the sparkling sea ushers you into Monaco, the glittering, legendary principality ruled by the Grimaldi family since the 13th century.

In Focus Higher up the mountainside, the **Moyenne Corniche** (Middle Coast Road), or N7, offers a dizzying drive with balcony views over cliff and sea. Around the midpoint of the drive, the medieval village of Èze rises 1,550 feet (472 m) directly above the sea. Its steep, shop-filled lanes wind up to the Jardin Exotique, with cactuses sprouting among castle ruins. Higher still, the **Grande Corniche** (Great Coast Road), or D2564, rides the cliff tops at 1,600 feet (487 m), following the Roman Via Aurelia, used to conquer the west. Today, it's the playground of race-driver wannabes and fearless cyclists.

FROM: Nice, France
TO: Monaco
ROADS: D6098, D25, D125
DISTANCE: 20.5 miles (33 km)
DRIVING TIME: 1 hour
WHEN TO GO: The prettiest time is April and May. Avoid summer, when congestion can be maddening.
PLANNING: Return to Nice on the A8, a 30-minute drive; or, to see the same views from a different angle, take one of the other corniches (see In Focus). www.beyond.fr

The bright colors of Villefranche-sur-Mer's harbor perfectly offset the green mountains and blue sea.

The mellow-brick medieval town of Tossa de Mar marks the starting point for exploring the beautiful Catalonian coastline.

SPAIN

Costa Brava

Given the rugged beauty of the extreme northeast coast of Spain, it's not surprising that it has been the target of cheap resort development. The delightful surprise is that long stretches of cliffs and white beaches remain intact, to be enjoyed in peace.

The medieval watchtower of Tossa de Mar recedes into the distance as you set out on the GI-682 coast road, climbing a series of switchbacks cut into the cliffs. After the seaside town of Sant Feliu de Guíxols, you come upon a run of popular beaches, starting with Platja d'Aro and, after exiting onto the C-31 inland highway at Palamós, the delightful sands of Calella de Palafrugell, Llafranc, and Tamariu. The last is the quietest, with limpid water backed by thick woods. A little farther on lies the cove of Aiguablava. Take the GIP-6532 to Fornells and the bustling town of Begur. From here, take the GI-653 and GIV-6502 to Pals, with its Gothic defensive walls and centuries-old mansions. The castle ruins of Torroella de Montgrí appear high above, as the GI-632 leads north to L'Escala, a pleasant seaside spot, before the GI-623 cuts inland and north past the nature reserve of Parc Natural dels Aiguamolls de l'Empordà. A little farther on, Castelló d'Empúries awaits you, its old center dominated by the Gothic Església de Santa Maria. Continue east on the C260 and GI-618 through the highlands of the Cap de Creus Peninsula to reach the chic town of Cadaqués and Port Lligat, former home of surrealist artist Salvador Dalí.

Unexpected Pleasure The marine nature reserve of the **Illes Medes,** with its labyrinth of underwater tunnels and caves and more than 1,400 species of animal and plant life, lies off the coast town of L'Estartit—east of Torroella de Montgrí on the GI-641. The islets are a favorite diving and snorkeling spot—the deepest dive is 164 feet (30 m), where you may encounter rays as well as octopuses.

FROM: Tossa de Mar, Spain
TO: Cadaqués, Spain
ROADS: GI-682, C-31, GIP-6532, GI-653, GIV-6502, GI-632, GI-623, C260, GI-618
DISTANCE: 83 miles (133 km)
DRIVING TIME: 3 hours
WHEN TO GO: Year-round
PLANNING: www.catalunya.com

SOUTH AFRICA

The Garden Route

This stretch of South Africa's coast must have seemed like the Garden of Eden to early Dutch settlers, with its hidden coves and endless beaches edging lakes, rivers, and wetlands, the entire sweep nestled between mountains and ocean.

After climbing to the top of Mossel Bay's St. Blaize Lighthouse to spot whales and dolphins, and exploring the town's excellent museums, head northeast on the N2 Garden Route to George. The town, 5 miles (8 km) inland at the base of the Outeniqua Mountains, boasts some world-class golf courses and beautiful colonial buildings. The Garden Route Botanical Garden shows off the local flora, including cape reeds, daisies, and Afromontane forest. After the town of Wilderness, which no longer lives up to its name, pass through Wilderness National Park, a 13-mile (20 km) stretch of forest interspersed with lagoons and lakes. This is a paradise for birdlife, including five types of kingfisher, gray heron, and the brightly colored Knysna loerie. After the seaside resort of Sedgefield, the road passes Buffalo Bay, where you can go horseback riding through the surf. Next stop is Knysna, which has plenty of bars and restaurants and sits on a beautiful lagoon surrounded by one of South Africa's largest indigenous forests, with many Afromontane species. About a half-hour drive onward brings you to Knysna Elephant Park, where orphaned elephants roam among 148 acres (60 ha) and guides allow access to the animals. Farther along the N2 is the seaside village of Plettenberg Bay, with almost 6 miles (10 km) of immaculate sandy beaches. After crossing Nature's Valley, a small village on the Groot River estuary surrounded by dense forest, the road meanders into Storms River. This small village is a center for outdoor activities such as mountain biking and river tubing. The adventurous can throw themselves off Bloukrans Bridge in one of the world's highest bungee jumps.

FROM: Mossel Bay, South Africa
TO: Storms River, South Africa
ROAD: N2 Garden Route
DISTANCE: 121 miles (196 km)
DRIVING TIME: 2.5 hours
WHEN TO GO: Year-round, although it can be crowded in the summer months, especially December; the region is also popular at Easter.
PLANNING: www.gardenroute.co.za

Unexpected Pleasure Take a ride from George to Knysna on the **Outeniqua Choo-Tjoe,** South Africa's last fully operational steam train. The line goes through scenery that is otherwise inaccessible: dense forest, fern-covered hills, lakes, rivers, and lagoons. It also stops off at interesting places, including small towns, museums, places of historical interest, an aquarium, and a railway workshop. The round-trip need not be completed in one day, giving you the chance to stay in Knysna.

The mighty Indian Ocean meets the Great Brak River at Mossel Bay.

Also Recommended

❶ Atlantic Coast Drive, Nova Scotia, Canada

Starting out from Halifax, the landscape is bleak, passing remote fishing ports battered by the ocean and cottages perched beside harbors. The road sticks to the coast, passing a string of small towns, including much-photographed Peggy's Cove. Watch out for sea mist unexpectedly rolling in as you head 225 miles (362 km) south to Barrington.

www.novascotia.com

❷ Great Lakes Seaway Trail, Ohio

Niagara Falls are the undisputed highlight along this famous route marked by green and white signs. But with water in view for much of the route between Erie and Thousand Islands and a succession of pretty lakeside ports and towns, this legendary drive has plenty more to offer.

www.seawaytrail.com

❸ East Shore, Lake Tahoe, Nevada

This drive has earned a description as "the most beautiful drive in America." And it's no wonder. As you cruise along Rte. 28, crystal clear Lake Tahoe is breathtaking, the pine trees bristle, and the mountains are often dusted with snow. Stop along the way for watersports, golfing, and skiing.

www.visitinglaketahoe.com

❹ Santa Monica to Zuma Beach, California

This drive along California's Pacific Coast Highway brings a heady mix of mountains, cliffs, beaches, and dramatic seascapes. Stop at Malibu Pier and Surfrider Beach to get your toes in the sand. Back on the road, you pass Paradise Cove and Broad Beach on the way to Zuma Beach.

www.pacific-coast-highway-travel.com

❺ Hamakua Coast, Hawaii

Beginning at Hilo, the drive passes spiny black rocks and crashing waves at Onomea Bay before reaching Waipo Valley overlook. Head north on Hawaii 19, keeping an eye out for sea turtles, and visit Akaka Falls State Park and Kolekole Stream. Farther on you come to Laupahoehoe Beach—a unique lava peninsula pounded by surf.

www.gohawaii.com

❻ Baja Peninsula, Mexico

The route from Tijuana south to Cabo San Lucas—historically popular with adventurous naturalists and anglers—was finally paved in 1974. Hwy. 1 still isn't the smoothest ride, but it's excellent for whale watching from Laguna Ojo de Liebre or snorkeling at Caleta San Lucas.

www.visitmexico.com

❼ Punta Cana to Sabana de la Mar, Dominican Republic

Begin at Cabo Engaño for an exhilarating drive through sand, then follow signs for Bavaro inland to reach Playa Monaco. Continue along the coastal road passing beaches and coconut trees for 105 miles (169 km) until you reach Sabana de la Mar.

www.godominicanrepublic.com

❽ Chacarita to Carate, Costa Rica

To visit such paradises as Rincón, where views reach all the way to Panama, or Playa Sombrero, where only the most skilled surfers dare enter the ocean's extreme swells, drive along Osa Hwy. 245. After curling 73 miles (117 km) around the peninsula you reach Carate, perched at the edge of Parque Nacional Corcovado.

www.tourism.co.cr

❾ Bariloche to El Bolsón, Argentina

The lakes of Parque Nacional Nahuel Huapi along RN40 offer sparkling clear waters among snowcapped peaks. When you arrive in El Bolsón visit the famous street markets and hike in the nearby mountains. Spend the night back along the water at Lago Puelo.

www.patagonia-argentina.com

❿ Paihia to Cape Reinga, New Zealand

To explore the famous 90 Mile Beach, you'll need to join a tour or bring your own 4WD. There's more to this drive than simple surf and sand—watch out for quicksand streams, and in Waiharara, investigate an ancient, buried kauri forest. Bring a boogie board for sliding down dunes.

www.explorenz.co.nz/Dune-Rider

⓫ Great Nature Trail, Tasmania

Spend some time spotting wallabies and wombats at Narawntapu National Park, just east of Devonport. Then take Bass Highway to Burnie, stopping off en route in the small town of Penguin to see—you guessed it—penguins! Continue west to Wynyard, famous for its October tulips, and on to Stanley, a fishing village dominated by a volcanic plug known as the "Nut."

www.discovertasmania.co.uk

⓬ Northeast Loop, Phuket, Thailand

From Two Heroines Monument traffic circle, go east on Hwy. 4027, passing small Thai communities built around fishing areas and shrimp farms. Just 7.5 miles (12 km) after the circle, turn to follow signs for Ao Po and enjoy a loop with views into the bay and across to grey-green islands.

www.phukettourist.com

⓭ Gower Peninsula, Wales

The Gower was Britain's first designated Area of Outstanding Natural Beauty. The 18-mile (29 km) stretch west of Swansea (mostly along the A4118) brings coves, cliffs, the sweeping beaches of Oxwich and Port Eynon, and the crowning glory of Rhossili Bay at the end of the peninsula. Stop off to swim, surf, picnic, and hike.

www.enjoygower.com

⓮ Antrim Coast, Northern Ireland

Snaking through geological formations, the A2 runs 53 miles (85 km) from Ballygalley to Bushmills. At Carrick-a-Rede, walk across a precarious rope bridge—the only thing separating you from a chasm foaming with surf 98 feet (30 m) below. At the famous Giant's Causeway, tall columns of solidified lava rise from the sea. End the drive with a relaxing ferry ride to Larne.

www.discovernorthernireland.com

CHAPTER 3

Rivers, Valleys, & Canyons

THE ROUTES FOR SOME OF THE WORLD'S most memorable drives are those created by nature herself, inscribed by the slow but implacable movements of water and rock across vast stretches of time. Rivers are journeys all their own, their routes to the sea having provided the stage for endless human dramas and stunning geological change. Some of the journeys on the following pages lead deep into the world's wild places, where the scarcity of human traffic allows for spectacular surprises: the Ultimate Road Trip through rainbow-colored rock formations of unearthly beauty in southern Utah's Canyonlands; a visit to a dinosaur's nest in the Canadian province of Alberta; a quest into the heart of East Africa for a visit to Lake Victoria and the source of the Nile. Others are gentler, more reflective journeys through the highways and byways of social history, folklore, architecture, and the arts: a music-lover's meander through the Mississippi Delta, birthplace of the blues; a sampling of New England mansions, riverboats, and a gem of a Victorian opera house in the Connecticut River Valley; and a stately progress along Germany's River Elbe, with its Saxon castles, opulent palaces, and old-world spas.

Clouds of spray rise from the Victoria Falls as the Zambezi River plunges into a gorge more than 300 feet (100 m) deep. Visitors can enjoy a breathtaking view from the Victoria Falls Bridge.

The Qu'Appelle River Valley meanders through a graceful landscape of grasslands.

CANADA

Saskatchewan Prairies

This leisurely drive through southern Saskatchewan combines rolling plains, a pretty river valley, forested hills, and small towns redolent with the history of the fur trade and the lives of early immigrant settlers.

FROM: Loop route from Regina, Canada

ROADS: Trans-Canada 1, Hwys. 2, 202, 20, 99, 22, 310, 52, 47, 247, 9, 13

DISTANCE: 575 miles (925 km)

DRIVING TIME: 6.5 hours

WHEN TO GO: May through October

PLANNING: www.sasktourism.com

Beginning in the provincial capital, Regina, take Trans-Canada 1 west to Moose Jaw, which, during Prohibition, became a paradise for gangsters from across the U.S. border. The smuggling tunnels in this "Little Chicago" are now open as a tourist attraction. Head north on Hwy. 2 and turn onto the 202 to visit Buffalo Pound Provincial Park, where you can sometimes see wild buffalo roaming the hills. The park also includes the Nicolle Flats Interpretive Area, where wetlands provide a home for a variety of birds, such as grebes, ducks, bitterns, and coots. Return to Hwy. 2 and drive to Craven. Turn north on Hwy. 20 to Last Mountain House Provincial Historic Park, a former provisioning post for the Hudson Bay Company, where demonstrations re-enact the life of a 19th-century fur trader. Pick up Hwy. 22 via Hwy. 99, turn north on Hwy. 310 (a gravel road), and then east on Hwy. 52. The Western Development Museum in Yorkton tells the stories of immigrants who settled Saskatchewan, drawn by the promise of free land and religious freedom. From Yorkton, take Hwy. 47 to Hwy. 247 through the most scenic part of the drive—the verdant valley of the Qu'Appelle River. A kiosk just above the road in the lower Qu'Appelle has information on a 950-year-old Indian burial mound. Old George's Authentic Collectibles down Hwy. 9 in Whitewood is a prairie mansion packed with an eccentric collection of antique furniture, toys, Native American artifacts, and more. Follow Hwy. 9 through Moose Mountain Provincial Park, a plateau of lakes, marshes, and forest, and continue to Cannington Manor Provincial Historic Park. Founded in the 1880s, this prairie village is an attempt to re-create a version of English country life. At Carlyle, turn onto Hwy. 13 heading west through flat plains back to Regina.

CANADA

Beyond Calgary

This remarkably diverse journey through southwestern Alberta combines the dazzling alpine scenery of the Canadian Rockies—dramatic cliffs, lakes, waterfalls, and valleys—with a fascinating excursion into the world of the dinosaurs.

After exploring Calgary's many museums, head south on Hwy. 2 to High River. Cross Highwood River on Rte. 543, then pick up Hwy. 22 south to Bar U Ranch National Historic Site, an immense open-range ranch dating from 1882. Continue south, turning west on Hwy. 3 toward the Rockies and Crowsnest Pass, revered for its mining history and natural beauty. Double back to Pincher Creek, then turn south on Hwy. 6 toward Waterton Lakes National Park where the great plains push against the Rockies, creating a dramatic landscape of cliffs, waterfalls, lakes, valleys, and streams. Pick up maps from the visitor center and hike up nearby Bear's Hump Trail, which offers excellent views of the valley. From Waterton, Hwy. 5 crosses the prairie to Cardston and the Remington-Alberta Carriage Centre. North on Hwy. 2 is Fort Macleod, the first outpost of the North West Mounted Police and home to the Fort Museum. West of town is Head-Smashed-In Buffalo Jump, where prehistoric peoples hunted by herding hundreds of animals over the cliff. East on Hwy. 3, Lethbridge, perched above Oldman River, is Alberta's third largest city, with several museums, including Fort Whoop-Up, which chronicles the 19th-century whiskey trade. Hwy. 4 leads southeast to Warner and the Devil's Coulee Dinosaur Heritage Museum, which conducts tours of a dinosaur nesting site. Head northeast on Hwy. 36, then northwest on Trans-Canada 1, and follow Hwy. 56 to Rosedale in the Drumheller Valley and the Royal Tyrrell Museum of Palaeontology, one of the world's finest dinosaur museums with a complete Tyrannosaurus Rex skeleton. Return to Calgary via Hwy. 9.

Hidden History Take Hwy. 544 off Trans-Canada 1 northeast of Brooks and you come to **Dinosaur Provincial Park** in the heart of one of the world's preeminent deposits of Cretaceous dinosaur bones. The area contains more than 200 bone beds that have yielded the remains of dinosaurs, crocodiles, turtles, flying reptiles, and small mammals, some of which are on display in the Field Station Visitor Centre. Interpretive tours of the area (mid-May to mid-October), conducted on foot and by bus, are popular (book ahead). The fossil display buildings and five self-guided trails are open all year.

FROM: Loop route from Calgary, Canada

ROADS: Hwy. 2, Rte. 543, Hwys. 22, 3, 6, 5, 4, 36, Trans-Canada 1, Hwys. 56, 9

DISTANCE: 750 miles (1,200 km)

DRIVING TIME: 12 hours

WHEN TO GO: May through September

PLANNING: Bring boots for hiking. www.tourismcalgary.com

The sun goes down on the ancient landscape of Dinosaur Provincial Park, home to hoodoos and beds of dinosaur bones.

The Goodspeed Opera House in East Haddam is the birthplace of musicals such as *Annie* and *Shenandoah.*

Highlights

- The **Goodspeed Opera House** in East Haddam, restored in the late 1950s to its Victorian grandeur, has been the birthplace of many top Broadway musicals.
- The **Connecticut River Museum** in Essex traces the area's nautical heritage through displays of model ships, navigational instruments, paintings, and a model of the *American Turtle*, the first submarine in the world to be used in battle.
- **Essex Steam Train and Riverboat** run tours along the river on restored locomotives and riverboats, evoking the atmosphere of 19th-century travel.
- **Thankful Arnold House** in Haddam provides a glimpse into the daily life of Thankful, widow of local businessman Joseph Arnold, in the early 19th century. Tours take in the house and herb and vegetable gardens.

CONNECTICUT

Connecticut River Valley

At the end of its 400-mile (644 km) journey south from the Canadian border, the Connecticut River flows through peaceful farmland, past old towns and villages that once hummed with activity, and into Long Island Sound.

Perched on a bend in the Connecticut River, Middletown was one of the biggest ports in the U.S. in the 18th century. From here, head east on Conn. 66, crossing the river into Portland, and continue to the small village of Cobalt. Turn right onto Conn. 151, heading south, before turning onto Conn. 149 to the small riverside town of East Haddam, famous for its opera house (see Highlights). Pick up Conn. 82 and follow signs for Gillette Castle State Park, where the 1919 castle overlooks the river. Leaving the park, turn left onto Conn. 148, through the small town of Hadlyme, where a ferry has transported people and vehicles across the river for two centuries. After exploring the village, return to Conn. 82, continue east, then turn south onto Conn. 156 and cross Eightmile River near Joshua's Rock. Continue through Hamburg and into Old Lyme, a historic town on Long Island Sound with grand mansions that were owned by 18th- and early 19th-century sea captains. Continue south a short way on I-95, crossing the river and taking the first exit onto Conn. 9, and then the second exit off Conn. 9 onto Conn. 154, toward the historic harbor of Essex, where in 1775 the first Connecticut warship, the *Oliver Cromwell*, was built. Back on Conn. 9, continue north and turn west onto Conn. 148 and follow signs to Cockaponset State Forest, home to rare tulip trees. Back on Conn. 154, follow the river to the picturesque town of Haddam and on to the Seven Falls Highway State Park, which has a waterfall and, beyond it, the flat stone slabs of Bible Rock, resembling an open bible. From the park entrance, take Conn. 9 back to Middletown.

FROM: Loop route from Middletown, Connecticut
ROADS: Conn. 66, 151, 149, 82, 148, 156, I-95, Conn. 9, 154
DISTANCE: 56 miles (90 km)
DRIVING TIME: 2 hours
WHEN TO GO: May through October
PLANNING: www.enjoycentralct.com

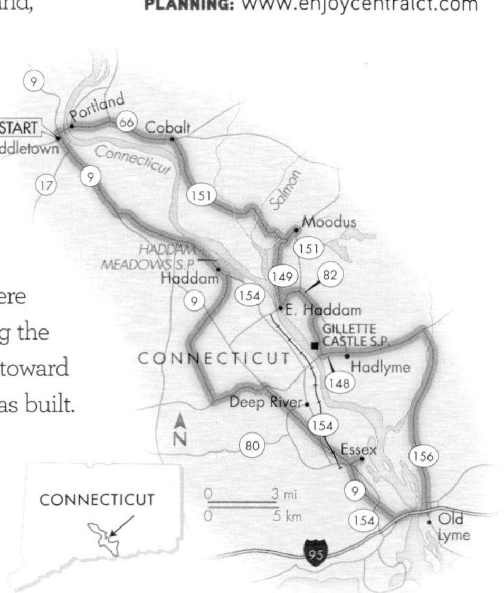

NORTH CAROLINA

Cullasaja River Gorge

This short, winding stretch of road in the southwestern corner of North Carolina runs upriver from Franklin through a narrow, steep-sided gorge at the southern edge of the Smoky Mountains, and past a series of dramatic waterfalls.

Franklin is a mountain town set in some spectacular scenery, and calls itself the "gem capital of the world" because of the ruby, garnet, and sapphire mines nearby (see Unexpected Pleasure). Pick up U.S. 64 here and head south through gentle countryside that gives no hint of the steep climbs ahead. After around 7 miles (11 km), the pastureland disappears and the road climbs to the towering granite mass of Higdon Mountain, then enters a narrow, curving gorge. Drive along the north side of the gorge, high above the Cullasaja River, navigating frequent sharp bends—there are places to pull off and enjoy views of the river and the Nantahala National Forest. The first waterfall along the way is Lower Cullasaja Falls. It's unmarked, but the 250 feet (76 m) of terraced, cascading white water makes a marker unnecessary. You'll spot it easily, but there is nowhere here to pull off and park. The road continues its meandering ascent along the path of the river, between towering cliffs and through forests of pine, hemlock, and maple. At Dry Falls, get out and take the small trail that tunnels under the 75-foot (23 m) falls, where you can look out through the surging water without getting wet. Drive a little farther to come to the 120-foot (36 m) Bridal Veil Falls—an elegant spray of white water gives the falls their name. If you wish, you can drive along an old road that goes behind the waterfall. The tour ends in the mountain resort of Highlands, the highest and wettest town in North Carolina and filled with mountain flowers and lush foliage. It is also known for its antique shops, fine restaurants, and vibrant art scene.

FROM: Franklin, North Carolina
TO: Highlands, North Carolina
ROAD: U.S. 64
DISTANCE: 18 miles (29 km)
DRIVING TIME: 0.5 hours
WHEN TO GO: Spring through fall
PLANNING: www.cs.unca.edu/nfsnc

Unexpected Pleasure If you'd like to try your hand at gem mining, visit one of the mines in the Franklin area, such as **Cowee Mountain Ruby Mine** (just off Hwy. 441, 4 miles/6.4 km north of Franklin), **Gem Mine at Gem World** (on Hwy. 441), **Gold City Gem Mine** (on Hwy. 441, 6 miles/9.6 km north of Franklin), or **Jackson Hole** (just above the Cullasaja Falls). Most mines sell buckets of gem dirt, and provide equipment for sifting through the mud as well as advice on technique for novices. They'll also help you identify your haul—which may include rubies, sapphires, garnets, and moonstones.

At Dry Falls, you can stand behind the waterfall and look out through a solid sheet of cascading water.

THE TOP 10 African River Drives

Drives that follow the great rivers of Africa offer the chance to see famous waterfalls, spectacular wildlife, and remote and dramatic scenery.

❶ Draa River Valley, Morocco

Located at the junction of three rivers, the modern city of Ouarzazate is an excellent starting point. Known as the Hollywood of Africa, the Draa Valley has been the set for many movies, including *Lawrence of Arabia* and *Gladiator*. Follow the N9 south through the valley and watch as the lush green landscape around the oasis town of Agdz slowly turn to desert as you reach the edge of the Sahara at Zagora.

PLANNING: Visit the holy village of Tamegroute, 13.5 miles (22 km) south of Zagora, where cultural artifacts from the 11th century are preserved in the library. *www.gonomad.com*

❷ Gambia River, The Gambia

In Banjul, The Gambia's capital, take the ferry across the mouth of the Gambia River to Barra Point, and drive inland along the river on the North Bank Road. At the town of Juffureh, you can break the drive with a boat trip on the river to James Island, which has a 17th-century fort.

PLANNING: It is best to hire a guide for this trip. *www.hiddengambia.com*

❸ Victoria Nile, Uganda

Start at the source of the Nile River on the northern shore of Lake Victoria, near the town of Jinja, and drive to the Bujagali Falls, the first rapids on the river and popular for white-water rafting. Then take the main highway west to Kampala and turn north to the Murchison Falls National Park, where you can see the river pounding through the magnificent Murchison Falls.

PLANNING: Aim to arrive at Murchison Falls around sunset, when scores of fish can be seen crossing the Nile. *www.cycadssafaris.com*

❹ River Galana, Kenya

From Mombasa, head 70 miles (113 km) northwest to Tsavo East National Park, entering at the Bachuma Gate. Drive northeast across savanna to the Lugard Falls, a series of white-water rapids on the River Galana. Follow the road along the river as it flows to the Indian Ocean, and exit the park at the Sala Gate. Malindi, the closest big town, is 73 miles (118 km) east.

PLANNING: You will need a 4WD for this drive and you are not allowed to leave your car while in the park. *www.africanconcept.co.ke*

❺ Lake Malawi and the Shire River, Malawi

Cape Maclear, on the southern coast of Lake Malawi, is a small fishing village popular with travelers. You can go on a fishing trip or visit Mumbo Island, the uninhabited tropical retreat 2.5 miles (4 km) offshore. Drive south along the edge of the lake until you reach Mangochi, where the lake empties into the Shire River. From here, the river runs south through Liwonde National Park, where you can take hippo- and crocodile-spotting boat trips.

PLANNING: You could spend up to a week enjoying this 125-mile (200 km) drive. *www.safaridrive.com*

❻ Zambezi River, Zambezi

Victoria Falls on the Zambezi River marks the border between Zambia and Zimbabwe. Heading south from Livingstone toward the falls you pass a viewing point on the side of the road, but the 5,604-foot (1,708 m) wide cataract—the largest on earth—is best viewed from Victoria Falls Bridge. A short spin west of the falls brings you to Mosi-Oa-Tunya National Park, where you can drive along beside the river and see the park's wildlife.

PLANNING: The falls are at their most spectacular in March and April, when peak flooding occurs. *www.victoriafalls.biz*

OPPOSITE: A herd of elephants makes its way across the Olifants River in Kruger National Park, South Africa.

❼ Fish River Canyon, Namibia

Using Hobas as your base, drive across the arid, desert-like plateau of the Nama Karoo for 6 miles (10 km) until you reach the main viewing point of this 500-million-year-old canyon. Continue to the spa resort at Ai-Ais, where, from February to October you can take a dip in the thermal springs.

PLANNING: The trip is best done between January and April, when the Fish River rages through the canyon in a great torrent. *www.namibian.org*

❽ Olifants River, South Africa

Northeast of Johannesburg, the Olifants River meanders through several national parks. Drive west from the city of Polokwane to Tzaneen, where a dam across the river has created a wilderness area that attracts over 350 varieties of birds. Continue through the fertile valley to Klaserie, stopping off at one of the smaller game reserves to enjoy a more intimate safari experience before reaching Kruger National Park, where you can see all of the Big Five game species.

PLANNING: Allow at least a day for a safari in Kruger National Park, which has a plethora of birds and wildlife. *www.places.co.za*

❾ Orange River, South Africa

Start from Upington, a town on the edge of the Kalahari Desert, and take the R359 that runs beside the Orange River, passing vineyards and fruit farms along the way. After 50 miles (80 km) you reach the Augrabies Falls National Park, meaning "place of the big noise," where you can watch as the Orange River plunges 230 feet (70 m) into the ravine below.

PLANNING: The 162-mile (260 km) drive from Upington and back makes a good day trip. *www.kalaharisafaris.co.za*

❿ Breede River, South Africa

Easily accessible from Cape Town, this drive through the heart of the Cape Winelands follows the Breede River from historic Tulbagh to Robertson. A relaxing way to spend half a day, this 65-mile (105 km) drive passes through magnificent mountain scenery and is usually less congested than the better-known wine routes to the south.

PLANNING: The town of Worcester, halfway along the route, is a perfect place to stay if you want to spend more time in the area. *www.places.co.za*

TENNESSEE/MISSISSIPPI

Mississippi Blues Highway

Highway 61 follows the Mississippi River through the Delta, home of the blues. It became known as the Blues Highway because it is the route musicians traveled from the Delta to Memphis to escape their harsh lives in the Delta and seek fame and fortune.

The blues, which came out of America's deep south in the early 20th century, revolutionized popular music, and its soulful tunes reached a much wider audience than the black community from which it emerged. Start in Memphis (see Stay a While), the home of Elvis Presley, whose immersion in blues music helped him evolve his unique rock-and-roll sound. Before leaving town, search out Wild Bill's, one of the coolest blues bars around, and take a walk through Beale Street, the city's thriving heart, where B. B. King and Howlin' Wolf made their names and which still has some great blues music. Head south on Hwy. 61—the Blues Highway—to Clarksdale, Mississippi, one-time home of John Lee Hooker, Muddy Waters, and Ike Turner. The town has many authentic "juke joints" (blues bars), so take a look at the listings board at Cat Head, a blues music and folk art store, to see who's playing where. For a taste of what life on a plantation may have been like, spend a night at the Shack Up Inn, a collection of restored sharecropper shacks on the Hopson Plantation off Hwy. 49 outside Clarksdale. The plantation also hosts many blues gigs. In Cleveland, 45 minutes south of Clarksdale, you can visit the old Dockery Plantation, considered the birthplace of the Delta Blues because of the influence of several musicians who lived there, including Charley Patton and Howlin' Wolf. At Leland, turn west to Greenwood, in the heart of blues country. Walk past the WGRM radio station on Howard Street, where B. B. King made his first live recording in 1940, before heading into the Greenwood Blues Heritage Museum and Gallery, which focuses on the "King of the Delta Blues," Robert Johnson. Return to Hwy. 61 and continue south to Vicksburg, an important Civil War city.

Stay a While Spend a day exploring Memphis's musical past. You can take a tour of **Sun Studios,** often called the birthplace of rock-and-roll, but also famous for its blues history. The **Rock 'n' Soul Museum** in the Gibson Guitar Factory tells the story of the area's music pioneers who overcame racial and socio-economic adversity to shake the world. The **Stax Museum of American Soul Music,** in the refurbished Stax recording studios, is dedicated to the rich history of soul in the area.

FROM: Memphis, Tennessee
TO: Vicksburg, Mississippi
ROADS: Hwys. 61, 49
DISTANCE: 230 miles (370 km)
DRIVING TIME: 4.5 hours
WHEN TO GO: October, for the Cotton Capital Blues Festival in Greenwood
PLANNING: Allow time to enjoy performances at the blues joints en route. www.blueshighway.org

Sun Studios is filled with memorabilia from the days when music legends such as Howlin' Wolf, B. B. King, and Elvis Presley recorded here.

A paddleboat plies the Illinois River in Starved Rock State Park.

ILLINOIS

Illinois River Road

The historic Illinois River was an early water-highway used first by Native Americans and later by French explorers. This route through central and northern Illinois follows the river on both banks, passing parks, wildlife areas, and historic sites.

Begin in the old city of Ottawa and head west on Ill. 71 to Starved Rock State Park to look at its canyons carved into sandstone bluffs. The park was the site of a 17th-century French fort, situated across the river from the Grand Village of the Kaskaskia tribe. It gets its name from a Native American legend that said the Illiniwek tribe was besieged and starved to death here. When the fort and village existed, much of the Illinois River was flanked by shallow backwaters and had a wide array of wildlife. Drainage has eliminated many of these areas, but some have been preserved. To see one, take Ill. 71 west to Ill. 26 and drive south before turning west onto Hennepin Farms Road. The wetlands of the Hennepin and Hopper Lakes Restoration have brought back many birds, amphibians, and plants not seen in the area for decades. Continue south on Ill. 26, 116, and 29, which run on the east and west sides of the river respectively, passing mostly hillside bluffs and cropland as well as several more wetland areas. Ill. 29 traverses forested hillsides before entering Peoria, whose riverfront features plenty of restaurants, festivals, and concerts. From Pekin, on the east side of the river, travel southwest along local roads to the historic town of Havana. Cross the river and turn north on Ill. 78/97 to the Dickson Mounds Museum, with exhibits showing the 12,000-year history of the Native Americans in the Illinois River Valley. The neighboring Emiquon Preserve is one of the country's largest floodplain restoration projects, and has a wide variety of flora and fauna. Return to Ottawa on the western bank of the river via U.S. 24, Ill. 29, and U.S. 6.

FROM: Ottawa, Illinois
TO: Havana, Illinois
ROADS: Ill. 71, 26, 116, 29, 78/97, U.S. 24, 6, local roads
DISTANCE: 291 miles (468 km)
DRIVING TIME: 7 hours
WHEN TO GO: Late spring through fall
PLANNING: Bring binoculars to see the river's abundant birdlife.
www.illinoisriverroad.com

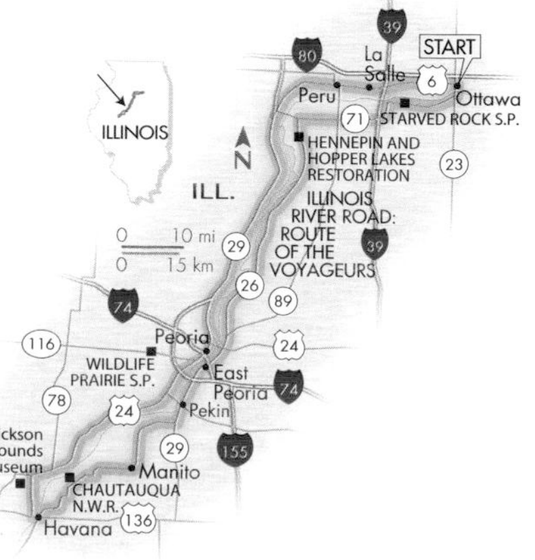

MINNESOTA

Great River Road

From a small trickle, the Mississippi River matures into the Great River, flowing for 2,552 miles (4,107 km) from Minnesota's North Woods to the Gulf of Mexico. This drive follows the first stages of the river's winding journey, starting in Lake Itasca State Park.

The city of St. Paul has 26 miles (42 km) of Mississippi shoreline and extensive riverside trails.

Highlights

- In the town of Little Falls, just beyond Brainerd, the **Charles A. Lindbergh Historic Site** preserves the house where the famous aviator grew up, and displays artifacts from his life.
- The **St. Anthony Falls Historic District** in downtown Minneapolis includes St. Anthony Falls, Mill Ruins Park, and Stone Arch Bridge, which is the best place to see the Minneapolis skyline at sunset.
- **Bald Eagle Bluff Scientific and Natural Area** is an important wintering site for bald eagles. During the day they perch by the river to feed. Look for them in the upper branches of taller stands of cottonwood trees.

In Lake Itasca State Park, Minnesota's oldest, you can wade across the ankle-deep Mississippi River where it starts in Lake Itasca, and visit the Mary Gibbs Mississippi Headwaters Center to find out about the continent's longest waterway. From the park, local roads take you north briefly, past large boulders that were deposited at the end of the last ice age, and on to Bemidji, the first city of any size along the river's route. The Mississippi is just a stream here as it flows into the waters of Lake Bemidji, which, according to legend, is the footprint of mythical lumberjack Paul Bunyon. Giant, colorful statues of Paul Bunyan and his companion, Babe the Blue Ox, stand on the shores of the lake.

The Great River Road heads southeast past many lakes and angling resorts before traversing Chippewa National Forest and turning south at Grand Rapids. The river winds ceaselessly as you follow it on a series of county roads through croplands and on to Brainerd, and has widened considerably by the time you reach St. Cloud. Situated on the river's east bank, the Munsinger and Clemens Gardens are great places to take a walk before entering the twin cities of Minneapolis (see Highlights) and St. Paul. Both have an abundance of attractions, including St. Paul's Mississippi National River and Recreation Area, just down the road from the Science Museum of Minnesota. Beyond the old river city of Hastings, the route joins U.S. 61. As you wind among bluffs several hundred feet above the river, you catch stunning views of the Mississippi between steep headlands. At Frontenac State Park, south of Red Wing, trails offer broad vistas of Lake Pepin, which is popular with boaters; Lake City's large marina is a good place for sailing and jet-skiing. Watch for a roadside sign near Reads Landing marking Bald Eagle Bluff Scientific and Natural Area (see Highlights), as in winter you may spot a bald eagle around here. Or you can try to catch sight of one at the National Eagle Center in Wabasha. Continue south through the 19th-century lumber town of Winona and on along bluffs above the river to Lamoille, with a view of the Trempealeau Mountains. Cross I-90 here to La Crescent. For the last 20 miles (32 km) to the Iowa border, the byway follows Minn. 26 as the Mississippi widens into the Great River.

FROM: Lake Itasca State Park, Minnesota
TO: Iowa State Line south of La Crosse, Minnesota
ROADS: Local county and state roads, U.S. 61, I-90, Minn. 26
DISTANCE: 575 miles (925 km)
DRIVING TIME: 8 hours
WHEN TO GO: April through November
PLANNING: Unpaved roads may be unsafe in bad weather. www.greatriverroad.com

OPPOSITE: Rocks mark the place where water spills over the banks of Lake Itasca at the start of the Mississippi.

The Eisenhower Center in Abilene includes the family home in which the future president and his brothers were raised.

KANSAS

Prairie Lands

Traveling through the northeast section of this frontier state, you'll get a taste of the region's rich history, including tales of the Wild West and the Chisholm and Santa Fe Trails, and you'll discover the area's role as hometown to an American president.

FROM: Lawrence, Kansas
TO: Topeka, Kansas
ROADS: I-70, U.S. 24, Kans. 99, 18, 177, 15, 4, U.S. 77 56, I-335
DISTANCE: 210 miles (338 km)
DRIVING TIME: 4.5 hours
WHEN TO GO: Spring through early fall
PLANNING: Allow time to explore the route's many museums. Lawrence hosts various music festivals throughout the summer. www.visittopeka.com

Start in Lawrence, home to several excellent museums such as the Watkins Community Museum of History, which focuses on the conflict between free-state Kansas and pro-slavery Missouri in the pre-Civil War era. Head west on the Kansas Turnpike (I-70) to the state capital, Topeka. The Historic Ward-Meade Park has an 1870s mansion with a botanical garden and a reconstructed turn-of-the-20th-century town square. Head west on U.S. 24 to the city of Wamego, where the Oz Museum has the world's largest collection of Wizard of Oz memorabilia. From here, take Kans. 99 south to Kans. 18, turning west to Manhattan, where the Riley County Historical Museum includes a prefabricated settler's house that was shipped in by steamboat in 1855. Next, take Kans. 177 south and I-70 west to Fort Riley, a military base that houses the U.S. Cavalry Museum and the First Infantry Division Museum. Continue west until you reach Kans. 15 and turn south to Abilene, the terminus of the Chisholm Trail and boyhood home and final resting place of President Dwight D. Eisenhower. At the Eisenhower Center, you can tour the home where young Ike grew up, and the Eisenhower Museum, which traces his story from boyhood to military hero to president. The museum includes the First Lady's Gallery, and features clothing, jewelry, and other items that belonged to Mamie Eisenhower. The site also contains the Presidential Library, the Place of Meditation, where the couple are buried, and the 11-foot (3.3 m) Ike Statue. The town's Wild West history is told at the Dickinson County Heritage Center. From Abilene, head south and east on Kans. 15 and 4, then on U.S. 77 and 56, to Council Grove, an important stop on the Santa Fe Trail. Visit the Kaw Mission State Historic Site and Museum, before returning to Topeka via U.S. 56 and I-335.

IDAHO/MONTANA

Salmon River Scenic Route

The route follows central Idaho's largest river, the Salmon, north from its headwaters in the Sawtooth Mountains, snaking through canyons and gorges to the Idaho/Montana border, where the river swerves west.

From the small city of Stanley, head northeast on Idaho 75, following the Salmon River as it descends into a forested gorge. The river drops 15 feet a mile (2.9 m/km) here as it comes down off the Sawtooth Mountains. It flows past several hot-spring pools between the river and the road and seeps into emerald-green and turquoise pools in the town of Sunbeam. Follow the river east, past Indian Riffles, which overlooks former salmon spawning grounds, and on through small canyons that get wider and drier as you descend. Beyond the old mining town of Clayton, the river turns northwest through a valley surrounded by desert hills. Approaching the junction with U.S. 93, you pass under a towering, rust-colored cliff over which Native Americans drove herds of buffalo. As you head north on U.S. 93, past the town of Challis, watch out for pronghorn on the desert floor and hawks circling overhead. Soon you cross the Pashimeroi River and then pass the northern flank of the Lemhi Range. Approaching the ranching city of Salmon, the road and river cut through a narrow gorge that widens into a spectacular, high-walled canyon. Continuing north, the river plunges into the Salmon River Canyon, one of the deepest gorges on the continent. The Salmon River Scenic Route ends at the Idaho/Montana border, but the drive continues west along U.S. 93 through dense forest to Lost Trail Pass (7,014 feet/2,138 m), named by the bewildered explorers Lewis and Clark in 1805. From here, you descend into the forested Bitterroot Valley. Approaching Darby, you'll see the high peaks of the Bitterroots to the left and the low-lying Sapphire Mountains to the right.

Hidden History At Lost Trail Pass you can turn east onto Idaho 43 for 17 miles (27 km) to reach **Big Hole National Battlefield.** In 1877, during their failed attempt to reach Canada, the Nez Percé tribe crossed the Bitterroot Mountains into the Big Hole Valley, where the U.S. Army attempted to cut them off. In the ensuing Battle of Big Hole, the Nez Percé beat back the soldiers and escaped. The park is a memorial to the dead on both sides. From the parking area, walking trails take you to the Nez Percé Camp, the Siege Area, and the Howitzer Capture Site. Each walk takes about an hour.

FROM: Stanley, Idaho
TO: Darby, Montana
ROADS: Idaho 75, U.S. 93
DISTANCE: 200 miles (322 km)
DRIVING TIME: 4.5 hours
WHEN TO GO: Spring through fall
PLANNING: www.idahobyways.gov

The Salmon River with the Sawtooth Mountains in the background

MONTANA

Going-to-the-Sun Road

Crossing Glacier National Park in northwest Montana from east to west, Going-to-the-Sun Road climbs from the fringe of the Great Plains to the Continental Divide, then drops into the lush rain forests of the McDonald Valley.

A hoary marmot in Glacier National Park

Highlights

- At **Sun Point,** about 3 miles (4.8 km) beyond Wild Goose Island Turnout, a short path climbs to a lake overlook where a mountain peaks chart identifies the main summits. The effects of glaciation—cirques, horns, knife-edge crests, and broad U-shaped valleys—can be seen on all of them.
- From the visitor center at Logan Pass you can hike 1.5 miles (2.5 km) to the **Hidden Lake Overlook.** A boardwalk trail climbs through a wide basin of rock terraces overgrown with wildflowers and ends at the brink of a spectacular hanging valley. This is a good place to spot mountain goats.

The spectacular Going-to-the-Sun Road starts at St. Mary, just off U.S. 89 on Glacier National Park's eastern edge. The route heads west along the north shore of St. Mary Lake before curving through wildflower meadows bordered by aspen and lodgepole pine to reach Wild Goose Island Turnout, which has an elegant view of an islet dwarfed by mountains. About 5 miles (8 km) farther on, look toward the left for a short trail leading to St. Mary Falls, one of the loveliest cascades in the park, and for views across the lake of Virginia Falls dropping through the forest. Continue on through deep subalpine forest, where black bears, red squirrels, marmots, and great horned owls thrive, to Jackson Glacier Turnout, where a sign explains how the glacier has shrunk considerably in recent years. A short drive on, the road breaks out of forest and onto a broad slope rimmed by mountains, including Mount Siyeh, and Going-to-the-Sun Mountain. Grizzlies roam the area and bighorn sheep and mountain goats graze the upper slopes. Approaching 6,646-foot (2,025 m) Logan Pass, the road edges round the cliffs of the Piegan Mountains, with sweeping views of Glacier's expansive mountain ranges.

From Logan Pass, you descend along Garden Wall, a knife-edged crest running down the Continental Divide that separates the Atlantic and Pacific watersheds, and come to Bird Woman Falls Overlook, with views of the falls framed by Mounts Oberlin, Clements, and Cannon. You can also see the deep, glaciated McDonald Valley. Next, traverse an area recovering from a 1967 wildfire, and then make a sharp turn to glide through the forest to McDonald Creek on the valley's floor. One of the most enjoyable short walks on Glacier's west side involves a stop at Avalanche Creek; pick up the short Trail of the Cedars from the roadside to the swift-moving creek, which winds through a deep gorge of boulders. A little farther on, several pull-offs provide views of McDonald Creek and the rapids at Sacred Dancing Cascade. After pulling away from the creek, the road drills through a dense forest, emerging at Lake McDonald Lodge. Lake McDonald itself is 10 miles (17 km) long, with several turnouts that have paths leading down to broad pebble beaches. At the end of the lake, follow signs to the village of Apgar the end of the drive.

FROM: St. Mary, Montana
TO: Apgar, Montana
ROAD: Going-to-the-Sun Road
DISTANCE: 50 miles (80 km)
DRIVING TIME: 1.5 hours
WHEN TO GO: Late spring through fall (closed October to early June)
PLANNING: There is an admission fee to Glacier National Park. Vehicles longer than 21 feet (6.4 m) or wider than 8 feet (2.4 m) are prohibited between Avalanche Creek and Sun Point.www.visitmt.com

OPPOSITE: St. Mary Lake is surrounded by the towering peaks of Glacier National Park.

UTAH

Arches and Canyons

Southern Utah's canyons, chasms, arches, and spires, finely crafted over millions of years, are among the most dramatic landscapes in the U.S. This route travels through geological wonderlands, passing prehistoric and Native American sites.

From Mesa Arch in Canyonlands, you can see the canyon sides of Island in the Sky Mesa.

Begin in Utah's spectacular Dead Horse Point State Park, 2,000 feet (610 m) above the Colorado River with grand views of the eroded cliffs, winding river, and bare-rock scenery below.

Follow Utah 313 to The Neck entrance road into Canyonlands National Park's Island in the Sky district and stop at the Grand View Point Overlook. The 6,080-foot (1,853 m) ledge falls away to the rim of a basin filled with tall rock towers. Return to Utah 313, turn back onto U.S. 191, and enter Arches National Park to discover some of the area's most dazzling scenery. From here, you can take take a short detour up Utah 279, driving past Canyonlands rock formations until you reach a sign announcing "Indian Petroglyphs," where viewscopes focus on ancient drawings carved into the stone by prehistoric hunters. Farther up the road, follow signs to "Dinosaur Tracks" to see some three-toed dinosaur footprints.

Now turn back toward the town of Moab, which is a good base for hikes, mountain biking, river trips, and outdoor adventuring. Around 35 miles (56 km) farther down U.S. 191, then right along Utah 211, you pass Newspaper Rock, a sandstone wall crowded with 1,500-year-old petroglyphs. Soon you'll reach The Needles District, a bewildering maze of red and yellow sandstone spires protruding high above the sandy mesas and flat valleys. You can find a shaded picnic spot with distinctive views at the end of Elephant Hill Road, off Utah 211. Continue south on U.S. 191 through Blanding (see Highlights), where Edge of the Cedars State Park/ Museum has collections of Native American artifacts and charts the history of the Pueblo, Ute, and Navajo peoples.

> "Long before Colorado, New Mexico, Arizona, and Utah were created, the forces of time were busy carving and painting this desert into a geological pastiche of natural wonders."
>
> -JOHN ROSENTHAL
> NATIONAL GEOGRAPHIC WRITER

Take a left turn onto Utah 262 and continue to the Native American ruins of Hovenweep National Monument, which was a Puebloan metropolis from about the 5th to the 13th century. The square, circle, and D-shaped fortress-like towers were probably used for star-gazing, an important skill for agrarian tribes. Continue south on Utah 262, turn east on Utah 162 and Colo. 41, and then right onto U.S. 160 to Four Corners Monument, where Utah, Colorado, New Mexico, and Arizona meet. People assume ungainly—and entertaining—positions in order to get a limb in each state.

The route turns west here into Arizona and enters the red rock country of the Navajo Indian Reservation, crossing open-range farming landscape. Turn north at Kayenta onto U.S. 163. The road across Monument Valley is what makes vacation

A Wonderland of Arches

Over hundreds of millions of years, the forces of nature have created a masterpiece: wildly shaped towers, fins, balanced rocks, and petrified sand dunes. And, of course, arches. The **Arches National Park** contains the world's largest concentration of them—some 2,000 arches, ranging in size from 3 to 300 feet (0.9–90 m) wide; included is Utah's signature formation, Delicate Arch. The 18-mile (30 km) Arches Scenic Drive provides access to viewpoints and a variety of trails, such as a short walk around The Windows section of the park, and the Devil's Garden Trail at the end of the drive. Information on self-guided walking tours are available at the park visitor center.

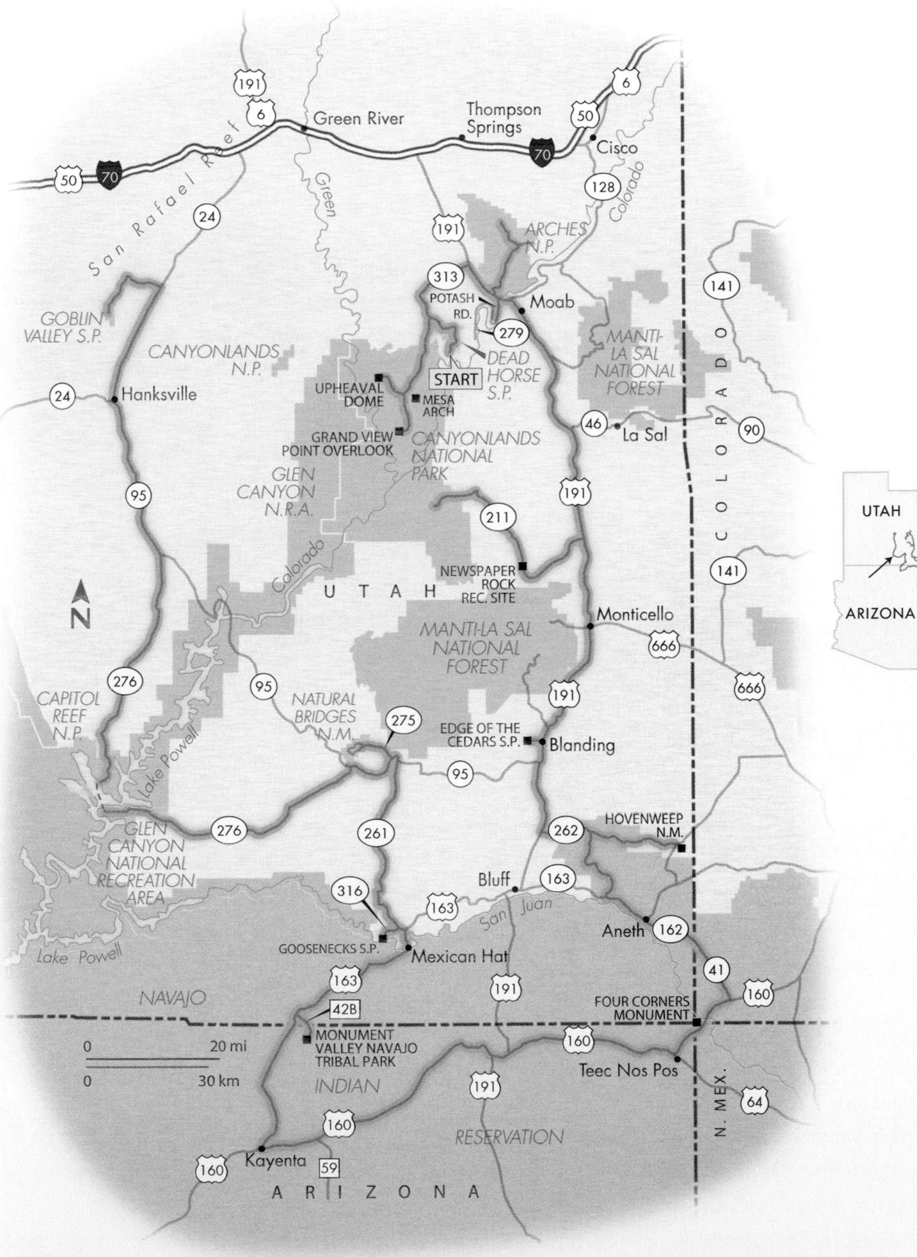

Ancient petroglyphs cover the face of Newspaper Rock in The Needles District.

driving so special. Colossal orange, red, and yellow sandstone buttes tower overhead and sagebrush dots the desert floor for miles on end.

Crossing back into Utah, head north on Utah 261, crossing the zigzagging San Juan River with its 1,000-foot (305 m) deep canyon at Goosenecks State Park, before exploring Natural Bridges National Monument. The natural bridges of Sipapu, Kachina, and the world's second largest, Hopi, were formed by streams washing away the soft, underlying sandstone over hundreds of millions of years. Then take Utah 276 west through Glen Canyon National Recreation Area, where the 200-mile (322 km) long Lake Powell, the U.S.'s second largest man-made lake, offers water sports, hiking, camping, biking, and amazing views.

Take the ferry across the lake and continue north on Utah 276, 95, and 24 to see the bizarre mushroom formations of Goblin Valley State Park. These sandstone structures, many looking like mushrooms, some reaching 200 feet (60 m) high, are a geological formation unique even in this special part of the world.

FROM: Dead Horse Point State Park, Utah
TO: Goblin Valley State Park, Utah
ROADS: I-70, U.S. 191, Utah 313, 279, 211, 262, 162, Colo. 41, U.S. 160, 163, Utah 261, 276, 95, 24
DISTANCE: About 860 miles (1,384 km)
DRIVING TIME: 18 hours
WHEN TO GO: Late spring through fall
PLANNING: Set out with a full tank of gas and plenty of water. www.discovermoab.com

Highlights

- **Blanding** is known for its Native American art and handicrafts. Watch tribe members work at **Cedar Mesa Pottery,** and purchase some handmade pots in the gift shop.

- Take Reservation Road 42B off U.S. 163 to reach **Monument Valley Navajo Tribal Park,** near Kayenta, which includes more than 100 archaeological sites. An unpaved, 17-mile (27 km) loop drive starts from the visitor center.

ALASKA

Seward Highway

This scenic byway in Chugach National Forest in south-central Alaska takes you through the full glory of the state's natural wonders, including fjords, glaciers, mountains, lakes, meadows, forests, and wildlife-rich wetlands.

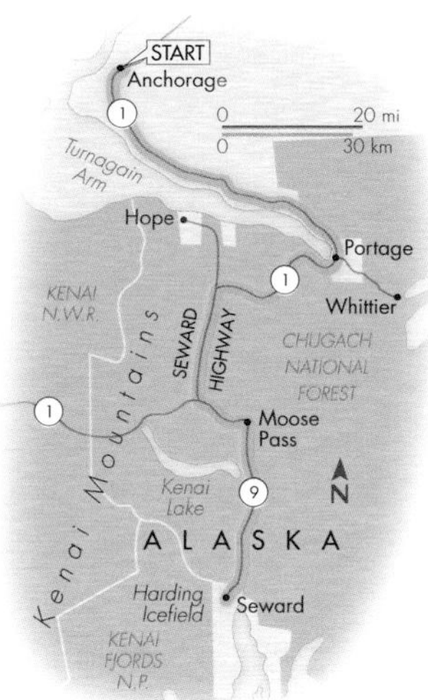

Take Old Seward Highway south from Anchorage, joining Alas. 1 at Turnagain Arm. Stop at the Anchorage Coastal Wildlife Refuge to spot a large variety of birds, as well as moose and muskrats. To the west stands the active volcano Mount Spurr; to the east are the Chugach Mountains, 13,000 feet (3,962 m) high and burdened with glaciers. Across Turnagain Arm, an extension of Cook Inlet, are the peaks of the Kenai Mountains and the spruce and hemlock of Chugach National Forest. Continue south to Potter Marsh, a wetland of sedges and willows that is often teeming with fish. A little farther on, you pass Potter Section House, a former railroad lodge now serving as the Chugach State Park headquarters. For the next 36 miles (58 km), follow Turnagain's northern shore. At Beluga Point, you can enjoy sweeping views and there is a chance you may see some of the white whales for which the point was named. Continuing south, you'll pass Portage, a village that was abandoned in the 1960s after an earthquake dropped it onto a tidal plain, and then Portage Glacier. Continue past Explorer and Middle Glaciers to the Begich Boggs Visitor Center, where you can find out more about these ice rivers. Hook around the end of Turnagain Arm, cross the Placer River delta and begin the ascent up the steep Ingram Creek Canyon to alpine meadows and the 988-foot (301 m) Turnagain Pass. You soon come to Hope Highway, where you can make a 17-mile (27 km) detour to the old goldmining community of Hope. To stay on the byway, bear left and continue to Tern Lake Junction, taking a left onto Alas. 9 for Seward, soon passing Tern Lake and Kenai Lake. Farther on, the road runs beside the backwaters of the Snow River before arriving in Seward.

FROM: Anchorage, Alaska
TO: Seward, Alaska
ROADS: Alas. 1 and 9, Hope Highway
DISTANCE: 127 miles (204 km)
DRIVING TIME: 3.5 hours
WHEN TO GO: June through mid-September
PLANNING: www.dot.state.ak.us

Excursion Just before you arrive at Seward, a 9-mile (14 km) road (open from early May through mid-November) takes you to **Exit Glacier** in Kenai Fjords National Park. Several short walks lead from the Nature Center to different views of the glacier, while a 0.5-mile (800 m) hike ends at the glacier's 150-foot (46 m) seracs, or spires, of broken blue ice along its base. A 3.5-mile (5.6 km) route takes you to the **Harding Ice Field,** the third largest in North America.

Turnagain Arm, part of Alaska's Cook Inlet, is surrounded by forested and snowcapped mountains.

Moss-covered cliffs tower above Oneonta Creek in the Columbia River Gorge.

Highlights

- **Bonneville Dam,** on I-84, was completed in 1937 as part of President Roosevelt's New Deal, and is a good place to look for the river's abundant salmon stocks.
- **Cascade Locks Marine Park,** by the Bridge of the Gods, has a museum on the history of the gorge as well as trips aboard the stern-wheeler *Columbia Gorge*.
- **Horsethief Lake State Park,** near Murdock, is a perfect place to pitch a tent, and has ancient Native American petroglyphs and pictographs.
- The **Maryhill Museum of Art,** founded in the 1920s, houses a diverse collection of art from Europe and the U.S.A. and an extensive collection of Native American art and artifacts.

OREGON/WASHINGTON

Columbia River Highway

This drive through the Columbia River Gorge National Scenic Area, near the Oregon/ Washington border, combines natural beauty, river views, waterfalls, mountain scenery, local history, wildlife, and 20th-century art.

FROM: Troutdale, Oregon
TO: Maryhill, Washington
ROADS: Historic Columbia River Highway (HR30), I-84, Wash. 14
DISTANCE: 90 miles (145 km)
DRIVING TIME: 1.5 hours
WHEN TO GO: Spring through late fall
PLANNING: Bring boots for hiking.
www.columbiariverhighway.com

From Troutdale in western Oregon, head east on the longest original 1922 section of the Historic Columbia River Highway still in use. For the next 9 miles (14 km) the drive passes parks, farms, and small towns. At a pulloff at the Portland Women's State Park, you'll catch your first view of the Columbia River, whose basalt cliff gorge is covered in dense foliage. Not far on is Vista House, the highest point on the drive, perched atop a promontory overlooking the river. The winding highway then descends through imposing forests to the river's edge, soon reaching Latourell Falls, the first of several impressive waterfalls along the drive. Eight miles (13 km) on, you can see Multnomah Falls from a short, steep, paved trail. Back on the highway, you're soon greeted by the narrow cliffs of Oneonta Gorge rising hundreds of feet above your head. The cool, moist conditions where the Oneonta Creek squeezes between the cliffs suit a wide variety of ferns, mosses, and lichens—some unique to this spot. As the historic section of the highway ends, continue for around 9 miles (14 km) east on I-84. Cross the river on the steel-strutted Bridge of the Gods (toll) into Washington and pick up Wash. 14 heading east. Under the looming shadows of the mountains, the road passes small towns and wetlands rich with birdlife. To rejoin the byway that runs along U.S. 30, re-cross the river at White Salmon to the farming city of Hood River on the Oregon side, popular for its orchards and wineries and known for great windsurfing. Or you can remain on the Washington side of the gorge and continue to the Maryhill Museum of Art (see Highlights).

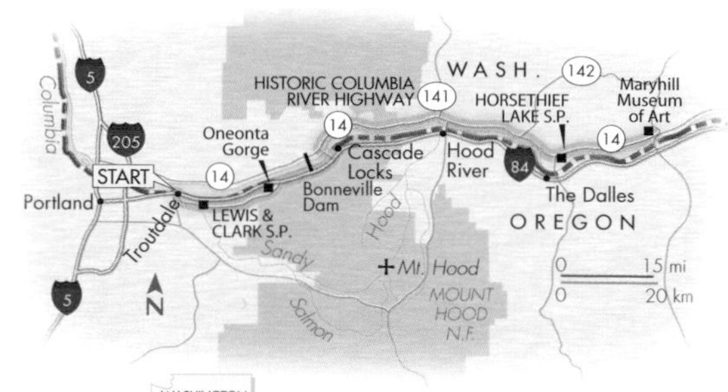

CALIFORNIA

Lost Coast and Redwoods

The little-explored route along northern California's Lost Coast takes you to Cape Mendocino and then turns inland to wind through redwood forests, linking up with the famous Avenue of the Giants in the Humboldt Redwoods State Park.

The village of Ferndale is famous for its beautiful Victorian architecture.

Begin in the historic Victorian village of Ferndale, just south of Eureka in the Eel River Valley. In the mid-19th century, the village grew rich from dairy farming, and the resulting building boom left a treasure-trove of Victorian houses and false-front architecture. Take Main Street (Calif. 211) to Ocean Avenue and turn left on Mattole Road (look for the arch that says Capetown) to leave town, zigzagging up slopes covered with maples and evergreens. Before long, a wide view opens up across forested valleys and grassy hills. The road then descends to Bear River and passes the Capetown ranch and a former stage stop. Continue down a precipitous stretch of road toward Cape Mendocino, the site of many shipwrecks. This is one of the continent's most active earthquake zones, where three tectonic plates rub against each other just off the coast.

For the next 5 miles (8 km) you drive south along a tidal zone that rose 4 feet (1.2 m) during the 1992 Cape Mendocino earthquake, giving the appearance of a perpetual low tide. In 1895, the state's first commercial oil wells were drilled in Petrolia, now a small community surrounded by farms. Continue on to Honeydew, which is no more than a store yawning in the shade. The road then climbs up to the 2,744-foot (836 m) Panther Gap, crossing the Mattole River on the way, and continues to Humboldt Redwoods State Park and Rockefeller Forest, home to many of the world's remaining old-growth redwoods, some more than 350 feet (107 m) high (see Highlights).

At South Fork, the Mattole Road intersects Calif. 254, known as the Avenue of the Giants, which runs from Pepperwood southward to Phillipsville. First turn left to reach Pepperwood, then turn around to complete the route. From Pepperwood, head south past the Drury-Chaney Groves, and then through Weott, a town surrounded by redwoods on all sides. At Williams Grove there's river access for fishing, and the park's visitor center has exhibits on local wildlife and history. You'll now drive along a stretch of road lined with redwoods, bigleaf maples, and black cottonwoods, with views of the South Fork Eel River to the right. Get a good look at the redwoods from the F. K. Lane Grove before reaching the end of the drive at Phillipsville.

OPPOSITE: California's coastal redwoods are among the tallest in the world.

Highlights

- Just beyond Petrolia, you can take a 5-mile (8 km) drive along Lighthouse Road to the shore. From here, a 3.5 mile (5.6 km) trail (part of the Lost Coast Trail) leads to the now-abandoned **Punta Gorda Lighthouse** and views of the coast.
- From the Big Trees Area on Mattole Road you can take a short trail to the **Giant Tree,** which, at 363 feet (110 m) high, is the tallest redwood in the park.
- The **Grieg-French-Bell Trail** and the **Drury-Chaney Loop Trail,** at the northern end of the Avenue of the Giants, both take you through old-growth forest.

FROM: Ferndale, California
TO: Phillipsville, California
ROADS: Calif. 211, Mattole Road, Calif. 254
DISTANCE: Lost Coast 65 miles (105 km); Avenue of the Giants 31 miles (50 km)
DRIVING TIME: 2 hours
WHEN TO GO: Year-round, but winter rains can create difficult driving conditions.
PLANNING: Best driven north to south, for views of the Pacific. www.humboldtredwoods.org.

The spires of Cathedral Rock rise high above the desert, glowing red as they catch the sun.

ARIZONA

Red Rocks of Arizona

This short route winds through central Arizona's Red Rock Country, near the town of Sedona, a desert wonderland of massive, richly colored rock formations set against red earth and green juniper trees.

FROM: Coconino National Forest, Arizona
TO: Chapel of the Holy Cross, Arizona
ROAD: Ariz. 179
DISTANCE: 7.5 miles (12 km)
DRIVING TIME: 0.5 hour
WHEN TO GO: Year-round
PLANNING: To hike, you need a pass from one of the Gateway Visitor Centers. www.visitsedona.org

The rock formations south of Sedona are a happy accident of geology. Millennia of wind and water dug deep canyons out of the soft sandstone of the Colorado plateau and sculpted the rock into an endless variety of shapes, giving rise to names such as Chimney Rock, Rabbit Ears, and Cathedral Rock. The glorious red color comes from iron in the rock and is intensified when caught by the sun. The drive begins in the diverse Coconino National Forest, which has campgrounds and hiking trails through ponderosa pine forests and alpine tundra. From the intersection with I-17, take Ariz. 179 north. Soon you pass through the Village of Oak Creek (Big Park on some maps), and will be in no doubt that the butte ahead is Bell Rock, one of the region's most famous and recognizable landmarks, with its large and impressive bell-like shape. Some people believe that this is the site of a vortex, a spot where energy from within the Earth is thought to be conducted and amplified. Yavapai Indians, whose ancestors first roamed the region more than six centuries ago, believed that the red rocks were the bodies and blood of monsters slain by the shaman Skatakaamcha. Those mythical monsters included a giant bird that lived on a mountaintop—which some people say is now Bell Rock. To see Bell Rock and nearby Courthouse Butte close up, park at the Bell Rock Vista & Pathway southern trailhead, just north of Oak Creek. The trail has options for a short stroll and longer hikes of up to 4 miles (6.5 km). The road re-enters the forest and continues past towering rock formations on both sides. A mile (1.5 km) farther down the road, the Little Horse Trailhead offers views of more formations, including Cathedral Rock to the west, which is revered by some Native Americans as the birthplace of the first man and woman. The byway ends at the Chapel of the Holy Cross, a concrete-and-glass monolith tucked into rocks in a canyon to the east of the road.

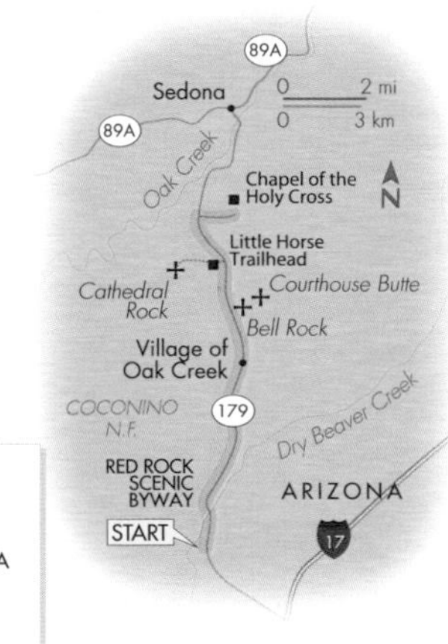

DOMINICAN REPUBLIC

Samaná to Sánchez

This short yet very sweet drive through the Cordillera Samaná on the north of the island takes in sandy beaches around Las Terrenas and a mountain road with breathtaking views of coconut groves and the ocean far below.

Begin in Samaná, a center for whale-watching tours, and take the turnoff for El Limón signposted 0.75 miles (1.2 km) west of town. The road curves uphill, offering the first views of Samaná Bay with the *mogotes* (eroded limestone hills) of the Parque Nacional Los Haitises on the horizon. The potholed highway descends to the community of El Limón, famous for its beautiful waterfall. Past here, turn right at the T-junction beside Santi Rancho and then, after 1.5 miles (2.4 km), left down a dirt road to Playa Morón, where fishing boats rest on the sandy beach. Return to El Limón and continue northwest to the shores of Playa Punta Popy, whose windy beaches are popular with kiteboarders. When you reach the center of Las Terrenas, turn right onto Avenida Alberto Caamaño Deno. The road runs along the Playa las Ballenas, where you can snorkel in the clear waters. Then backtrack into town, following the one-way system along Calle Principal. Turn right onto Calle Fabio Abreu and follow signs to Playa Bonita, a nice place to linger with your feet in the water. Return again to Las Terrenas and turn south along the main road, heading uphill toward a ridge at the top of the Cordillera Samaná with a beautiful view of the coast. After the mountain village of Los Puentes, the road descends down sweeping curves and past a series of farmed valleys. You are now in the dramatic landscape of the mogotes, and views suddenly open up of the Bahia de Samaná far below. The island's largest coconut plantation stretches out beneath you. The road switchbacks sharply, with views of the foothills blanketed with palms, as you wind down the steep gradient onto Carretera 5 on the west side of Sánchez.

FROM: Samaná, Dominican Republic
TO: Sánchez, Dominican Republic
ROADS: Local roads
DISTANCE: 31 miles (50 km)
TIME: 3 hours
WHEN TO GO: Year-round
PLANNING: Visit the Salto del Limón waterfall early in the day to avoid the crowds.
www.godominicanrepublic.com

Unexpected Pleasure You can take a horseback ride from El Limón to the magnificent 165-foot (50 m) **Salto del Limón waterfall.** Well-mannered horses carry you most of the way along paths, some of which can be slippery, and across rivers. Some hiking up steep, rocky paths is also involved. The journey to the falls takes about 40 minutes, and the entire excursion lasts three hours, so you can swim and relax once you're there. The trip can be arranged through Santi Rancho, a local tour operator in El Limón.

Playa Bonita near Las Terrenas is a tranquil spot to break the drive.

PERU

Lima to Tacna

The Pan-American Highway South forms the backbone of Peru's southern lowlands. This route follows it down the coast from Lima, then cuts inland through the driest desert in the world, passing ancient oases and pre-Inca sites, to the Chilean border.

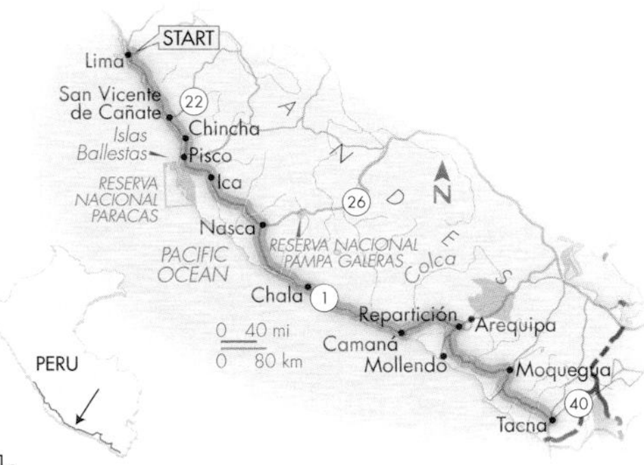

Begin in the Peruvian capital, Lima, and head southeast down Rte. 1. At San Vincente de Cañate, a short detour leads to the fishing village of Cero Azul, popular for surfing and the remains of pre-Inca mud buildings. Back on the highway, continue through Chincha, where Afro-Peruvian folk culture thrives, and on to the city of Pisco, famous for the eponymous Peruvian brandy. Pisco is Quechua for "bird," and the city was named for the birdlife in the region. From El Chaco, south of Pisco, you can take a boat tour around the Ballestas Islands to see large colonies of seabirds and sea lions. Pisco was badly affected by the 2007 earthquake, with many buildings demolished. The road heads inland now through arid desert, yet as you approach the canal-irrigated Rio Ica Valley, the desert falls away dramatically. Wine and pisco are two of the main industries here, and there are plenty of opportunities to sample both. Ica was once the capital city of the pre-Incan Nasca people, and an interesting stop is the Museo Regional de Ica, which charts the area's history and displays an unusual collection of skulls highlighting some very early brain surgery. Just along the road, the oasis of Huacachina is a tree-lined lagoon dwarfed by sand dunes. This tranquil spot is a good base for touring the region's *bodegas* (wineries), and to try sandboarding. Continue to Nasca, where you can see the Nasca Lines and other ancient sites (see Hidden History). Past Chala, the road hugs the Pacific coast once again, before heading north at Camaná. At Reparticion Junction, head south toward Moquegua, a town with some excellent 18th-century wattle-and-daub architecture, before continuing to Tacna.

Hidden History The origins of the giant pictographs known as the **Nasca Lines,** which include a hummingbird in flight, a whale, and a spider, are still a mystery to scholars. The images, some more than 656 feet (200 m) across, can be seen from a 40-foot (12 m) observation tower, but are best viewed from the air. Light aircraft leave from Nasca airport daily on 30-minute flights. To the east of Nasca, you can visit the ancient aqueduct of **Cantalloc;** to the west, the 34 Nasca pyramids of **Cahuachi.**

FROM: Lima, Peru
TO: Tacna, Peru
ROAD: Pan-American Highway South (Rte. 1)
DISTANCE: 827 miles (1,330 km)
DRIVING TIME: 3 days
WHEN TO GO: Year-round, although the weather is best from December through March.
PLANNING: There is an Afro-Peruvian folk festival in Chincha in February, and a wine festival in Ica in March. Off the main road, other roads are mostly unpaved.
www.peru.info

Swap your vehicle for a dune-buggy to explore the sand dunes around the town of Ica.

The 400-year-old Matsumoto Castle is one of the most intact and attractive castles in Japan.

JAPAN

Tokyo to Kyoto

Whether adorned by the cherry blossoms of spring time or the snows of winter, this drive is a delight, taking in the beautiful Japanese Alps and the Sea of Japan coast, historic cities, hot springs, enchanting gardens, and culinary pleasures.

From energetic Tokyo, take the Chuo Expressway west toward Nagano. Leave the expressway at Kofu City to see museums and temples, including Kai Zenjoki Temple, which was founded by the *daimyo* (warlord) Takeda Shingen in 1558. Continue west on the expressway and at Okaya junction take Nagano Expressway toward Matsumoto Interchange. The Matsumoto Kamikochi exit brings you to Nagano prefecture, home to the crumpled beauty of the Japanese Alps and the city of Matsumoto with its splendid castle. Matsumoto is also a starting point for hikes through the Japanese Alps via Kamikochi. Follow National Route 158 to the city of Takayama, where you will find a well-preserved Old Town and the acclaimed hot springs of Gero-onsen town. Next, take the alpine pass toward Kou Takayama Bypass, then Takayama-Kiyomi Road and Tokai Hokiruku Expressway. Stop off at the mountain villages of Shirakawa-go and Gokayama, famous for their *Gasshyo Zukuri* (traditional thatched houses). Continue north and at Oyabe Tonami junction take Hokuriku Expressway toward Kanazawa. The Kanazawa Morimoto interchange road and Rte. 159 bring you to Kanazawa City, where you will find Kenrokuen Garden, one of three great gardens of Japan. From Kanazawa, follow the Sea of Japan route along the western coast for glorious views and delicious seafood such as *Ama-ebi* (sweet shrimp). Head southeast from Kanazawa on Rte. 25, then take Hokiruku Expressway and Meishin toll road. This portion of the drive nears Lake Biwa, the largest freshwater lake in Japan. Finally, take Rte. 1 into Kyoto, the former imperial capital city.

FROM: Tokyo, Japan
TO: Kyoto, Japan
ROADS: Chuo Expy., Nagano Expy., National Rte. 158, Takayama-Kiyomi Road, Tokai Hokiruku Expy., Rtes. 159, 25, Hokiruku Expy., Meishin toll road, Rte. 1, local roads
DISTANCE: 261 miles (420 km)
DRIVING TIME: 7.5 hours
WHEN TO GO: Year-round
PLANNING: Pleasure boat rides leave from Otsu port at the southern tip of Lake Biwa.
www.japan-guide.com

GERMANY

The Valley of the Elbe

This drive along the banks of the Elbe River in Saxony takes in historic palaces and castles, fine old towns, and the dramatic sandstone scenery of the National Park of Sächsische Schweiz (Saxon Switzerland).

Eighteenth-century Schloss Pillnitz has a beautiful riverside setting and fanciful architecture.

Highlights

- You can walk up to the ramparts of **Festung Königstein** or take the shuttle from the parking lot. Whichever way you get there, the views from the top are magnificent.
- The visitor center at **National-park Sächsische Schweiz** in Bad Schandau is a conservation and geology museum that has exhibits on the park.
- The hikes around **Bastei,** including the walkway across the sandstone **Bastei Bridge,** offer sumptuous views.
- In the grounds of the waterside Schloss Pillnitz stand a church known as the **Weinbergkirche,** and the **Kunstgewerbemuseum,** which exhibits furniture, silverware, and woodcarving.

The Elbe is one of Europe's most important rivers, and its eminence can be seen in the castles and palaces gracing its banks. Start in Dresden, once one of Germany's most beautiful cities but destroyed by Allied bombers during World War II. Take the busy B172 southeast to the riverside town of Pirna, whose church has some intricate vaulting. Continue along the B172, turning right into Festung Königstein, a 13th-century fortress whose stone walls were once considered impregnable (see Highlights). Cross the Elbe to Bad Schandau (see Highlights), with a popular thermal spa, botanical garden, and museum. Turn north on the S163 to the small village of Rathsmannsdorf, and carry straight on at a junction. The narrow road (K8723) up through woods brings you to the hilltop town of Hohnstein, whose castle houses a local history museum and offers wonderful views. Turn west on the S165 here and follow signs to Bastei, eventually turning off the highway to the left. Walk up to the weather-sculpted sandstone scenery of the Bastei (see Highlights), a great natural curiosity of cliffs, crags, and pillars towering 1,000 feet (305 m) above the Elbe. To enjoy the pathways and their views of the abyss beneath without the crowds, avoid visiting at noon. Back on the S165, drive on to Lohmen, and take the S167 to Schloss Pillnitz (see Highlights). This mock-Chinese riverside palace was built by Augustus the Strong, Elector of Saxony, in 1720 as his summer residence; guests arriving by boat from Dresden disembarked via a stunning waterside stairway. Carry on up the S167 toward Dresden, crossing the Elbe via the Blaues Wunder (the Blue Miracle), a steel suspension bridge built in 1893.

Excursion If you have time, you can take the little electric tramway that runs from Bad Schandau up the valley known as the **Kirnitzschtal,** in the eastern section of the **National-park Sächsische Schweiz.** The tram runs along the Kirnitzsch River, through one of the prettiest Elbe valleys, past historic mills that have been renovated and turned into restaurants or pensions, and terminates at the Lichtenhain Waterfall. The journey takes about 25 minutes and stops at inns along the way.

FROM: Loop route from Dresden, Germany
ROADS: B172, S163, K8723, S165, S167, local roads
DISTANCE: 87 miles (140 km)
TIME: 2 hours
WHEN TO GO: Spring through fall
PLANNING: Summer months may be busy. A boat trip along the River Elbe from Dresden offers beautiful views of the valley. www.saechsische-schweiz.de

OPPOSITE: The footbridge linking the Bastei rock towers provides extraordinary views of the Elbe River.

The road through the Altmühl Valley passes below the Twelve Apostles rock formation.

GERMANY

The Altmühl Valley

This drive in northern Bavaria takes you along one of Germany's most unspoiled river valleys. The Altmühl River cuts deep into a limestone plateau, creating a varied landscape of sheep-grazed pastures overlooked by limestone cliffs, interspersed with delightful towns.

Begin in the small town of Ellingen, which is dominated by a great 18th-century baroque castle. Head south on the B2 to the enchanting medieval town of Weissenburg, which has a nearly complete set of ramparts and gateways and a well-preserved old town center, as well as the remains of Roman settlements. Continue south on the B2 for 7 miles (11 km), turning left at a railway bridge onto the road that follows the river through the Altmühl Valley. Pappenheim, much of whose center dates from medieval times, is dominated by the ruins of a 12th-century castle, and is almost completely encircled by a bend in the river. Beyond Esslingen, 6 miles (9 km) on, the river curves past a series of rocks known as the Twelve Apostles, which were once part of a great reef in an ancient sea. Situated on top of a wooded hill, the white castle of Willibaldsburg dominates the approach to the elegant town of Eichstätt. Continue along the valley, past the village of Pfünz, beside limestone cliffs and under the A9 autobahn, toward the hilltop palace of Hirschberg in the old town of Beilngries. Beyond here, the Altmühl joins the Main-Danube waterway, a system of canals linking the rivers that flow to the North Sea with those that feed southern Europe and the Black Sea. Farther on, situated on a sheer cliff above the river, the castle at Prunn is one of the most spectacular in the valley. One of the drive's most picturesque vistas is just downstream from Prunn, at the riverside village of Essing, which has a perfectly preserved watchtower and an ancient timber bridge. End the drive at the city of Kelheim, where the Altmühl joins the Danube and the Befreinungshalle, or Hall of Liberation, keeps watch across the two rivers. This neoclassical rotunda, built by Ludwig I of Bavaria, commemorates the part played by the German states in victories over Napoleon in 1813 and 1815.

FROM: Ellingen, Germany
TO: Kelheim, Germany
ROADS: B2, local roads
DISTANCE: 84 miles (34 km)
DRIVING TIME: 2 hours
WHEN TO GO: Year-round
PLANNING: www.naturpark-altmuehltal.de.

FRANCE

Routes des Abbayes

This route follows the north bank of the Seine River as it snakes westward through Normandy from Rouen to the coast, passing wooded valleys, chalk cliffs, and apple orchards.

Pick up the D982 from Rouen, once the largest city in medieval Europe and the place where Joan of Arc met her unfortunate end, and go west to the village of St.-Martin-de-Boscherville, where you can see the Romanesque Abbaye de St.-Georges. The abbey has a simple interior with a beautifully carved apse, and the remains of a 12th-century chapterhouse with superbly carved capitals. Continue on the D982 to Duclair, where you can gaze at fine views of the Seine before forking left to detour along the D65. Follow the meandering river past apple and cherry orchards around the old village of Le Mesnil-sous-Jumièges and you'll soon spot the great towers of the Abbaye de Jumièges standing tall above the distant trees. The atmospheric ruins of this once great monastery bear witness to a turbulent past. It was founded in A.D. 654, raided by Vikings in the ninth century, and rose to pre-eminence in the 13th and 14th centuries. The French Revolution brought about its downfall, and only the two 11th-century towers and part of the nave remain. Head northwest on the D143 to the Fontenelle Valley and the Abbaye de St.-Wandrille (see Hidden History). Take the D982 west to the riverside town of Caudebec-en-Caux with its fine 15th-century church, then take the D81 to the village of Villequier to visit the Musée Victor Hugo, dedicated to the great French literary figure. Continue west to Lillebonne, which has some impressive Roman remains. The drive ends at Tancarville's suspension bridge with stunning views of the Seine estuary.

FROM: Rouen, France
TO: Tancarville, France
ROADS: D982, D65, D143, D81
DISTANCE: 51 miles (82 km)
DRIVING TIME: 2 hours
WHEN TO GO: Spring through fall
PLANNING: Mass at the Abbaye de St.-Wandrille is held weekdays at 9:25 a.m. and Sunday at 10 a.m. www.normandy-tourism.org

Hidden History The **Abbaye de St.-Wandrille** was founded in the seventh century by St. Wandrille, sacked by the Vikings, refounded in the tenth century, destroyed during the French Revolution, and revived again in 1931. It has a restored 14th-century cloister, while the atmospheric 13th–14th century Gothic church remains in ruins. In the 1960s, the monks founded a new church in a 15th-century wooden tithe barn. There is a guided tour most days of the year. If you enjoy Gregorian chant, time your visit to the abbey so that you can attend a sung Mass.

The Musée Victor Hugo in Villequier, in the writer's home, displays memorabilia about his life.

FRANCE

Dordogne Valley Drive

This drive travels east along the great Dordogne River as it flows through a region famous throughout the world for fine food and wine, and loved locally for its wooded valleys, historic towns and villages, and craggy limestone cliffs.

A boat navigates the Dordogne River as early-morning mist hangs low on the water.

The drive starts in Bergerac, where medieval houses grace the town center and the old port spans both banks of the Dordogne River. Take the D660 east along the river's north bank, crossing to the Château de Lanquais on the D37 at St.-Capraise-de-Lalinde. The structure—part-medieval castle and part-Renaissance palace—sits above the village of Lanquais, and still bears the cannonball scars from the 16th-century Wars of Religion. To the east of the papermaking town of Couze-et-St.-Front, the village of St.-Front-de-Colubri is perched above the river, offering superb views of the Gratusse rapids. Cross back to the north bank for the best views of one of the Dordogne's extraordinary horseshoe bends, or *cingles*, at the Cingle de Trémolat. Take the D31 from Trémolat to the hilltop village of Limeuil with its Renaissance houses and 12th-century church. From here, follow the D51 along the cliff-flanked Dordogne, then cross on the D25 toward the Cistercian abbey of Cadouin, home to some fine Gothic cloisters. Take a small road east to Urval to see a huge, 12th-century, fortified church, and then return to the D25 and drive east to the river town of Siorac-en-Périgord. Cross to the north bank again, and take the D703E upstream to St.-Cyprien, a market town clustered around a 14th-century church. Continue upstream on the D703E; as the valley narrows, you can see the fortress châteaus of Beynac-et-Cazenac and Castelnaud high above you. Continue east to La Roque-Gageac, a village built under, and in places carved into, the cliffs lining the riverbank, where you can relax in one of the riverside cafés or climb the narrow streets up to the 12th-century church for a good view of the river. From here, continue on the D50 to Sarlat-la-Canéda.

Highlights

- **Bergerac** is known for its tobacco, history, and wine. The **Musée du Tabac** documents the history of tobacco and its uses, while local wines are celebrated at the **Maison des Vins**.
- During the Hundred Years War, **Castelnaud** was an English stonghold. It now houses a museum on the history of siege warfare.
- The 15th-century **Château les Milandes** (south from Castelnaud on the D53) was the home of the 1920s American jazz singer Josephine Baker. The château has an exhibition on her life, and the park and formal garden are also open to visitors.

FROM: Bergerac, France
TO: Sarlat-la-Canéda, France
ROADS: D660, D37, D31, D51, D25, D703E, D50
DISTANCE: 90 miles (145 km)
DRIVING TIME: 2 days
WHEN TO GO: Spring through fall. Summer is the busiest, and fairs and festivals are held at this time
PLANNING: The Dordogne River offers many leisure activities such as canoeing and kayaking.
www.bergerac-tourisme.com

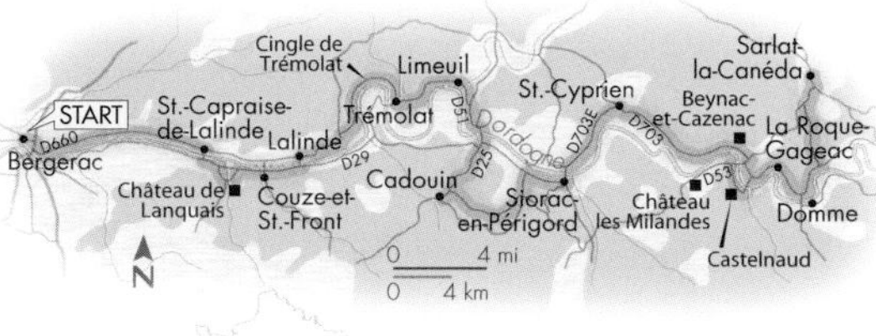

Hidden History If you turn south onto the D46 a few miles east of La Roque-Gageac, you come to **Domme,** one of the best preserved *bastides* (walled towns) in the area. Perched high on a crag on the south bank of the river, the town's narrow streets and 17th-century marketplace are sheltered within 12th-century walls. The Belvedere de la Barre at the end of the Grand-Rue has views of the river and the main châteaus in the area.

OPPOSITE: The Dordogne River winds through farmland and vineyards below the hilltop town of Domme.

Carvings in the Ermita of Quintanilla de las Viñas include the figures of Christ and the Evangelists.

Highlights

- The **Monasterio de Santo Domingo de Silos** is world famous for its beautiful cloisters and the Gregorian chants of the monks, which can be heard at the daily Mass. Its museum has many treasures.

- The church of **San Cosme y San Damián** in **Covarrubias** is an elegant white-stone Gothic building dating from 1474. The 400-year-old organ still plays, and the church houses a museum of papal documents, bishops' capes, and paintings.

- The oldest religious structure in the region is the late seventh-century **Ermita Visigótica of Quintanilla de las Viñas,** which is decorated with Visigothic carved friezes of grapes, birds, and monograms.

SPAIN

Drive to Arlanza

From its source in the Sierra de Urbion in northern Spain, the Arlanza River meanders westward through a dramatic valley to Lerma. This drive, which begins in Burgos, takes you through beautiful, often wild, countryside and past old villages and medieval churches.

Leave Burgos on the A1/E5 south towards Madrid, crossing the Arlanza River after 22 miles (34 km). Turn off at the Lerma-Estacion exit and follow signs to Lerma, entering the town through the medieval arch of Cárcel. Head up to and across the Plaza Mayor, graced by the austere Palacio Ducal (following *Todas direcciones* signs). Turn right downhill to take the left turnoff onto the BU900 for Santo Domingo de Silos. Drive through a landscape of rolling hills, wheat fields, and typical stone villages, until you reach the tiny hamlet of Santibáñez del Val. A right turn across the Ura River brings you to a charming little stone hermitage, the Ermita Mozarabe de Santa Cecilia de Barriosuso. Return to the BU900 and drive to the beautiful medieval village of Santo Domingo de Silos, home of the Monasterio de Santo Domingo de Silos (see Highlights). Then backtrack along the BU900 and turn right onto the BU902 through forested, rocky hills towards medieval Covarrubias, home to the 15th-century church of San Cosme y San Damián (see Highlights). Leaving Covarrubias, follow signs to San Pedro de Arlanza, on the BU905/CL-110. Dating from the 11th century, this evocative site was one of Castile's largest monasteries. The road continues through a pretty valley, crisscrossing the Arlanza River before joining the N234 at Hortigüela. Take a left here and drive 4.4 miles (7 km) to a right-hand turnoff down a narrow, twisting road past wheat fields to Quintanilla de las Viñas; take a right fork to see the remarkable seventh-century stone chapel, the Ermita Visigótica (see Highlights). Return to the N234 and turn right. Pass the cave houses of San Clemente before returning to Burgos, reconnecting with the A1/E5 at Saldaña de Burgos.

FROM: A loop from Burgos, Spain
ROADS: A1/E5, BU900, BU902, BU905/CL-110, N234
DISTANCE: 89 miles (142 km)
DRIVING TIME: 2.5 hours
WHEN TO GO: Year-round
PLANNING: www.turismoburgos.org

Also Recommended

❶ The James River, Virginia

In 1607, the James River opened up the American interior to the first successful English colonists. Follow the river from Richmond, along Rte. 5, to the reconstructed Jamestown settlement, then head to Yorktown, home to museums and a 1720s customs house.

www.dcr.virginia.gov

❷ Ashley River, South Carolina

Ashley River Road is an 11-mile (17 km) section of Hwy. 61, running alongside water shaded by the overarching branches of green trees. Marvel at the gardens at Magnolia Plantation and Middleton Place, and stop off at the old churches of St. Andrew's Parish and Springfield Baptist Church.

www.byways.org

❸ Mark Twain Country, Missouri

Mark Twain grew up in Hannibal at the edge of the Mississippi River. Start at his boyhood home, move on to a museum in his honor, and end at the Mark Twain Cave, a spot that featured prominently in *The Adventures of Tom Sawyer*. Drive south on Mo. 79 to reach Louisiana's art galleries, then on to Clarksville, where barges still chug up and down the river.

www.marktwaincountry.com

❹ Paradise Valley, Montana

From Livingston, head south on U.S. 89 through Paradise Valley. Follow Rte. 540 for stunning views of the Gallatin Range, returning to U.S. 89 to reach Gardiner. End your journey with the roaring falls, slicing chasms, and grassy flats of Yellowstone National Park—home to plenty of wildlife.

www.yellowstoneparknet.com

❺ Oak Creek Canyon, Arizona

From Flagstaff, follow the 12-mile (19 km) long and subtly colored Oak Creek Canyon to Sedona along Ariz. 89A. You'll reach points like Oak Creek Overlook, on a precariously projecting lip known as Mogollon Rim, where slanting walls of ponderosas stretch down to the river flowing along the bottom of the canyon.

www.americansouthwest.net/arizona/sedona

❻ Canada Hope to Kamloops, British Columbia, Canada

This is the route taken by 19th-century travelers who performed remarkable feats to cross the Fraser and Thompson canyons to reach the almost desert-like interior of British Columbia. Now, the 200-mile (322 km) trek is Trans-Canada Hwy. 1. The road traverses impressive geology such as Hells Gate, where the river gushes at unbelievable speeds and pressures through narrow, rocky walls.

www.canada.travel

❼ Valle de Coto Brus, Costa Rica

Hwy. 237 traces a deep gorge worn between the Talmanca and Fila Costeña Mountains, as it moves from Paso Real to Ciudad Neily, before climbing 11,660 feet (3,554 m) to towering Cerro Kamuk. Take the turnoff for Estación Tres Colinas, and at Jabillo follow signs to Coto Brus at the bottom of the valley. Continue up to high coffee fields and then through San Vito to connect with Hwy. 16. Admire herons and frogs in the nearby reserve before making your way back down to Ciudad Neily.

www.tourism.co.cr

❽ Huon Valley Trail, Australia

Follow the Huon Highway through "green-gold" pines, beloved of 19th-century shipbuilders, to reach Geeveston and nearby Tahune Forest Airwalk, where a walkway high in the treetops looks out across rivers and mountains. Continue the drive right into Hartz Mountains National Park, where you can explore and hike until joining the Channel Highway to Kettering to go through Margate and Kingston to Hobart, Tasmania's largest city.

www.discovertasmania.co.uk

❾ Rugova Gorge, Kosovo

Bright purple wildflowers cling to dark granite walls rising 2,000 feet (610 m) above the Drini River at the bottom of Rugova Gorge. At points the rock actually arches over the pavement as engineered tunnels take the road forward and earth momentarily blocks your view.

www.mkrs-ks.org

❿ Wachau Valley, Austria

From Melk and its fabulous baroque monastery, drive north along either Rte. 3 or Rte. 33, following the Danube River—one of Europe's longest rivers. On your way to Krems, you'll meander through the rolling Wachau Valley, a wine-growing region dating back to the Romans. The monasteries that dot the area were critical to the history of wine making in Wachau—the monks oversaw the original vineyards and were the first to trade wine upstream.

www.donau.com

⓫ Rhine Valley, Germany

The B9 follows the Middle Rhine between Koblenz and Mainz, a stretch of the river that is home to the valley's most majestic medieval castles, built here to levy tolls on traders plying the river. Riesling (a white grape unique to the region) vineyards cling to steep terraces along the slanting walls of the valley. Visit Boppard to enjoy a promenade along the river and explore its winding historical streets.

www.cometogermany.com

⓬ Marne Valley, France

Wander the historic streets of St.-Dizier, whose secrets include fine examples of decorative ironwork by art nouveau architect Hector Guimard. Follow the N67/E17 south along the valley of the Marne River, stopping in Vignory to admire the 11th-century Church of St. Etienne, an exceptional example of Romanesque architecture. Finish in Chaumont, sitting on a spur above the Marne.

www.tourisme-hautemarne.com

⓭ Exe Valley, England

Drive north-to-south across England's southwestern peninsula, starting in picturesque Dunster, dominated by its castle, revamped in the 18th century. From here, take the A396 into Exmoor National Park. After Wheddon Cross, the road follows the wooded valley of Quarme River, which joins the Exe. Twist and turn as you follow the Exe south through Tiverton to the cathedral city of Exeter.

www.visit-exmoor.co.uk

CHAPTER 4

The Road Less Traveled

For travelers with a true spirit of adventure, the back of beyond has a lot to commend it. Here lie the lonely highways and hidden byways leading to remote or little-known—but delightful—destinations. Some lie just off the beaten track, overlooked by the crowds who flock to more famous landmarks. Others are challenging forays into genuine wilderness that demand a cool head and careful preparation, but that reward those who undertake them with a powerful sense of achievement. Under boundless blue skies patrolled by eagles, a high-rising route enters Montana's National Bison Range, where a protected herd of the great beasts grazes undisturbed in the company of wild horses and bighorn sheep. Deep in the rain forests of Costa Rica, a network of rugged—and often difficult—dirt roads offers encounters with leatherback turtles, crocodiles, mangrove swamps, and jungle-covered seashores. For those eager to navigate one of the world's most formidable routes, complete with remote roads and the chance to experience fascinating cultures, there's a passage down the entire African continent—a spectacular expedition from the Egyptian capital, Cairo, south to Cape Town.

In northwestern Argentina, a lonely and beautiful road heads into the rocky landscape of Quebrada de las Conchas, known for its contrasting colors and extraordinary formations.

Hikers admire the barren, rugged landscape of Gros Morne National Park.

CANADA

Canada's Viking Coast

The west coast of Newfoundland is a place of staggering elemental beauty, where you'll find ancient mountains, fjords, cliffs and crashing seas, beaches, forests, and windswept barrens alongside a panoply of wildlife and a history of human habitation dating back 4,000 years.

After the six-hour ferry ride from North Sydney, Nova Scotia, leave Channel-Port aux Basques north on Trans-Canada 1, past the stark, windy, and fog-shrouded Long Range Mountains. Beyond are the fertile wetlands of the Codroy Valley—the Grand Codroy Ramsar Site. At Hwy. 490, head west and cross the causeway to take the 85-mile (137 km) scenic loop around the francophone Port au Port Peninsula. Follow Hwy. 463 north toward Lourdes and Piccadilly, past Long Point, and then turn southwest down the increasingly barren coast to Mainland (La Grande Terre). Descend to Cape St. George and return to Trans-Canada 1 via Hwy. 460. It's a scenic stretch north to the lumber town of Corner Brook, home to an art gallery, railway museum, and the Captain James Cook Monument. From here, continue for 30 miles (48 km) northeast through the strawberry-growing Humber Valley, then head north on Hwy. 430 to the beautifully wild Gros Morne National Park. Just beyond, The Arches Provincial Park has a triple-arch limestone formation by the sea. Farther north, explore the prehistoric Port au Choix National Historic Site, then continue through fishing villages, veering east at Eddies Cove. Turn left onto scenic Hwy. 436 and stop at L'Anse aux Meadows National Historic Site (see In Focus) 18 miles (29 km) north. Finally, visit St. Anthony and Fishing Point, a lookout for icebergs, whales, and seabirds, before returning to Channel-Port aux Basques.

In Focus Norse explorer Leif Eriksson established a settlement at **L'Anse aux Meadows National Historic Site** more than 1,000 years ago—a good 500 years before Christopher Columbus reached the Americas in 1492—making it the first known European settlement in the New World. Today, the site focuses on three reconstructed Norse buildings, where costumed interpreters explain the life of the early settlers.

FROM: Channel-Port aux Basques, Canada

TO: St. Anthony, Canada

ROADS: Trans-Canada 1, Hwys. 490, 463, 460, 430, 436

DISTANCE: 620 miles (1,000 km)

DRIVING TIME: 2 days

WHEN TO GO: From mid-June through mid-October

PLANNING: Take binoculars for watching birds and sea life. www.visitnewfoundland.ca

GEORGIA

Crossing Chattahoochee

Travel through the forested foothills, mountains, and valleys of northern Georgia's Chattahoochee National Forest, following the park's dramatic, wild river and climbing to the top of the state's highest peak, Brasstown Bald.

Begin in charming Helen, a former sawmill town that has recast itself as a faux-Bavarian alpine community, before heading north on Ga. 17/75. Follow the Chattahoochee River through the southern end of the Chattahoochee National Forest, one of the most productive hardwood forests in the world. At Robertstown, detour 3 miles (5 km) on Ga. 356 to the wilderness haven of Unicoi State Park and the beautiful Anna Ruby Falls. Back on Ga. 17/75, the road wends its treelined way beside Andrews Creek, becoming steeper and cresting at 2,949 feet (3,947 m) at Unicoi Gap. Beyond High Shoals Scenic Area, turn left onto Ga. 180, which climbs the lower slopes of Brasstown Bald, Georgia's highest mountain, measuring 4,784 feet (1,458 m). Take the Ga. 180 spur to the parking lot to hike or be shuttled the last half mile (800 m) to the treeless summit (the bald) and the visitor center. Return to Ga. 180, and continue through some of Georgia's most spectacular Blue Ridge country before entering a rolling, mountain-fringed valley. At Ga. 348, turn left onto the Richard Russell Scenic Byway, which follows the headwaters of the Nottely River. The countryside gives way to hills, then steep mountains, as the road climbs to 3,480 feet (1,061 m), past Tesnatee Gap and Hogpen Gap, to the top of the Blue Ridge Divide. The steep, rugged drainage you can see on the left is Lordamercy Cove. Descending Piney Ridge, with views of the wilds to the right, you come to Dukes Creek Falls, about 4.5 miles (7 km) ahead, where a short trail wanders to an observation platform. Soon after, turn left onto busy Ga. 75Alt, which leads back to Helen.

Excursion The first gold rush in the U.S. occurred in 1828 in the town of **Dahlonega,** around 30 miles (48 km) southwest of Helen (via Ga. 9, U.S. 19, and Ga. 75). Several mines remain open as tourist attractions, including the Consolidated Gold Mine, where you can take a tour to experience what it may have been like for those early miners—you'll get to see original equipment used by the miners and can even pan for gold. You can learn more about the historic goldrush at the Dahlonega Gold Museum in the center of town.

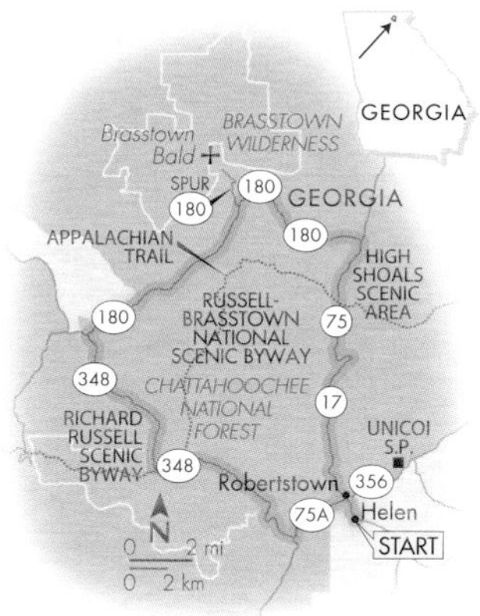

FROM: Loop route from Helen, Georgia

ROADS: Ga. 17/75, 356, 180, 348, Richard Russell Scenic Byway, 75Alt

DISTANCE: 41 miles (66 km)

DRIVING TIME: 1 hour

WHEN TO GO: Spring through fall

PLANNING: There is a shady picnic spot at Andrews Creek. Take boots if you plan to hike. www.byways.org

Cloud-filtered sunlight sparkles on ice-coated trees, with the dramatic Blue Ridge Mountains in the distance.

MINNESOTA/CANADA

North Shore Loop

Marked by forests, lakes, and rugged shores, the northwestern coast of Lake Superior is a chance to get away from it all in an environment where, over the centuries, humans have struggled to harvest natural resources, from furs to timbers and minerals.

One of Superior National Forest's gray wolves stares out from the snowbound trees in winter.

Highlights

- In Duluth, the Vista Fleet sightseeing cruise around the harbor passes the famous **Aerial Lift Bridge.** Also visit the marvelous **Lake Superior Museum of Transportation,** which displays classic trains, along with a recreation of Duluth's turn-of-the-century downtown.
- Explore the depths of the state's first underground mine at **Soudan Underground Mine State Park** (which lies off Minn. 169). A caged elevator lowers you a good half mile (800 m) underground, after which you'll take a train ride into the deepest part of the mine. An underground physics laboratory also has tours.

Drive into Minnesota's great outdoors on Minn. 61 from Duluth (see Highlights), following the northwest shore of Lake Superior. After exploring Gooseberry Falls State Park, with five waterfalls and an ancient landscape of lava, continue to Split Rock Lighthouse. The coastline becomes more mountainous around Tettegouche State Park and Superior National Forest, where you can pick up camping and hiking maps at the Tofte Ranger District Office. Sawbill Trail and other roads let you drive deep into the forest. Just before you reach Grand Portage near the Canadian border, visit the harbor area at Grand Marais and the Grand Portage National Monument (off Minn. 61), commemorating the 18th-century fur traders and explorers who toiled to reach this spot. Nearby, Gunflint Trail runs 63 miles (102 km) west into Boundary Waters Canoe Area Wilderness. Cross into Canada and head north toward Thunder Bay, a bustling lake port, where you can hike in Sleeping Giant Provincial Park (Hwy. 587) and visit Old Fort William, a reconstructed trading post from the early 19th century. From here, take Trans-Canada 11/17 west to Kakabeka Falls Provincial Park for spectacular waterfalls, hiking trails, and campgrounds. Continue west to the Dawson Trail entrance to the 1.1-millon-acre (454,154 ha) Quetico Provincial Park, whose ancient rock paintings are accessible only by boat. Head back into the U.S. along Trans-Canada 11 to International Falls, then continue south on U.S. 53 to Voyageurs National Park, packed full of lakes, rivers, and wildlife. The Mesabi Range, south on U.S. 53 and Minn. 73, is an early mining region. The Ironworld Discovery Center, off U.S. 169, is a museum and amusement park, while the Minnesota Museum of Mining in Chisholm's Memorial Park has traditional museum exhibits. Continue to Hibbing (Bob Dylan's childhood home), then take U.S. 169 east and Minn. 169 north to Soudan Underground Mine State Park (see Highlights). Continue east to Ely for the Boundary Waters Canoe Area Wilderness for a paddle on the lakes. Finish up with a trip to the International Wolf Center (Minn. 169), where you can see a pack of wolves.

FROM: Duluth, Minnesota
TO: Ely, Minnesota
ROADS: Minn. 61, Hwy. 587, Trans-Canada 11/17, Trans-Canada 11, U.S. 53, Minn. 73, U.S. 169, Minn. 169
DISTANCE: 740 miles (1,191 km)
DRIVING TIME: 2 days
WHEN TO GO: May through October
PLANNING: Permits must be acquired months in advance for canoe trips in Boundary Waters Canoe Area Wilderness and Quetico Provincial Park. www.northshorevisitor.com

OPPOSITE: Fall brings a riot of flaming color to the roads across Superior National Forest.

WISCONSIN

Wisconsin's North Woods

Beginning at Lake Superior's southern shore, this tour loops inland south and east through woods, across tumbling streams, and past some wondrous waterfalls. You can fish on the rivers and lakes or hike the woodland trails.

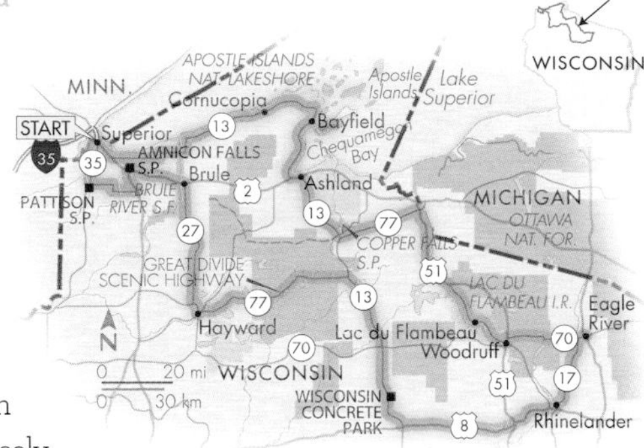

From the lakeside city of Superior, it's not far south on Wis. 35 to Pattison State Park, where the Black River roars over Big Manitou Falls. This is your first taste of the North Woods, which stretch southeast toward Lake Michigan. From here, local roads lead to Amnicon Falls State Park, off U.S. 2, which has spectacular waterfalls. Drive east on U.S. 2 to Brule River State Forest, then head south on Wis. 27 to Hayward and the National Fresh Water Fishing Hall of Fame. The route then heads east on Wis. 77 to the Great Divide Scenic Byway, which passes for 30 miles (48 km) through densely packed maples and aspens as you drive through Chequamegon National Forest. Wisconsin Concrete Park on Wis. 13 is home to 250 life-size concrete figures embellished with glass and mirrors, and farther south and east on U.S. 8 lies Rhinelander Logging Museum, surrounded by mountains, lakes, and trails. Eagle River, north on Wis. 17, has a string of resort-lined lakes and is a winter snowmobile hotspot. Drive west on Wis. 70 and briefly on U.S. 51 to pick up Wis. 47 at Woodruff and reach the town of Lac du Flambeau on Lac du Flambeau Indian Reservation. The George W. Brown, Jr. Ojibwe Museum and Cultural Center here exhibits Ojibwe indigenous people's traditional way of life. Continue north on Wis. 47 and U.S. 51, then head west on Wis. 77 and north on Wis. 169 to Copper Falls State Park for trails along steep-walled canyons by the Bad River. Backtrack and follow Wis. 13 north to the Lake Superior shore. At Ashland, the region's story is told at the Northern Wisconsin History Center. Visit Apostle Islands National Lakeshore (see In Focus), just off the Bayfield Peninsula, and the fishing port of Bayfield. Return to Superior on Wis. 13.

In Focus The 21 islands of the **Apostle Islands National Lakeshore** have provided refuge from Lake Superior's storms for centuries. There is plenty to explore, including Bayfield's Cooperage Museum, the Madeline Island Historical Museum and bus tour, the wind-battered cliffs and caves of Devils Island, the 1881 Sand Island Lighthouse, and a restored fishing camp on Manitou Island. You can also camp, hike, fish, hunt, and kayak. Tour boats go around the islands.

FROM: Loop route from Superior, Wisconsin
ROADS: Wis. 35, U.S. 2, Wis. 27, 77, 13, U.S. 8, Wis. 17, 70, U.S. 51, Wis. 47, 169, 13, local roads
DISTANCE: 500 miles (805 km)
DRIVING TIME: 12 hours
WHEN TO GO: Spring through fall
PLANNING: Take boots, swimsuits, and anything else you may need for outdoor activities, including sailing. www.explorewisconsin.com

The striated cliffs of Lake Superior's Sand Island are wonderful to explore by kayak.

The National Bison Range is one of the oldest wildlife refuges in the U.S., established in 1908 to protect the American Buffalo.

MONTANA

Where the Buffalo Roam

This scenic drive takes in outstanding alpine scenery with plenty of opportunities to glimpse western Montana's ample wildlife. You'll also see museums of pioneer and Native American history, towns with splendid Victorian neighborhoods, and a dinosaur dig.

To reach the forested Jocko Valley, take I-90 west of Missoula to U.S. 93 and turn north. At Ravalli, a detour west on Mont. 200 brings you to the National Bison Range, which has a protected herd of up to 500 bison. From Ravalli, continue north on U.S. 93 to an 1854 Jesuit log mission at St. Ignatius Mission National Historic Site (off U.S. 93 on Flathead Indian Reservation) and continue to Doug Allard's Flathead Indian Museum and Trading Post to admire Native American art. Drive on to Pablo, whose People's Center interprets the region's past and present through Native American eyes. Just north of Polson, you reach Flathead Lake, the largest natural freshwater lake in the west. Go west around the lake on U.S. 93 past vineyards, Flathead Lake State Park, and Dayton, which overlooks Wild Horse Island—noted for its bighorn sheep, wild horses, deer, eagles, and falcons. North of the lake, follow U.S. 93 through Kalispell to Whitefish and head east, taking the Mont. 40 cutoff to U.S. 2. Enter Glacier National Park from West Glacier and take U.S. 2, which is largely a canyon drive that skirts the glacier's southern border and follows the powerful Middle Fork of the Flathead River through a scenic corridor to East Glacier Park. Continue to Choteau on U.S. 89 and detour west to Egg Mountain to see the first dinosaur nests discovered in North America. From Choteau, follow U.S. 287 south to I-15 and take the exit for Gates of the Rocky Mountains, one of the Missouri River's most scenic areas. Back on I-15, visit the state capital Helena, with many lavish Victorian buildings, then go north on I-15 and take U.S. 279 over Flesher Pass to Mont. 200. Visit the ghost town of Garnet (10 miles/16 km west of the junction with Mont. 83) before returning to Missoula.

FROM: Loop route from Missoula, Montana

ROADS: I-90, U.S. 93/Mont. 200, Mont. 40, U.S. 2, 89, 287. I-15, U.S. 279

DISTANCE: 650 miles (1,046 km)

DRIVING TIME: 1.5 days

WHEN TO GO: Early summer to fall

PLANNING: www.glaciermt.com

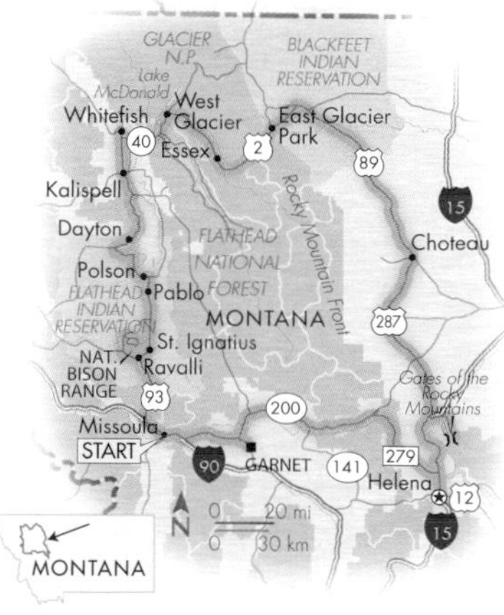

THE TOP 10 U.S. Wildlife Adventures

Along with excellent roads through delightful scenery, the U.S. is blessed with some of the world's finest wildlife drives. Here's our top 10.

1 Victory Basin, Vermont

In fall, drive the Victory Road south of Gallup Mills. This part-paved, part-dirt route crosses Victory Basin, where vibrant colors of broad-leaved trees—yellow birch, American beech, and sugar maple—are interspersed with sphagnum bog and stands of black and red spruce. White-tailed deer spend the winter here, and watch out for moose and the rare black-backed woodpecker.

PLANNING: *www.vtfishandwildlife.com*

2 Mouth of the Delaware, Delaware

Start at New Castle, founded by the Dutch in 1651, and follow Rte. 9 over the high bridge across the Chesapeake–Delaware Canal toward Penn Port, named for William Penn, the founder of Pennsylvania. The road passes through salt marshes—be sure to visit Woodland Beach's tidal marshes, which have blue herons and snowy egrets. Also stop by Bombay Hook National Wildlife Refuge to see migrating birds before joining Rte. 8 to Dover.

PLANNING: *www.fws.gov/northeast/bombayhook*

3 Indian River Lagoon Scenic Highway, Florida

On the Atlantic coast of Florida, drive on Rte. 1 and Rte. A1A between Wabasso and Titusville through a habitat with more species of estuary wildlife than anywhere else in North America. And if three national wildlife refuges and several state parks and sanctuaries fail to impress, there's always the Kennedy Space Center, and the McLarty Treasure Museum, with shipwrecked Spanish treasures.

PLANNING: *www.dot.state.fl.us*

4 Loess Hills Scenic Byway, Iowa

This route in western Iowa between the small communities of Akron and Hamburg follows the Missouri River through prairie and forest-covered bluffs made of wind-blown silt. To the north of Akron (the northern terminus of the byway) lies the Broken Kettle Grasslands, famed for its profusion of prairie butterflies such as the dusted skipper.

PLANNING: *www.traveliowa.com*

5 Creole Nature Trail, Louisiana

Passing bayous, marshlands, and beaches in the Louisiana Outback along the Gulf of Mexico, this 180-mile (290 km) route—accessed via I-10—has been designated an All-American Road by the U.S. Department of Transportation. It crosses three wildlife refuges and a bird sanctuary, and with two major bird migration flyways passing through, the area is one of the best birding places in the U.S. More than 300 species stop here, including tree swallows, kingbirds, kingfishers, Orchard Orioles, and Yellow-billed Cuckoos. On warm, sunny days, however, a favored local activity is alligator spotting.

PLANNING: *www.creolenaturetrail.org*

6 Witchita Mountains Scenic Byway, Oklahoma

This route (Okla. 49) passes through one of the U.S.'s oldest wildlife reserves—Wichita Mountains Wildlife Refuge, which with its remnants of mixed grass prairie is reminiscent of the unspoiled Wild West. Along with more than 50 species of mammals, 240 species of birds, and 64 species of reptiles and amphibians, you'll see North American bison in their native habitat. There is also a chance you'll spot Rocky Mountain elk and white-tailed deer, as well as Texas longhorn cattle.

PLANNING: *www.okscenicbyways.org*

Opposite: An alligator crouches by a bayou in Louisiana's Sabine National Wildlife Refuge, part of the Creole Nature Trail.

7 International Selkirk Loop, Washington/Idaho/British Columbia

This 280-mile (450 km) loop route follows rivers and lakeshores, cuts through narrow canyons, passes forested hillsides, crosses lowland meadows, and skirts snow-capped mountains. In fall, thousands of Canada geese stop off to refuel before heading off on their migration route southward.

PLANNING: *www.selkirkloop.org*

8 Volcanic Legacy Scenic Byway, Oregon/California

From Oregon's Crater Lake to California's Mt. Lassen, this 500-mile (804 km) volcano-to-volcano route is a birder's paradise. In addition to showcasing volcanic and geothermal features, this drive takes you past Klamath Lake, where a million migrating birds stop each fall; Clear Lake, where white pelicans and double-crested cormorants nest; Tule Lake, where you may spot a golden eagle; Crater Lake, home to red-tailed hawks and horned owls; and Bear Valley, which has the biggest concentration of bald eagles in the lower 48 states.

PLANNING: *www.volcaniclegacybyway.org*

9 Wetlands and Wildlife Scenic Byway, Kansas

Two of the largest wetland systems in the world are to be found at Cheyenne Bottoms and Quiviri. More than half of all migrating shorebirds east of the Rockies pass through here, and during spring migration 500,000 birds put down at Quiviri, including impressive sandhill and whooping cranes.

PLANNING: The route is 77 miles (124 km) long. *www.kansaswetlandsandwildlifescenicbyway.com*

10 Nebo Loop Scenic Byway, Utah

From Nephi to Payson, this drive climbs to 9,000 feet (2,743 m) in 37 miles (60 km). Overlooks with interpretive signs offer above-the-clouds views of the Utah Valley, Mount Nebo (the highest peak in the Wasatch Mountains), and Uinta National Forest. A mile (1.6 km) hike from the road takes you to the natural red sandstone amphitheater and spires of Devil's Kitchen.

PLANNING: *www.utah.com/byways/nebo_loop.htm*

Snowy peaks and blue sky reflected in a mountain lake add to the symphony of glowing color in the Alaskan landscape.

ALASKA

Alaskan Wilderness

Although Anchorage has the modern amenities of any U.S. city, the rugged surrounding mountains are a constant reminder that wild country is all around it. This drive through southern Alaska takes in isolated communities, mountains, forests, and glaciers.

From Alaska's largest city, Anchorage, head north on Glenn Highway (Alas. 1) through shrubby woodlands toward the wilderness. After 13 miles (21 km), make a detour east to follow Eagle River Road through Chugach State Park, where urban sprawl gives way to glacier-molded mountains, lakes, waterfalls, and forests. Back on the main road, continue a short way to Eklutna Historical Park, a preserved 17th-century, Russian-influenced Athabaskan settlement. Guided tours take in St. Nicholas Russian Orthodox Church and a brightly decorated native cemetery. Continue north through the fertile Mat-Su Valley, to the agricultural town of Palmer. Farther north, take a turnoff onto Archie Road for Independence Mine State Historical Park, a well-preserved early 20th-century gold mine. Back on the main road, follow the wide curves of the Matanuska River through broad, snow-capped mountains to reach Matanuska Glacier—Alaska's largest road-accessible glacier. The highway now descends through scrawny conifers leaning at crazy angles, which give rise to the local name of "drunken forest." After the town of Glennallen, turn south onto Alas. 4 and past a lookout point on the Wrangell Mountains. Stop at the historic town of Copper Center, where you'll find the George I. Ashby Memorial Museum, full of pioneer and native artifacts. Around 10 miles (16 km) on at Willow Creek, turn east onto Alas. 10 and follow the Copper River southeast to Chitina and McCarthy Road. The main attraction along this 60-mile (96 km) bumpy dirt road, aside from beautiful scenery, is the wondrously isolated town of McCarthy. A footbridge across the Kennicott River is the only thing linking the road to the town, which is a great base for treks, river-rafting, or flightseeing trips deeper into the Alaskan wilderness.

FROM: Anchorage, Alaska
TO: McCarthy, Alaska
ROADS: Alas. 1/Glenn Highway, Eagle River Road, Archie Road, Alas. 4, 10, McCarthy Road
DISTANCE: 303 miles (488 km)
DRIVING TIME: 8 hours
WHEN TO GO: Spring through fall
PLANNING: www.travelalaska.com

NEW MEXICO

Into the Heart of the Sands

The distant, towering peaks of the San Andreas Mountains surround waves of ever-shifting brilliant white sandy crests, making this southern New Mexico drive through the world's largest gypsum sand dune one of the most unusual in the southwest.

This drive through the white sands of New Mexico is a unique experience that takes you into the heart of one of America's true wildernesses. Before trekking into this harsh and demanding environment, stop by the visitor center of White Sands National Monument, which offers information about the unusual geological features of the area and tips on staying safe. The sands are created when the sun evaporates water from nearby Lake Lucero and Alkali Flat, leaving a thin crust of tiny gypsum crystals that the wind blows into dunes. In this devilishly hot and dry environment, species of mice, lizards, snakes, and scorpions have adapted light coloration to survive. The road skirts the edge of the dunes for about 3 miles (5 km), as saltbush encroaches close to the highway and fine flakes of sand float across the tarmac. On the left, the Big Dune Trail, a 1-mile (1.6 km) hike up a 60-foot (18 m) dune, leads past cottonwood shrubs and offers the chance to follow animal tracks made in the sand, including those of the roadrunner. As the road pushes farther into the dunes, vegetation gradually disappears, although you will see the occasional soaptree yucca plant, whose roots burrow down as far as 30–40 feet (9–12 m). A little farther on, the Interdune Boardwalk is a short stroll to view some of the sand's fragile wildflowers. In the heart of the dunes, swirling sand prevents plants from taking root (and the absence of roots causes the sand to swirl). At the end of the 8-mile (13 km) road, wide pullouts provide ample opportunities to hike or sand surf down some of the steep dune faces. The Alkali Flat Trail leads 2.3 miles (3.7 km) through the dunes out into the empty sands beyond—if you're looking for wilderness, this is it. The trail traverses wave-like dunes, and ends up at the Alkali Flat, the dried-up bottom of Lake Otero. If you can, stay until sunset, when fading light bathes the sands in soft hues of pinks and blues, and lengthened shadows across the darkened dunes create an exquisite experience, evocative of an Arabian fairy tale.

FROM: Visitor Center, White Sands National Monument, New Mexico
TO: End of the Alkali Flat Trail, New Mexico
ROAD: Dunes Drive
DISTANCE: 16 miles (26 km)
DRIVING TIME: 30 minutes
WHEN TO GO: Fall through winter
PLANNING: Bring water, sunglasses, and sunscreen.
www.nps.gov/whsa

A soaptree yucca lives a lonely existence in the barren, pure white sands.

CALIFORNIA

Delve into Death Valley

One of the world's great desert realms is Death Valley, the hottest, lowest, and driest place in North America, where the fascinating landscape reveals vanished Lake Manly, which existed here more than 12,000 years ago.

This drive, slightly longer than the officially designated Death Valley Scenic Byway, starts west of Death Valley in Olancha. Head past Owens Lake Bed, along Calif. 190, and climb 5,000 feet (1,524 m) to Death Valley National Park. Descend into the Panamint Valley, where you may see low-flying military jets, before climbing into the Panamint Range. At Emigrant Compound, turn right for a trip up Emigrant Canyon; after 12 miles (19 km), follow an unpaved road past Harrisburg, a vanished boomtown, and the Eureka Mine to reach Aguereberry Point, which has dizzying views of the Black Mountains and Sierra Nevada. Return to the highway and drive into Death Valley and tiny Stovepipe Wells Village. At Mosaic Canyon, up a 2-mile (3 km) long gravel road, you can walk through halls of breccia and white marble that were carved out by an ancient river. Drive on to the junction where Calif. 190 turns south; take a short detour to Scotty's Castle, a 19th-century villa, or continue to the turnoff for Salt Creek. Along a short nature trail at the creek, you'll see tiny desert pupfish whose ancestors swam here tens of thousands of years ago. From Furnace Creek—home to natural springs, date palms, a visitor center, and a golf course—drive 9 miles (14.5 km) south on Badwater Road for a walk in Golden Canyon, then on to Devil's Golf Course and Badwater (see In Focus). Back on the highway, turn right to Zabriskie Point and walk to an overlook of tilted and eroded badlands created by ancient lake beds. Continue on Calif. 190 until you reach a turnoff for a 13-mile (21 km) side trip to Dantes View, 5,475 feet (1,669 m) above the valley, for a spectacular lookout. Return to the highway and turn right: the drive ends at Death Valley Junction.

FROM: Olancha, California
TO: Death Valley Junction, California
ROADS: Calif. 190, Badwater Road
DISTANCE: 130 miles (209 km)
DRIVING TIME: 3 hours
WHEN TO GO: Year-round, but summer is extremely hot
PLANNING: Carry plenty of drinking water and set out with a full tank of gas. www.visitcalifornia.com.

In Focus The loop detour to **Badwater** takes in several fascinating sites: Devil's Golf Course (a jumble of rock-hard salt pinnacles) and pools that, at 279 feet (85 m) below sea level, are saltier than the ocean. One-way Artists Drive, best seen at sunset, winds for 10 miles (16 km) back to the highway through terrain that is streaked with iron oxides (red, yellow, pink) and volcanic minerals (green, purple), and then through canyons cut into the valley's many alluvial fans.

Only insects and algae can survive in low-lying Badwater's salty pools.

A farmer drives an ox-drawn cart, still a common sight in the region around Holguín.

CUBA

Cuban Byways

Dipping down to the shore and into the lush vales of eastern Cuba's Grupo Montañoso Maniabon mountains, Rte. 6-241 is one of the island's most picturesque roads, carving a path though a landscape of irregular limestone hummocks *(mogotes)* and ridges.

From the suburbs of Holguín, drive east onto Avenida XX Anniversario to reach Rte. 6-241. The road soon begins to dip and rise through an open country of thatched huts, cacti, and steep-faced mogotes. About 20 miles (34 km) on, detour left at Rafael Freyre to Frey Benito, and turn right for Parque Monumento Nacional Bariay, where Christopher Columbus landed in 1492. Backtrack to Rafael Freyre, which has a sugar and steam train museum, and continue northeast past the Bahía de Naranjo nature park to the popular resort of Guardalavaca. The road immediately heads south and cuts inland over the northernmost mogotes of the Grupo Montañoso mountains. At Yaguajay, turn right at the sign for Museo Aborigen Chorro de Maita, Cuba's largest pre-Columbian archaeological site. Back on Rte. 6-241, the road drops down to the village of Cañadón in the Valle de Samá. Tousled royal palms stand sentry over lime-green tobacco fields backed by rounded hills on the approach to El Salado, where freestanding knolls tower over the highway. The snaking road deposits you 18 miles (29 km) beyond Guardalavaca, on a broad plain that sweeps east to the Bahía de Banes. Follow the road as it curves eastward to Banes, past lush green sugarcanes that ripple in the breeze. In Banes, you can swim with dolphins and visit the church of Iglesia de Nuestra Señora de la Caridad, where Fidel Castro was married in 1948. The Museo Indocubano has a collection of pre-Columbian artifacts, including a unique gold figurine with a feather headdress. The town's wooden and concrete houses are full of color, and the numerous classic U.S. cars add plenty of character, so it's a delight just to walk around the town and soak up the Cuban atmosphere.

FROM: Holguín, Cuba
TO: Banes, Cuba
ROADS: Avenida XX Anniversario, Rte. 6-241, local roads
DISTANCE: 60 miles (96 km)
DRIVING TIME: 4.5 hours
WHEN TO GO: Spring through fall
PLANNING: Take your swimsuit; be prepared for potholes, ox-drawn carts, and bicycles on the road. www.dtcuba.com

A local worker climbs the steep slopes rising from the startling blue waters of Lake Atitlán, the deepest lake in Central America.

GUATEMALA

Villages and Volcanoes

The volcanoes of central Guatemala stand watch over a landscape of gentle hills, elegant coffee plantations, and one of the world's most beautiful lakes, as well as fascinating colonial towns and quaint villages.

From Antigua (see In Focus), head south on Ruta Nacional 14, which runs between the towering Volcano Agua and the smoking Volcano Fuego, to the industrialized city of Escuintla. From here, head west on C.A. 2 through small farming communities, then turn north onto Ruta Nacional 11 at Cocales. Soon you'll reach the beautiful coffee plantation (*finca*) called Los Tarrales, which stands in the lee of two 11,000-foot (3,353 m) volcanoes. Stay the night and then head toward the town of Chicacao, turning off the highway and down a cobblestone lane (Hwy. 14) toward Santiago Atitlán. This takes you along the old Camino Reale, built on top of Indian footpaths by conquistadores to link Mexico City with their outer territories. Several hours and many steep mountain roads later, you'll reach Santiago Atitlán in the southern highlands, on the shores of Lake Atitlán, a flooded caldera that is regarded as one of the world's most beautiful lakes and is surrounded by picture-perfect volcanic cones. The town is startlingly barren, yet somehow compelling, and crowded with local Tzutujil Indians in colorful dress. Like the massive Catholic church built in 1547 with stones taken from Mayan temples, local religious beliefs and rituals are a mixture of both cultures.

FROM: Antigua, Guatemala
TO: Santiago Atitlán, Guatemala
ROADS: Ruta Nacional 14, C.A. 2, Ruta Nacional 11, Hwy. 14
DISTANCE: 56 miles (90 km)
DRIVING TIME: 2 hours
WHEN TO GO: Year-round
PLANNING: www.atitlan.com

In Focus The Spanish ordered the former colonial capital of **La Antigua Guatemala** to be abandoned in 1776, after earthquakes had wrecked the city, yet not everyone left. Today it remains full of historic buildings, such as the 17th-century San José Cathedral and the 16th-century Church San Francisco; the old colonial streets are a delight to explore. The Parque Central is also worth a visit, and El Mercado, a maze-like market, has everything from gifts to livestock.

COSTA RICA

Costa Rican Coast

This challenging drive along the rugged southwestern shore of Nicoya is one of Costa Rica's best adventures, but it is not for the fainthearted. The rutted dirt road clambers over mountainous headlands and along crocodile-infested rivers.

Don't leave the funky fishing hamlet of Sámara in anything less than a sturdy vehicle appropriate for the bumpy road ahead. The stretch of Hwy. 160 to Estrada is paved, running inland and parallel to the coast by the white sands of Playa Carrillo. The fun begins beyond Playa Islita, where leatherback and Ridley turtles nest along the jungled shore, as a narrow dirt track begins a stiff climb that would challenge even a goat. It then spirals down to the hamlet of Islita—home to the Open-Air Contemporary Art Museum—and climbs again over Punta Barranquilla before swooping down to Playa Corozalito. The road continues to run inland parallel to the shore, which is backed by wetland swamps teeming with wildlife, on past Playa Bejuco, the hamlet of Pueblo Nuevo, and Playa Coyote, toward the crossroads of San Francisco de Coyote. Here, the going begins to get tricky. Unpaved Hwy. 162 heads southeast along the Río Jabillo and is subject to flooding, but as long as you avoid the wildlife-filled mangroves (home to crocodiles, snakes, turtles, and egrets), you should get through. After twisting for 4 miles (6 km), turn right at the Y-fork beside the sugarcane field. This will bring you to the Río Bongo, a shallow crossing that will make your heart race. A little beyond the river, you will pass Salon La Perla India at a road junction. Drive inland back across the Río Bongo to Bajos de Ario, and drive 300 feet (90 m) upriver to the hamlet of Betel. Turn right, and after 1.5 miles (2.5 km), you'll reach Bello Horizonte. The rough-and-ready track claws over Punta Pochote and follows Playa Santa Teresa. Beware of deep mud after rain. Keep straight to arrive at the offbeat surf resort of Malpaís.

FROM: Sámara, Costa Rica
TO: Malpaís, Costa Rica
ROADS: Hwys. 160, 162, rough dirt roads, Hwy. 21
DISTANCE: 57 miles (91 km)
DRIVING TIME: 4 hours (one way)
WHEN TO GO: The dry season (December through April)
PLANNING: Take drinking water, spare clothes, shoes, and a flashlight.
www.nicoyapeninsula.com

Excursion A short drive south of Malpaís is **Cabo Blanco Nature Reserve,** at the peninsula's southern tip. The reserve was Costa Rica's first, established in 1963, and covers 2,896 acres (1,172 ha) of mostly moist tropical forest. There is plenty of wildlife here, such as white-tailed deer, pacas, armadillos, coyotes, porcupines, and raccoons. There are also two hiking trails: the short Danes Trail and the longer Sueco Trail that winds through the forest and drops down to the beach.

The white sands of Playa Carrillo and the eponymous fishing hamlet are a great base for sportfishing.

THE TOP 10 Untamed Roads

Celebrate extremes of human—and automotive—endurance with our pick of the most back-to-nature and bone-rattling rough tracks.

1 Parc national du Mont-Tremblant, Quebec, Canada

Gravel roads pass spectacular lakes, streams, rivers, and waterfalls tumbling down mountains. The maple forests in the province of Quebec's largest and oldest national park are among the finest in North America for viewing fall foliage. Prepare your eyes for a riot of yellows, greens, oranges, and reds.

PLANNING: While the forest foliage is prettiest in fall, the park is open year-round. *www.sepaq.com*

2 Dempster Highway, Canada

From Yukon's Dawson City, head north through 457 miles (736 km) of icy wilderness. The track brings you to Inuvik—the largest town in the Arctic Circle. In winter, the S.U.V.-testing odyssey extends another 121 miles (194 km), as a river and the Atlantic freeze to form an ice road to the even remoter Tuktoyaktuk.

PLANNING: Eagle Plains, midway along, has the only gas station and hotel between Dawson and Inuvik. *www.nunavuttourism.com*

3 Hole-in-the-Rock Scenic Backway, Utah

This 57-mile (92 km) dirt road abruptly terminates at Hole-in-the-Rock, a 1,200-foot (366 m) crevice blasted and chiseled by 250 Mormon pioneers in 1880. Pass Devil's Garden (a picnic spot surrounded by unusual rock formations), a sandstone amphitheater called Dance Hall Rock, and the Escalante Canyons.

PLANNING: The route starts 5 miles (7 km) east of Escalante on Scenic Byway 12. Allow time for hiking off the main trail. *www.scenicbyway12.com*

4 Land Rover Experience, Carmel Valley, California

Whether you are a beginner or a veteran, this unusual environment offers the chance to hone your off-road driving skills in safety and comfort. On a specially adapted 80-acre (32 ha) course, the school's instructors offer customized lessons and programs that last from one hour to several days.

PLANNING: The school is open year-round. *www.landroverschool.com*

5 Boranup Drive, Western Australia, Australia

Skyscraping karri forests, the surfer-friendly Cape Leeuwin coastline, spring wildflowers, and (for nondrivers) forays into Australia's prime Margaret Valley vineyards—all these tempt visitors to meander through the serene Leeuwin-Naturaliste National Park.

PLANNING: It takes three hours to drive to Margaret Valley from Perth. There is a campground just south of Boranup Drive in Hamelin Bay. *www.westernaustralia.com*

6 Kalupahana-Horton Plains, Sri Lanka

Nicknamed Satan's Steps in colonial times and ascending 4,236 feet (1,291 m) over just 15 miles (24 km), this jaw-chattering jeep track through Sri Lanka's highest plateau has steep switchbacks, including one called the Devil's Staircase. Experienced drivers can expect glorious hill-country landscapes, with tea plantations, waterfalls—including Sri Lanka's highest, Bambarakanda—and a refreshingly cool climate.

PLANNING: The road leads from Kalupahana on the Colombo-Badulla highway to the Horton Plains National Park visitor center via the Udaweriya Estate. To drive farther into a protected part of the park requires a permit from the visitor center. The best driving conditions are January through March. *www.srilanka.travel*

Opposite: The canyons of Escalante in Utah's Grand Staircase National Monument boast some of the United States' least tamed roads.

7 Nature Explorer 4x4 Training, Iceland

Follow in the tracks of elite special forces and aid workers training for service in Afghanistan and other fields of combat as you learn advanced 4WD skills in a country with vastly varied terrains, no motorways, and few surfaced roads at all.

PLANNING: In addition to offering 4WD military training, Nature Explorer is an all-round outdoor tour company run by wilderness experts. *www.natureexplorer.is*

8 Specialist Vehicle Training, Norfolk, England

For true adventure, driving a tank is hard to beat. Various adventure centers around the U.K. offer short tank drives, but this one can claim to be truly authentic. It trains soldiers for the U.K. H license, which is for tracked vehicles.

PLANNING: Intensive training lasts two days, with the driving test on the third day. *www.svtraining.co.uk*

9 Sharm al-Sheikh to St. Catherine's Monastery, Egypt

As you drive northwest from Sharm al-Sheikh through the Sinai Desert to Mount Sinai and the sixth-century Greek Orthodox St. Catherine's Monastery, believed to be where God revealed the Ten Commandments, you pass Bedouin encampments, camel trains, and curious brightly colored sandstone formations.

PLANNING: Only a few roads traverse the desert; a 4WD is essential. Allow six hours for a nonstop round-trip, and another six to scale Mount Sinai's summit by foot or partly by camel. *www.sinaimonastery.com*

10 Wadi Dhaiqah, Oman

Lying in a canyon about 56 miles (90 km) east from Muscat—and with more than 100 lesser wadis (gullies) in between—Wadi Dhaiqah presents a remarkably mixed terrain of lofty cliffs, narrow valleys, and deep pools fed by natural springs. It's one of Oman's driving—and visual—highlights.

PLANNING: It's safest to go in a convoy of experienced drivers or with a tour group or local expert. Dry summer months offer the best driving conditions. *www.omantourism.gov.om*

ARGENTINA

Argentina's Heart

Red-rock canyons, shifting dunes, verdant vineyards, colonial towns, ancient ruins, and cardón cacti are highlights along this varied loop drive through northwestern Argentina. You will need at least three days to take it all in, and ideally much more.

From Salta, skirt Embalse Cabra Corral reservoir, whose whitewater outlets are popular with kayakers, and head south on RN 68. About 60 miles (96 km) on, the smooth, paved road begins its ascent through the striking canyon country of Quebrada de las Conchas (see Stay a While). You pass through the dune fields of Los Médanos as you approach the town of Cafayate, which has a colonial ambience and is surrounded by wine country, making it the ideal place to stay overnight. Before leaving, take a detour 34 miles (54 km) south to the pre-Columbian fortress of Quilmes, one of Argentina's most important archeological sites. From Cafayate, the northbound RN 40 is paved only as far as the village of San Carlos. Then follow the narrow, dusty road as it weaves through dramatically folded sedimentary strata, occasionally emerging onto alluvial flats whose greenery contrasts with the monochrome hills. Stop at the village of Molinos, 55 miles (88 km) north of San Carlos, and visit Estancia Colomé, 11 miles (18 km) west—possibly the world's highest vineyard. To reach the city of Cachi, 29 miles (46 km) farther on, continue north through the picturesque hamlet of Seclantás. The RN 40 is paved for another 7 miles (11 km) east, to the village of Payogasta, where it intercepts paved RP 33, an arrow-straight road that climbs to Parque Nacional Los Cardones, home to the saguaro-like cacti that dot the landscape at altitudes over 11,000 feet (3,400 m). The pavement ends about 5.5 miles (8.8 km) into the park, and the road peaks at 10,985 feet (3,348 m) at the Cuesta del Obispo. It then follows an awesomely steep, zigzag route that drops from high desert into subtropical woodlands on one of the country's most spectacular descents. Turn north onto the RN 68 back to Salta.

FROM: Loop route from Salta, Argentina
ROADS: RN 68, RN 40, RP 33
DISTANCE: 380 miles (611 km)
DRIVING TIME: 8 hours
WHEN TO GO: Year-round
PLANNING: Leave with a full tank of gas. www.norteargentino.gov.ar

Stay a While The fabulous landscape of **Quebrada de las Conchas,** also known as Quebrada de Cafayate, recalls Utah's Bryce Canyon with its stunning and colorful rock landforms such as El Sapo (The Toad) and Los Castillos (The Castles). There are no services on the route, so take a picnic and plenty of water in readiness for exploring sites such as the Garganta del Diablo (Devil's Throat) and El Anfiteatro (Amphitheater).

Many interesting rock formations punctuate the fertile valley of Quebrada de Cafayate.

The red-colored Gibb River Road—still known as the "beef road"—was built so that cattle could be driven to market from distant ranches.

AUSTRALIA

Gibb River Road

The long, lonesome Gibb River Road cuts though the heart of the Kimberley region of Western Australia. This rough track is one of the continent's greatest adventure drives, offering a tremendous sense of freedom as you pass through wide-open country.

FROM: Kununurra, Australia
TO: Derby, Australia
ROADS: Great Northern Highway, Gibb River Road
DISTANCE: 420 miles (676 km)
DRIVING TIME: 9 hours
WHEN TO GO: April to September; the road is blocked at other times
PLANNING: A 4WD is recommended; book places to stay in advance. www.gibbriverroad.net

From Kununurra, take the Great Northern Highway through pretty scrubland west for 25 miles (40 km) to the marked turnoff toward Wyndham. Head north for a couple of miles, before turning left onto the Gibb River Road. The road's first 150 miles (240 km) are the roughest stretch, with several potentially treacherous river crossings, but the surrounding countryside is magnificent. Fifteen miles (24 km) west from the road's start is the turnoff for El Questro Station, a working cattle station that can arrange fishing trips, horseback riding, and wildlife and rock art drives. Your next refueling stop will be Mount Barnett Roadhouse, 209 miles away (337 km), while there are other places to stay at Imintji Wilderness Camp, near the turnoff to pretty and popular Bell Creek Gorge, and farther on at the Mount Hart Wilderness Lodge. West of Mount Barnett Roadhouse, you enter the dramatic King Leopold Ranges. For supplies and accommodations, turn off 40 miles (64 km) past Mount Barnett Roadhouse and head 40 miles (64 km) north to Beverly Springs, or continue another 40 miles (64 km) along the road before turning onto a rough bushtrack for 30 miles (48 km) to Mount Hart Homestead. A turnoff goes 20 miles (32 km) to the spectacular Windjana Gorge National Park and, farther on, to Tunnel Creek National Park, one of the oldest cave systems in western Australia and home to Aboriginal rock paintings. Over the ages, the Lennard River cut its way though the rock here to form the gorges, and at Tunnel Creek you can wade through the tunnel to see flying foxes. The last 40 miles (64 km) of the Gibb River Road into Derby are paved.

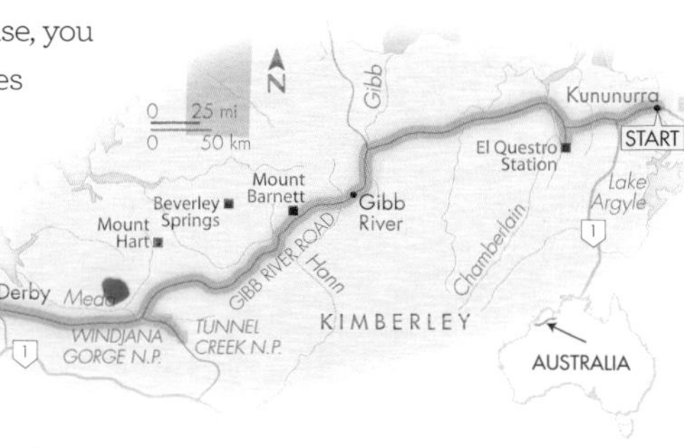

AUSTRALIA

Across Australia's Outback

Follow in the footsteps of explorer John McDouall Stuart through the desolate saltbush country of Australia's deserts, across the Red Centre to Alice Springs and on through the peaceful archipelago of outback settlements in the north.

Visitors explore the varied merchandise in a gift shop in Coober Pedy.

Highlights

- The opal-mining town of **Coober Pedy** stands in a weirdly desolate desert landscape. There is plenty to see, including the underground housing, which most residents favor to escape the high daytime temperatures of the region.

- **Alice Springs** is an oasis town in the heart of the dramatic MacDonnell Ranges in Australia's Red Centre. It is the hub of many outback attractions, with scenic hiking trails nearby. If you want to go to Adelaide without driving, load the car onto the Ghan train and ride back from here.

Leave Port Augusta on the two-lane Stuart Highway, driving north to the scruffy town of Pimba, with Lake Gardner National Park, a vast saltpan, sprawling off to your left. You're likely to be alone with the big blue sky and your thoughts as you approach the convenient night stop of Coober Pedy (see Highlights), keeping an eye out for scores of kangaroos on the road at dusk. Head north in the morning, passing by Cadney Homestead roadhouse and the tiny hamlet of Marla (the hottest place in Southern Australia), and through the desert to Alice Springs (see Highlights). On the remaining 950 miles (1,529 km) to Darwin, you'll roll north across the lonely, reddish, stony immensity of the Northern Territory outback, past the hamlet of Ti Tree, Central Mount Stuart Historical Reserve, and Devil's Marbles Conservation Reserve, where you can camp and walk amid the eerily rounded boulders—the eggs of the Rainbow Serpent, according to Aborigine lore.

Keep going through Tennant Creek, once home to a lonely telegraph station (now open to visitors) and the site of a 1930s gold rush, and past the tiny settlement of Renner Springs, where the dry desert climate of Australia's center yields to the tropical north. Although scrubby, the bush becomes greener and taller from here on. The small town of Daly Waters was once a vital refueling stop for pioneering aviators, and you should visit the Daly Waters Pub (where early Qantas passengers en route to Singapore received their meals) for good food and a chance to admire early aviation memorabilia. Larrimah, a major military post in World War II, was once the terminus of the North Australia Railway. Head north, passing through Mataranka, which has thermal springs and a pocket of rain forest, and Katherine—a large town famous for nearby Nitmiluk National Park and its beautiful 13-gorge river system, popular with kayakers. The last 200 miles (320 km) crosses rolling bushland. At the old goldmining town of Pine Creek, a paved road leads into the heart of the Kakadu National Park. Turnoffs lead to Douglas Hot Springs, the beautiful Robin Falls, and the pretty gorges of Daly River Nature Reserve, which is an ideal camping spot. Housing becomes more frequent and suddenly you are at the end of the line: Darwin's palm-ringed esplanade and the coast at King Sound beckon.

OPPOSITE: The granite boulders known as the Devil's Marbles (Karlu Karlu) are sacred to the Aborigines.

FROM: Port Augusta, Australia
TO: Darwin, Australia
ROAD: Stuart Highway
DISTANCE: 1,700 miles (2,735 km)
DRIVING TIME: 7 days
WHEN TO GO: Year-round
PLANNING: Take basic spares and extra water for yourself and the car. If you head into the bush, you'll need a 4WD, and get local advice. www.exploringaustralia.com.au

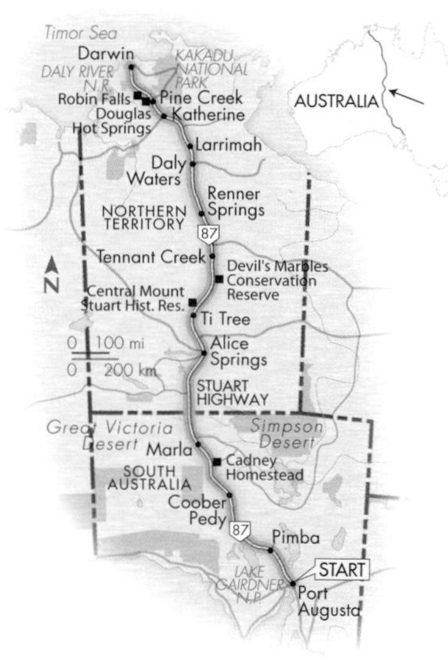

THE TOP

10 Wilderness Drives

Military-style planning is essential for this pick of the world's most challenging, but rewarding, 4WD wilderness odysseys.

1 Wilderness Road Heritage Highway, Kentucky

A drive from Middlesboro to Berea, through Cumberland Gap, an 800-foot (244 m) break in the Pine Mountains, offers heady Appalachian views, complete with pine-clad mountains, elk, and remarkable geological formations.

PLANNING: The road spans 94 miles (151 km). Summer and fall are the best times to visit. *www.byways.org, www.kentuckytourism.com*

2 French Line, Simpson Desert, Australia

Running east-northeast from Dalhousie Springs to Birdsville, the 271-mile (437 km) French Line was built through the world's longest parallel dunes, with around 1,200 red sandy crests to negotiate, most notably the 130-foot (40 m) high Big Red (or Nappanerica).

PLANNING: Dalhousie has a campground and Birdsville a hotel—expect little else between. Entry permits are necessary. The desert closes November through February. *www.southaustralia.com*

3 Outback Way, Australia

One of Australia's great 4WD adventures, this 1,686-mile (2,713 km) road leads from Laverton, Western Australia, to Winton, Queensland, and passes Uluru (Ayers Rock), Kata Tjuta (the Olgas), Alice Springs, central Australian deserts, and Aboriginal territories.

PLANNING: The best conditions are April through October. Entering Aboriginal territories requires a permit. *www.outbackway.org.au*

4 Ulaanbaatar-Elsen Tasarkhan-Karakorum, Mongolia

Drive through the steppes of the Gobi from Mongolia's capital to Karakorum, Genghis Khan's 13th-century seat, through a curious mix of mountains, forests, and towering sand dunes. On the road, look out for unique natural formations, dinosaur remains, yurts, and wildlife such as Bactrian camels, Asiatic wild asses, and gazelles.

PLANNING: Allow two days. The Naadam festival of wrestling, archery, and horse racing (July 11–13) is a good time to visit Ulaanbaatar. *www.mongoliatourism.gov.mn*

5 Trans-Siberian Highway, Russia/Kazakhstan

This paved Eurasian artery runs for more than 6,835 miles (11,000 km) from St. Petersburg on the Baltic Sea to the Sea of Japan, crossing seemingly endless Siberian taiga. Built atop permafrost, the most challenging stretch is the partly unsurfaced 1,345-mile (2,165 km) long M58, or Amur Highway, between Chita and Khabarovsk.

PLANNING: It's safest to spend the night at truck stops near police stations. Expect much camping—hotels are few and far between. Allow plenty of time for Kazakh and multiple-entry Russian visa applications. *www.kazakhstan-tourist.com*

6 Kerman-Bam, Iran

Driving along this 120-mile (194 km) road between the oasis towns of Kerman, Mahan, and Bam will give you an appreciation of the Persian love of gardens, and the ingenuity of Iran's engineers, who toiled to bring fresh water extraordinary distances. The highway flanks the western edge of the Dasht-e Lut (Desert of Emptiness)—one of the Earth's least hospitable regions. Although seriously damaged in the 2003 earthquake, the wonderful Citadel of Bam is one of the world's largest mud buildings.

PLANNING: It's best to visit March through June, and September through November. U.S. citizens normally go in a group. *www.tourismiran.ir*

Opposite: It's easy to get lost among the high sand dunes of Saudi Arabia's Empty Quarter.

7 Empty Quarter, Saudi Arabia/United Arab Emirates/Oman/Yemen

Crossing ill-defined frontiers, the world's largest sand sea is the ultimate driving challenge. Among the perils are abrasive winds, extremely low humidity, temperatures more than 122°F (50°C), and dunes the size of small mountains.

PLANNING: This is only for the hardiest of drivers. Saudi Arabian visas are difficult to obtain. *www.sauditourism.com.sa*

8 Ring Road, Iceland

An 832-mile (1,339 km) highway around the rim of Iceland showcases extraordinary natural phenomena, including sulfur pits, hot springs, icebergs, icecaps, and laval outcrops. You'll find lots of evidence of human habitation on the way: sheep-dotted farmlands, fish smokeries, and gaily colored houses and churches.

PLANNING: Visit in summer as icy roads are a winter hazard. The road is narrow and much of it is unpaved. *www.visiticeland.com*

9 Addis Ababa-Jinka, Ethiopia

This challenging 474-mile (762 km) road through the Omo Valley crosses some of Ethiopia's most isolated ethnographic areas. Tribes include the Mursis, known for terracotta dishes embedded in the women's lower lips; the Dorze, who inhabit beehive-shaped bamboo houses; and the Gurage, who live in thatched-roof villages.

PLANNING: The road leads southwest from Addis Ababa to the town of Jinka, near the Kenyan border, via Debre Zeyit, Hawassa, and Arba Minch. *www.tourismethiopia.org*

10 Skeleton Coast Road, Namibia

This gravel road passes through desolate wilderness with plenty of scenic drama. While they initially appear barren, the variously colored sand dunes support a variety of life, including plant-like lichen, gemsbok, jackals, zebra, springboks, ostrich, and even lions, while whales and dolphins may be spotted offshore.

PLANNING: The coastal road (C34) starts at the town of Swakopmund, 225 miles (362 km) west from Windhoek by national highway, and follows the coast up to the Ugab River. *www.skeletoncoastsafaris.com*

UZBEKISTAN

The Silk Road

For more than 2,000 years, trade routes ran across Asia, connecting China to the Mediterranean. Precious goods were transported by caravans of camels, horses, and mules, and with them came new religions and fresh ideas.

Turquoise domes top the minarets of Bukhara's early 19th-century Chor Minor (Four Minarets) Madrassa.

The length of the storied Silk Road falls between China and the Mediterranean. The Silk Road was never actually just one road but several, each of which followed a different path across a forbidding terrain of high mountains and deserts, where travelers had to take refuge from ferocious weather and bandits in a series of trading centers. Some of these became powerful and wealthy, and turned into centers of art, craftsmanship, learning, and faith. This was nowhere more true than in Uzbekistan, where three fabled cities—Samarqand, Bukhara, and Khiwa—flourished in the golden age of Islamic architecture. The route also evokes the memory of the great conqueror Timur (1336–1405), better known as Tamerlane—heir to the marauding Mongols, ancestor of the powerful Mughals of India.

Begin in Tashkent, Uzbekistan's capital—a brash, modern city rebuilt since a 1966 earthquake, but still containing an atmospheric old town and interesting monuments and museums. These include the Khazret Imam complex of mosques and madrassas (religious schools), which date from the 16th century; the History Museum of the People of Uzbekistan; and the Museum of Applied Arts, introducing the region's crafts and architecture.

The M-39 heads southwest for 180 miles (290 km) to Samarqand, passing through farmland. The stately dignity of Samarqand is reflected in its famous central square, the Registan (see Highlights), described in 1889 by British statesman Lord Curzon as "the noblest public square in the world." Samarqand contains Tamerlane's burial place at the Guri Emir mausoleum, adorned by a ribbed, blue-tiled dome and tiled minaret. Among the other attractions are the huge Bibi Khanum mosque, the Shakhi-Zinda complex of mausoleums, noted for glittering tile decorations; the Afrosiab, site of a ruined pre-Islamic city, with a museum; and the remains of the extraordinary Observatory of Ulugbek.

> "Bukhara is a maze of dusky mosques, teahouses, and bazaars; its mesmerizing sand tones and amorphous shapes lend an organic feel, as if the city rose from the desert of its own accord."
>
> -SHERMAKAYE BASS
> NATIONAL GEOGRAPHIC WRITER

From Samarqand, the M-37 heads west for 175 miles (282 km) through wooded hills and pasture to Bukhara, nicknamed "The Divine" because of its many 15th- and 16th-century mosques and madrassas. The 1514 Kalon mosque is the most impressive of these for scale alone: it has a 157-foot (48 m) high minaret. Lyabi-kauz Square, at the heart of the old center, has two 16th-century madrassas and a mosque. The old citadel, where the emirs lived, now contains a museum.

The A-380 follows the course of the Amu Darya (Oxus River), taking you northwest to the regional center, Urganch,

History of the Silk Road

For more than 3,000 years, traders, soldiers, pilgrims, and missionaries crossed the heart of Asia on the silk trails, transporting luxury goods and new ideas from east to west. The route, extending 4,000 miles (6,437 km) from China to the Mediterranean, was integral in developing the great civilizations of China, India, Persia, and Rome, and takes its name from the much-coveted Chinese silks that stimulated trade between the far-flung nations. The road's most famous traveler was Marco Polo, a Venetian whose epic 24-year journey inspired his fellow Europeans to explore the world, including Christopher Columbus, who owned a copy of *The Travels of Marco Polo*.

and then to Khiwa. Only toward the end of this 390-mile (628 km) stretch from Bukhara to Khiwa does the landscape soften from hilly desert and scrub to farmland, with shady trees and mud-brick farms. Most buildings in Khiwa date from the 19th century, although many stand on the sites of more ancient structures. The city's impressive brick walls were built in the 17th century on foundations laid some 700 years earlier. The rectangular Ichon-Qala (old town) contains the Kuhna Ark (fortress), where architectural beauty provided an incongruous setting for the tyrannical rule of the khans of Khiwa. The mosques, minarets, and madrassas in the Ichon-Qala include the Juma mosque, which has ranks of 212 carved wooden pillars, some of which date back a thousand years. Outside the old town, the Tash Chauli (see Highlights) is the large and intriguing 19th-century palace of the khans; the beautiful harem, throne room, and courtyards are evidence of their immense power.

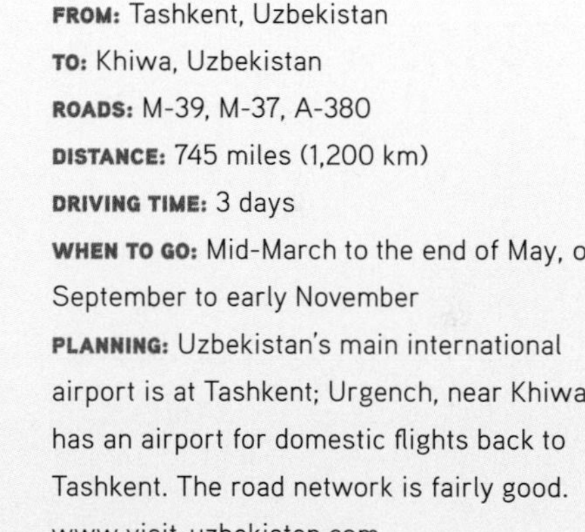

FROM: Tashkent, Uzbekistan
TO: Khiwa, Uzbekistan
ROADS: M-39, M-37, A-380
DISTANCE: 745 miles (1,200 km)
DRIVING TIME: 3 days
WHEN TO GO: Mid-March to the end of May, or September to early November
PLANNING: Uzbekistan's main international airport is at Tashkent; Urgench, near Khiwa, has an airport for domestic flights back to Tashkent. The road network is fairly good. www.visit-uzbekistan.com

Highlights

- Samarqand's **Registan** is surrounded on three sides by the towering, tile-decorated arches, domes, and minarets of madrassahs dating from the 15th to the 17th century.
- Khiwa's **Tash Chauli** palace of the khans contains exquisite harem quarters, famed for being some of Central Asia's finest secular architecture.
- Also at Khiwa, the 18th-century **Pahlavan Mahmud Mausoleum,** dedicated to a revered ancient wrestler, doctor, and poet, has a tiled interior of extraordinary opulence.

Uzbek sheep herders tend their flock in Navoiy.

ITALY

Umbria's Rural Heartlands

The lesser-known hill towns between the cities of Assisi and Spoleto in central Italy are the highlights of this bucolic drive off Umbria's beaten path. Attractions include wonderful medieval buildings, while the views from Monte Subásio are not to be missed.

Glorious 15th-century frescoes by Pinturicchio adorn the walls of Santa Maria Maggiore in Spello.

Head east from Assisi to the Eremo delle Carceri (see Highlights), and turn left just beyond the monastery to follow the Subásio road as it climbs through the woods to the open slopes of Monte Subásio. The road is mostly gravel, but generally sound, and reaches 4,232 feet (1,290 m) with unforgettable views. Park by the road and stroll the mountain's grassy meadows, then descend to Spello (see Stay a While), where you should park and explore the medieval center on foot. Most sites, such as the Roman gateway, are ranged along the town's main street. From here, take the SS75 toward Foligno, leaving it at the first major junction and following signs to Bevagna on the SS316. The town is a rural backwater with a stunning medieval square, where two beautiful 12th-century churches face each other. Also visit the remains of a Roman temple and amphitheater, as well as the local history museum. A scenic road leads from Bevagna to the hilltop wine town of Montefalco (see Highlights), which offers vast views of the Vale of Spoleto. To leave the town, head south and turn left at the intersection just beyond San Fortunato and follow signs up to the village of Trevi, which soon appears before you on a spectacular pyramidal hill. The highlights here include the sleek Pinacoteca Comunale, featuring magnificent Umbrian paintings, and an olive oil museum. Return to the valley and turn south on the SS3 toward Spoleto. South of Trevi, stop off at the Tempio del Clitunno, an eighth-century church, and the limpid pools and springs of Fonti del Clitunno, renowned since classical times. From the Fonti, continue south 7 miles (11 km) on the SS3 to Spoleto, one of central Italy's most charming towns, replete with Romanesque churches.

Stay a While There are some wonderful sites in **Spello.** Don't miss Santa Maria Maggiore and the famous fresco cycle showing the Life of the Virgin by Pinturicchio, one of Umbria's leading Renaissance artists. For more superb art, visit the Pinacoteca Civica, which showcases the town's religious and artistic history. Walk up to the Arco Romano for its excellent views of the old Roman amphitheater, which is unfortunately closed to the public, and visit Villa Fidelia for its furniture, costumes, and sculpture. If you have time, climb to the top of the town for some superb views.

OPPOSITE: Enjoy dramatic views from the medieval bridge and aqueduct of Ponte delle Torri in Spoleto.

Highlights

- The medieval Franciscan monastery of **Eremo delle Carceri,** just south of Assisi, was the first home of St. Francis and his followers. You can see the small cave where Italy's patron saint prayed; the surrounding woods have plenty of tranquil trails to explore.

- **Montefalco** has splendid frescoes—visit the superb gallery in the former church of San Francesco, which has a marvelous cycle by Benozzo Gozzoli. Also worth seeing are the churches of Sant'Agostino (Via Umberto 1), Sant'Illuminata (Via Verdi), and San Fortunato (just south of town).

FROM: Assisi, Italy
TO: Spoleto, Italy
ROADS: Local roads, SS75, SS316, SS3
DISTANCE: 53 miles (86 km)
DRIVING TIME: 2 hours
WHEN TO GO: Year-round
PLANNING: www.aboutumbria.com

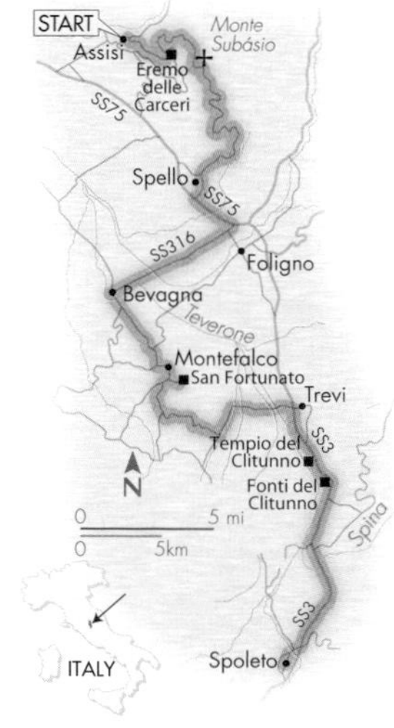

ROMANIA

The Calm of Cerna Valley

Wind your way through the impressive mountains and breathtaking scenery of western Romania for an adventurous rural excursion with a strong artistic flavor and some picturesque country towns.

Târgu Jiu's most famous son, legendary artist Constantin Brâncuși, whose emphasis on revealing the essence of his subjects led him to become the father of modern sculpture. The town is closely associated with the artist, and the World War I memorials here are some of his most poignant works. Head west on the DN67D through gentle farmland to the village of Peștișani. Turn left on a local road to Hobița and visit Brâncuși's well-preserved childhood home—Timber House, now a small museum. Return to Peștișani and continue west, with the grand Cerna Mountains rising to the northwest, then turn right onto a road signposted for Tismana. Drive through the hillside town until you reach the 14th-century monastery of Mănăstirea Tismana and enjoy the stunning mountain scenery. Return to the main road and head west through the pretty wooded tablelands of Plaiul Cloșani to Baia de Aramă, one of the most charming country towns in Romania. Back on the DN67D, continue west, passing through the villages of Brebina, Titerlești, and Mărășești. The highway then climbs steeply to a 3,150-foot (1,050 m) pass, making a series of tight, serpentine loops through bucolic countryside strewn with houses, orchards, hayfields, and more small villages, with tall ridges rising to the northwest. At the pass, leave your car and take a trail west through beech woods and meadows to the Mehedinți Plateau, which is ringed with spectacular karstic outcroppings dotted with isolated black pines. Return to the road and head on to the Valea Cernei (Cerna Valley) beyond the pass, where brown bear and lynx live relatively undisturbed. Drive south along the Cerna River to the Roman spa town of Băile Herculane.

Excursion From Baia de Aramă, to get to **Ponoarele** and the forest reserve of Ponoare Lilac, turn left onto a country road that makes a sharp, right-hand bend. A little farther on is a massive natural stone bridge known as God's Bridge—so-called because several cars have slipped off the road here, but no one has yet died. South, between the bridge and Lake Zaton, is an impressive field of calcareous rocks.

FROM: Târgu Jiu, Romania
TO: Băile Herculane, Romania
ROADS: DN67D, country roads
DISTANCE: 70 miles (113 km)
DRIVING TIME: 2.5 hours
WHEN TO GO: Spring through fall; the DN67D is closed when there is heavy snowfall in winter.
PLANNING: Be prepared for rough, potholed road surfaces in places.
www.romaniatourism.com

N
Mănăstirea Tismana
Tismana
DN67D
Peștișani
Hobița
Târgu Jiu
timber house
START
Valea Cernei (Cerna Valley)
Obârșia-Cloșani
Titerlești
DN67D
Brebina
Mărășești
Baia de Aramă
Baia de Aramă
DN67D
Mehedinți Plateau
0 5 mi
0 5 km
Băile Herculane
ROMANIA

Rocky outcrops rise from the surrounding greenness of the Cerna Mountains near Băile Herculane.

Dusk is a wonderful time to explore Anghiari's medieval hilltop streets.

ITALY

Hidden Tuscany

Although southern Tuscany attracts a multitude of visitors, too few spend time in the outstanding countryside around Arezzo. With its wild hills, high mountains, remote abbeys, and ancient forests, this region is a delight to explore.

From Arezzo's delightful medieval heart, take the SS71 north to Ponte alla Chiassa and turn right, following signs to Chiassa and Anghiari. Just before Anghiari, take a minor road to the ninth-century Romanesque church of Pieve di Sovara. Return to Anghiari to explore its medieval center and the art at the Museo di Palazzo Taglieschi, before taking the only road north to the pretty, hilltop village of Caprese Michelangelo. The famous artist was born here, and his former home is now a modest museum. From here, take the mountain road northwest through Chiusi della Verna to the junction with the SS208. Follow signs to La Verna, one of Italy's most important Franciscan sanctuaries, where St. Francis of Assisi is said to have received the stigmata. There is a hiking trail to the top of Monte Penna offering fantastic views of the Arno Valley. Return to the SS208 and turn right for Bibbiena, 16 miles (26 km) west. Here, pick up the SS71, then the SS70, and head north to Poppi and the medieval fortress of Palazzo dei Conti Guidi and the 12th-century church of San Fedele. Leave Poppi the way you came, and turn left toward Camaldoli and another monastery (the Eremo) in the heart of the Parco Nazionale delle Foreste Casentinesi. The park has some of the region's most scenic mountains and forests, with many walks starting at Camaldoli. From near the monastery, take the only road west to Pratovecchio, and follow the minor road, signed to Firenze, a short distance to see San Pietro di Romena, a beautiful eighth-century church in an idyllic setting. A road from here leads to the magnificent views of the Castello di Romena. Return to Pratovecchio and drive the 28 miles (46 km) to Arezzo via the SS310/SS70/SS71.

FROM: Loop route from Arezzo, Italy
ROADS: SS71, minor roads, SS208, SS70, SS310
DISTANCE: 130 miles (208 km)
DRIVING TIME: 4.5 hours
WHEN TO GO: Year-round
PLANNING: Bring boots for hiking. www.discovertuscany.com

WY251

ENGLAND

Moors and More

This drive through the North York Moors National Park, in northern England, features stark but beautiful moorland, lonely green hills, and spectacular coastal cliffs, with gentle rolling pastures and plenty of pretty villages perfect for stopping off for a cup of tea.

The ancient Gothic arches of Rievaulx Abbey rise majestically from a terrace on the side of a tranquil valley.

Start at Pickering, a compact market town whose parish church of St. Peter and St. Paul contains interesting 15th-century frescoes. From here, you can enjoy a ride on the renovated steam trains of the fabulous North Yorkshire Moors Railways, through beautiful moor countryside. Take the A170 east from Pickering to Thornton-le-Dale, then turn left onto a side road to reach the Dalby Forest Drive, which winds for 9 scenic miles (14.5 km) through the moors and emerges at Hackness. Continue east to Scarborough, Yorkshire's premier seaside resort, sitting on a rocky promontory and with plenty of cafés, amusement arcades, theaters, and other attractions. The ruins of an 11th-century castle divides the town into the quiet North Bay and the more touristy South Bay.

The A165 leads north to Cloughton, where the coast road switchbacks to Staintondale and Ravenscar. From Ravenscar, you can enjoy a pretty walk on the abandoned railroad track or along the cliff-top path. Take the A171 north, and turn right down the steep B1447 to Robin Hood's Bay, a fishing village that was once a smuggling den and is now full of characterful pubs and cafés. The B1447 continues to Whitby (see Highlights), the setting for much of Bram Stoker's *Dracula*. From here, take the A174 north to the cliff village of Staithes, where the young Captain James Cook served as a grocer's assistant. Continue on the A174 to Easington, then turn onto the A171. A short drive later, turn left on minor roads through the idyllic villages of Danby, Castleton, and Westerdale. Farther south, pass Ralph Cross, where medieval travelers left coins "for those less fortunate;" bear left past White Cross (also known as Fat Betty) to the quaint village of Rosedale Abbey. From here, take side roads to Hutton-le-Hole, which has some restored local buildings at the Ryedale Folk Museum. Two miles (3 km) east is Lastingham, where the crypt of St. Mary's Church is believed to shelter the burial place of the seventh-century St. Cedd. From Hutton-le-Hole, take the A170 and turn right for the market town of Helmsley and nearby Duncombe Park (see Highlights) and the spectacular abbeys of Byland and Rievaulx (see Highlights). Return to Pickering via the A170.

OPPOSITE: Fishing boats lie moored in Roxby (or Staithes) Beck, which reaches the North Sea at Staithes.

Highlights

- The seaside town of **Whitby** is charm encapsulated, with fantastic 13th-century abbey ruins on the cliff, the Norman church of St. Mary, and the Captain Cook Memorial Museum.
- Finely restored **Duncombe Park**, the North Moors' preeminent stately home, boasts lavish interiors (open April–October) and lovely gardens.
- Owing to the difficult natural terrain, **Rievaulx Abbey**—a Cistercian foundation built in 1123—was designed to face north-south rather than the traditional east-west.

FROM: Loop drive from Pickering, England
ROADS: A170, Dalby Forest Drive, A165, A171, B1447, A174, minor roads
DISTANCE: 120 miles (193 km)
DRIVING TIME: 5 hours
WHEN TO GO: Spring through fall
PLANNING: Making a few overnight stops will help you get the most out of this national park.
www.moors.uk.net

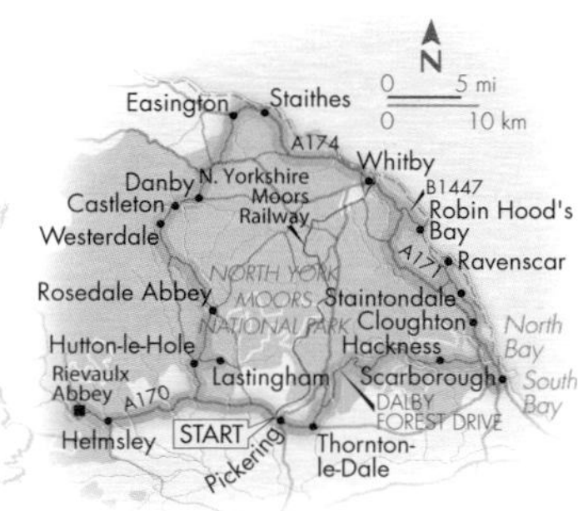

The beautiful rock colors of the Gorges du Tarn stand out against the verdant background of a tree-filled valley.

FRANCE

Gorges du Tarn

The Tarn and Jonte Rivers have cut through a limestone plateau in southern France, creating spectacular canyons and gorges, at times hundreds of feet deep. Considered one of France's most scenic spots, the area is also home to some wonderful medieval villages.

The old tanning town of Millau makes a good touring base for the plunging Gorges du Tarn, whose colored cliffs change subtly with the light. From Millau, follow the Tarn River north and east, on the N9-E11 and D907. Near Les Vignes, about halfway along the canyon, zigzag up the D995 and then take the D46 to the aptly named Point Sublime, with a terrific view of the gorge and river below. The gorge narrows dramatically at the spectacular channel of Les Détroits, before reaching La Malène, a pretty little village that is the main crossing point of the canyon, and is a good place to take a boat trip downriver. Farther on, the 15th-century Château de la Caze has an excellent restaurant. Enjoy the beautiful village of Ste.-Énimie, with its many old limestone buildings, and then continue to the town of Florac—south and east along the D907 and N106—with a 17th-century castle at its center. From here, head south along the D907 into the verdant mountains and wide-open spaces of Parc National des Cévennes, one of the most picturesque parks in France. Follow the D983, D9, and D260 along the stunning Corniche des Cévennes for 31 miles (50 km) to St.-Jean-du-Gard. Originally cut in the early 18th century, the Corniche des Cévennes offers superb views of green valleys and hills: perfect hiking and cycling country. St.-Jean-du-Gard has a good museum of local life, the Musée des Vallées Cévenoles (95 Grand Rue). Take the D907/996 and head west to Meyrueis. The Abîme de Bramabiau, southeast of Meyrueis, off the D986, is an abyss with an underground river. Northwest of the town lie the splendid Gorges de la Jonte and two famous caves—Aven Armand, a vast grotto full of colored stalactites, and the Grotte de Dargilan. Continue on the D996, D907, and N9-E11 to return to Millau, where the stunning Millau Viaduct, the world's highest bridge, designed by British architect Norman Foster and French engineer Michel Virlogeux, spans the valley of the River Tarn.

FROM: Loop route from Millau, France

ROADS: N9-E11, D907, D995, D46, D907, N106, D983, D9, D260, D986, D996

DISTANCE: 60 miles (90 km)

DRIVING TIME: 3 hours

WHEN TO GO: Go out of season (avoid summer) to miss the crowds.

PLANNING: www.gorgesdutarn.net

TANZANIA

Serengeti Safari

The incredible Serengeti in northern Tanzania covers 11,583 square miles (30,000 km²), and has the world's largest overland migration, when two million animals travel south to follow the rains.

Fetch your 4WD in Arusha and head west along Tanzania national route A104, flanked by maize fields and open grasslands where Masai herders graze their cattle. Reaching the town of Makuyuni, turn right onto the B144 (toward Oldeani). The entrance to Lake Manyara National Park, worth a detour for its flamingo population, is just ahead on the left. From Manyara, the B144 snakes up the Great Rift escarpment into the high plateau country. The route runs through a forest of baobab trees—their trunks as thick as a locomotive—and farmland. At Oldeani, the highway jags northward and begins a slow ascent up the lush southern slope of Ngorongoro Crater (about 38 miles/60 km from Manyara). Your first view of the massive crater interior comes at 7,500-foot (2,286 m) Hero's Point. Lodges and restaurants are scattered along the crater's southern rim. From here, the highway plunges down toward the Serengeti. The contrast with the crater's southern slopes could not be more dramatic—rather than thick green bush the countryside morphs into brown semi-desert. About 40 minutes along, the roadway tumbles into Olduvai Gorge, where in 1931, British anthropologists Louis and Mary Leakey discovered a series of human remains dating back more than two million years. An archaeological museum on the site celebrates their achievement. An hour west of Olduvai comes Naabi Gate, the eastern entrance to the Serengeti National Park (see Wildlife Encounter). All around are the short grass plains, where massive herds of zebra and wildebeest roam from December to May. Otherwise, it's another hour to Seronera in the heart of the park, home to numerous lodges and campgrounds, and some of the best game viewing.

FROM: Arusha, Tanzania
TO: Seronera, Tanzania
ROADS: Tanzania A104, B144
DISTANCE: 187 miles (302 km)
DRIVING TIME: 4.5 hours
WHEN TO GO: January through February and June through October
PLANNING: Book places to stay well in advance. www.madeintanzaniasafaris.com

Wildlife Encounter After checking into **Serengeti National Park** at Naabi Gate, veer south across the golden plains, heading for an isolated rock outcrop called the Moru Kopjes. Here, you have the chance to see vast herds of wildebeest and zebra in columns that stretch a mile (1.6 km) or more. At night, you may hear the far-off wail of a spotted hyena, the hiss of a leopard, and the persistent growls of a lion pride—deep, sonorous grunts that send chills down your spine.

On the flat floor of Ngorongoro Crater, herds of wildebeest and zebra pay scant attention to a tourist vehicle.

AFRICA

Cairo to Cape Town

This drive down the length of the continent reveals the extremes of Africa, from the fabled splendors of Egypt, to grasslands and mountain landscapes, rivers and lakes, through busy towns and empty deserts, eventually arriving in rambling, multicultural Cape Town.

Masai tribesmen drive donkeys across parched grassland in Tanzania.

This epic journey traverses ten countries: Egypt, Sudan, Ethiopia, Kenya, Tanzania, Malawi, Zambia, Botswana, Namibia, and South Africa. And where else to start it than the pyramids of Giza outside Cairo? Feast your spirit on their ancient majesty before hitting the road south to Luxor, stopping off to sleep under the stars in the White Desert on the way. Near Luxor, another world-famous sight is the tomb of the boy pharaoh, Tutankhamun, in the Valley of the Kings (see Highlights). Follow the great artery of the Nile south to Aswân, where you board a ferry for an 18-hour trip along Lake Nasser to Wadi Halfa in Sudan. Visit the ninth-century B.C. Meroe pyramids, then go southwest to the Sudanese capital, Khartoum, whose delights include freshly squeezed fruit juices and tea on sale at street corners. Cross into Ethiopia and visit the ancient cities of Axum and Lalibela. In the capital, Addis Ababa, drink steaming coffee and admire the exquisite local jewelry. Making your way ever southward, cross into Kenya, traversing lands occupied by nomadic Samburu tribespeople and eventually reaching paved roads, with Mount Kenya looming in the distance.

From the Kenyan capital, Nairobi, head on to Tanzania, passing Masai men herding livestock and Masai women selling crafts at the border town of Namanga. Arusha in northern Tanzania is the starting point for trips to Serengeti National Park and Mount Kilimanjaro. Continue to the capital, Dar Es Salam, and take a ferry to the fabled "spice island" of Zanzibar (see Highlights). Back on the mainland, drive to Iringa for Ruaha National Park, then continue across the Malawi border. Pause a while on the shores of Lake Malawi at the campground and lodge at Chitimba, from where you can try your hand at freshwater scuba diving at Nkata Bay. Across the border in Zambia, pass through the capital, Lusaka, on your way to Victoria Falls (see Highlights). Next up is Botswana: Head to Chobe National Park, then Maun, the gateway to the Okavango Delta (see Highlights). In Namibia, visit Etosha National Park and the town of Swakopmund, where you feel the unmistakable influence of its German colonists. In the south, admire the vast Fish River Canyon, then, as you near the end of your journey, cross into South Africa. The road south takes you through farmland and vineyards to Cape Town.

OPPOSITE: Light glints off a gold sacophagus in the tomb of Tutankhamun in the Valley of the Kings.

Highlights

- No trip to Egypt would be complete without a visit to the **Valley of the Kings** at Luxor, the burial place for the pharaohs of the New Kingdom.
- The island of **Zanzibar** off the coast of Tanzania has plenty to offer, including tropical beaches on the Indian Ocean, spice tours, and Arab architecture.
- Sending mist high into the air, the 5,600-foot (1,700 m) wide **Victoria Falls** on the Zambezi River form a natural border between Zambia and Zimbabwe.
- Watch out for hippos, elephants, and buffalo while you take a serene ride in a *mokoro* (dug-out canoe) through the **Okavango Delta** in Botswana.

FROM: Cairo, Egypt
TO: Cape Town, South Africa
DISTANCE: 11,600 miles (18,600 km)
DRIVING TIME: 10 weeks
WHEN TO GO: October through February
PLANNING: Use a 4WD as sections of the drive are off-road. Check with your embassy in advance for areas en route that may be dangerous.
www.africaexpeditionsupport.com

A lioness chastises her cub in Chobe National Park's Savuti area.

BOTSWANA

Discover Okavango Delta

Northern Botswana's Okavango Delta is one of Africa's most beautiful oases. Since the Kalahari Desert is irrigated by the waters of the Okavango River, all manner of wildlife flock there to enjoy the lush greenery of one of the world's largest inland deltas.

Count them one by one, the elephants that surround your Land Rover on the delta's grassy floodplain. They act as if you're not even there, as they graze, trumpet, or toss dirt on their backs. This moment will make all the miles you have logged worthwhile, since embarking on a road trip that skirts the Okavango's eastern edge and ventures into the heart of Chobe National Park. The journey starts by following the airport road north out of the town of Maun. When you reach a large roundabout, veer left onto a tarmac road for Shorobe, 29 miles (47 km) away. Not far beyond is a turnoff on the left for Okavango River Lodge and Crocodile Camp, a base for boat trips through the Okavango wetlands. Beyond Shorobe, the road deteriorates, first into gravel, then into sand and hard-baked dirt that becomes muddy after a shower. Just after the Veterinary Control Fence, you reach a fork marked by a green concrete pillar. Head left toward Moremi Game Reserve, which includes a large part of the delta's eastern side. Cruise the 12 miles (19 km) to the reserve's South Gate. One option here is to head west to Moremi's Third Bridge and Xakanaxa areas, where you are likely to see lions and wild dogs. Otherwise, make a sharp right after the South Gate and drive the arrow-straight road to the lush North Gate/Khwai River area, where the overnight possibilities include campgrounds and lodges. There is enough game around here for several days' viewing. Continue your journey, and exit the village of Khwai along the north side of the river valley. Beyond an aerodrome comes a junction, where you can fork right onto a road that leads up and over the Magwikhwe Sand Ridge to Mababe Gate, the south entrance to the vast Chobe National Park, famous for its 120,000-strong population of elephants. After you have signed in and paid your park fees, continue due north along the main road another 35 miles (57 km) to Savuti, with a collection of half a dozen campgrounds and lodges.

FROM: Maun, Botswana

TO: Savuti, Botswana

ROADS: Local roads

DISTANCE: 137 miles (220 km)

DRIVING TIME: 1 day

WHEN TO GO: May through October

PLANNING: Stock up on gas and water before you leave.

www.okavango-delta.net

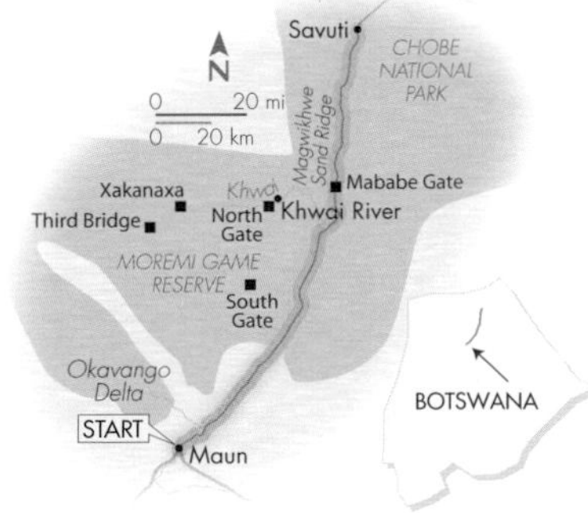

Also Recommended

❶ Drive on Ice, Northwest Territories, Canada

"Drive" may not be the best word for this 360-mile (600 km) frozen freeway—"glide" is more like it. Begin outside the city of Yellowknife, and head north to four remote Arctic diamond mines for a night in a cozy cabin. The Northern Lights will light your way at night, but if you need a break from the lonely Arctic just bring along a trucker radio and chat to the ice road regulars.

www.spectacularnwt.com

❷ Badlands Loop, South Dakota

The views along the Badlands Loop Road (S. Dak. 240 between Pennington and Jackson) take in desolate prairies and harsh geology, with sharply eroded buttes, pinnacles, and spires. Leave the road for a 10-mile (16 km) loop to Roberts Prairie Dog Town to see some wild prairie dogs.

www.badlands.national-park.com

❸ Grand Canyon View Scenic Drive, Arizona

A 25-mile (40 km) stretch of Ariz. 64 runs along the south rim of the Grand Canyon, connecting Grand Canyon Village with the easternmost viewpoints at Desert View. Stop for a steep hike up Grandview Trail, which lives up to its name, or just enjoy the vertigo-inspiring viewpoints along the road.

www.nps.gov/grca

❹ Moapa Valley Drive, Nevada

Nev. 169 leads directly into Valley of Fire State Park, where the sandstone has oxidized into fiery reds and oranges. The flame-colored landscape includes curious shapes, like the tall boulders of the Seven Sisters and the intricately shaped Elephant Rock. Rainbow Vista breaks from the usual red wash—its canyons, domes, towers, and ridges sparkle various colors in the sun.

www.parks.nv.gov/vf.htm

❺ Joshua Tree Journey, California

Drive amid 800,000 acres (323,749 ha) of California desert landscape along Joshua Tree National Park's Park Boulevard, connecting I-10 and Calif. 62. Midway, Queen Valley is a good place to linger and gaze at vast groves of trees. You may also take Geology Tour Road, 18 miles (29 km) of dirt track winding past the park's distinctive natural rock sculptures, rounded by erosion.

www.nps.gov/jotr

❻ Crater Rim Drive, Hawaii

A drive around the rim of Kilauea Volcano brings you up close to the simmering power of earthly creation. Start at Kilauea Visitor Center, where displays explain how the still-active volcano shaped the island. From here, the loop is just 11 miles (18 km), providing opportunities to hike Earthquake Trail to Kilauea Caldera or Devastation Trail, where a rain forest was obliterated by pumice and cinders in 1959.

www.nps.gov/havo

❼ Middle Earth, New Zealand

Fans of *The Lord of the Rings* can follow the small footsteps of Hobbits and set off for Mordor—New Zealand's North Island Volcanic Plateau. Leave from Hamilton in the idyllic Waikato region, and head east for Hobbiton (filmed around Matamata). Farther south is the brooding, tortured terrain of Middle Earth's Emyn Muil and Mount Doom, filmed around Mount Ruapehu. The end of the journey is Wellington, where Peter Jackson based his production.

www.tourism.net.nz

❽ Tropic of Capricorn, Australia

From Bundaberg—the "Gateway to the Great Barrier Reef"—drive 400 miles (644 km) north to Mackay, past lakes, coastal towns, and mountains. For a detour, take a ferry from Rosslyn Bay to reach the beautiful beaches of Great Keppel Island.

www.tourism.australia.com

❾ The Route to the Base of Everest, China/Tibet

Tibet's mystical capital, Lhasa, is an excellent place to adjust to the altitude before your ascent into the Himalayas. From here, take the Friendship Highway south, past isolated monasteries and enchanting villages to Everest's base camp at 17,087 feet (5,208 m).

www.visit-himalaya.com

❿ Central Highlands, Iceland

Folklore has it that supernatural beings await travelers along the interior roads of Iceland's Central Highlands. The current dangers of the Kjölur road (F35) between Haukadalur in the south and Blönduós in the north are flash floods and rough terrain, but let nothing stand in the way of the drive through a wonderland of ice caves and mountains colored black by geothermal forces.

www.icelandtouristboard.com

⓫ DN57B, Romania

Start in Oravița, following the quiet DN57B north through fabulous blooms in spring, and head round to the small mining towns of Steierdorf, via Anina, where Europe's oldest human remains (some 40,000 years old) were found.

www.romaniatourism.com

⓬ Toledo to Cáceres, Spain

Head west from Toledo into Extremadura, the starkly dramatic homeland of many of the *conquistadores*. Having explored Toledo's cathedral, its *alcázar* (castle), and the house of the painter El Greco, follow twisting mountain roads to Guadalupe, whose shrine of Our Lady is one of Spain's holiest pilgrimage sites. Continue west to the astonishing cities of Trujillo and Cáceres, enriched by the gold of the Americas.

www.spain.info

⓭ Parque Nacional da Peneda, Gerês, Portugal

The vistas on this easterly drive on the N203 from Ponte de Lima to Ponte de Barca are uniquely lush and pastoral. There are gorse, pine trees, black sheep, horses, goats, and long-horned *barrosau* cattle.

www.visitportugal.com

⓮ Cairo to Kharga, Egypt

Travel from Cairo between five different oases—Kharga, Dakhla, Farafra, Bahariya, and Siwa—and across the region of forgotten cites, tombs, and mummies. The journey stretches from soft dunes to the famous white desert with its contorted, wind-ravaged, pale ground.

www.egypt.travel

CHAPTER 5

VILLAGE BYWAYS

VILLAGES ARE LITTLE WORLDS WITHIN worlds that seem to lie outside time. Deep in the countryside, they perch precariously on rocky crags, hide themselves away up narrow green lanes, or dream their dreams in the shadows of ancient castles. On maps, their names are marked in the smallest print—if, indeed, they appear at all. But for travelers with a sense of romance, these are destinations worth getting lost for. Small they may be, but they are as varied as the landscapes in which they are set and throb with their own kinds of life. A journey to North Carolina's Outer Banks leads to tiny fishing villages tucked amid high sand dunes and seascapes stretching out to far horizons. The devout farmers and craftsmen of Indiana's Amish country preserve a world of horse-drawn buggies, carpentry workshops, and immaculate farms. Romanian shepherds in southern Transylvania paint their houses in extravagant colors and don costumes handed down through generations, while in the green heart of southern England, a leisurely tour of the Cotswolds reveals villages of honey-colored stone, with church towers and ruined abbeys dotted among gently rolling hills.

The lush green pastureland of Swaledale in England's Yorkshire Dales sweeps to the horizon, its fields threaded by dry-stone walls. The rich grazing here has given rise to some of the region's renowned cheeses.

CANADA

St. John River Valley Drive

Well-kept farms and historic communities of genteel Victorian homes punctuate a beautiful landscape of wooded hills and pastures along the valley of the mighty St. John River. Indulge in a game of croquet in Victorian Fredericton to complete the period feel.

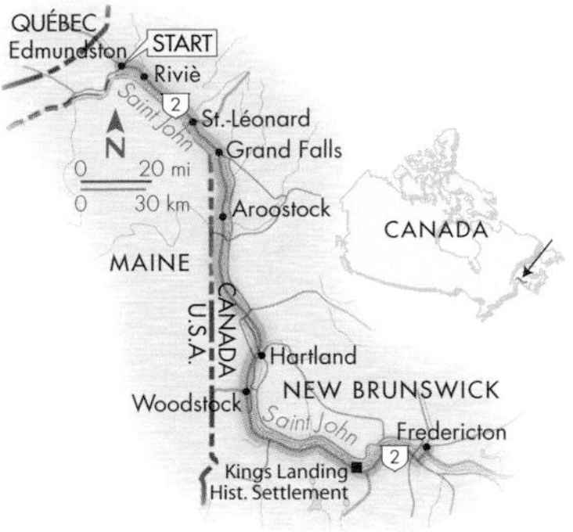

The wooded wilderness of the St. John River Valley basin attracted settlers from France, Britain, and the U.S. from around 1785. Begin in francophone Edmundston with a visit to the reconstructed Fortin du P'tit Sault Blockhouse, just one part of a long line of British defenses in the area. Both powers wanted sovereignty over the area, and you can see why as you follow Trans-Canada 2 south through lush, fertile countryside of forested hills with views of the grand St. John River. Much of the valley's farmland is devoted to potato growing. The river, which now forms the border between Canada and the U.S., changes dramatically at Grand Falls, where it plunges 80 feet (24 m) and rushes along a rocky chasm to a riverbed littered with huge wells worn into the rocks. Continue through pastoral landscapes and the village of Aroostook, once a major railroad junction, and on to the small community of Hartland, where the world's longest covered bridge crosses the river. Pass through Woodstock, the oldest town in New Brunswick and home to many fine Victorian buildings, and continue to Kings Landing Historical Settlement (see Hidden History).

The highway follows the waterway southeast to Fredericton, New Brunswick's riverside capital. The city, built well inland to avoid American incursions, has a strong neocolonial feel with elm-lined streets and regency homes. The British Army's presence is still felt in the Historic Garrison District, now Fredericton's cultural heart with a blend of museums, music, art, and historic re-enactments, including the Changing of the Guard (July and August). The city's fine historic buildings include the Second Empire-style Provincial Legislative Assembly Building and Christ Church Cathedral with its towering spire.

FROM: Edmundston, Canada
TO: Fredericton, Canada
ROAD: Trans-Canada 2
DISTANCE: 170 miles (273 km)
DRIVING TIME: 3.5 hours
WHEN: July and August
PLANNING: Although winters are beautiful, most attractions are open only in July and August. Fall color is best in September and October. www.tourismnewbrunswick.ca

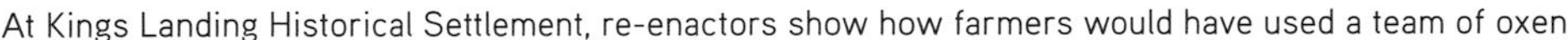

Hidden History A 300-acre (120 ha) living museum, **Kings Landing Historical Settlement** is a carefully re-created New Brunswick town from 1780–1910. Re-enactors tend the fields, meadows, fences, and gardens, and keep alive more than 70 buildings such as a variety of houses, a sawmill, gristmill, forge, store, church, pub, and theater. The costumed re-enactors demonstrate period skills, and they impart a detailed knowledge of life in the area to visitors.

At Kings Landing Historical Settlement, re-enactors show how farmers would have used a team of oxen.

At the heart of the tiny village of Stowe is its classic New England church, completed in 1863.

Highlights

- Beyond Amherst Lake, take Vt. 100A to **President Calvin Coolidge State Historic Site** in tiny Plymouth Notch. You can also tour **Plymouth Cheese Factory,** established by the president's father, the **Cilley General Store,** the post office, several barns displaying farming tools of the era, and the dance hall that served as the Summer White House.
- Just north of Waterbury village, after crossing I-89, you come to **Ben and Jerry's** ice cream factory, where you can take a tour to see gourmet ice creams being made and taste the flavors of the day.
- Just beyond Ben and Jerry's, on the right, is **Cold Hollow Cider Mill,** where you can watch apples being pressed into cider.

VERMONT

Vermont 100

Vermont 100 divides the state of Vermont in two, north to south, paralleling the rugged Green Mountains as it passes through beautiful, peaceful scenery and classic New England villages, with spectacular mountain views all the way.

Travel north along Vt. 100 from the village of Wilmington, past Haystack Mountain and the north branch of the Deerfield River, before climbing to West Dover, one of the loftiest villages in Vermont. Traverse the southern section of Green Mountain National Forest, descending through dense woods to North Wardsboro, a village of small restaurants, general stores, and craft stores. Continuing along the West River Valley and through the village of Jamaica, bear right at Rawsonville. Soon you reach Weston, a classic Vermont village with a bandstand on the green, white steeples, and cradling hills. Drive on through forested hills and the former factory town of Ludlow, passing tranquil, tree-lined Lake Rescue, followed by Echo and Amherst Lakes—strung together by the Black River. The road follows the river as it climbs past Killington Peak, a mecca for skiers, and heads into mountainous terrain along the edge of the northern section of Green Mountain National Forest, to the village of Pittsfield. Skirting pastures and cornfields along the floor of the steep White River Valley, the road passes through Talcville and Rochester, the prettiest town along this stretch. The valley narrows past Granville, and the road enters Granville Gulf Reservation, where summer foliage and jutting escarpments shade the road. At Moss Glen Falls, a series of cascades zigzags through the trees. After Waitsfield, drive past rolling farmland overlooked by the towering Green Mountain range, before crossing the Winooski River at Waterbury (see Highlights). Soon you reach Stowe, a romantic village clustered around a spire-topped church. After Morrisville, the terrain grows wilder as moose and bears abound. Beyond Lowell, the mountains open to broad vistas as you approach Newport.

FROM: Wilmington, Vermont
TO: Newport, Vermont
ROAD: Vt. 100
DISTANCE: 188 miles (303 km)
DRIVING TIME: 5 hours
WHEN: Late spring through mid-fall
PLANNING: www.visit-vermont.com, www.vermontvacation.com

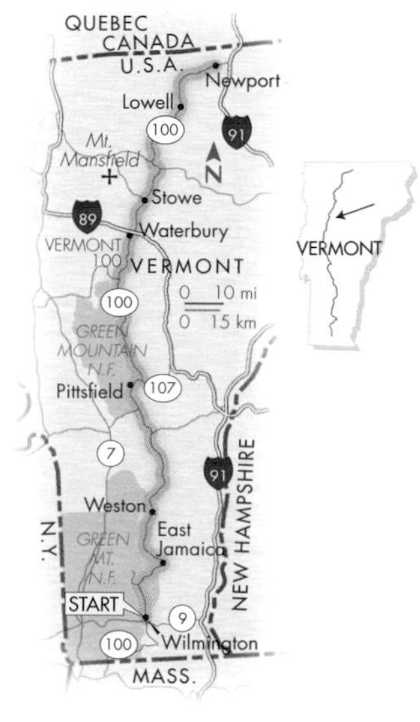

In Kent Falls State Park, a few miles north of Kent, a tributary of the Housatonic River has eroded a beautiful waterfall out of the marble bedrock.

CONNECTICUT

Litchfield Hills

Tucked into Connecticut's northwest corner, just hours from the bustle of New York City, the Litchfield Hills are the epitome of the pastoral New England landscape. This quiet drive meanders through picturesque villages and visits some of the state's finest parks.

The town of Litchfield, southwest of Torrington on U.S. 202, was settled in 1719 and is the picture of an ideal New England community, with a lovely village green surrounded by elm trees and colonial buildings. Continue southwest to the White Memorial Conservation Center, a wildlife sanctuary with 35 miles (56 km) of trails leading through fields, ponds, swamps, and woodlands. At Bantam, take Conn. 209 south along the shores of Bantam Lake, Connecticut's largest natural lake, popular with boaters and anglers. Turn south at the tiny town of Washington to pick up Conn. 199 as it twists its way to the Institute for American Indian Studies, where you can visit an authentically reconstructed Algonquian village. Follow Conn. 199 and 67 west to New Milford to stroll across Connecticut's largest village green and explore the riverside town's historic homes and churches. Continue on U.S. 202 through picturesque New Preston, packed with antiques shops, to the turnoff for Lake Waramaug State Park, where you can swim or picnic at one of Connecticut's loveliest lakes. Looping around the lake, you come to Hopkins Vineyard, where you can take a tour of the winery and enjoy a tasting. New Preston Hill Road rambles west to the covered Bulls Bridge over the Housatonic River. Take U.S. 7 north to reach Kent, and when you have explored its well-preserved old houses, antiques shops, and art galleries, continue north and then turn west on Conn. 4 to the Sharon Audubon Center, dedicated to the conservation of birds and other wildlife, where 11 miles (18 km) of trails wind past ponds, streams, fields, and marshlands. Continue through the town of Sharon on Conn. 41, past Lake Wononskopomuc, and stop off in Salisbury. Go through Canaan on U.S. 44, past the 1872 Union Station, and on through Norfolk, home of Yale School of Music and Art and Infinity Hall, and then on Conn. 8 to return to Torrington.

FROM: Loop route from Torrington, Connecticut

ROADS: U.S. 202, Conn. 209, 109, 199, 67, U.S. 7, Conn. 4, 41, U.S. 44, Conn. 8

DISTANCE: 188 miles (303 km)

DRIVING TIME: 5 hours

WHEN TO GO: Late spring through mid-fall

PLANNING: www.litchfieldhills.com

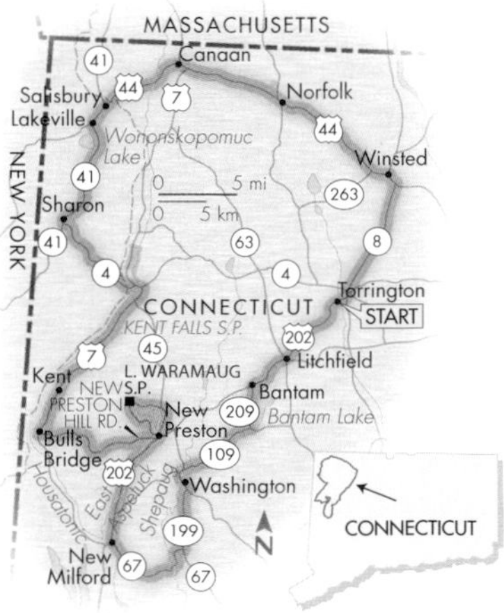

NORTH CAROLINA

Outer Banks Scenic Route

The arc of slim barrier islands, more than 100 miles (160 km) long, that stretches out from the mainland, protecting the coast from the battering Atlantic, includes Cape Hatteras National Seashore and coastal villages where history and beauty share the spotlight.

From the mainland, cross Albemarle Sound on U.S. 158 to reach the Outer Banks, then turn south. The road passes through Kill Devil Hills, where you can see the Wright Brothers National Memorial on the site where they made the world's first powered airplane flight in 1903. A little farther on, Jockey's Ridge State Park boasts the highest living sand-dune system (130 feet/40 m high) on the East Coast—a popular spot for hang gliding. Turn east here down one of the side roads that lead to N.C. 12, which hugs the coastline on its way south. The road passes beach houses at the resort town of Nags Head and then threads its way through Cape Hatteras National Seashore, a 70-mile (113 km) sweep of protected coastline that extends to Ocracoke Inlet. Driving through the grassy marshlands of Bodie Island, you pass more dunes at Coquina Beach, where you can stop to search for seashells, and lonesome Bodie Island Lighthouse on Albemarle Sound.

Cross Oregon Inlet onto Hatteras Island, taking in sweeping views of the Atlantic Ocean to the east and Pamlico Sound to the west as you approach Pea Island National Wildlife Refuge, which attracts more than a million migratory birds in spring and fall. It's also a nesting ground for the threatened loggerhead sea turtle. Pass through the quiet beachside villages of Rodanthe, Waves, and Salvo, with their weathered ocean-front houses, stacks of crabpots, and boats. Traveling south past an endless stretch of dunes and wind-pruned shrubs, you should find a quiet patch of beach. Farther on is Buxton, a mellow resort town popular with anglers and windsurfers, where you can visit the famous Cape Hatteras Lighthouse. The north end of Buxton Woods is here, and offshore you can see the Diamond Shoals, which have caused many ships to run aground. The road winds through the woods to Frisco and on to Hatteras, a unique fishing community and home to the Graveyard of the Atlantic Museum. From Hatteras, take the free ferry to Ocracoke Island and pick up N.C. 12 to Ocracoke. The island's only settlement, this fishing village has sandy, shaded streets and features the second oldest operating lighthouse in the U.S. It is also home to the ghost of Blackbeard, the notorious pirate, who was killed here in 1718.

FROM: Kill Devil Hills, North Carolina
TO: Ocracoke, North Carolina
ROADS: U.S. 158, N.C. 12
DISTANCE: 80 miles (129 km)
DRIVING TIME: 3 hours
WHEN: Spring and fall
PLANNING: During summer, the drive may take longer due to the route's popularity and occasional delays on the ferries. www.outerbanks.org

At 208 feet (63 m) high, Cape Hatteras Lighthouse is America's tallest brick lighthouse.

OAK & CHERRY FURNITURE ♦ 2 FLOORS
Mansfield
6529

INDIANA

Amish Culture and Crafts

This short drive across northern Indiana's Amish country features well-groomed farms and quaint villages, offering a look into a traditional, rural way of life, where religion and community thrive and modern machines are shunned.

An Amish store in Shipshewana sells a colorful array of goods.

If you're touring in an RV or mobile home, you'll be very welcome in the riverside community of Elkhart (see Stay a While), birthplace of automobile touring. From Elkhart, head east on busy U.S. 20. Veer north at Ind. 13, to reach Middlebury, a small town in the heart of Amish country. As you turn right onto East Warren Street (which begins as County Rd. 16, then turns into 250N), you'll immediately notice the difference, with hitching posts for horses outside the county store and shops selling locally made food. Here, barns have gambrel roofs and trim, white-frame houses line the road, horses graze in lush pastures, and corn, rye, oats, and hay grow in well-kept fields. Drive slowly as you're likely to come across horse-drawn buggies.

Three miles (5 km) east of Middlebury, you can stop by Guggisberg Deutsch Käse Hause to watch Colby and Colby Jack cheeses being made. Soon you enter bustling Shipshewana, where shoppers flock to the Midwest's largest flea market and the village's specialty retailers offer handcrafted items and home-style cooking. To learn more about the Amish, turn south at Van Buren Street (Ind. 5) to reach the Menno-Hof Amish/Mennonite Visitor Center (see Highlights). Then turn onto Farver Street (200N) and head east, back into farm country. The road passes Wana Cabinets and Furniture, custom builders of oak furniture. More than half of the area's Amish heads of household work as carpenters and in woodworking. Babers Blacksmith Shop and M&M Harness Shop, a mile (1.6 km) beyond Wana Cabinets, are typical of the local cottage industries. When you reach Ind. 9, turn right into Lagrange, where you can tour the County Courthouse, a marvelous redbrick building dating from 1878.

Stay a While **Elkhart** has a number of interesting museums, including the RV/MH Hall of Fame, with antique vehicles dating from 1913. The **Midwest Museum of American Art's** collection includes artists such as Norman Rockwell, George Luks, and Thomas Sully. The National New York Central Railroad Museum brings the history of the railroad to life with full-sized and toy trains and a collection of memorabilia from stations and railroad cars.

OPPOSITE: Horse-drawn buggies are a common sight in the Amish towns of Indiana.

Highlights

- South of Elkhart, along Ind. 19, is the divine **American Countryside Farmers Market,** housed in and around an Amish-built barn. Come hungry and snack on homegrown fruits, cheeses, pies, and many other tempting treats.

- The Hostetler Hudson Auto Museum in **Shipshewana** has more than 50 classic Hudson cars, race cars, and hot rods.

- The Menno-Hof Amish/Mennonite Visitor Center in **Shipshewana** tells the history of the Anabaptists and how they came to settle in Indiana.

FROM: Elkhart, Indiana
TO: Lagrange, Indiana
ROADS: U.S. 20, Ind. 13, County Rd. 16, 250N, Ind. 5, 200N, Ind. 9
DISTANCE: 28 miles (45 km)
DRIVING TIME: 1 hour
WHEN: Spring through fall
PLANNING: www.amishcountry.org

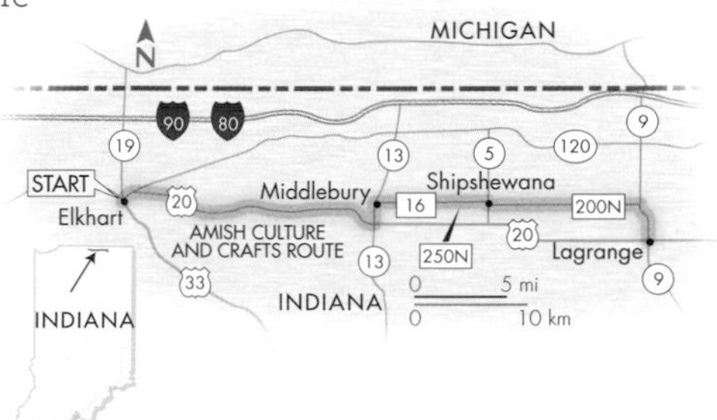

The small house where Lyndon B. Johnson was born is part of the LBJ Ranch near Johnson City.

TEXAS

Texas Hill Country

Rolling hills and plunging gorges are typical of the old-world charm of this area of central Texas. This route combines dramatic sections of road, colorful towns, and great sweeps of open countryside.

West out of Oak Hill, U.S. 290 heads into the hills. The first few miles provide glimpses of the plains as you ascend the Edwards Plateau. The landscape is scattered with limestone rubble, gnarled oaks, and shrubby hills and ridges. Just west of the little hamlet of Henly is a turnoff to the right toward Pedernales Falls State Park, where a glorious waterfall in pretty woodlands cascades over a series of tilted limestone steps. Farther north, on U.S. 290, is Johnson City, home of Lyndon B. Johnson (see Highlights), and Fredericksburg (see Highlights), a town with a 19th-century character and lingering German culture. Well worthwhile is an 18-mile (29 km) detour north on Farm Rd. 965 to Enchanted Rock State Natural Area, home of a 440-foot (134 m) high dome of pink granite, the second highest batholith on the continent. From Fredericksburg, head south on Tex. 16 across fertile country abutting the Pedernales River. Soon the landscape flattens and the road begins to twist and turn, descending to the Guadalupe River Valley. Beyond Kerrville (see Highlights), Tex. 16 sweeps through splendid countryside with exhilarating hairpin bends, grand vistas, craggy mountains, and clear streams, before entering Medina, "apple capital of Texas." Continue through ranchland to Bandera (see Highlights), a town with a real cowboy flavor, then turn left at the intersection with Tex. 46, heading through low hills to Boerne, an antiques hub with German heritage. Continue through rolling hills edged with oak and cedar to New Braunfels, Texas's oldest community.

Highlights

- At **Lyndon B. Johnson National Historical Park,** just west of Johnson City on U.S. 290, the frame house that was LBJ's childhood home has been lovingly re-created, along with the complex where his forefathers first settled. Thirteen miles (21 km) farther on, grazing buffalo mark the **LBJ Ranch,** where Johnson was born, and the one-room school he attended. Nearby, **Lyndon B. Johnson State Park and Historic Site** includes a living history farm and a nature trail with plenty of wildlife.
- The **Admiral Nimitz State Historic Site** and **National Museum of the Pacific War** in Fredericksburg honor the memory of Chester Nimitz, commander-in-chief of the Pacific Fleet during World War II.
- The **Museum of Western Art** at Kerrville focuses on art and artists from the American West.
- Bandera's **Frontier Times Museum** has exhibits on the Old West and on the town's 1852 founding.

FROM: Oak Hill, Texas
TO: New Braunfels, Texas
ROADS: U.S. 290, Farm Rd. 965, Tex. 16, 46
DISTANCE: 280 miles (450 km)
DRIVING TIME: 6 hours
WHEN: Year-round
PLANNING: www.travel.state.tx.us

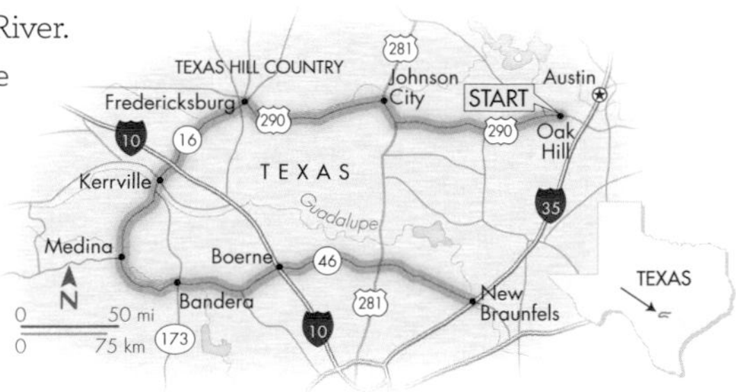

CALIFORNIA

The Gold Rush Trail

Tracing the rolling, river-streaked foothills of the Sierra Nevada, Calif. 49 is named after 1849, the year of the California gold rush, and this drive passes many of the mines and boomtowns that shaped the state's history.

Columbia State Historic Park captures the feel of the gold rush era and is your starting point. Take Parrotts Ferry Road north past Moaning Cavern, a multi-hued limestone cave, which you can descend by a rope or spiral stairwell. Go north on Calif. 4 to reach Angels Camp, a site once rich in gold-bearing quartz, then continue on Calif. 49 to Mokelumne Hill, one of the largest gold rush towns. At Jackson, you find the Kennedy Mine—the deepest mine in the U.S.—and a little farther north lies Sutter Creek, its charming main street lined with classic buildings of the era. Backtrack to Ridge Road, and head east through the oak-studded meadows of Indian Grinding Rock State Historic Park. Onward through the village of Volcano, take Rams Horn Grade, pass Daffodil Hill—resplendent with blooms in early spring—then turn left for the former stagecoach stop of Fiddletown. Return to Calif. 49, heading north to Placerville, where Hangtown's Gold Bug Park & Mine boasts the nation's only city-owned gold mine, and Coloma (see In Focus). Ahead lies well-preserved Auburn, whose Gold Country Museum has a model mine tunnel and a working miniature stamp mill. After another half-hour drive, you can gaze down the main shaft at Empire Mine State Historic Park, where the oldest and richest mine produced 5.8 million ounces (164.4 million gm) of gold. A quick hop along Calif. 49/20 brings Grass Valley's North Star Mining Museum, where the world's largest Pelton wheel extracted gold ore from quartz. The road threads through pine-clad hills to Nevada City, before passing through picturesque Downieville. A mile (1.6 km) beyond Sierra City lies Sierra County Historical Park and Museum at the Kentucky Mine, with exhibits on mining, skiing, logging, and Chinese settlers.

In Focus California gold was first discovered on January 24, 1848, by James Marshall at Coloma, on the land of local celebrity and sawmill-owner John Sutter, who planned to turn the area into agricultural land. Soon hordes of gold diggers swamped the area, destroying his plans. In **Marshall Gold Discovery State Historic Park,** Sutter's mill—the exact spot where gold was first seen—has been reproduced, together with a Chinese store, church, and other buildings of old Coloma.

FROM: Columbia State Historic Park, California
TO: Sierra County Historical Park and Museum at the Kentucky Mine, California
ROADS: Parrotts Ferry Road, Calif. 4, 49, local roads, Calif. 49/20
DISTANCE: 196 miles (315 km)
DRIVING TIME: 4.5 hours
WHEN: Year-round
PLANNING: www.parks.ca.gov

This print shop, one of many businesses in the gold rush town of Columbia, has been perfectly preserved.

CANADA/ALASKA

Yukon Golden Circle

Myriad prospectors flocked to the Yukon's southwest corner during the Klondike gold rush. Now scenic pleasures replace golden treasure along this glorious and varied drive in North America's wildest landscape.

Colorful, beautifully preserved wooden shops line a street in the former gold rush town of Skagway.

Highlights

- At Whitehorse, visit the **S.S. *Klondike* National Historic Site** to view a huge 1930s paddle wheeler. Guides lead you through the ship's cargo deck, engine room, cabins, and wheelhouse.
- From Skagway, take the **White Pass & Yukon Route Railroad,** a vintage narrow-gauge train that climbs up through the Skagway River gorge to emerge onto the alpine meadows of White Pass, ascending almost 3,000 feet (915 m) in just 20 miles (32 km). The railroad took miners to the Canadian border and still visits Bennett, a gold rush–era ghost town. A round-trip takes about three hours.

Begin in the Yukon's capital, Whitehorse (see Highlights), which sprang to life in 1897 during the gold rush, and head west along Alaska Highway (Hwy. 1) as it glides over Yukon Plateau's southern fringe. Stop at the Long Ago Peoples Place in Champagne, where traditions of the Southern Tutchone people, who avoided European contact until the mid-19th century, are still practiced. The road soon picks up the Dezadeash River and heads toward the Kluane Ranges. This line of glacial peaks dwarfs the crossroads town of Haines Junction and extends along the eastern front of Kluane National Park Reserve. Head south on Haines Road (Hwy. 3), stretching your legs at Kathleen Lake, where rocky peaks burst 5,000 feet (1,524 m) up from the water's edge. At the log-cabin village of Klukshu, watch Southern Tutchone trap, fillet, and dry fish during the summer and fall spawning runs. Farther south, Tutchone gather at Dalton Post to catch salmon with gaff hooks on long poles. The highway soon climbs into British Columbia and emerges from the trees.

Chilkat Pass marks the border with Alaska. From here, you begin a 4,000-foot (1,220 m) plunge, swinging past jagged, glacier-covered mountains and through forest to the broad floor of the Chilkat River valley. In late fall, around 4,000 American bald eagles—the world's greatest concentration—roost in the cottonwoods and feed on salmon. The small port of Haines overlooks a fjord gripped by 6,000-foot (1,830 m) peaks and includes the Chilkat Center for the Arts, where Tlingit dancers interpret their legends. Downtown, the Sheldon Museum and Cultural Center summarizes pioneer history and interprets Tlingit culture through artifacts such as woodcarvings. From here, board the Alaska Marine Highway ferry, and cross the water to Skagway (see Highlights). A major gateway during the gold rush, this town was once a lawless place, controlled by gangster "Soapy" Smith. The prospector's story is told at the Klondike Gold Rush National Historical Park. Take South Klondike Highway (Hwy. 2), climbing out of the gorge at the 3,292-foot (1,003 m) White Pass. The descent follows a gentler landscape, shimmering with huge lakes. In Carcross, explore the Matthew Watson General Store, Yukon's oldest shop, before returning across the Canadian border to Whitehorse.

FROM: Loop route from Whitehorse, Canada
ROADS: Hwys. 1, 3, 2
DISTANCE: 487 miles (785 km)
DRIVING TIME: 9 to 10 hours
WHEN: Mid to late summer
PLANNING: Fit your trip around the ferry schedule from Haines. Ferries are not daily, often run at inconvenient times, and fill up in advance. Bring your passport as the route crosses international borders. www.travelyukon.com

OPPOSITE: Motorcyclists travel the deserted Alaska Highway 1 toward Kluane National Park Reserve.

A man totes vegetables in Yaviza near the frontier with Colombia.

PANAMA

To the End of the Highway

This stretch of the world-famous Pan-American Highway delivers you, quite literally, to the end of the road. Along the way, you'll witness the colorful clothes and traditional dances of the area's indigenous peoples and pass some gorgeous jungle and mountain scenery.

Begin in the quiet yet colorful town of Chepo, hidden just south of the highway, 33 miles (53 km) from Panama City. A police checkpoint and a statue of St. Christopher, the patron saint of travelers, mark the junction where you should turn east as the highway undulates along the southern lee of the Serrania da San Blás mountains. At the silvery lake of Lago Bayano 24 miles (39 km) on, the traditional costumes of indigenous Kuna women add plenty of color. After crossing the lake on an iron bridge, you enter the Comarca de Kuna de Madugandi Kuna tribal territory, and for the next 20 miles (32 km), the road is flanked by a forest home to many butterflies and parrots. Vistas open up beyond Quebrada Cali, with views southward toward the Serrania de Majé mountains. Continue east, through the villages of Ipetí Kuna and nearby Ipetí Emberá, where you can watch traditional ceremonial dances and learn about the indigenous way of life. Pastures punctuated with free-standing mahoganies line the route as you approach the town of Tortí, where *talabarterias* (leather workshops) face each other across the street as they handcraft saddles in preparation for the town's rodeo in late March. After passing teak plantations, you're greeted at Aguas Frías with a billboard saying "Welcome to Darién." Thirteen miles (21 km) farther on, pass the artistic community of Emberá Arimae, where you can buy arts and crafts, before the asphalt ends at the Afro-Antillean community of Zapallal. Farther south at Metetí, the police may discourage your onward journey. The town has a gas station and bank, but the road rapidly deteriorates from here, and you should call a halt in the wet season. Continue (if you dare) though Canglón to Yaviza, a dilapidated, vaguely menacing frontier town with a heavy (and heavily armed) police presence. The road fizzles out completely here, as the 99-mile (159 km) long Darién Gap of thick jungle prevents any further driving.

FROM: Chepo, Panama
TO: Yaviza, Panama
ROAD: Pan-American Highway
DISTANCE: 127 miles (204 km)
DRIVING TIME: 5 hours
WHEN: Dry season (mid-December through mid-April)
PLANNING: You'll need to present your passport at the regular checkpoints. Driving into the jungle is extremely dangerous due to heavily armed guerrillas.
www.panama1.com

NEW ZEALAND

The East Cape

New Zealand's East Cape, on the smaller North Island, has resisted European influence, retaining a strong Maori character along with its stunning coastline of isolated beaches, rocky outcrops, and characterful cliff tops with fabulous views.

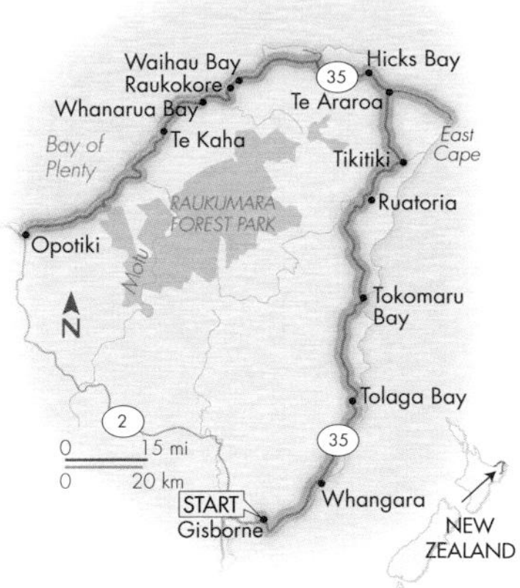

FROM: Gisborne, New Zealand
TO: Opotiki, New Zealand
ROAD: SH35
DISTANCE: 205 miles (327 km)
DRIVING TIME: 4.5 hours
WHEN: Year-round
PLANNING: Be sure to have a full tank of gas before you set out, and bring good walking boots if you plan to hike.
www.newzealand.com

From the pleasant wine-growing city of Gisborne, take the SH35 north past some fine surf beaches, before the road cuts inland through rolling green countryside. After 13 miles (21 km), turn east to Whangara, a coastal Maori town whose meeting house has a fabulous carved figure of a man riding a whale, depicting the legend of the tribe's arrival in the bay. Return to the main highway, which hits the coast again on a beautiful sweep of Tolaga Bay's mudstone cliffs. Turn off to the Tolaga Bay Wharf and hike on Cook's Walkway, around the top of the cliffs and down to where Captain Cook landed in 1769 at Cook's Cove. Continue up the highway to Tokomarù Bay, a dilapidated town set on an inlet surrounded by gorgeous mountains. The atmospheric old wharf and derelict buildings here are relics from the town's better days. Farther on, Ruatoria, lying inland off the main road, is a center for the indigenous Ngati Porou people, while Tikitiki is notable for the beautiful St. Mary's Church, with its carved Maori entrance and interior of woven panels and carvings.

About halfway along the drive, tiny Te Araroa lies on the scenic Kawakawa Bay and is home to the country's largest pohutukawa tree, at 131 feet (40 m) around. From here, a 12-mile (19 km) detour to East Cape brings you to a lighthouse that's the first building in the world to see sunrise. Return to the SH35, and soon you'll reach a great beach at Hicks Bay and, farther on, some incredible views at Lottin Point, which lies 2.5 miles (4 km) from the road. The SH35 follows the coast from Waihau Bay, past 65 miles (105 km) of beaches and rocky bays and cliff-top ocean views. You'll also pass many small Maori settlements, *maraes* (Maori meeting places), and historic churches. A particularly picturesque church with a carved entrance and a steep spire stands on a promontory overlooking the ocean at Raukokore. The road now winds and dips its way past a number of secluded beaches and beautiful Whanarua Bay. Continue down the coast to the town of Te Kaha with a stunning marae. Farther along is the Motu River, with views of mountains and sea. The SH35 ascends Maranui Hill, offering panoramas of the coast, and passes more small settlements and lonely beaches before finishing in the Maori town of Opotiki.

Drive along the unpaved road between Te Araroa and East Cape to witness the world's earliest sunrise.

ROMANIA

Transylvanian Villages

A leisurely drive in southern Transylvania takes you into the pastoral landscapes of the Cindrel Mountains. The route passes through some of the traditional villages that make up the so-called Boundaries of Sibiu, where shepherding is the chief vocation.

Colorful town houses with "eye" windows in the roofs edge the main square of Sibiu.

A 15-minute drive south from medieval Sibiu (see In Focus) lies Rășinari, a classic Romanian village with cobbled streets and neat old houses. After exploring its attractive museum, set out in the direction of Sibiu, but take a left turn down a country lane, crossing the Sebeș River, onto the 106D toward Poplaca. Continue to the next village of Orlat, dominated by a 14th-century earth fortress, Cetatea Scurtă, and turn left onto the 106E. After 2 miles (3 km), turn left for Fântânele (see Highlights), its multicolored houses tucked into the surrounding hillside. Head west to Sibiel (see Highlights), where the Biserica Sf. Treime (Church of the Holy Trinity) rises up, its 18th-century exterior belying the Byzantine flavor of the interior. Farther on, in Săliște, you can see ancient Transylvanian dances, such as the *căluș*, *brâu*, or *sârbă lui Ghiboi*, performed in the streets by men in black-and-white costume. From here, head west to Tilișca, a village of wooden houses and once the site of strong resistance, under the Dacian king, Burebista, to Julius Caesar's army. Follow the road through the mountains past Rod and Poiana Sibiului, to reach Jina, one of the most remote villages in the Mărginimea (Boundaries) region. Winding onward via Dobra, turn right at the next intersection, where the Dobra River runs beside the road. Turn right again at the 67C through Șugag and Mărtinie toward Căpâlna, where one of Transylvania's finest Dacian citadels, Dealul Cetății, lies just over a mile (2 km) south of the village. Continue through Săsciori, staying with the Sebeș River to Sebeș, centered on a Romanesque-Gothic church with some fine stone carvings. Drive east from here for 6 miles (9 km) on the DN1 and DN7, then turn right on the 106F for Cetatea Câlnic, a restored 12th-century fortress designated a World Heritage Site and now serving as a cultural center.

In Focus Hidden in the Dumbrava Forest, about 4 miles (6.5km) south of Sibiu, lies the **ASTRA Museum of Traditional Folk Civilization,** Romania's largest ethnographic open-air museum. Its 237 acres (96 ha) of gentle rolling swards, woodlands, boating lakes, and ponds showcase the inventiveness of Romania's rural people, especially their clever use of wood. There is even a "witch's house," although, sadly, no witch.

OPPOSITE: Wooden windmills, as well as workshops and forges, are on view at Sibiu's ASTRA Museum.

Highlights

- An ideal side trip is the 12th-century town of **Sibiu,** with its colorful buildings characteristically arcaded and with "eyes" in the roofs—small oval windows half-covered by tile "eyelids." Visit the splendid main square and the museum, which has excellent examples of Romanian art.

- **Fântânele's village museum** has a cheerful collection of icons and rural crafts displayed in two rooms of a former 18th-century inn.

- **Sibiel's** church grounds house the charming Zosim Oancea Museum, named for the local priest who created it, displaying more than 700 folk icons painted on glass.

FROM: Rășinari, Romania
TO: Cetatea Câlnic, Romania
ROADS: 106D, 106E, 67C, DN1, DN7, 106F
DISTANCE: 66 miles (105 km)
DRIVING TIME: 2 hours
WHEN: Year-round
PLANNING: A 4WD vehicle is recommended for this trip. www.romaniatourism.com

The tower of the church of the Taxiarchis (Archangels) overlooks a shady side street in Areopolis.

GREECE

On the Peloponnese

The harsh yet compelling landscape of the Mani, on a finger of the Peloponnese, is dotted with deserted villages of strange tower houses, Frankish castles, and aged Byzantine churches smothered inside with colorful icons—a hidden culture to intrigue the curious.

From the Mani's largest west-coast town, Areopolis (see Highlights), head south on the main road, avoiding turnoffs. Even if you do accidentally go wrong, most roads will return to the main road as they usually just loop through villages. En route, you will often see tiny churches worth a visit. It takes about half an hour to reach the village of Alika, where you turn right for Vatheia, a cluster of narrow, stone tower houses atop a hill. Now silent and empty, the houses were once inhabited by feuding families—internecine warfare was endemic and such houses are characteristic of the peninsula. The adventurous can drive on via Porto Kagio to the southernmost tip of the Mani and admire the hill of Akra Tenaro—aka Cape Matapan, the legendary gateway to Hades. Retrace your steps to Porto Kagio, where a castle sits above the bay, then take the switchback road running up to join the main route just below another village of tower houses, Lagia. This stretch of coast feels very remote, with mountains dropping down to the sea. Continue north then west back to Areopolis via the pass at Pirichos. Pick up Hwy. 39 for lively Githio, the main town on the east coast. It has some good restaurants around its fishing harbor, the remains of a Roman theater, and great beaches nearby.

Hidden History Around 30 miles (48 km) north on the E961 from Githio, **Mystras** is a ruined Byzantine city, set on a hill at the edge of the Taygetos Mountains. The dominant feature of this atmospheric site is the castle, or Kastro, offering superb views. The Despots' Palace is well preserved, with a 14th-century throne room where several Byzantine kings were crowned. At the bottom of the hill lies the Mitropolis, a cathedral dating from 1309, with original frescoes.

Highlights

- Follow the signs south from Areopolis for **Spilia Dirou** (Diros Caves), 5 miles (8 km) away; a 30-minute boat ride takes you into a labyrinth festooned with stalagmites and stalactites. Waiting time for the boat increases in high season.

- Another 5 miles (8 km) beyond the Diros Caves, turn right for Agios Georgios and the village of Mezapos. From here, you get a splendid view of **Tigani,** or "frying pan"—named for its shape—a low-lying neck of rocky land supporting the **remains of a Frankish castle.** A 15-minute drive from Mezapos brings you to Agia Kyriaki, from where you can hike to Tigani, which takes about an hour.

FROM: Areopolis, Greece
TO: Githio, Greece
ROADS: Local roads, Hwy. 39
DISTANCE: 70 miles (110km)
DRIVING TIME: 3 hours
WHEN: Year-round
PLANNING: Be sure to have a full tank of gas and a supply of drinking water before setting out. Winds can be fierce, and it is usually baking hot in summer. Churches are sometimes locked, so you may need to track down the key holder to visit them. www.zorbas.de/maniguide

ITALY

The Valle d'Aosta

This exhilarating drive in northwestern Italy follows one of Europe's most beautiful valleys, justly renowned for its romantic villages and medieval castles set in high alpine scenery, and ends at the foot of Mont Blanc.

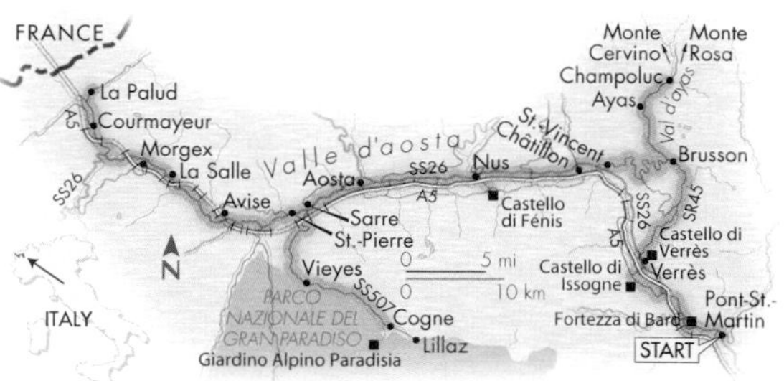

Loved for its vineyards, Pont-St.-Martin is a village built around a small first-century B.C. Roman bridge. Set out from here on the SS26, and in a few minutes you pass Fortezza di Bard, one of 70 or so fortresses for which the Valle d'Aosta is known. Yet more superb is the Castello di Issogne, a little farther along, built in 1498 by Georges de Challant, whose family controlled much of the valley for centuries. Across the river lies the Castello di Verrès, of gaunt, military aspect. Take the SR45 at the village of Verrès, and head north to explore the Val d'Ayas, the prettiest of the side valleys en route. The village of Champoluc is 17 miles (27 km) away, where you can take a cable car to see Monte Rosa and Monte Cervino, the two highest Alpine peaks after Mont Blanc (15,781 feet/4,810 m). Return toward Brusson, and take the vertiginous route westward to St.-Vincent, home to one of Europe's largest casinos. Here, you meet the SS26 again and soon pass the Castello di Fénis, renowned for its exquisite frescoes and furniture. After around 18 miles (30 km), you reach Aosta, its center a delightful mix of Roman ruins, medieval churches, and tranquil old squares, with an impressive tally of monuments. Another 10 minutes along a local road takes you to Sarre castle (1710), used as a hunting lodge by Vittorio Emanuele II. Back on the SS26, you find two more castles at St.-Pierre, where the highway begins to climb into high Alpine country. The ski resort of Courmayeur is about 18 miles (30 km) away, with tiny La Palud just beyond. From here, the cable-car ride over Mont Blanc makes a dazzling end to the drive.

FROM: Pont-St.-Martin, Italy
TO: La Palud, Italy
ROADS: SS26, SR45, local roads
DISTANCE: 90 miles (145 km)
DRIVING TIME: 3 hours
WHEN: Year-round
PLANNING: If you take the full cable-car ride, you will need your passport to cross into France. www.regione.vda.it

Stay a While Italy's oldest national park, the **Parco Nazionale del Gran Paradiso,** extends across 270 square miles (700 km^2) of majestic mountain scenery, encompassing several alpine villages. Take the side road from Sarre to Cogne, a good place to stay although the best scenery is a little deeper into the park. Lillaz is a peaceful village, and from here a short hike eastward along the valley brings you to the dramatic waterfall of Cascata di Balma. Valnontey is a busier village, and the trailhead to the Vittorio Sella mountain refuge, one of the park's most popular hikes.

A chamois obligingly poses in the Valle d'Aosta's Parco Nazionale del Gran Paradiso, a haven for wildlife.

THE TOP

10 Mediterranean Drives

Explore the facets of this important sea, from its easternmost shore through historic ports and villages to the cliffs and coves of its islands.

❶ Tiberias to Tel Aviv, Israel

From the ancient city of Tiberias, on the Sea of Galilee, home to the tomb of the 12th-century sage Maimonides, meander eastward to the coast, a gold expanse of sand. The 100-mile (160 km) long journey takes you through modern Haifa, on the slopes of sacred Mount Carmel, and on to Herod's port city of Caesarea Maritima, full of ancient ruins, to end in bustling Tel Aviv.

PLANNING: May and October are the best months to visit (but avoid holidays). *www.goisrael.com*

❷ Chania to Palaiochora, Crete

From the beautiful waterfront city of Chania, craggy mountain roads wind 50 miles (80 km) through the heart of Crete, passing ancient villages, including Alikianos and Aghia Irini, where men still wear traditional black baggy pants and high mountain boots. Stop for a peek at Samaria, Europe's longest gorge, before ending in the pink-sand seaside resort of Palaiochora.

PLANNING: Chania has plenty of places to stay. *www.cretetravel.com*

❸ Mount Pelion Peninsula, Greece

Begin this tortuous, stunning drive in Volos, twisting up Pelion's slopes to the village of Makrinitsa, its 18th-century homes hanging from the green mountainside. Passing slate-roofed villages, ancient churches, and fruit orchards, head up and over the mountain to the peninsula's east coast, where narrow lanes lead to beautiful beach towns, including Agios Ioannis. Return to Volos via Milies.

PLANNING: June is the best month to go: warm and not crowded. *www.aroundpelion.com*

❹ Jadranska Magistrala, Croatia

Lauded as Croatia's most scenic drive, the Jadranska Magistrala (Adriatic Road) snakes south more than 300 miles (480 km) along a rocky coast between Rijeka and Dubrovnik. Admire national parks, battered peaks, and peaceful medieval villages, and don't miss the most stunning section—running beneath Velebit Mountain, with a view of the island of Pag.

PLANNING: The road briefly crosses Bosnia, so keep your passport handy. *www.croatia.hr*

❺ Dingli Cliffs, Malta

In Malta's prettiest, most unspoiled corner, the narrow road southwest of Dingli village skirts vertical cliffs that plummet 980 feet (300 m) to the sea. Visit in late afternoon, as the fiery sun drops into the ocean.

PLANNING: Stay in Dingli village or Rabat. Be warned that GPS mapping of Malta isn't always reliable. *www.visitmalta.com*

❻ Leuca to Otranto, Italy

At the heel of Italy, rambling between the seaside towns of Otranto and Santa Maria di Leuca, this 50-mile (80 km) road has been dubbed the "Little Amalfi Coast" for its jagged coastline and secret beaches. Swim, hike, and picnic along the way. In Leuca, climb the headland for the staggering vista where the Adriatic and Ionian Seas meet.

PLANNING: Spring and fall are the best times to go. *www.italiantourism.com*

❼ Genoa to La Spezia, Italy

This 50-mile (80 km) drive begins in Genoa, a powerful Mediterranean city in medieval times. Eastward along the Gulf of Genoa, be sure to stop in the red-tile-roofed villages of Santa Margherita Ligure and Portofino, clustered on a green peninsula along boat-dotted waters. From La Spezia, hike the Cinque Terre fishing villages, connected by paths overlooking the sea.

PLANNING: In winter, lodging is cheaper and crowds are few. *www.italiantourism.com*

Opposite: Krapanj, a small, low-lying island only 5 feet (1.5 m) high just off the Croatian coast, basks in the warm sunshine.

❽ Route des Crêtes, France

Teetering on cliffs high above the Mediterranean—certainly not for the faint-hearted—this 12-mile (19 km) drive between the pastel-painted fishing village of Cassis and the coastal city of La Ciotat heads over the Cap Canaille, at 1,300 feet (396 m) Europe's highest maritime cliff. From roadside viewpoints peer down into the gorgeous turquoise *calanques* (inlets) that line the coast from here to Marseille.

PLANNING: Cassis has beautiful beaches, and there are plenty of places to stay—Les Roches Blanches is a popular hotel with amazing views. Be sure to hike along the calanques (trails are signposted), as well as take a boat ride out to them. *www.ot-cassis.com, www.beyond.fr*

❾ Camargue, France

Long-horned black bulls and white horses with flowing manes run semi-free through the Camargue, wild marshland south of ancient, artsy Arles. Here, too, congregate 300 species of birds, including flocks of pink flamingos, and soaring eagles, hawks, and harriers. High points include the Camargue Museum and the area's capital, Stes.-Maries-de-la-Mer, full of Spanish charm. In May, thousands of Roma (gypsies) from all over Europe come to the town to venerate their patron saint, Sara, in colorful processions to the sea.

PLANNING: Stay in Stes.-Maries-de-la-Mer. Spring and late fall are best for bird-watching and seeing the bulls and horses. *www.saintesmaries.com*

❿ The Griffon's Route, Sardinia

The rugged road running south from the medieval town of Alghero edges eroded, lavender-covered cliffs that dive down to the sea. Scan the skies above for the rare griffon vulture. From the ancient town of Bosa, 30 miles (48 km) south of Alghero, topped by a medieval fortress, return to Alghero along the inland mountain route. It is fraught with hairpins and switchbacks but passes the prehistoric settlement of Nuraghe Appiu.

PLANNING: Griffons may be seen in early morning or at sunset. Spring and fall are good times to visit for driving, though if you also want the beaches, summer is best. *www.italiantourism.com*

The landscape of the Val d'Orcia inspired some of the finest artists of the Renaissance.

ITALY

Renaissance Landscapes

Southern Tuscany is full of charming sun-drenched communities set amidst rolling hills where art and architecture have flourished for centuries. The region's fine wines and delicious cuisine provide a literal as well as visual feast.

From Siena, head southeast through a distinctive landscape of bare, clay hills to the village of Asciano and its late 13th-century Romanesque-Gothic church. Take the scenic minor road south to Abbazia di Monte Oliveto Maggiore, a Benedictine abbey with some excellent medieval art. A few miles on you reach Buonconvento, a village whose ugly outskirts conceal a pretty medieval center. The road now climbs up to Montalcino, a walled village perched on a hilltop, crowned by its picture-perfect castle. Six miles (10 km) south is the Abbazia di Sant' Antimo, a glorious medieval abbey, isolated amidst verdant countryside. Drive east into the picturesque Val d'Orcia and the first community you reach on the SS323 is Castiglione d'Orcia, a small town of cobbled streets huddled around an imposing fortress. Close by is Bagno Vignoni, whose famous town square is not, in fact, a square at all but a large open *piscina*, or pool, that bubbles with water from the sulfurous hot springs below. Once you have passed San Quirico d'Orcia, Pienza is the next stop. In the 15th century, Pope Pius II tried to turn the village into a model Renaissance city. The cathedral, papal residence, and a palace-ringed piazza still remain, forming the heart of one of Italy's most charming villages. Continue on the SS146 to Montepulciano, a classic hill town of 16th-century churches and palaces.

Stay a While No drive through Tuscany is complete without a visit to the sky-rise towers of **San Gimignano.** Dubbed the "medieval Manhattan," the village is situated an easy hour's drive west of Siena. The famous towers—part status symbol, part defense system—began to appear around 1150. The walled town also has some truly impressive churches and the excellent Museo Civico, where a number of Sienese and Florentine masterpieces are on display. The village is very popular during peak season (July and August) and parking can be a problem, so plan your trip carefully.

FROM: Siena, Italy
TO: Montepulciano, Italy
ROADS: SS438, SS451, SS323, SS146, local roads
DISTANCE: 76 miles (120 km)
DRIVING TIME: 2.5 hours
WHEN: Year-round
PLANNING: Wine-lovers should visit in fall. www.turismo.intoscana.it

FRANCE

A Drive around Les Dentelles

The villages in northern Provence seem trapped in a time warp: cobbled streets lead past charmingly ramshackle houses, while medieval hilltop castles grandly survey the countryside dotted with vineyards and historic wineries.

After exploring the small but lively town of Vaison-la-Romaine, cross the Roman bridge over the River Ouvèze as you leave the lower town, and turn left on the D938. Just after the hamlet of Crestet, turn right on the D76 and head up the hill to Le Crestet, with an 11th-century church and a 9th-century castle standing on top of the hill. Return to the D938, continuing to the old town of Malaucène, then take the D90 west, through the sweeping vistas at the Col de la Chaîne and up past Les Dentelles de Montmirail, the crests of chiseled limestone named for their resemblance to lace (*dentelles*). Soon you'll arrive at the hamlet of Suzette, where the view over Crête de St.-Amand and the mountains is the star attraction. Pass through tiny Lafare to reach Beaumes-de-Venise, best known for its Muscat wine, which you can taste in cellars along Avenue Raspail. The nearby Cathédrale Notre-Dame-d'Aubune was built in the 8th century, with its unusual tower added in the 12th.

Continue through flat wine country before taking the turnoff for sleepy Gigondas. The village is famous for its robust, powerful wine, and there are many wine cellars and cafés around the shaded central square, Place Gabriel Andéol. Leave the car and wander around the pretty lanes until you come across Ste.-Catherine's parish church. The hilltop town of Séguret awaits just down the road. Celebrated as one of France's most beautiful villages, its narrow streets wind past noble houses, restaurants, and galleries, as well as santon shops, where you can watch master artists create tiny painted ceramic figures. Continue north to the D88, heading east on the D975 to return to Vaison-la-Romaine.

In Focus Throughout the region, almost every town stages a weekly traditional **Provençal market,** where everything from regional specialties, clothing, and souvenirs are available to sample and buy. For a morning at least, these historic towns spring to life as stalls take over the streets and cars are almost absent. The market comes to Vaison-la-Romaine and Beaumes-de-Venise every Tuesday, and to Malaucène on Wednesday. Try to arrive early in the morning to grab the best bargains.

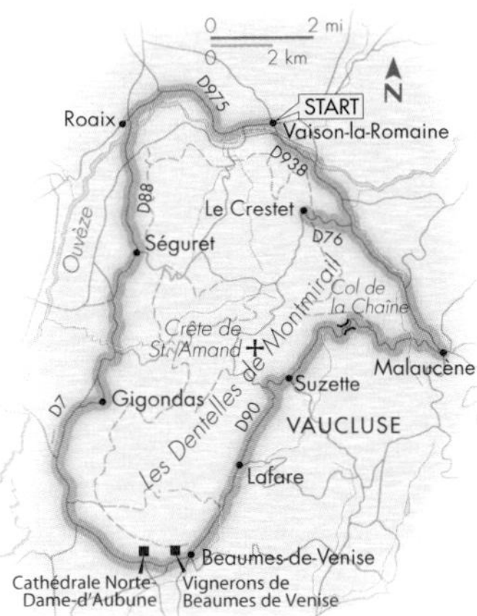

FROM: Loop route from Vaison-la-Romaine, France

ROADS: D938, D90, D88, D975

DISTANCE: 40 miles (65 km)

DRIVING TIME: 2 hours

WHEN: Year-round

PLANNING: Explore Séguret on foot. There is a parking lot on the right as you enter the village. www.provencebeyond.com

Climb the steeply sloping streets of Séguret and enjoy the medieval architecture.

ENGLAND

Two Cotswold Drives

Easily accessible from London or Oxford, the tiny Cotswold villages, with their trademark golden-hued stone buildings, have retained their individual characters and remain some of the most beautiful and remote spots in England.

The River Windrush flows through the peaceful town of Bourton-on-the-Water.

The villages of the Cotswolds are quintessentially English, with old pubs looking out onto grassy greens or fantastic views that stretch for miles. This is two drives in one, centered around the 18th-century spa town of Cheltenham.

From Cheltenham, head east on the A40 through fields divided by hedgerows. Pass Northleach, where the impressive church of St. Peter and St. Paul, endowed by 15th-century wool merchants, reminds visitors of the town's role in medieval times. Wander through nearby Burford, a stone-built Georgian town with a buzzing high street. Then take the A424 north, following signs to Bourton-on-the-Water, where tiny footbridges span the River Windrush. To escape the crowds, drive through the twin villages of Upper and Lower Slaughter, just northwest of Bourton, where picturesque cottages line the banks of the River Eye.

The B4068 takes you north to Stow-on-the-Wold, the area's highest town, with an imposing marketplace where sheep are still sold. It is also famous for its antiques shops and as the site of some fierce fighting in the English Civil War. Take the A424 northwest, before turning right to Chipping Campden, where a splendid Domesday painting dominates the 15th-century church of St. James. From here, take narrow minor roads east to elegant Broadway, one of the showcase villages of the Cotswolds. Elizabethan houses and the historic Lygon Arms Hotel, patronized by both King Charles I and Oliver Cromwell, surround the village green. For a great view of the Severn Valley, climb up Broadway Tower at the top of Fish Hill.

> "These picturesque communities evoke an England of timeless calm... To the visitor, [the Cotswolds] remains the rural fantasyland pictured in my childhood books, a Brigadoon of Britishness."
>
> -STEPHEN McCLARENCE, NATIONAL GEOGRAPHIC WRITER

Just to the south are the villages of Stanton and Stanway, built completely out of Cotswold stone, which glows gold on a sunny day. A little farther south, in Winchcombe, gargoyles surround the church, where Saxon carvings from the former Benedictine abbey are preserved. Walk up the well-marked Cotswold Trail to visit Sudeley Castle (see Highlights), then drive on to Belas Knap, a 5,000-year-old chambered cairn. Descend Cleeve Hill to return to Cheltenham. The town has a broad, tree-lined central promenade and some of Britain's best Regency architecture, including the domed Pittville Pump Room, built for balls, galas, and social intercourse.

The second drive heads south from Cheltenham on the A46 to Painswick,

Sinking a Pint or Two in a Pub

England is renowned for its country pubs, and nowhere are they more common than in the Cotswolds. As you tour the area, you cannot fail to stumble across pubs hidden away in villages or perched unexpectedly on hillsides. The **Donnington Way** is a 62-mile (100 km) circular hike through the North Cotswolds that links the 15 public houses owned by the local Donnington Brewery—a delight for those who enjoy a well-earned, locally brewed pint (or two) after rambling through the pristine countryside. Traditionally, the hike begins in the ancient market town of Stow-on-the-Wold. Of course, the route can be done in sections, with the two closest pubs less than 2 miles (3 km) apart.

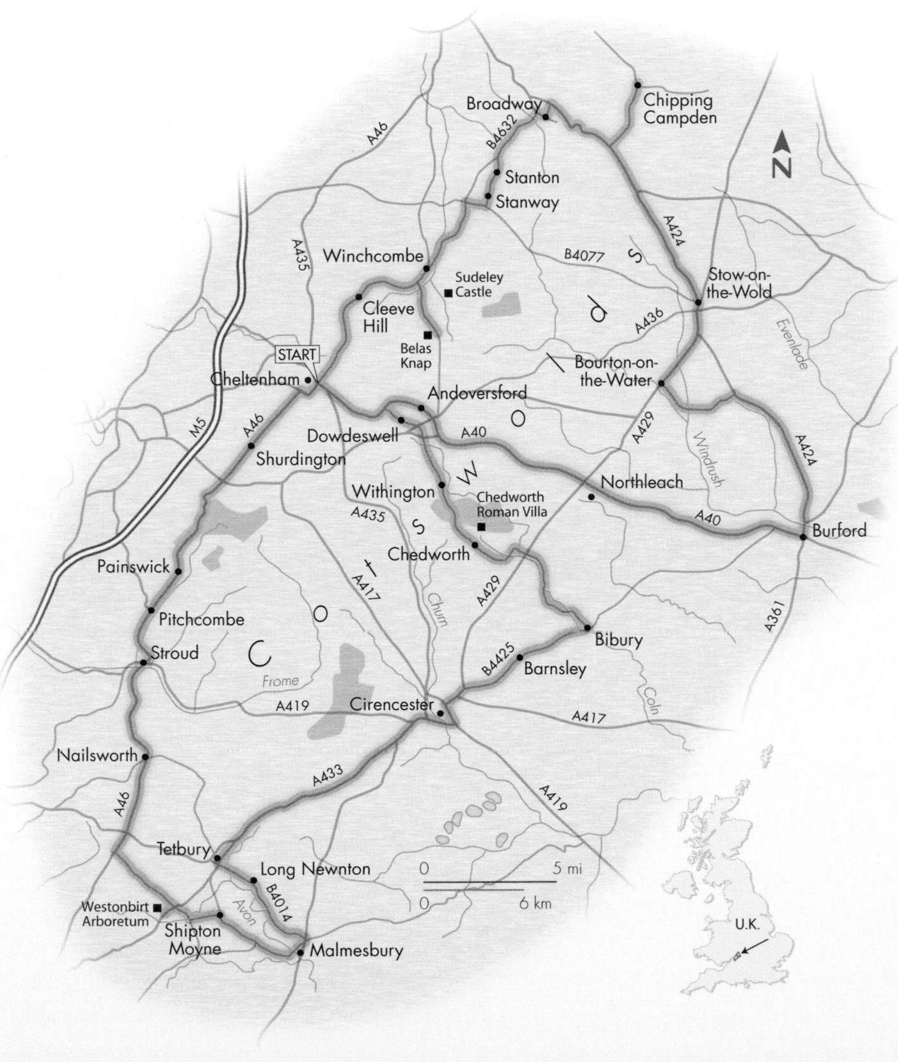

a pretty town sitting on a ridge, where gray limestone houses line the steep streets. Continue on to Stroud, where huge old textile mills dot the wooded Golden Valley. The road climbs up over the Cotswold Hills bringing panoramic views. Take a left turn 4 miles (6 km) south of Nailsworth to reach Westonbirt Arboretum, one of the world's largest collections of trees, including maples, a Lebanese cedar, and the so-called "toffee-apple" tree. Turn left from here onto the A433, then pass through Shipton Moyne to Malmesbury, which has a beautifully carved Norman abbey.

Follow the B4014 northwest to Tetbury, another charming small town with a Georgian church, and rejoin the A433 toward the market town of Cirencester. In Roman times, Cirencester was the second largest city in Britain, and it is still known as the Capital of the Cotswolds. The Corinium Museum has a fine collection of Romano-British material, and the Church of St. John the Baptist is one of the grandest in the region.

The B4425 heads to Bibury, where a row of 17th-century weavers' cottages is one of the area's most photographed sites. Then take the pretty Coln Valley road northwest to Chedworth Roman Villa. Passing Withington and Dowdeswell, you pick up the A40 back to Cheltenham.

FROM: Double loop from Cheltenham, England
ROADS: A40, A424, B4068, B4632, A46, A433, B4014, B4425, minor roads
DISTANCE: 140 miles (225km)
DRIVING TIME: 4.5 hours
WHEN: Year-round
PLANNING: www.the-cotswolds.org

Highlights

- **Sudeley Castle,** dating from the tenth century, has impressive gardens and fine paintings. Guided tours are available three days a week from March through October.
- **Snowshill Manor,** near Broadway, is home to an extraordinary collection of 22,000 objects, including full suits of Samurai armor, amassed by architect, poet, and collector Charles Wade.

Chipping Camden is one of the best-preserved towns in the Cotswolds.

ENGLAND

O'er Hill and Dale

This tour in the north of England visits charming historic towns and the remote villages of the Yorkshire Dales, offering a great opportunity to escape the crowds and delight in a peaceful rural landscape that teems with wildlife.

Start in Knaresborough, a town on the edge of the Dales that dates back to Norman times, where ruins of the 10th-century castle remain. Take the A59 west through the elegant gray-stone town of Harrogate, and continue to the Yorkshire Dales National Park. The Dales are some of England's lushest countryside, with green fields dissected by dry-stone walls. Wharfedale runs northwest from the village of Bolton Abbey, home to the 12th-century Bolton Priory, whose great east window stands flanked by tall arches. Two miles (3 km) north, at the Strid, the River Wharfe crashes through a narrow, rocky channel around 6 feet (1.8 m) across. The B6160 runs up Wharfedale to the honeypot village of Grassington, where there are plenty of craft shops, cozy cafés, and hotels around a cobbled square. Continuing north, you see Kilnsey Crag rising dramatically from the roadside—the spectacular rock formation is popular with climbers. Next is pretty Kettlewell, a classic Yorkshire village with some excellent tearooms. Soon you'll reach Hubberholme, with its humpback bridge and a little church with a rare Tudor rood loft. Continue east as the road climbs up and over the hillside to West Burton. Wensleydale, famous for its cheese, is to the west on the A684. Stop in the village of Aysgarth to marvel as the River Ure tumbles down two long falls of limestone steps. In Bainbridge, head north briefly, then take the first road on the left. Just before Hardraw, turn north and pass through High Shaw and some of the most spectacular scenery in the park. At the B6270, head east, passing the unspoiled villages of Swaledale, the most rugged of the Dales, as you approach Reeth. Finish the tour in Richmond, northeast of the National Park.

Hidden History One of England's finest small cities, **York,** 17 miles (27 km) east of Knaresborough on the A59, has ancient walls, old narrow streets, and a fabulous cathedral (or minster). There is a host of historical attractions close to the center, including York Castle Museum where you can see a reconstructed Victorian street. Another top attraction is the Jorvik Viking Centre, with a "time-travel machine" taking you back to the city's Viking days, smells and all.

FROM: Knaresborough, England

TO: Richmond, England

ROADS: A59, B6160, A684, B6270, local roads

DISTANCE: 67 miles (108 km)

DRIVING TIME: 2 hours

WHEN: Year-round

PLANNING: Take care on these narrow, winding roads—you may need to stop for oncoming traffic. www.yorkshiredales.org.uk

The market town of Knaresborough features a 19th-century viaduct 90 feet (27 m) above the River Nidd.

The long sandy beach and tranquil water make Playa de los Genoveses hugely popular in summer.

SPAIN

The Secret Spanish Coast

This southeastern corner of Spain is the setting for a gentle drive along a coast where secluded communities and ancient fishing villages have resisted the lure of mass tourism and still practice their traditional crafts.

FROM: Níjar, Spain
TO: Mojácar, Spain
ROADS: Local roads
DISTANCE: 70 miles (110 km)
DRIVING TIME: 2.5 hours
WHEN: Year-round
PLANNING: www.degata.com

From the 15th-century church at Níjar, head down the main street where shops sell *jarapas* (woven rugs), grass baskets, and ceramics. Follow signs to Almeria and San Isidro, meandering through the yucca, aloe, and windmill-dotted landscape of the Parque Natural de Cabo de Gata-Níjar. Just before Pozo de los Frailes, turn left toward Rodalquilar. After the 18th-century coastal fort of Los Escullos, take a right to the tiny fishing village of Isleta del Moro. Continue north, past the coastal views at Mirador de la Amatista, before arriving at Rodalquilar, a curious former gold-mining village. Farther north on the main road is a right turn for Las Negras—drive straight down to the beach. Return to the main road and drive northwest to Fernán Pérez, turning right toward Agua Amarga, passing farmland with almond trees, goats, and prickly pears. As the sea appears beyond the rocky hills, continue on to a junction with a paved road that brings you to Agua Amarga, a pleasant beach resort. Moving ever northward, pass Carboneras to skirt Playa la Galera, backed by clefts of high sierra, and find the most memorable views of the drive. At the built-up sweep of Mojácar Playa, strike inland to Mojácar village, perched spectacularly high above the blue Mediterranean.

Stay a While Ideally placed to explore the southeasterly tip of the country, **San José** is a short drive south from Pozo de los Frailes. The easily negotiable dirt track circles around the headland. Turn off left to explore the beautiful cove at Playa de los Genoveses, or continue to Playa de Monsul (with black sand) and enjoy the great view south to the Cabo de Gata lighthouse. These popular beaches have both been locations for numerous films, including *Indiana Jones and the Last Crusade*.

SPAIN

Spain's Whitewashed Villages

Explore the undulating landscape of southern Spain as the road winds through the Sierra de Grazalema, where clusters of gleaming white villages speckle the countryside, perilously located on imposing cliff edges or overlooking deep ravines.

Sample local specialties of this region, famed for its wine, cheese, and cured ham.

The western gateway to the Parque Natural de la Sierra de Grazalema is Arcos de la Frontera, a town set on a dizzying clifftop, with winding streets best explored on foot. The main square has a beautiful Gothic-Mudejar church and a mirador (lookout point) with views over olive groves and orchards. The square also has the Moorish walls of the Castillo de los Duques and numerous baroque and Renaissance facades. Leave Arcos on the beltway, following signs for El Bosque, 19 miles (31 km) east on the A372. You'll pass a densely cultivated landscape of olive groves, vegetable farms, and horse ranches before the Sierra de Grazalema comes into view. The scenery becomes increasingly more spectacular en route to El Bosque, a small town at the base of the mountains where people flock for hiking, rock climbing, trout fishing, and hang-gliding adventures. Leave town on the A372, and stay on the road as it turns left toward Grazalema. The road immediately climbs through eucalyptus and pine trees. After passing the village of Benamahoma, views of the valley open up and forest alternates with rock. The stark granite peak of Monte Simancón accompanies you to the 3,618-foot (1,103 m) pass of Puerto del Boyar, with its superb views of mountain ridges receding to the west. You may spot a roe deer here, or even a mountain goat, Griffon vulture, or eagle. As the road descends, the dazzling whitewashed houses, red-tile rooftops, and church towers of Grazalema appear, wedged between the sierras of El Pinar and El Endrinal. Continue to Ronda (see Highlights), 20 miles (33 km) east. If you fancy a winding detour to a delightful village, take a turnoff to the left to Zahara, 1 mile (1.6 km) beyond Grazalema. Otherwise, continue through the rock-strewn valley where cork and holm-oak forests line the road and views of farmland dotted with white *fincas* (farms) open before you. Turn right onto the A376, which twists past granite cliffs to Ronda. Split in two by a steep gorge, this popular tourist town is home to Spain's oldest bullring still in use and a museum devoted to bullfighting.

OPPOSITE: Ronda sits on a rocky precipice nearly 500 feet (150 m) above the Guadalevín River.

Highlights

- Hike the **Garganta Verde** between Grazalema and Zahara. The gorge is 1,320 feet (400 m) deep, and trails are steep in places.
- Ronda is the center of Spain's bullfighting heritage. Visit the **Museo Taurino** in the 18th-century Plaza de Toros. The Feria Goyesca de Pedro Romero, held in early September, is the best time to watch a bullfight.
- The wonderful **Palacio de Mondragón** mansion in Ronda, built in 1314, was the residence of the great Moorish king, Abb el Malik.

FROM: Arcos de la Frontera, Spain
TO: Ronda, Spain
ROADS: A372, A376
DISTANCE: 47 miles (76 km)
DRIVING TIME: 2 hours
WHEN: Year-round
PLANNING: The houses are meticulously whitewashed each spring, so visit in early summer to see the region at its finest. www.andalucia.com

SPAIN
START
Arcos de la Frontera
A372
Prado del Rey
El Bosque
Benamahoma
PARQUE NATURAL
Puerto del Boyar
A372
A376
Grazalema
Sierra de Grazalema
Montejaque
Ronda
0 5 mi
0 5 km
N

A stone figure of Jesus presides over the village of Castelo Rodrigo and the surrounding valley.

PORTUGAL

Medieval Strongholds

This loop through northeastern Portugal links four fortified medieval villages that guarded the border with Spain and, despite their relative proximity, developed distinct histories and styles of military architecture.

FROM: Loop route from Guarda, Portugal
ROADS: N221, N332, N340, N324, A25/N16
DISTANCE: 87 miles (140 km)
DRIVING TIME: 2 hours
WHEN: Year-round
PLANNING: www.visitcentro.com

From Guarda, follow the N221 to Pinhel, past dry-stone walls, vineyards, and orchards, before the landscape evolves into barren, granite-strewn slopes. Huge boulders dominate the entrance to Pinhel, a venerable town where the remains of a 14th-century castle stand guard over the steep, cobbled streets, lichen-clad houses, and a flattened hilltop dominated by two sturdy towers. Leave on the main road past the cemetery and turn left at the bottom of the hill, following the N221 as it meanders north. Soon Castelo Rodrigo, a peaceful village with commanding views, comes into sight. Visit the citadel and the semi-ruined palace of Cristóvão de Moura, an evocative sight. The villagers burned the palace down in 1640, when they suspected their ruler of conspiring with the Spaniards. Head south on the N332 toward Almeida, where the massive, moated fortress, built in the Vauban form of a six-pointed star, was later used as an ammunition depot. Walk the ramparts and remember how Napoleon's troops laid siege to this stronghold in 1810 and blew up the depot. Head south on the N340 and N324 to the fortress-village of Castelo Mendo (see Hidden History), whose stone archway is guarded by two granite boars. It was named after the first commander of the fort, Mendo Mendes, appointed in the 14th century. The A25/N16 returns you to Guarda, about 24 miles (39 km) west.

Hidden History In the Battle of Fuentes de Oñoro in May 1811, the French forces were prevented from relieving the besieged Almeida, which marked a turning point in the fortunes of British General Wellington's Peninsular Campaign. The village's narrow streets remain almost as they were at the time of the battle, and it's easy to imagine the bloody carnage that took place. You are recommended to bring a guide to the battlefield with you to find the key spots. **Fuentes de Oñoro** is 11 miles (18 km) east from Castelo Mendo, just over the border in Spain.

Also Recommended

❶ Cape Breton Villages, Canada

The Nova Scotia fishing village of Neils Harbour connects to South Harbour along a rickety coastal road that is worth some bumps for its fantastic views. Lobster pots line the vistas. To taste their catch, carry on along the Cabot Trail to Pleasant Bay, where the Rusty Anchor is a popular restaurant.

www.cbisland.com

❷ Mohawk Trail, Massachusetts

The Mohawk Trail follows the path of a centuries-old trade route linking the Connecticut and Hudson River valleys. This section of U.S. 2—one of the oldest highways in the United States—is filled with pilgrim churches and more modern village charms, such as the Bridge of Flowers at Shelburne Falls.

www.mohawktrail.com

❸ U.S. 169, Connecticut

Head south from Woodstock, Connecticut, on U.S. 169 to enjoy a 30-mile (48 km) drive through farmland and historic communities that are even more beautiful in fall when the leaves are changing. The town of Brooklyn is on the National Register of Historic Districts. At the route's southern end is Canterbury with a classic New England town green.

www.byways.org

❹ Door County, Wisconsin

This peninsula drive offers a choice between cozy harbors on the Green Bay shore or the rolling surf of Lake Michigan. Bailey's Harbor, founded in 1851, has one of the largest wildflower preserves in North America. Enjoy the white steeples and picket fences of Ephraim, "the fruitful land." Continue south on U.S. 42 to reach Alogma, with views of fishing boats, shanties, and an impressive lighthouse.

www.doorcounty.com

❺ Blue Mountains, Australia

Along New South Wales's Great Western Highway, a string of villages starting with Glenbrook welcomes you with art galleries and gardens. The Falls Gallery is one of these establishments—housed in a turn-of-the-century cottage a few minutes' walk from the picnic area at Falls Reserve. Leura hosts an annual garden festival in October. End the drive at Katoomba for views of the sandstone formations called the Three Sisters.

www.openroad.com.au

❻ Himalayan Villages, Nepal

About 50 miles (80 km) southwest of Kathmandu, the Tribhuvan Highway reaches Daman with a superb panorama of the world's highest peaks—use the long-range telescopes in the viewing tower. To see traditional pagodas and woodcarvings, head west to Bandipur and Sirubari. Contact the tourist board for information about staying with village families.

www.visit-nepal.com/Villagetour.htm

❼ Corfu, Greece

From the island's capital, also called Corfu (Kérkyra), a coastal road travels north through the resort of Gouvia. Fork left to pass through Sgombou. Wind upward through the tranquil mountain villages of Skripero and Troumbeta. The road descends to the seaside village of Ropa on the edge of a fertile plain. From here, head east to quietly chic Agios Stefanos. Return south along the coast to Corfu Town.

www.greeka.com/ionian/corfu/index.htm

❽ Iezer Mountains, Romania

North of the city of Curtea de Argeș, lonely villages and monasteries lie folded into the valleys of the Iezer-Păpușa massif. Road signs are often lacking, but villagers are friendly if you have a problem navigating along the DN73C to Brădet. In Brădet explore the 15th-century wooden *skete* (Orthodox monastery). The next village is Domnești, followed by isolated Corbi.

www.romaniatourism.com

❾ Fairy-tale Route, Germany

This route from Bremen in northwest Germany to Hanau, near Frankfurt, links more than 70 towns and villages associated with the Brothers Grimm fairy tales. Stop in Hameln, famous for the Pied Piper. Romantic Trendelburg Castle, now a hotel, boasts a Rapunzel's Tower. The museum in Schwalmstadt has displays of regional costumes, including the outfit associated with Little Red Riding Hood. Finally, in Hanau, you come to the birthplace of the brothers, Jacob and Wilhelm Grimm.

www.germany-tourism.de

❿ La Gaume, Belgium

Begin in the pink-roofed, hilltop village of Torgny. Head north through the pastoral Gaume region for the Abbey of Our Lady of Orval, best known for its Trappist beers. Farther north comes the scenic valley of the Semois River, where you drive through Mortehan to Bouillon, whose magnificent castle stands above a bend in the river.

www.belgiumtheplaceto.be

⓫ Hilltop Villages, France

In the Middle Ages, hilltop locations meant easier fortification. Gordes, Lacoste, Roussillon, Bonnieux, and Ménerbes are the best known of southern Provence's *villages perchés* (hilltop villages). In Roussillon, stone mined nearby gives the buildings a unique reddish hue. Castle remains, turrets, and towers are part of the view in each of the villages.

www.frenchriviera-tourism.com

⓬ Dorset, England

Begin in Dorchester, heart of the region made famous in the novels of Thomas Hardy. Continue northeast to Milton Abbas, a village of thatched cottages laid out in the 18th century by the landscape architect "Capability" Brown. Continue north to Shaftesbury, a hill town founded in A.D. 800 by King Alfred the Great.

www.dorsetforyou.com

⓭ Ring of Kerry, Ireland

From Killarney, head west along this loop route around the Iveragh Peninsula. At Caherciveen, turn off the N70 for Doulus Head. Return to the N70, then turn right to Valentia Island, with patchwork fields and needle-towered rocks. Loop past St. Finan's Bay and out to scenic Bolus Head. Take a pub break in Caherdaniel before heading back via Kenmare to Killarney.

www.ringofkerrytourism.com

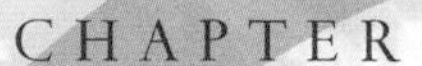

CHAPTER 6

URBAN EXCURSIONS

CITIES PRESENT SPECIAL CHALLENGES for drivers. Few historic centers are car-friendly; many have created pedestrian-only zones within their mazes of narrow streets and hidden squares. The journeys on these pages show you how to do what the locals do—find the best routes (and best times) for exploration and reveal the particular delights of escaping for leisurely trips into the surrounding countryside. In Los Angeles, a cruise along Sunset Boulevard offers a journey through a sprawling megalopolis that only the automobile age could create, encompassing Pacific beaches, mesquite-filled canyons, the bright lights of the Sunset Strip, and the architectural extravaganzas housing movie moguls and stars. A journey between three Texan cities—Houston, Beaumont, and Galveston—offers dazzling contrasts, from the Houston Space Center to world-class art museums, from oil barons' mansions to the birthplace of legendary rock diva Janis Joplin. Bedazzlement of another kind can be found on a seasonal trip through the rainbow-colored glories of Holland's tulip-fields, set like necklaces around townscapes straight out of paintings by the Dutch Masters.

In Colmenar el Viejo, north of Madrid, the Church of the Assumption is a fine example of late Gothic Spanish architecture. Notice the gargoyles on the four corners of the 160-foot (50 m) tower.

CANADA

East from Montreal

Cross the St. Lawrence River on Montreal's Pont Champlain (Champlain Bridge) and head out into the beautiful and historic regions that lie southeast and east of the city: pastoral Montérégie and the picturesque, British-settled Eastern Townships.

Leaving behind the sophisticated charms of Quebec's first city, follow the A-10 out into the open plains of Montérégie, famous for its cider apple orchards, maple groves, vineyards, and forests. About 11 miles (18 km) east of the Pont Champlain, take the exit for Chambly to visit Fort Chambly National Historic Site, an 18th-century, French-built fortress in a superb position on the banks of the Richelieu River. Continue 25 miles (40 km) south through the Richelieu valley on Rte. 223. Just beyond the town of St.-Paul-de-l'Île-aux-Noix, stop off for another fascinating historic site: the early 19th-century, British-built Fort Lennox, on an island in the Richelieu River, which you reach by ferry. Back on Rte. 223, carry on south for 5 miles (8 km), then turn east onto Rte. 202. The road takes you through Quebec's rolling wine country, along the northernmost shores of Lake Champlain, and on to the village of Dunham, set on a forested plain with a backdrop of Appalachian peaks. Beyond Dunham, continue on Rtes. 104, 243, and 245 for about 40 minutes to Bolton Centre, where you turn onto local roads to Austin, then follow signs to the Abbaye de St.-Benoît-du-Lac. Spend some contemplative time in the grounds of the Benedictine monastery magnificently situated above Lac Memphrémagog, before heading northeast along the lovely Chemin Nicholas-Austin to Magog in the Eastern Townships (Cantons de l'Est). Rte. 112 leads to Sherbrooke, the graceful regional capital, built at the meeting point of the Magog and St.-François Rivers. North of Sherbrooke, Rte. 143 follows the course of the St.-François River to Drummondville and its Village Québécois d'Antan, a delightful open-air museum that re-creates life in a 19th-century Quebec village. Head back to Montreal along the A-20.

Excursion After Drummondville, you can continue along Rte. 143 to the northwest, where the land levels out and the air is grassy sweet. **Odanak** has a good museum dedicated to the culture of the Wabanaki (Abenaki) nation. Take Rte. 132 northeast, then cross the St. Lawrence to **Trois-Rivières,** Quebec's second-oldest city. The historic Rte. 138—Chemin du Roy (King's Way), opened in 1737—leads southwest beside breathtaking **Lac St.-Pierre,** a lake in the St. Lawrence. At St.-Ignace-de-Loyola, a ferry takes you back across the river. Drive south along Rte. 133, which follows the **Richelieu River,** then back to Montreal on the A-20.

FROM: Loop route from Montreal, Canada

ROADS: A-10, Rtes. 223, 202, 104, 243, 245, Chemin Nicholas-Austin, Rtes. 112, 143, A-20

DISTANCE: 268 miles (432 km)

DRIVING TIME: 6.5 hours

WHEN TO GO: Mid-May through October. Spring is good for the maple harvest, fall for the colors and the apple harvest.

PLANNING: If you tire of driving, rent a boat to explore the numerous navigable rivers and lakes. www.bonjourquebec.com

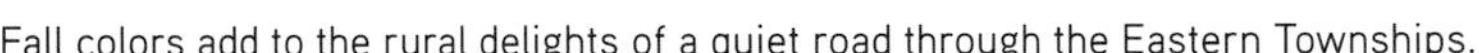

Fall colors add to the rural delights of a quiet road through the Eastern Townships.

A rainbow forms in the spray of Niagara Falls.

CANADA

Two Lakes from Toronto

An easy weekend loop route from Toronto includes shoreline highlights along two of the Great Lakes, Ontario and Erie, and the thundering splendor of Niagara Falls. Stroll along the boardwalk in Port Dover, then watch classic drama in Niagara-on-the-Lake.

From downtown Toronto, head southwest along the shore of Lake Ontario on historic Hwy. 2, one of Ontario's King's Highways that follow the routes of old foot-trails and wagon roads. After 45 miles (72 km), you reach Hamilton, the central town of the lake's Golden Horseshoe, its arc-shaped southwestern fringe. Allow yourself time to explore Hamilton's pleasant downtown and visit the Royal Botanic Gardens, the Art Gallery (with a good collection of Canadian art), and Dundurn Castle, a handsome 19th-century mansion that now houses a museum. After these urban delights, head across open countryside on Hwy. 6 to the harbor town and resort of Port Dover on the north shore of Lake Erie. From here, head east on Hwy. 3 past tobacco farms and rustic villages to Port Colborne and on to Fort Erie, where the Old Fort Erie is a restored British fortress. Standing on its ramparts and looking east across the Niagara River toward the U.S., you will understand the fort's strategic importance during the frontier's less peaceful days. Head north along Hwy. 116 into Niagara Falls—enjoy the city's glitz, and of course don't miss views of the Horseshoe Falls, the spectacular cataract on the Canadian side of the border. In the town of Niagara-on-the-Lake to the north, the British-built Fort George, completed in 1802, is the centerpiece of a historic district, which includes the site where the first parliament of Upper Canada met in 1792. You are now back on the shores of Lake Ontario. Head west on Hwy. 87 until you join the Queen Elizabeth Way, a freeway that whisks you across the Burlington Bay James N. Allan Skyway at the southwestern end of the lake and back to Toronto.

Highlights

- A detour southwest of Port Dover takes you to **Long Point Provincial Park** on a wild, 20-mile (32 km) sandspit poking into Lake Erie. Long Point is home to turtles and many bird species. In spring and fall, it is a staging area for thousands of migratory songbirds and waterfowl.

- In Niagara Falls, don't neglect a trip on ***Maid of the Mist,*** one of four sturdy boats that have been ferrying visitors around the falls for 150 years.

- Capital of Upper Canada in the 1790s, burned by the Americans in 1813, a summer resort at the turn of the 19th and 20th centuries—**Niagara-on-the-Lake** has been through many incarnations, most recently as home of the **Shaw Festival** (April through October), devoted to works by the playwright George Bernard Shaw and his contemporaries. The Shaw Festival Theatre company is one of North America's finest acting ensembles.

FROM: Loop route from Toronto, Canada
ROADS: Hwys. 2, 6, 3, 116, 87, Queen Elizabeth Way
DISTANCE: 280 miles (450 km)
DRIVING TIME: 7 hours
WHEN TO GO: Mid-April to October
PLANNING: Port Dover is a good place to stop overnight.
www.ontariotravel.net

THE TOP

10 City Circuits

Follow in the wheel tracks of some of the world's greatest racing drivers in a selection of Grand Prix and other famous auto-racing street circuits.

❶ Trois-Rivières, Canada

The 1.5-mile (2.4 km) circuit skirts the grounds of the Trois-Rivières' exhibition center near the St. Lawrence River. Start in Avenue Gilles-Villeneuve and drive counterclockwise. Head past the swimming pool under the concrete Porte Duplessis, then up by the baseball stadium, before taking a 90-degree left down Rue Calonne. Navigate the sharpest of the circuit's ten turns to head back to Avenue Gilles-Villeneuve and the finishing line.

PLANNING: Check to see if there are races, fairs, or other entertainments at the grounds. *www.gp3r.com*

❷ St. Petersburg, Florida

The current Grand Prix circuit in St. Petersburg takes in a length of landing strip at Albert Whitted Airport, so you'll have to go back to the original 1985 Trans-Am course, starting beside the Bayfront Arena parking lot. Head up Beach Drive Northeast to 5th Avenue Northeast, then back down past the pier on Bayshore Drive.

PLANNING: Start early, especially in peak season (December through April). *www.gpstpete.com*

❸ Los Angeles, California

TV host and car-lover Jay Leno recommends a 13-mile (21 km) circuit of his home city. He starts at Mulholland Drive, where so many Hollywood movies have been shot and where Steve McQueen and other stars used to race. Head east to Laurel Canyon, turning right and right again onto Sunset Boulevard. Carry on through Beverly Hills, turning up Coldwater Canyon to complete the circuit.

PLANNING: Get up early for clear roads. *www.jaylenosgarage.com*

❹ Montevideo, Uruguay

By the beach in Montevideo, lively Parque Rodó has played host to Grand Prix contests and occasionally becomes the focus of a motor-racing circuit. Drive along the seaside *ramblas* (promenades) of the Punta Carretas neighborhood, with its golf course (look out for parrots in the trees), from Playa Ramirez to Playa Pocitas.

PLANNING: Punta Carretas has the best dining in Montevideo. *www.welcomeuruguay.com*

❺ Melbourne, Australia

The distinct pleasure of the Australian Grand Prix road circuit in Melbourne is that it surrounds the lake in Albert Park, a large area of outdoor activity enjoyed by joggers, skateborders, cyclists, rowers, yachtsmen, and picnickers using public barbecues. The circuit runs for 3.3 miles (5.3 km) around the park, with 15 turns and few long straits for overtaking—not a problem for the civilian driver.

PLANNING: Albert Park is a couple of miles from the center of Melbourne. The Grand Prix is in March, when there is also a carnival. *www.grandprix.com.au*

❻ Bucharest, Romania

Communist dictator Nicolae Ceauşescu's extraordinary Palace of the Parliament, the world's largest civilian administrative building, is the centerpiece of the Bucharest Ring, designed in 2007 and host to auto-racing events that year and the next. The circuit of around 2 miles (3 km) heads off down Calea 13 Septembrie—the street to the left as you look at the building—then right up Strada Izvor and along Bulevardul Națiunile Unite and back to the front of the parliament building.

PLANNING: A tour of the palace is highly recommended. It's open every day, though you may have to book some hours in advance, and it can be closed for state occasions. *www.bucharest-ring.com*

Opposite: The foothills of the Maritime Alps plunging into the Mediterranean create a dramatic setting for Monte-Carlo and its circuit.

❼ Paris, France

Nobody today could get away with the tour of Paris shot in a single take by filmmaker Claude Lelouch at dawn one day in 1976. *C'était un Rendez-vous* lasts nine minutes, the time it took Lelouch to hurtle across the city from Porte Dauphine to Sacré Coeur, taking in the Champs-Élysées and Place de l'Opéra. Reaching speeds of 85 mph (137 km/h), and sometimes on the wrong side of the road, he was afterward arrested.

PLANNING: *www.virtualglobetrotting.com/map/route-during-the-rendez-vous-movie*

❽ Monte-Carlo, Monaco

Monte-Carlo seems to have been built for the roar of its springtime race. At just over 2 miles (3 km), the slowest and toughest of the F1 Grand Prix circuits starts at the back of the harbor (two drivers have ended up in the drink), twists up and around the casino and Grand Hotel hairpin, then roars through a tunnel back to the harbor.

PLANNING: You might want to stay over the border in France, where prices are lower and parking is easier. *www.grand-prix-monaco.com*

❾ Valencia, Spain

The Grand Prix street circuit in Valencia covers 3.3 miles (5.3 km) of the city by the marina, which has become one of the most prestigous berths in the Mediterranean after being spruced up for the 2007 America's Cup. The circuit starts at the back of the marina, goes over a specially built swing bridge, then heads for an inland loop before returning to the port.

PLANNING: Valencia has good temperatures year-round. *www.valenciastreetcircuit.com*

❿ Marrakech, Morocco

The medieval walls of Marrakech form the backdrop for a recently designed 2.8-mile (4.6 km) circuit, located five minutes from the medina (old city). Head up Avenue Mohammed VI, then navigate a hairpin bend onto Route de l'Ourika and loop back to the start. When you've finished, how about drinks at the world-famous Hotel La Mamounia?

PLANNING: The Grand Prix event takes place in April. *www.raceofmorocco.com*

Against a suitably dramatic background of heavy cloud, a shaft of sunlight illuminates some of the log shelters at Valley Forge.

PENNSYLVANIA

Philadelphia Freedom Trail

Memories of the Revolutionary War abound in this history-rich region. An easy day trip takes in the Liberty Bell, two battlefield sites, George Washington's Valley Forge encampment, and the magnificent Longwood Gardens.

FROM: Loop route from Philadelphia, Pennsylvania
ROADS: U.S. 1, Pa. 52, U.S. 202, 422, Valley Forge Road, I-76, I-476, Germantown Pike, Germantown Avenue
DISTANCE: 95 miles (153 km)
DRIVING TIME: 2.5 hours
WHEN TO GO: Year-round
PLANNING: Check opening times—many sites are closed on Mondays. www.visitphilly.com

Start in Philadelphia's Chestnut Lane, with its cluster of historic sites, including Independence Hall (where the Declaration of Independence was signed and the U.S. Constitution drafted), Congress Hall, and the Liberty Bell Pavilion. Enter the chateau country of the Brandywine Valley as you head west out of the city on U.S. 1. Here, the mansions of the du Pont family stand amid a landscape of rolling pastures, woods, and streams. Near Chadds Ford, Brandywine Battlefield State Park contains the farmhouses that served as headquarters for George Washington and his French ally, the Marquis de Lafayette, during the Battle of Brandywine in September 1777. Continue west to Longwood Gardens, the life's work of Pierre du Pont, who died in 1954. This is a glorious chance to relax as you wander through more than 1,000 acres (405 ha) of outdoor gardens or admire the 20 indoor gardens. Wind northeast along Pa. 52 to the elegant town of West Chester. From here, U.S. 202/422 and Valley Forge Road bring you to the primitive log shelters used by George Washington's Continental Army. Valley Forge National Historical Park encompasses 3,500 acres (1,416 ha), including the encampment where Washington and his army spent the bitter winter months of 1777–78 after their defeat at Brandywine and stalemate at Germantown. Don't miss the Valley Forge Historical Society Museum, located inside the park's Washington Memorial Chapel. From Valley Forge, pick up I-76/476 and the Germantown Pike until you reach Germantown Avenue, which runs through the once fashionable enclave of Germantown, also the site of the October 1777 battle. For a clearer picture of the engagement, visit Cliveden, a mansion fortified by the British against American bullets. Continue south along Germantown Avenue into downtown Philadelphia.

TEXAS

Out from Houston

Head from Texas's biggest city—rich, rowdy, and sprawling—on a loop route that shows off wildlife reserves, historic sites, and NASA's Space Center Houston. Stretch your legs and explore Big Thicket National Preserve or Galveston's elegant mansions.

After absorbing Houston's many attractions (see In Focus), take I-45 north to Huntsville. A memorial museum on the campus of Sam Houston State University has several attractions related to Sam Houston, one of the heroes of Texas history, who drove Santa Anna and the Mexicans out of Texas in 1836. After Huntsville, follow U.S. 190 east to the Alabama-Coushatta Indian Reservation, where tribe members guide you through natural woodland, perform traditional dances, and demonstrate tribal crafts. To reach Big Thicket National Preserve, one of Texas's most ecologically diverse areas with pines, savanna, and swampy woods, continue east, then south on U.S.-69/287. Another 30 miles (48 km) south, the city of Beaumont stands at the apex of the Golden Triangle, transformed by the discovery of "black gold" (oil) there in 1901. Beaumont's McFaddin-Ward House leaves you in no doubt of the riches acquired during that time. Follow U.S. 287 to Port Arthur, birthplace of U.S. music icon Janis Joplin, then Tex. 73/124 to High Island. Anahuac National Wildlife Refuge—reached via a short side trip—is 33,000 acres (13,355 ha) of marsh and ponds populated by alligators, wading birds, and waterfowl. High Island is famous for its woodlands, which attract small birds crossing the Gulf of Mexico northward during spring migration. From here, head west on Tex. 87 to Port Bolivar and ride the ferry to Galveston Island, a busy 19th-century port until devastated by a hurricane in 1900. Explore its historic legacy at sites such as the Texas Seaport Museum, the Railroad Museum, and the turn-of-the-century architectural splendors of Moody Mansion and Bishop's Palace. From here, take I-45 back to Houston, with a break south of the city at Space Center Houston, whose exhibits include the Apollo 17 command module.

In Focus Houston's attractions are numerous. For art lovers, the most outstanding is the **Rothko Chapel,** where 14 huge paintings by Mark Rothko combine with natural lighting in an octagonal interior to create an aura of contemplation. Also notable are the **Menil Collection** of art and antiquities and the **Museum of Fine Arts Houston.** The **Museum of Natural Science** offers the walk-through Cockrell Butterfly Center, with hundreds of brilliant species flitting through the greenery.

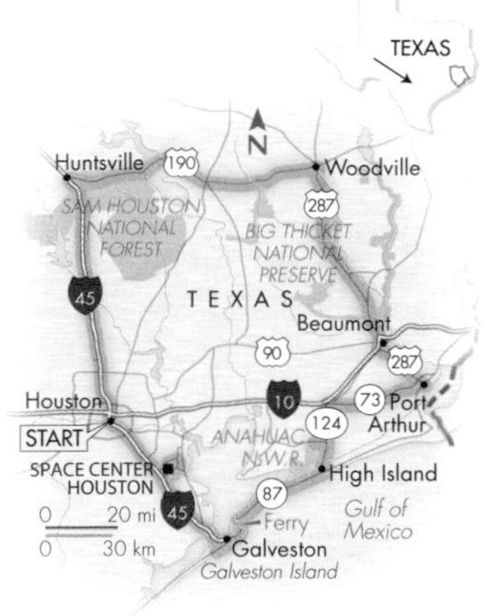

FROM: Loop route from Houston, Texas

ROADS: I-45, U.S. 190, 69, 287, Tex. 73, 124

DISTANCE: 413 miles (665 km)

DRIVING TIME: 8.5 hours

WHEN TO GO: Year-round, though summer humidity is intense

PLANNING: Houston has a lively performing arts scene, with resident opera and ballet companies. www.visithoustontexas.com

At Space Center Houston, you can listen to live communications between NASA Mission Control and a space shuttle, if one is currently in orbit.

WASHINGTON

Seattle's Sound to Mountains

The first half of this stunning drive follows the beautiful Mountains to Sound Greenway, a band of preserved forest and farmland bordering historic highway I-90 from Puget Sound across the Cascades. The return loop leads through high passes and by limpid rivers and lakes.

Seattle's Pike Place Market covers four city blocks and is still very much a working market.

Highlights

- Numerous hiking trails strike out from the 3,022-foot (821 m) Snoqualmie Pass and its vicinity. Many forge north to the **Alpine Lakes Wilderness,** but this area can get crowded during summer and on weekends. Try the trails south of I-90, such as the **Annette Lake Trail** and the **Asahel Curtis Nature Trail**.

- The **Château Ste. Michelle Winery** just outside Woodinville is one of Washington state's largest and most acclaimed wineries. Here, you can walk the 87-acre (35 ha) sprawl of formal gardens and experimental vineyards while arguing the merits of your favorite vintages.

Where better to start your trip than Seattle's renowned Pike Place Market (see Hidden History)? Stock up with victuals for a roadside snack, then head out of the city on I-90. After 25 miles (40 km), turn off for a short side trip to admire the 268-foot (82 m) Snoqualmie Falls. Back on I-90, you start climbing the western flank of the Cascades until you reach Snoqualmie Pass (see Highlights). Pause for a while to take in the spectacular panorama of snowy peaks, old-growth forest, and mountain tundra. Beyond the pass, you briefly traverse Wenatchee National Forest, then drive alongside Keechelus Lake and descend to the valley of the Yakima River. From the town of Cle Elum, Wash. 970 and U.S. 97 take you back into Wenatchee National Forest for a drive northward through forests and farmland. Turn west onto U.S. 2, where mountain-encircled Leavenworth was transformed in the 1960s from a moribund timber town into a mock-Bavarian Alps village in order to attract tourists—even the Mexican restaurant maintains the Bavarian theme. Beyond Leavenworth, U.S. 2 enters the dramatic Tumwater Canyon, carved by the tumbling waters of the Wenatchee River. After 15 miles (24 km), Wash. 207 leads north to beautiful Wenatchee Lake and its state park. Continue along this road until it rejoins U.S. 2 before recrossing the Cascades watershed in Stevens Pass. As far as Monroe, the road mostly parallels the course of the Skykomish River as it meanders westward down the mountainsides. Turn southwest on Wash. 522 to the leafy town of Woodinville, from which an easy half-hour drive along I-405 and Wash. 520 deposits you back in downtown Seattle.

FROM: Loop route from Seattle, Washington
ROADS: I-90, Wash. 970, U.S. 97, 2, Wash. 207, 522, I-405, Wash. 520
DISTANCE: 274 miles (441 km)
DRIVING TIME: 5.5 hours
WHEN TO GO: Late spring through fall
PLANNING: The I-90 part of the route should be drivable in winter, but take snow chains and other traction devices for Snoqualmie Pass. www.mtsgreenway.org

Hidden History When exploring **Seattle,** take your cue from the city's founding settlers and begin at the waterfront, the 1.5-mile (2.4 km) stretch along **Elliott Bay** that holds shops, restaurants, parks, ferry docks, boat-tour departure points, and piers barnacled with businesses. On Pier 59, visit Puget Sound habitats and a working salmon ladder at the **Seattle Aquarium**. Just behind the waterfront, **Pike Place Market** was founded in 1907, when outraged housewives campaigned to remove price-gouging middlemen.

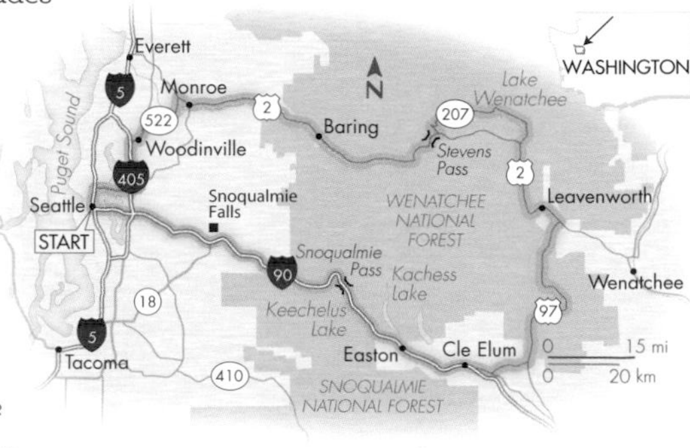

OPPOSITE: Snow covers the shoreline and forests around Lake Wenatchee.

CALIFORNIA

Sunset Boulevard

Follow the quieter western half of legendary Sunset Boulevard, from the Pacific shore in Santa Monica Bay to the fabled heights of Beverly Hills. Sample the fabulous art treasures of the Getty Center, and gaze at the homes of stars in Bel Air.

Take a side trip to North Beachwood Drive for the best views of the Hollywood sign in Griffith Park.

Before setting out on your drive, pull into Gladstone's Malibu, the renowned oceanside restaurant in Pacific Palisades, where a brunch of French toast and orange mimosas (only one, please) will get you into the proper mood.

Thus fortified, head east out of the parking lot onto the Pacific Coast Highway, then almost immediately left onto Sunset Boulevard at its western end. You soon reach the unobtrusive entrance to one of Los Angeles's secret treasures—the beautiful gardens and lake of the Self-Realization Fellowship Lake Shrine. Don't be put off by the cumbersome name. In this exquisite 10-acre (4 ha) haven of peace, you will forget the hustle and bustle of the rest of L.A. as you wander past waterfalls, grottoes, a memorial to Mahatma Gandhi, and a Court of Religions, with monuments dedicated to each of the world's major faiths.

Back on Sunset, follow the road as it loops through the foothills of the Santa Monica Mountains, whose mesquite and sage-covered upper slopes are preserved within the confines of Topanga State Park, crisscrossed with a multitude of hiking trails. If that makes you want to get out and stretch your legs, Bienveneda Avenue, 1.4 miles (2.3 km) beyond the Lake Shrine, offers the first of a number of opportunities. Turn north up the avenue, drive 1.2 miles (1.9 km) to the end of the road, and park on the street. A nearby sign points to the Phil Leacock Memorial Trail, a hiking route into Topanga that starts with a sharp, lung-bursting climb, but brings the reward of fantastic ridgetop views over Pacific Palisades and the ocean.

> "From the sparkling Pacific to neon-clad nightclubs, famed hotels, and Beverly Hills mansions, Sunset Boulevard's 20 windy miles serve as a microcosm of all that is L.A."
>
> -LARRY PORGES
> NATIONAL GEOGRAPHIC EDITOR

Return to Sunset Boulevard, where after just over half a mile (800 m) you pass the small Temescal Gateway State Park, which also links up with Topanga State Park and its trails. Next up, on the right, is the famous Gelson's Market, a store in the iconic California supermarket chain, where you can buy picnic provisions. Beyond Gelson's, look out for the turnoff left to Will Rogers State Historic Park (see Highlights). The beloved humorist deeded his estate to California, which has maintained his home and private polo field. A free audio tour of Rogers's living quarters, with its charming cowboys-and-Indians decor, is a must.

On Sunset again, carry on for just over 3.5 miles (5.6 km) to Brentwood Village, where you can stop for an espresso in one of its many coffee shops. Continue to the San Diego Freeway (I-405)

Pink's: A Legend for Chili Dogs

Beyond Beverly Hills, you enter West Hollywood and the part of Sunset Boulevard called the **Sunset Strip**, famous for its lurid billboards, clubs, and restaurants. Turn south down North La Brea Avenue, where on the corner with Melrose you'll find **Pink's**, probably the world's only hot dog stand with a parking attendant. This is Hollywood, after all, and that limo pulled up alongside may belong to a star. Specialties of the stand, which opened in 1939, include its trademark chili dog (with mustard, chili, and onions), the 10-inch (25 cm) stretch chili dog, and the chili cheese dog. Go in, place your order, and watch your dog being built before your eyes.

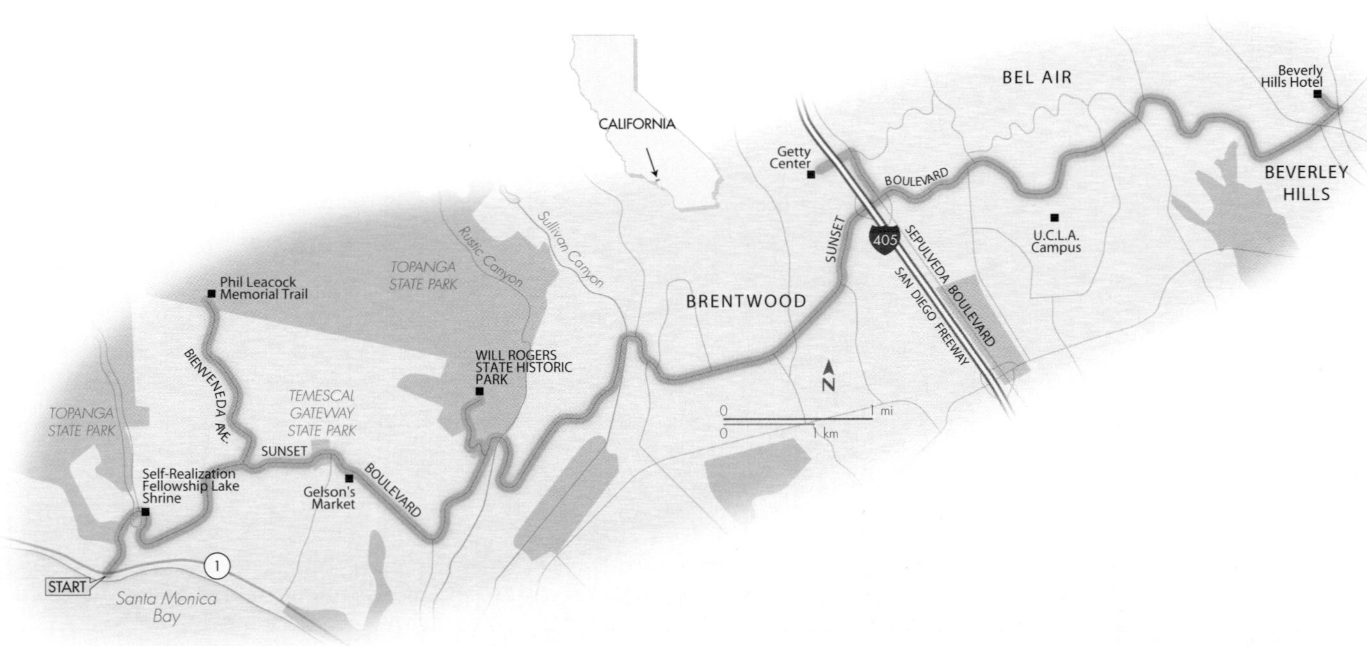

and North Sepulveda Boulevard, which takes you to the gates of the Getty Center (see Highlights). Set on a hilltop amid 110 acres (45 ha) of grounds, the center is worth a visit if only for the views across L.A. with the majestic backdrop of the San Gabriel Mountains behind and the ocean beyond. Relish the panorama, the gardens, the striking modernist architecture, and of course the superb collections of European and North American art.

Return to Sunset Boulevard, where you now enter Bel Air, home of the rich and famous. Two ornate "gates" on the north side of Sunset admit the curious to a maze of small streets that are lined with some of L.A.'s priciest (if sometimes aesthetically troubling) estates—note that the "star maps" hawked here are likely to vary in accuracy. South of Sunset, you can explore the campus of U.C.L.A. or carry on east for more celeb-spotting in Beverly Hills. Here, the perennially "pink palace," the Beverly Hills Hotel, makes a stylish finishing point for your drive. Watch Hollywood dealmakers schmooze in the famous Polo Lounge, or enjoy a salad or sandwich in the poolside Cabana Café.

FROM: Pacific Palisades, California
TO: Beverly Hills, California
ROADS: Pacific Coast Highway, Sunset Boulevard, Bienveneda Avenue, San Diego Freeway (I-405), North Sepulveda Boulevard
DISTANCE: 20 miles (32 km)
DRIVING TIME: 1 hour
WHEN: Year-round, but spring and fall are best if you want to include some hiking
PLANNING: Admission to the Getty Center is free, but for parking you have to pay $15 per car, except on Saturday evenings when parking is also free. The Center is closed on Mondays. www.latourist.com

Highlights

- At **Will Rogers State Historic Park,** there is another chance for a hike–a 2-mile (3 km) loop to and from **Inspiration Point.** Walking the trail as the wispy late-afternoon fog rolls into the park will put a flush of sun and wind on your face.

- Among the treasures at the **Getty Center,** you will find European paintings (including Vincent van Gogh's "Irises"), drawings, French decorative art, and medieval manuscripts. Architect Richard Meier designed the museum, which opened in 1997. Don't miss the glorious **Central Garden,** created by artist Robert Irwin, at the heart of the complex.

The Santa Monica Mountains provide an ever-present backdrop to the beaches of Pacific Palisades.

PANAMA

Panama City to Azuero

Relish the old colonial towns and villages and striking landscapes of Panama's Azuero Peninsula. Step back in time as you share the road with ox-drawn carts and encounter artisans pursuing traditional crafts, from pottery to special five-stringed guitars.

From Panama City's fabled Puente de Las Americas (Bridge of the Americas), follow the Pan-American Highway west for 3.5 hours until you reach the town of Divisa. Turn south onto the Carretera Nacional (National Highway), which takes you into the Azuero Peninsula. After the town of Parita's quaint colonial streets and historic church, you reach La Arena, a village famous for its ceramic workshops. Pause for a while to explore its artisan stores, where the pottery ranges from reproductions of pre-Columbian images to wind chimes and vases. Farther south, the Carretera enters the city of Chitré, where modern commercialism surrounds a colonial center with whitewashed churches. From here, continue to Los Santos. The town of "the saints" is close to the hearts of Panamanians, as the *grito de la Villa de Los Santos* ("shout of the town of Los Santos")—the first public call for independence from Spain—emanated from here in November 1821. The town's compact main square, Plaza Simón Bolivar, is dominated by the Iglesia de San Atanasio, with a simple wooden interior and a baroque gilt altar. Farther on, Guararé is known for producing five-stringed guitars called *mejoranas*. Continue to the city of Las Tablas, famous for *polleras*, the gathered skirts and tops that are a national costume for Panamanian women. From here to the sleepy town of Pedasí, you pass through an increasingly remote landscape, where the only other vehicles on the road are likely to be creaky ox-drawn carts. To make a loop back to Las Tablas, continue west from Pedasí and follow the southern shore of the Azuero Peninsula to El Cacao, then turn north to Las Tablas. The last section of road winds upward through mountain scenery, with magnificent views of the coastal plains and Pacific Ocean.

Excursion Reached by turning left off the Carretera Nacional 14 miles (23 km) south of Divisa, the 20,000 acres (8,100 ha) of **Sarigua National Park** combine a sculpted arid environment—in stark contrast to the backdrop of lush green mountains—with salty lagoons and mangroves along the Pacific shore. More than 160 bird species flock to the lagoons and mangroves. You may also see armadillos. For sweeping views of the park, head for the mirador at its ranger station.

FROM: Panama City, Panama
TO: Pedasí, Panama
ROADS: Pan-American Highway, Carretera Nacional, minor roads
DISTANCE: About 250 miles (400 km)
DRIVING TIME: 5 to 6 hours
WHEN: Year-round
PLANNING: Pack your swimsuit. There are a number of good swimming and surfing beaches near Pedasí. www.panamainfo.com

In Sarigua National Park, a lone tree stump stands erect in a landscape of rocks, wind-tossed sand, and deeply eroded gullies.

The Torre del Cabillito in Mexico City is one of a number of striking modern skyscrapers along the Paseo de la Reforma.

MEXICO

Paseo de la Reforma

The short drive along Mexico City's elegant principal thoroughfare offers a fascinating insight into the country's multicultural character, which dates back centuries: from the Aztecs and Spanish colonialism to French occupation and contemporary Mexican culture.

Built in the reign of the Emperor Maximilian during the French occupation of Mexico in the 1860s, the Paseo de la Reforma, originally modeled on the Champs-Élysées in Paris, slices northwest-southeast through the capital. Start in the Zócalo, the huge square that marks the city's ceremonial center, where Diego Rivera murals adorn the walls of the National Palace (seat of Mexico's government). From here, Avenidas Francisco I Madero and Juárez lead to the Paseo. Turn southwest and reach the first of the *glorietas* (traffic roundabouts) that occur every third block. This one, at the corner with Morelos, has a monument to Christopher Columbus. Watch out for the monument to Cuauhtemoc, the last Aztec emperor, at the corner with Insurgentes, and the golden Angel of the Revolution at the corner with Florencia. Rising ahead of you is the country's tallest skyscraper, the 740-foot (225 m) Torre Mayor, whose curved glass facade has become an architectural icon—it also has the city's highest public observatory on the 52nd floor. Beyond that, the Paseo enters Chapultepec Park (see Unexpected Pleasure), which spreads out around a hill topped by the neoclassical Chapultepec Castle. This one-time home of the Emperor Maximilian now houses the National Museum of History.

Unexpected Pleasure Chapultepec Park has superb outdoor sculptures and three of Mexico City's most fascinating museums: the Modern Art Museum, the Rufino Tamayo Museum, and the National Anthropology Museum. There are also lakes with paddle boats, an old-style wooden roller coaster, and a zoo.

FROM: The Zócalo, Mexico City, Mexico
TO: Chapultepec Park, Mexico City, Mexico
ROADS: Avenidas Francisco I Madero and Juárez, Paseo de la Reforma
DISTANCE: 9 miles (14 km)
DRIVING TIME: 30 minutes
WHEN: Anytime except Sundays, when the Paseo becomes a pedestrian walkway
PLANNING: Ideally, hire someone else to drive—this will allow you to enjoy the sights. www.mexicocity.com.mx

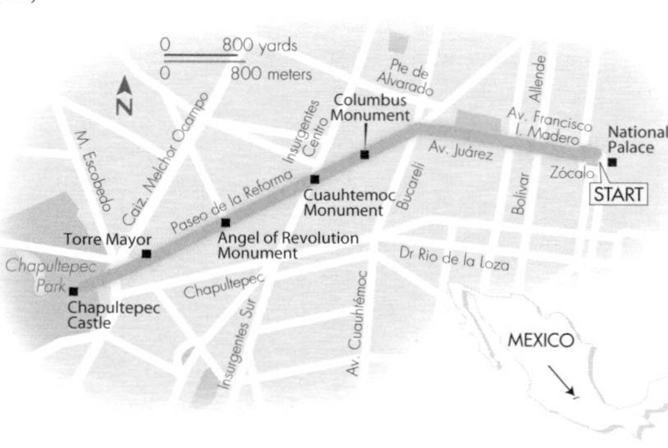

10 Music Drives

The world is blessed with many different rhythms and sounds that make you dance and smile. Here's our pick of the world's top music drives.

1 Hip-Hop Tour—New York, New York

A short drive around the Bronx and Harlem takes you past the sites where hip-hop was born, such as 1520 Sedgwick Avenue, where DJ Kool Herc developed break beats from soul and funk records in the 1970s. Also visit the Graffiti Hall of Fame, the Cotton Club, and the legendary Apollo Theater, where many hip-hop artists performed.

PLANNING: Organized tours with hip-hop experts are available. *www.hushtours.com*

2 Country Tour—Nashville, Tennessee

Nashville is the home of country music, and the whole city is full of it. A stop at the Grand Ole Opry, the world's longest-running live radio show and country's most famous stage, is a must. There is also the Country Music Hall of Fame, Tootsies Orchid Lounge, which has been popular with stars over the years, and Printers Alley with its many music clubs.

PLANNING: The popular CMA Music Festival is held each June. *www.visitmusiccity.com*

3 Cuban Beats—Santiago de Cuba, Cuba

The Casa de la Trova in Santiago de Cuba's Calle Heredia district is perhaps the country's most famous music venue, with regular live shows of Cuba's creolized mix of African and European sounds. Then head north to Casa de las Tradiciones for some real authentic Cuban beats.

PLANNING: The best time to visit the city is July, during its carnival. *www.cuba-junky.com*

4 Rajasthani Music—Jaipur to Jodhpur, India

Start your trip with a visit to Jaipur's Nād Sādhna, a music school that teaches the melodic tunes of Rajasthani folk music. Continue to Jodhpur, where music is a way of life and you'll often see performers on the streets. If you time your trip right, you can visit the world famous RIFF Folk Music Festival, held every October in Jodhpur's impressive Mehrangarth Fort.

PLANNING: Book tickets for the RIFF festival well in advance. *www.nadsadhna.com, www.jodhpurfolkfestival.org*

5 Classical Tour—Vienna to Salzburg via Linz

Beethoven and Mozart, among others, wrote, performed, and lived in these proud musical cities. Start with Vienna's Theatre an der Wien, where Beethoven had rooms and premiered many of his works, and take in a concert at the State Opera House. Also visit the Museum of Sound to learn about the great composers. Head west to Linz, where the Brucknerhaus holds performances most evenings. Continue west to Salzburg, which has Mozart's birthplace and home. Attend the city's Grosses Festspielhaus for more great classical music.

PLANNING: To ensure seeing the famous Vienna Philharmonic , be sure to make reservations at least six months in advance. *www.wien.info, www.visit-salzburg.net*

6 Opera Tour—Parma to Cremona, Italy

From Monteverdi to Verdi, northern Italy was home to some giants of opera. In Parma, visit the home of Verdi and the Museum of Opera before watching a performance in the famous Teatro Reggio. Head northwest to Cremona, home of Stradivarius, and visit the Stradivari Museum to see the artisan's tools and learn about the art of violin making.

PLANNING: Book concerts in Parma early. *www.parmaitaly.com*

Opposite: Renowned fado singer Ana Maria brings a tear to the eye at the Taverna del Rey in Lisbon's Alfama district.

7 Chapel Music Tour—Oxford to London to Cambridge, England

The choral services at the medieval chapels of Magdalen College in Oxford and King's College in Cambridge are an extraordinary delight. When driving between the two cities, detour to London for a classical performance at St. Martin-in-the-Fields in Trafalgar Square or, for contemporary music, at Islington's Union Chapel.

PLANNING: *www.kings.cam.ac.uk, www.magd.ox.ac.uk, www.visitengland.com*

8 Irish Folk Tour, Ireland

Watching a fiddle-player in an Irish country pub is even more enjoyable than drinking the Guinness. From Donegal's Leo's Tavern, the starting point for some of Ireland's folk stars, such as Enya and Clannad, head south to the Coleman Traditional Irish Music Centre, which often has big-name acts. Then drive west to Matt Molloy's Bar in Westport. Farther south, County Clare has many small country pubs with regular music nights.

PLANNING: County Clare's Corofin Music Festival is held in March. *www.discoverireland.com*

9 Fado Music—Lisbon to Coimbra, Portugal

Fado, music with a lonesome voice and acoustic guitar, is known as the soul of Portugal. The most popular version, Lisbon fado, is best found in the Alfama and Mouraria districts of the city. A more refined version of fado is from the university town of Coimbra, where Bar à Capella hosts many top local acts.

PLANNING: Fado music is often played in restaurants. *www.enterportugal.com*

10 Sounds of Bamako, Mali

Ali Farka Toure and Salif Keita thrust Mali's capital, Bamako, onto the world music map. With a mix of traditional West African sounds and bluesy rhythms, the city is a musical wonderland. From legendary Club Djembe in the Lafiabougou district, continue up to Route de Koulikoro, which has some unmissable clubs, and on to the Hippodrome district, with yet more.

PLANNING: Music clubs can be hard to find, so ask local people for inside knowledge. *www.africaguide.com/country/mali*

Lush green vegetation frames a view of Iguazú Falls from the Argentinian side of the gorge.

ARGENTINA

Heading to Iguazú Falls

Skirting the borders of Uruguay and Paraguay, this epic drive climbs from Buenos Aires into Argentina's far northeast, swapping the epitome of urbanity for "outback" scenery en route to Iguazú Falls, a natural wonder that is taller than Niagara Falls and twice as wide.

Leave the intoxicating sprawl of Buenos Aires behind as you take the three-lane Avenida General Paz and head northwest out of the city on R.N.-9. At Zárate, turn north on R.N.-12 across the wide delta of the Paraná River. You have now entered the province of Entre Ríos, a fertile "island" region wedged between the Paraná to the west and the Uruguay River to the east. At Ceibas, take R.N.-14 to the city of Gualeguaychú, renowned for its annual carnival—those in the know prefer it to Rio's bigger bash. For the next 260 miles (420 km), the road runs through lush, wild landscape alongside the Uruguay River, which marks the border first with Uruguay, then with Brazil. Shortly after crossing from Entre Ríos into Corrientes province, follow R.N.-14 east at the junction with R.N.-119 and 127. A little more than 50 miles (80 km) beyond that, take care where a spur of R.N.-14 bears right toward the Brazilian city of Uruguaiana: Keep left on the northerly branch. After another 124 miles (200 km), R.N.-14 finally parts company with the Uruguay River to push more directly northward. You now have the vast Esteros del Iberá (Iberá wetlands) spreading out for more than 4,000 square miles (10,360 km²) to your west, while the terrain around you becomes more hilly. Near San José, shortly after entering the province of Misiones, turn left onto R.N.-105 toward the city of Posadas, standing by the Paraná River on the border with Paraguay. A few miles before Posadas, turn northeast near Villalonga onto R.N.-12. This is the road that leads to your ultimate goal, following the curve of the Paraná and taking you into mountainous scenery for the first time. On the Brazilian border, you cross the Iguazú River—a tributary that joins the Paraná here—on the Puente de la Fraternidad (Fraternity Bridge), a fittingly dramatic end to an epic trip. Take a day or two to rest and see some of the 275 cascades that make up the falls.

FROM: Buenos Aires, Argentina
TO: Puerto Iguazú, Argentina
ROADS: R.N.-9, 12, 14, 105, 12
DISTANCE: 810 miles (1,295 km)
DRIVING TIME: 16 hours
WHEN TO GO: October through March
PLANNING: All Rutas Nacionales (R.N.) are toll roads, so keep small change handy. www.turismo.gov.ar

BRAZIL

Rio to Itatiaia National Park

The pulsing urban beat and pounding surf of Rio de Janeiro seems much farther away than a three-hour drive, along which you'll pass coffee plantations and a Finnish town before reaching Itatiaia National Park.

This is a journey of extremes. Joining the Via Dutra expressway (B.R.-116) from Avenida Brasil in the port district of downtown Rio, you behold a portrait of urban grit that few tourists experience. These neighborhoods of drab concrete and bleak tenements—in which the majority of Rio's working class lives—are in sharp contrast to the picturesque hillside homes of the city's affluent seaside communities of Copacabana and Ipanema. As you depart metropolitan Rio, the urban corridor gradually gives way to rural stretches of small farms where residents hand-cultivate bananas, manioc, and other produce in much the same way as their colonial predecessors. This portion of Via Dutra passes by rolling hillsides, provincial towns, and the occasional remnants of coffee plantations—reminders of a bygone era when slave labor here produced three-quarters of the world's coffee supply. Just past the town of Resende is Penedo, Brazil's only Finnish colony. Head north on R.J.-163 and then east for a short distance on Rua Ribeirão das Pedras to visit Pequena Finlandândia, or "Little Finland," a small community of artisan shops, restaurants, and well-kept streets that offers a glimpse of Finnish life as it existed during the community's heyday in the 1930s. Here, you can observe weavers at work on their looms, tour a chocolate factory, and take one of the many nature trails outside of the village. Next stop is Itatiaia National Park, founded in 1937 and home to an incredible range of plants and animals. Back on Via Dutra, turn off for the upper park at Km 330, or wait until Km 316 and visit the lower park (see Stay a While).

Stay a While Itatiaia National Park offers diverse landscapes. The lower park has a wide array of tropical flora and fauna as well as hikes along **verdant trails** with numerous waterfalls, while the upper park, or *planalto*, offers stunning vistas of rugged peaks and tropical hillsides. In the upper park, venture along the dirt road that leads steadily upward to **Abrigo Rebouças,** a shelter on the slopes of **Pico das Agulhas Negras,** the country's fifth highest peak, 9,157 feet (2,791 m) above sea level.

FROM: Rio de Janeiro, Brazil
TO: Itatiaia National Park, Brazil
ROADS: B.R.-116/Via Dutra, R.J.-163, Rua Ribeirão das Pedras, local roads
DISTANCE: 155 miles (250 km)
DRIVING TIME: 3 hours
WHEN TO GO: May through September
PLANNING: The upper park can be cold during winter (June through August); its trails are for experienced trekkers only. www.embratur.gov.br

In Penedo—a handy base for touring Itatiaia National Park—Finnish immigrants make a corner of Brazil their own.

INDIA

India's Coastal Capital

Showcasing temples, churches, courts, a fort, and a Victorian-era ice house, this drive through Chennai (Madras) follows the Marina, a promenade that sweeps along the waterfront of India's fourth largest city and ends at the Government Museum Complex.

Fishermen and their boats add to the color of the scene along Chennai's Marina.

Begin with a visit to San Thome Church, where relics said to be those of St. Thomas the Apostle are housed. The saint is believed to have come from Palestine to India in about A.D. 52 and to have been murdered in 78. From the cathedral, drive along the Marina, built in 1881–86 and now renamed Kamaraj Road. In the evenings, Chennai's residents come here to chat, snack on freshly barbecued fish, and stroll along the 3-mile (5 km) promenade. Look out on the left for the circular former Vivekananda House, once the Ice House, where the Tudor Ice Company used to store blocks of ice imported from North America. Also on the promenade are the University Examination Hall and Presidency College, built in the style of British architect Edwin Lutyens. Farther along are the Public Water Works and the Chepauk Palace, an extravaganza erected in the 1760s for *Nawab* (prince) Mohammed Ali. The Senate House was constructed in the 1870s in a Gothic-Saracenic hybrid style, with polychrome stones and arcades—a Golden Jubilee statue of the Queen-Empress Victoria stands outside. Continue north to Fort St. George, the first British fortress in India, founded in 1639. Drive or walk through it to find St. Mary's Church, the spiritual heart of old Chennai and Asia's oldest surviving Anglican church (see Highlights). Almost opposite the fort is the spectacular Indo-Saracenic warren of the High Courts. Upstairs by the statue of the first Indian judge, Sir T. Muthasamy Iyer, the public courts have beautiful stained glass and tiles. Finally, drive past Chennai Central Station on High Road to find, on the right, the 19th-century St. Andrew's Kirk, considered India's finest neoclassical church; the circular interior still has its original louvered doors and cane pews. Finish at the Government Museum Complex (see Highlights) on Pantheon Road.

Excursion West of San Thome is Chennai's famous **Kapaleeshwar Temple,** main shrine to the supreme god Shiva. The 16th-century temple buzzes with festivals, singing, and busy bazaars. Enthusiasts can detour southwest to see **St Thomas's Mount,** believed to be where the saint was stoned to death. The Old Cantonment, with lots of old flat-topped Madras villas, is nearby. Return via the racetrack and Raj Bhawan, the former Government House built for Sir Thomas Munro.

OPPOSITE: The Kapaleeshwar Temple's facade teems with brightly colored statues of Hindu gods and goddesses.

Highlights

- Step inside **St. Mary's Church,** built in 1678–80, to see the impressive original teak gallery balustrade and the black Pallavaram granite font, as well as a stunning collection of funerary monuments.
- Visit the **Government Museum Complex,** whose collections are some of the finest of their kind in India. They include superb early Buddhist sculptures, bronze figurines, Indian miniature paintings, musical instruments, and early photographs.

FROM: San Thome Church, Chennai, India
TO: Government Museum Complex, Chennai, India
ROADS: Kamaraj Road, High Road, Pantheon Road
DISTANCE: 4 miles (6 km)
DRIVING TIME: 20 minutes
WHEN TO GO: November to February.
PLANNNG: Hire a driver; Chennai traffic is not for the faint-hearted.
www.tamilnadutourism.org

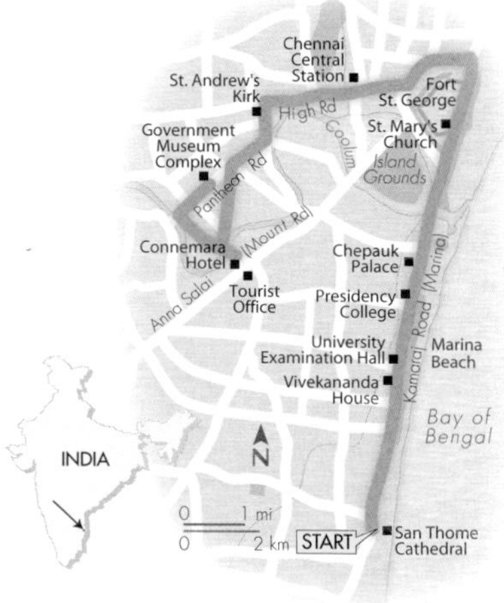

One of India's ubiquitous yellow taxis flashes past the elaborately decorated white-stucco facade of a Raj-era mansion block.

INDIA

Oh Kolkata!

Feel the pulse of Bengal's rich culture, past and present, on this drive through the decaying grandeur of a once-great colonial city. You'll pass some of the public buildings, churches, monuments, and houses built in Kolkata's prime in the 18th and 19th centuries.

Rise with the sun and see dawn break at Babu's Ghat on the Hooghly River. Look across the Maidan (the open space in front of the 18th-century Fort William) to Jawaharlal Nehru Road and you can imagine the city as it once was. Drive along Esplanade past the refurbished Town Hall (dating from 1813) and the grandiose Raj Bhavan (Government House), then pass the Oberoi Grand Hotel on Jawaharlal Nehru Road, and turn left down Lindsay Street to shop in the bustling lanes around New Market. Back on Jawaharlal Nehru Road, the now slightly shabby Indian Museum holds exceptional stone and metal sculptures rescued from sites in eastern India. Farther on, you pass the Asiatic Society of Bengal, founded by the Oxford-educated scholar and judge Sir William Jones in 1784. Turn left on Park Street, then right on to Middleton Row to see the Convent of Our Lady of Loreto. Beyond Camac Street, on Shakespeare Sarani, the Royal Calcutta Turf Club (founded in 1820) is one of the many British clubs that have changed little since the days of the Raj apart from the nationality of the members. Take a stroll around South Park Cemetery, then head back the way you came, stopping off at St. Paul's Cathedral. Finally, you reach the symbol of British imperialism in the East, the now-restored Victoria Memorial, fronted by a statue of the Queen-Empress seated in regal glory.

In Focus The most spectacular of Kolkata's many festivals, **Durga Puja,** falls in September and October and brings the city to a near standstill to celebrate Durga, the god Shiva's wife in her destructive form. Idol-makers work all year to create hundreds of Durga images, painting their straw and unbaked clay models in gaudy colors to look like film stars. People create glitzy settings for the fierce and furious ten-armed goddess, and crowds stroll the streets to view them for ten days before Maha Ashtami, the day when the images are paraded down to the Hooghly River and immersed in its waters.

FROM: Babu's Ghat, Kolkata, India
TO: Victoria Memorial, Kolkata, India
ROADS: Esplanade, Lindsay Street, Jawaharlal Nehru Road, Park Street, Middleton Row, Camac Street, Shakespeare Sarani
DISTANCE: 6 miles (10 km)
DRIVING TIME: 20 minutes
WHEN TO GO: September to March
PLANNING: Get to the Indian Museum when it opens at 10 a.m.
www.westbengaltourism.gov.in

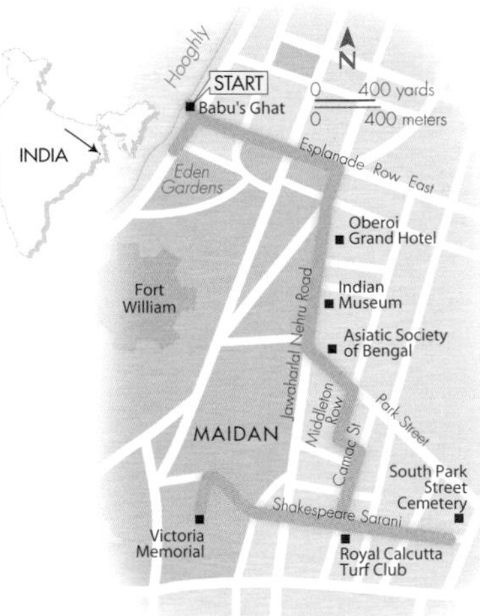

NORWAY

From Oslo to the Fjords

Say goodbye to vibrant Oslo and head for Norway's wild south, with deep-blue fjords, mighty snow-capped mountains, and powerful waterfalls. Here, you'll find both high-octane adventure and ample space for calm contemplation.

The E18 leads west out of Oslo toward Drammen. After about 15 minutes, turn north on the E16, which climbs steadily higher to the village of Sollihøgda. As you descend on the other side, panoramic views of the agricultural Ringerike Plain and its ring of mountains open up before you. At the large roundabout outside Hønefoss, take the forested tourist route RV7 toward Gol. Stop in Krøderen to see the 19th-century railway station, now a museum and part of a heritage railway line. In summer, take a steam train to Vikersund and back. After hugging the long eastern shoreline of misty and tranquil Lake Krøderen, you'll enter the deep, narrow Hallingdal Valley, a prime skiing area in winter and good hiking country in summer. Drive up to the municipalities of Flå and Gol and continue along the north shore of Strandafjorden. When approaching the wooden, red-painted Hol church, the largest in the area, stay on the RV7 for another steep climb to the ski resort of Geilo, and finally an ascent to the edge of the Handangervidda plateau. The distinctive flat-topped Hallingskarvet mountain range is in view to the north. The road descends to the Måbødalen Canyon—where you can take a path to Vøringsfossen waterfall, a white-water cascade that drops about 600 feet (183 m) into the canyon—and then drops down to sea level at Hardangerfjord, the world's third largest fjord. Continue on the RV7 along the shoreline, and take the ferry across the fjord from Brimnes to Bruravik. Head for Voss on the RV7/13 through the Vallavik Tunnel, taking the RV13 to rejoin the E16 at Voss (see Excursion) for the two-hour drive to Bergen, gateway to the fjords.

FROM: Oslo, Norway
TO: Bergen, Norway
ROADS: E18, E16, RV7, RV7/13
DISTANCE: 300 miles (480 km)
DRIVING TIME: 7.5 hours
WHEN TO GO: Year-round
PLANNING: Snow may close roads in winter. The ferry from Brimnes to Bruravik will be replaced by a suspension bridge in 2013. www.visitnorway.com

Excursion Canyons and hairpin bends await you beyond Voss. Driving northeast along the E16 takes you to the **Stalheim Canyon,** lined by one of the steepest roads in Norway. On either side of the canyon are the Stalheimfossen and Sivlefossen waterfalls, with 413-foot (126 m) and 541-foot (165 m) cascades respectively. Farther on is the world-famous **Flåm Railway**. The spectacular 50-minute journey between Flåm and Myrdal passes towering mountains, thundering waterfalls, and green meadows. At Flåm, you can also take a cruise on the narrow **Nærøyfjord,** hemmed in by high, steep-sided mountains.

The calm waters of Hardangerfjord reflect sky, mountains, and the pretty village of Eidfjord nestled on the shore.

THE TOP

10 Cities in Your Headlights

Bright lights in big cities—as darkness falls, lights start to blaze and dazzle, transforming great metropolises into nocturnal wonderlands.

1 Fifth Avenue, New York, New York

At night, shop windows on Fifth Avenue have a million-dollar sparkle. Traffic goes one way, so start at the top of this fabled 5-mile (8 km) stretch, at Frawley Circus at the north end of Central Park. Beyond the Metropolitan Museum of Art, you reach the Plaza Hotel and the shopping legends: Bergdorf's, Tiffany, Bulgari, Furtunoff. Then on to Saks Fifth Avenue, past Madison Square Park, and into Washington Square.

PLANNING: Traffic eases off after 8 p.m. *www.visit5thavenue.com*

2 Washington, D.C.

Impressive by day, D.C.'s monuments are even more so when lit up at night. The Capitol and White House take on their full majesty unruffled by the arguments of the day. Make the circuit from the Lincoln Memorial to the Capitol down Independence Avenue and back along Constitution Avenue beside the White House.

PLANNING: If you don't want to drive, night tours are available. *www.washington.org*

3 South Beach, Miami, Florida

When the shimmering sand and deep-blue sea are lost to the night, South Beach shines brightest. Three parallel roads—Washington Avenue, Collins Avenue, and fabled Ocean Drive—offer a fine confectionary of art deco buildings, with boutiques, bars, nightclubs, and restaurants that stay wide awake till dawn.

PLANNING: To get the full South Beach effect, go when it's busiest—in winter and on weekends. *www.miamibeachfl.gov*

4 Lakeshore Drive, Chicago, Illinois

On your side of the road as you head north is inky black Lake Michigan, scattered with the pinprick lights of ships, fishing boats, and leisure vessels. On the other side, by the southbound lanes, are the soaring lights of the city's famous skyscrapers, including the 1,450-foot (440 m) Willis Tower (formerly known as Sears Tower), the tallest building in the U.S.

PLANNING: Avoid the evening rush hour, which lasts until around 7:30 p.m. *www.cityofchicago.org*

5 The Strip, Las Vegas, Nevada

"Welcome to Fabulous Las Vegas," says the sign by the road from the airport. This is Las Vegas Boulevard South, better known as the Strip, a 4-mile (6 km) dazzler that becomes neon heaven at night. From the replica Eiffel Tower of the Paris Las Vegas Hotel and St. Mark's Tower at the Venetian Resort Hotel Casino to the classic Flamingo (lit up in pink, of course) and Caesar's Palace, it's hard to take it all in at one go—you'll need to drive up and down several times.

PLANNING: Avoid holiday weekends. *www.vegas.com*

6 Sydney, Australia

Sydney's waterside setting around a magnificent harbor makes it great to tour at night, which is why evening tours of all kinds are offered, from romantic limousines to motorbikes. Take the Sydney Harbour Tunnel to the bright lights of Luna Park, then turn back across the Sydney Harbour Bridge for views of the Opera House. Coming off the bridge, head up Observatory Hill for a panorama of the nighttime city—the Observatory Park is open until 10 p.m., and you can see the night sky close up from the Observatory.

PLANNING: There is a toll on southbound traffic on Sydney Bridge. Observatory visits need to be pre-booked. *www.sydneyobservatory.com.au*

Opposite: A floodlit replica of the Statue of Liberty stands outside the New York-New York Hotel and Casino on Las Vegas's famous Strip.

7 Rome, Italy

Always spectacular, Rome's fountains and monuments are particularly appealing when lit up at night. Start with a circuit of the Colosseum, then head past the Forum to Piazza Venezia. Join Corso Vittorio Emanuele to cross the Tiber, where Castel Sant'Angelo looks ready for the final act of *Tosca*, and head for St. Peter's Basilica.

PLANNING: Traffic should be less chaotic on Sunday evenings, and in August. *www.rome.info*

8 Kurfürstendamm, Berlin, Germany

Berlin's most exciting street in the bohemian 1920s and 30s, Ku'dam—flanked by rows of plane trees on wide pavements—is still the place to promenade in the evening. Start at the quieter west end. As you head east, restaurants, shops, and clubs animate the scene, culminating in the dramatically lit belfry of the Kaiser Wilhelm Memorial Church, bomb-damaged in World War II and rebuilt in the 1960s.

PLANNING: The street comes alive every evening until around midnight. *www.visitberlin.de*

9 London, England

A 2-mile (3 km) drive from Buckingham Palace to St. Paul's Cathedral takes in some of the city's brightest lights. From the palace, The Mall leads past snow-white Carlton House Terrace to Admiralty Arch and Trafalgar Square, where the spotlights are on Admiral Nelson at the top of his column. The Strand, along the southern edge of the West End, leads past the Savoy Hotel to Fleet Street, where St. Paul's, majestically lit, comes into view.

PLANNING: If The Mall is closed, take Birdcage Walk to Parliament Square, and go up Whitehall to Trafalgar Square. *www.visitlondon.com*

10 Cape Town, South Africa

Sunsets in Cape Town are famous. Start on Blouberg Beach for the classic view of the warm evening light playing on Table Mountain. Then head back into town and wind your way to Signal Hill, where you can watch the Southern Cross start to shimmer above the mountain while Cape Town twinkles at your feet.

PLANNING: The drive is about 15 miles (24 km). *www.tourismcapetown.co.za*

GREECE

Exploring Attica's Coastline

Leave behind the snarled traffic and smog of Athens as you wind your way along the coast to Akra Sounion, then north to Agios Stefanos. This is a snapshot of Greece in miniature—high hills, beach resorts, small villages, old churches, and fascinating classical sites.

In Athens, follow Leof. Syngrou southwest to Hwy. 91, then turn left at the port of Pireás and head south on the coastal route, with the clear, sparkling Aegean to your right. South of the suburban sprawl is Vouliagméni, a popular beach resort and escape from the city. A small temple to Apollo lies just south of town. Continue south along the coastal road until the imposing Temple of Poseidon, dating from about 440 B.C., comes into view at the peninsula's southern tip. When visiting the temple, don't follow the example of the British Romantic poet, Lord Byron, who carved his name on the ruins. Back on Hwy. 91, turn right and almost immediately the route number changes to 89 and the road heads north, following the coast before veering inland through fertile lands toward the small town of Markopoulon. After Markopoulon, backtrack to Hwy. 89 and turn left. Turn right onto Hwy. 85 almost immediately, which brings you to the port of Rafina. Head for the harbor, following signs for "Ferries," and try one of the waterside restaurants. Return to Hwy. 85 and continue north to the smaller resort of Nea Makri, where you join Hwy. 83 and turn right toward Marathon, site of the Battle of Marathon in which the Athenian army defeated the Persians (see Hidden History). To visit Tymfos Marathona, the simple burial mound under which the Athenian dead were interred, drive about 2.5 miles (4 km) south of Marathon and look for the sign. There is a small but worthwhile Archaeological Museum farther north on Hwy. 83 on the left. From Marathon, continue on the now winding Hwy. 83 until you reach the leafy village of Agios Stefanos. Take a right onto the main Athens–Thessaloniki highway (Hwy. 1/E75) to return to Athens.

Hidden History In 490 B.C., 10,000 Athenians defeated an army of 25,000 Persians at **Marathon;** the Athenians lost only 192 men, the Persians 6,400. News of the victory was carried back to Athens by one of the soldiers, Phedippides, who ran all the way from Marathon to the Acropolis in full armor. After relaying the information, he died on the spot from his exertions. The present-day term "marathon" commemorates that brave feat, and each October a marathon is run along the original route.

FROM: Loop route from Athens, Greece
ROADS: Leof. Syngrou, Hwys. 91, 89, 85, 83, 1/E75.
DISTANCE: 120 miles (190 km)
DRIVING TIME: 4 hours
WHEN TO GO: Year-round
PLANNING: During the summer months, carry drinking water. www.visitgreece.gr

The ruined Temple of Poseidon on the headland of Akra Sounion is visible from miles away.

A fairy-tale castle complete with cylindrical towers looms over the village of Manzanares el Real.

SPAIN

Madrid Mountain Drive

Take a day trip from Madrid and drive northwest of the city past dramatic landscapes. There are plenty of places to stop and breathe the mountain air in the Sierra de Guadarrama, a range of granite mountains that runs between the plains of La Mancha and Castile.

Having sated your appetite on Madrid's jaw-dropping trio of great art galleries—the Prado, the Thyssen-Bornemisza, and the Reina Sofía—head north up the Paseo de la Castellana and take the M-607. After Colmenar el Viejo, turn right onto the M-609, then follow the M-608 through the Cuenca Alta del Manzanares nature reserve toward Manzanares el Real, with its imposing and well-preserved 15th-century castle. Continue toward Cerceda, then take the M-607 toward Navacerrada. The road starts to climb as you drive past a reservoir on the left. With a 16th-century church and some good restaurants, Navacerrada is popular with weekenders from Madrid. After the village, take the M-601 up to the mountain pass of Puerto de Navacerrada. At the top, turn right onto the M-604 toward Cotos, the valley on your left. The former ski station of Puerto de Cotos mountain pass, now the Peñalara nature reserve, is 10 minutes farther on. Stop to stretch your legs on one of the well-marked hiking routes (leaflets available at the information center). The winding road drops 2,300 feet (700 m) into the Lozoya valley where, just before Rascafría, you reach the Real Monasterio de Santa Maria de El Paular, founded in 1390. Leaving Rascafría, which has several restaurants, take the M-611 toward Miraflores de la Sierra. After crossing the Río Lozoya, the road climbs again with a series of sharp bends to the 5,892-foot (1,796 m) pass of Puerto de Morcuera, with superb views over the plains of Castile. The road winds down to the village of Miraflores de la Sierra, surrounded by oak forests and a pleasant place for a stroll and a coffee. To return to Madrid, retrace your steps from Soto del Real.

FROM: Loop route from Madrid, Spain
ROADS: Paseo de la Castellana, M-607, M-609, M-608, M-601, M-604, M-611, M-609
DISTANCE: 110 miles (177 km)
DRIVING TIME: 3 hours
WHEN TO GO: Spring through fall
PLANNING: www.whatmadrid.com

THE NETHERLANDS

Springtime in Holland

In spring, Amsterdam's parks, window boxes, and flower markets overflow with tulips. For a yet more spectacular display, take a tour of the bulb fields of Haarlem, where a rainbow-colored patchwork of blossoms lights up the flat Dutch landscape.

A moat still guards the medieval keep that was once the stronghold of the van Teylingen family.

Highlights

- Visit the small seaside town of **Noordwijk aan Zee** with miles of glorious sand beaches backed by dunes. The conditions here are perfect for windsurfing.
- Haarlem's most famous son is the portraitist of Holland's Golden Age, Frans Hals (1581–1666). Visit the **Frans Hals Museum** to see the world's largest collection of his paintings.
- The late Gothic **church of Sint Bavokerk** in Haarlem dates mainly from the 16th century and has a richly decorated organ built in 1738.

Head out of the center of Amsterdam along Vijzelstraat, then take the S100, the S106, and the A10/E22 until you reach the A4/E19, heading southwest. At Junction 4 (Nieuw Vennep), take the N207 exit, toward Lisse. When you meet the N208, turn left for Lisse, a small, pretty small town in the middle of the Bloembollenstreek, the bulb-growing district, whose flat, multicolored fields stretch for nearly 20 miles (32 km) from Haarlem in the north to Leiden in the south. In Lisse, the Museum de Zwarte Tulp (Grachtweg 2A; closed Mondays) is devoted to the fascinating history of the tulip, introduced to the Netherlands from Turkey in the 1550s and so highly valued that small fortunes were once paid for prize blooms. Head north out of town for the entrance to Keukenhof (mid-March to mid-May), the 80-acre (32 ha) park that serves as a showcase for the Dutch flower industry. Spectacular colors (and heady scents) are the theme of this park, where bulbs are planted in layers to ensure continuous color from March through May. Some of the gardens are themed—natural, water, secret, and historical—and there are even mazes. From Keukenhof, turn right back into Lisse, then follow the N208 southward through the bulb fields to Sassenheim. On the edge of the town is the pretty Ruïne van Teylingen, the remains of a 13th-century castle. Follow the N443 until it meets the N206 near Noordwijk aan Zee (see Highlights). The N206 will take you northeast to Haarlem through some of the bulb district's most colorful fields. Visit Haarlem (see Highlights) before returning to Amsterdam on the A9/10.

FROM: Loop route from Amsterdam, the Netherlands
ROADS: Vijzelstraat, S100, S106, A10/E22, A4/E19. N207, N208, N443, N206, A9
DISTANCE: 62 miles (100 km)
DRIVING TIME: 2.5 hours
WHEN TO GO: Late March to mid-May
PLANNING: Keukenhof shuts when the season ends in mid-May. www.holland.com, www.keukenhof.nl

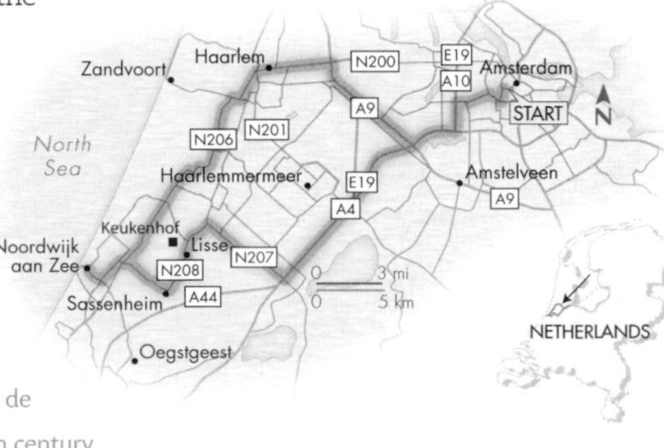

Excursion Detour to **Zandvoort,** Amsterdam's nearest beach resort, on N206 and N201. Behind the beach strip, the **Nationaal Park de Kennerduinen** (Kennemer Dunes National Park) has varied habitats and attracts many rare and unusual birds, such as the great ringed plover. Well-marked trails meander through a landscape of dunes, ponds, and small forested areas. The long, sandy beach on the other side of the dunes is a pleasure to walk along. Return to Amsterdam on N201 via **Hoofddorp,** where the Museum de Cruquius (March to October) is worth a stop to learn how Holland's bulb fields were created in the mid-19th century.

OPPOSITE: Muscaria (grape hyacinth) and glowing tulips form a river of color in the Keukenhof gardens.

Stirling's famous castle is perched dramatically at the town's highest point.

SCOTLAND

Glasgow to St. Andrews

This pleasant drive takes you north and east from Glasgow past gently rolling hills to Stirling and its magnificent castle. From here, you follow a rural route south of the Ochil Hills to the historic university city of St. Andrews, also the home of golf.

Leave gritty yet cultured Glasgow behind, and from Junction 17 of the M8 motorway, follow the A82 Dumbarton road to the A81, heading north out of the city. Follow the valley of Strath Blane, then turn right onto the A811, which descends into the wide Forth Valley. Ahead of you, Stirling climbs along the spine of a long volcanic crag. Among the attractions lining the city's cobbled streets are the 15th-century Church of the Holy Rude (Rood), where the 13-month-old James VI (later James I of England) was crowned king of Scotland in 1567 as successor to his deposed mother, Mary, Queen of Scots. Also worth seeing are Argyll's Lodging, the 1632 townhouse of the Dukes of Argyll, and the ornate 16th-century facade of Mar's Wark, a grand residence planned but never completed by the first Earl of Mar. Pride of the town, though, is Stirling Castle, home to the Scottish Royal Court between 1488 and 1625. From Stirling, the A91 leads east under the green and brown rampart of the beautiful Ochil Hills. At Dollar, turn left and walk up steep, narrow Dollar Glen. High on the hillside is the stark, atmospheric ruin of Castle Campbell, an imposing 15th-century stronghold. The A91 continues into the flatter farming country of Fife and reaches the small city of St. Andrews, looking out onto the North Sea (see Stay a While).

Stay a While Set above broad sands and rocky bays, **St. Andrews,** known for having the world's oldest golf course, is a golfer's paradise. History buffs will also adore the cathedral ruins on the headland and the two university quadrangles of St. Salvador and St. Mary's. St. Andrew's Castle is noted for its grim "bottleneck" dungeon and mine tunnels dug in 1546, when besiegers were attacked underground by their foes, who had dug a counter tunnel from inside the castle's walls.

FROM: Glasgow, Scotland
TO: St. Andrews, Scotland
ROADS: M8, A82, A81, A811, A91
DISTANCE: 95 miles (153 km)
DRIVING TIME: 3 hours
WHEN TO GO: Year-round
PLANNING: Daylight driving time is limited in winter when days are shorter. www.visitscotland.com

N
Cupar
A92
St. Andrews
Ochil Hills
Auchtermuchty
Milnathort
Castle Campbell
Stirling Castle
A811
A91
Dollar
M90
Loch Leven
Buchlyvie
M9
Stirling
Forth
Strathblane
0 4 mi
0 8 km
A82
A81
Glasgow
START
M8
U.K.

Also Recommended

❶ South from Ottawa, Canada

From Ottawa, head southwest to the old cotton town of Almonte, then to historic Perth on the Tay River. Carry on to Kingston, at the northeast end of Lake Ontario, whose sights include Bellevue House—a period gem that takes you back to the 1840s when it was the home of John A. Macdonald, later Canada's first prime minister. End the day with a leisurely boat cruise from Gananoque.

www.ontariotravel.net

❷ Long Island, New York

Drive east on Long Island, past the trendy bustle of the Hamptons, to North Fork and Shelter Island. Following N.Y. 25 from downtown Manhattan to Riverhead, keep an eye out for farm fresh berries, peas, tomatoes, and pumpkins sold from roadside stands. In Greenport, a 10-minute ferry trip takes you to Shelter Island with good beaches for swimming at West Neck Harbor and hiking trails in Mashomack Preserve.

www.northfork.org

❸ Ohio & Erie Canalway, Ohio

Cleveland lies at the northern end of the Ohio & Erie Canalway, built in the 1820s and 30s as a goods route to link Lake Erie with the Ohio River. It is now a National Heritage Area that encompasses parks, trails, museums, and local roads as well as waterways in the valleys of the Cuyahoga and Tuscarawas Rivers. Cuyahoga Valley National Park is the gem of the region, with waterfalls, streams, and abundant wildlife.

www.ohioanderiecanalway.com

❹ Brandywine Valley, Delaware/ Pennsylvania

The idyllic Brandywine Valley's many museums include Rockwood Park and Museum, one-time home of banker Joseph Shipley, who built it in the 1850s in the Gothic style. If museums don't appeal, enjoy hotdogs at a Wilmington Blue Rocks minor league baseball game. In early May, savor tea and sandwiches while watching the Devon Horse Show, the oldest horse and dog show in the U.S.A.

www.brandywinevalley.com

❺ Turquoise Trail, New Mexico

Connecting Santa Fe and Albuquerque, this drive along N.M. 14 owes its name to the blue-green stone first mined in the region by the Pueblo people. Stop at the quirky Tinkertown Museum, protected by unusual walls—50,000 glass bottles. The Garden of the Gods is a spectacular area of sandstone deposits, running alongside a 4-mile (6 km) stretch of the road.

www.turquoisetrail.org

❻ Damnoen Saduak, Thailand

Take a break from the swelter of Bangkok, though not from noise and crowds, by driving west for 62 miles (100 km) along the Phetkasem Road (Rte. 4) to the floating market in Damnoen Saduak. The market takes place in a *khlong* (canal), packed tight with narrow boats that brim with delicious strawberries, dragon fruit, spices, meats, bowls of noodles, spicy salads, and sticky rice. Return to Bangkok via Nakhon Pathom, which has the largest pagoda in Southeast Asia.

www.bangkok.com

❼ Colombo to Galle, Sri Lanka

Head south from Sri Lanka's commercial capital, Colombo, along the coastal A2. Break for sun-worshiping and surfing at the resort town of Hikkaduwa, then continue along the coast to the ancient port city of Galle in the far southwest of the island. Historic Dutch influence is still visible, with the addition of gorgeous luxury villas hovering on the edge of the sea.

www.srilankatourism.org

❽ Moscow's Golden Ring, Russia

The Golden Ring is a loop of historic cities northeast of Moscow. The first, Vladmir—also the first stop east of Moscow on the Trans-Siberian Railway—was the 12th-century capital of Russia. The 420-mile (678 km) route includes a huge variety of scenes, from industrial landscapes of the Soviet era to beautiful Pereslavl-Zalesskiy on Lake Pleshcheyevo, where Peter the Great amused himself by building a flotilla of small boats.

www.waytorussia.net

❾ Porvoo & Loviisa, Finland

Porvoo, Finland's second oldest town and its 13th-century trade hub, lies just 40 minutes east of Helsinki. Continue east along the E18 to Loviisa, with wooden houses and 18th-century fortifications, built as a defense against the Russians.

www.visitfinland.com

❿ Nelahozeves, Czech Republic

Drive 15 miles (24 km) north from Prague to stately Nelahozeves Castle, whose collections include original manuscripts by Mozart and Beethoven and paintings by Bruegel, Velázquez, and Rubens. In the village of Nelahozeves, visit the birthplace of the composer Antonín Dvořák.

www.aroundprague.com

⓫ Golden Circle, Iceland

A circular route, dubbed the Golden Circle, connects most of Iceland's best-known landmarks. The road passes Hveragerði with greenhouses heated by water from hot volcanic springs and the crater lake of Kerið. Stop off for the waterfall at Gullfoss (Golden Falls), where if the sun is shining dozens of rainbows emerge from the spray.

www.icelandtouristboard.com

⓬ Edinburgh to Newcastle upon Tyne, Scotland/England

Drive south on the A68 through the beautiful hills of the Borders. At Carter Bar, cross into England, where Northumberland National Park holds wonders large and small—from Hadrian's Wall to glimpses of otters in rivers and streams. Pause for a pub lunch in a village such as Falstone, before heading on to Newcastle upon Tyne.

www.northumberlandnationalpark.org.uk

⓭ Lisbon to Porto, Portugal

From Lisbon, head north to Leiria, dominated by a hilltop castle. Feast on fresh sardines in Figueira da Foz, then detour inland to the university city of Coimbra. Admire the canals and whitewashed houses of Aveiro. At the mouth of the Douro River, explore the atmospheric streets and music bars of the ancient city of Porto.

www.portugal-live.net

CHAPTER 7

DRIVING THROUGH HISTORY

EVERY ROUTE ON THESE PAGES has its own story to tell—whether it follows in the footsteps of explorers and pioneers, visits haunting battlegrounds, or uncovers long-vanished civilizations. A tour through the picturesque streets and leafy lanes of eastern Massachusetts follows the route taken by Paul Revere to warn of the British Army's advance on the eve of the Revolutionary War. It also traces the path of the march of the volunteer Minutemen, and visits the first battlefields of the war. An epic North Dakota road trip along the Missouri River shadows the frontier forays made in 1804 by explorers Lewis and Clark. On the other side of the world, a short drive in Goa, India, mingles gorgeous Hindu temples with the gleaming baroque churches of the state's once-thriving Portuguese colony. Moving into antiquity, an archaeological odyssey through Turkey brings you face to face with the remnants of civilizations as sophisticated and complex as our own—cities founded by Alexander the Great, and temples honoring the Greek and Roman gods. Meanwhile, in southwest France, remote Cathar castles testify to an extraordinary period of schism in the Catholic Church.

At the ancient site of Yagul in Mexico, the remains of the Zapotec city contain the Palacio de los Seis Patios (Palace of Six Courtyards), which may have served as a principal residence.

This monumental statue of a viking in Gimli serves as reminder of the town's Icelandic heritage.

Highlights

- If you're bringing the kids along for the ride, visit **Manitoba Children's Museum** at The Forks in Winnipeg for hands-on fun such as dressing up, seeing things through a mosquito's eyes, and clambering around a vintage locomotive.
- **Mennonite Heritage Village** is a 40-acre (16 ha) open-air museum that re-creates the feel of a Mennonite village of the 1800s and tells the story of Mennonite religious persecution and migration to the New World.
- The compound of **Lower Fort Garry National Historic Site,** near Lockport, was begun in 1830, making it the oldest intact stone fur-trading post in North America. Today's visitors are treated to a vivid and detailed portrait of the fur trade.

CANADA

Winnipeg Circle

Bursting with history and culture, this rich and varied loop drive around the prairies of southeastern Manitoba takes in some pretty scenery as well as a number of museums and heritage sites that reveal the region's eclectic past.

Lying along an ancient travel route at the confluence of the Red and Assiniboine Rivers, Winnipeg is one of the oldest settlements in western Canada. At the city's southern outskirts is Riel House National Historic Site, based around the small Red River frame house built for the mother of the founder of Manitoba, Louis Riel. As well as recounting the family's history, the site celebrates the culture of the Métis—descendants of native people and European fur traders. From Winnipeg, take Hwy. 75 south to the francophone village of Ste.-Agathe, then head east on Rte. 305 and Hwy. 52 to the regional hub of Steinbach and stop at Mennonite Heritage Village (see Highlights). Travel north on Hwy. 12, Trans-Canada 1, and Rte. 206 to the prairie hills, woodlands, and artificial lake at Birds Hill Provincial Park. From the park's west gate, turn south on Hwy. 59, west on Hwy. 101, then north on Hwy. 9 to Rte. 238—the River Road Heritage Parkway. This pleasant backroad hugs the Red River, passing buildings that reflect a strong 19th-century English presence. Wander among the 1840s gravestones at St. Andrew's Church (south of Lockport), then cross the lane to St. Andrew's Rectory National Historic Site, an 1854 house with exhibits on Anglican missionary activities. Continue north to Selkirk to climb aboard an 1897 steamship at the Marine Museum of Manitoba. Continue to Gimli, an old Icelandic fishing village on the shore of Lake Winnipeg, then take Rte. 231 west and Hwy. 7 south to Stonewall, where three kiln towers that were in use until the 1960s overlook a beach at Stonewall Quarry Park. Visit Oak Hammock Marsh Interpretive Centre to take a guided canoe outing through reclaimed marsh teeming with wildlife, before returning to Winnipeg.

FROM: Loop route from Winnipeg, Canada
ROADS: Hwy. 75, Rte. 305, Hwys. 52, 12, Trans-Canada 1, Rte. 206, Hwys. 59, 101, 9, Rtes. 238, 231, Hwy. 7
DISTANCE: 200 miles (322 km)
DRIVING TIME: 5 hours
WHEN: May through October
PLANNING: www.travelmanitoba.com

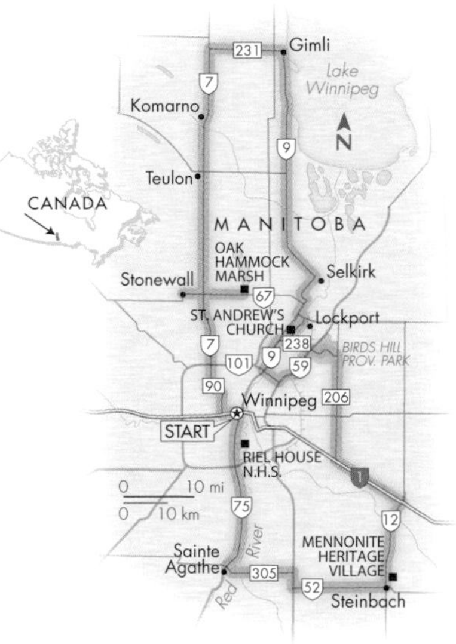

MASSACHUSETTS

Revolutionary Roads

In 1775, the revolutionary spirit was in the air in this corner of New England. Follow in revolutionary footsteps as you visit the locations where some of the most momentous events in the course of American history took place.

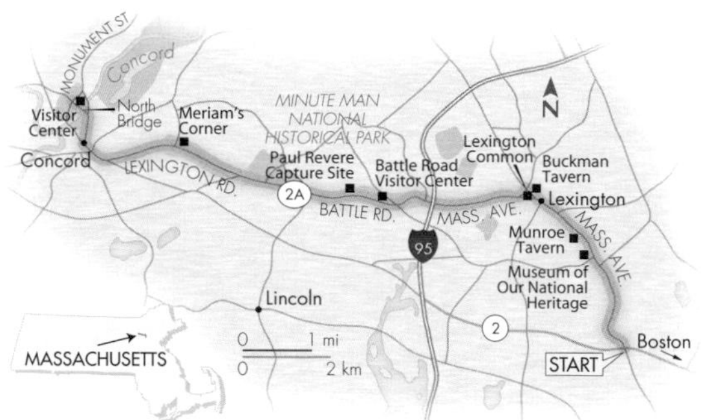

Drive northwest along Lexington's Massachusetts Avenue—the road Paul Revere traveled on his Midnight Ride to the town to warn of the approaching British Army—and stop at the National Heritage Museum for an overview of the events leading up to the start of the Revolutionary War. Back on the road, you pass Munroe Tavern—used as a field hospital for wounded British soldiers—then come to Lexington Common (or Battle Green), where the first shots of the war were fired on April 19, 1775. Nearby is Buckman Tavern, the headquarters of the Minutemen, with its interior restored to look as it did in 1775. Continue on Massachusetts Avenue out of Lexington. Following the route taken by the British on their way to Concord, cross over I-95/Mass. 12, turn right onto Wood Street, then left onto Old Massachusetts Avenue and left again onto Mass. 2A. The drive now falls within Minute Man National Historical Park, which preserves the landscape as it was during those tumultuous times. Park at Battle Road Visitor Center and take a short walk along Nelson Road, a section of Battle Road that retains the crushed stone surface that covered the entire road in 1775. Continue west on Mass. 2A, passing a memorial marking the spot where Paul Revere was captured. Veer right on Lexington Road toward Concord, and go past Meriam's Corner, where the Colonists attacked the British on their retreat to Boston. From Concord's green, turn right onto Mass. 62, then left, and right again onto Monument Street. The militia's first victory occurred at North Bridge, across the Concord River, as they blocked British progress. Explore the Visitor Center here, or return to Concord (see Unexpected Pleasure).

FROM: Lexington, Massachusetts
TO: Concord, Massachusetts
ROADS: Massachusetts Avenue, I-95/Mass. 12, Wood Street, Old Massachusetts Avenue, Mass. 2A, Lexington Road, Mass. 62, Monument Street
DISTANCE: 11.5 miles (18 km)
DRIVING TIME: 30 minutes
WHEN: May through October
PLANNING: www.visitlex.com

Unexpected Pleasure There is more to **Concord** than Revolutionary history. In the early 19th century, the town was the birthplace of Transcendentalism, a literary and philosophical movement espoused by residents, including Ralph Waldo Emerson and Henry David Thoreau. Find out more about both men at the Concord Museum, the Ralph Waldo Emerson House, and the Old Manse—the home of Emerson and author Nathaniel Hawthorne.

The restored 18th-century Hartwell Tavern stands on Battle Road, where the Colonists fought the British.

THE TOP 10 Historic Trails

Experience the rich history of the U.S., from Native American culture and the Civil War, to the gunslingers of the Wild West and the civil rights movement.

❶ George Washington Memorial Parkway, Virginia

A scenic gateway to Washington, D.C., this short drive begins at Mount Vernon, George Washington's home from 1754 to 1799. It then follows the Virginia shoreline of the wide Potomac River, through beech, maple, and oak woodlands, to the colonial port of Old Town Alexandria and on through wetlands cherished by birdwatchers.

PLANNING: Avoid rush hour. The 25-mile (40 km) route ends at the junction with I-495. *www.nps.gov/gwmp*

❷ Hallowed Ground, Pennsylvania/Maryland/Virginia

This tour, starting in Gettysburg, embraces an unmatched concentration of Civil War history. "Hallowed Ground" refers to President Abraham Lincoln's Gettysburg Address, and the drive takes in key battlefield sites including Antietam and Manassas, and passes Eisenhower National Historic Site and the homes of Presidents James Madison and Thomas Jefferson.

PLANNING: The 180-mile (290 km) route follows U.S. 15 and Va. 20. Best from spring through fall. *www.hallowedground.org*

❸ Washington Heritage Trail, West Virginia

A loop of 136 miles (218 km) in the Eastern Panhandle of West Virginia visits scenes from George Washington's life. It begins at Harpers Ferry, the site of John Brown's raid in 1859, then passes Shepherdstown, Martinsburg, the old spa center of Berkeley Springs, and the Cacapon Resort State Park. Another stop, Charles Town, was laid out in 1786 by Washington's brother, Charles.

PLANNING: Go from spring through fall. The drive follows U.S. 340, W. Va. 230, 480, 9, U.S. 522, W. Va. 11, 20, 51. *www.washingtonheritagetrail.org*

❹ Wilderness Road Heritage Highway, Kentucky

Pioneer and folk hero Daniel Boone blazed the Wilderness Road through the Cumberland Gap to settle Kentucky in the late 18th century. Start at Cumberland Gap National Historical Park and visitor center, near Middlesboro, then head north to Berea.

PLANNING: The 94-mile (151 km) route follows U.S. 25E, Ky. 229, U.S. 25. *www.byways.org*

❺ Selma to Montgomery March Byway, Alabama

This drive follows U.S. 80 through a landscape where some of the key events of the American civil rights movement took place. A march from Selma on March 7, 1965, attempting to reach the state capital of Montgomery 54 miles (87 km) away, ended in a brutal police confrontation called "Bloody Sunday." Martin Luther King, Jr., led another march on March 25; it started with 3,000 people and ended five days later with 25,000. Various memorials, landmarks, and exhibits can be seen along the route.

PLANNING: Allow at least four hours to give yourself plenty of stopping time along the way. *www.byways.org*

❻ Historic Route 66, Illinois

Route 66 was commissioned in 1926 to link Chicago to Los Angeles, a distance of 2,440 miles (3,927 km). It was updated and realigned over the years, but the Historic Route 66 can still be traced. The Illinois segment, the first to be completed, starts on Lake Shore Drive in Chicago and heads along I-55, past classic roadside architecture of the 1930s to 1950s, all the way to East St. Louis on the Mississippi.

PLANNING: Allow two to three days. Best from spring through fall. An alternative route after Springfield follows Ill. 4. *www.illinoisroute66.org*

Opposite: Majestic red sandstone formations rise above the scrubland in Monument Valley, Utah, along the Trail of the Ancients.

❼ Billy the Kid Trail, New Mexico

A mountainous loop from Ruidoso visits Wild West sites associated with the gunfighter Billy the Kid. The Byway Interpretive Center and Hubbard Museum of the American West provide background. At Lincoln State Monument, see the courthouse where, in 1881, Billy the Kid awaited hanging, before his escape. He died in a gunfight at Fort Sumner.

PLANNING: Allow at least three hours. The 84-mile (135 km) route follows U.S. 70, 380, and N. Mex. 48. *www.byways.org*

❽ Trail of the Ancients, Colorado/Utah

A double-loop route straddling the "Four Corners" takes in a region inhabited since ancient times by Native American peoples and passes through dramatic sculptural landscapes of bare, eroded rock. Covering 480 miles (772 km), it starts at Cortez and Mesa Verde National Park, and includes Monument Valley Navajo Tribal Park and the Anasazi Heritage Center.

PLANNING: The route follows U.S. 160, Colo. 145, 184, U.S. 491, C.R. 10, U.S. 191, Utah 95, 275, 261, U.S. 163, 162, 262. *www.byways.org*

❾ Pioneer Historic Byway, Idaho

Beginning at Franklin, drive across the southeastern corner of Idaho for 127 miles (204 km) to Freedom. For part of the way, the route follows the Oregon Trail along the Bear River. Conflict with the Shoshone led to the Bear River Massacre of 1863, near Preston. A detour leads to the ghost town of Chesterfield, an early Mormon settlement.

PLANNING: Allow at least half a day. The route follows U.S. 91, Okla. 34, U.S. 30. *www.pioneerhistoricbyway.org*

❿ San Luis Obispo North Coast Byway, California

Starting at the Mission San Luis Obispo de Tolosa, founded in 1772, head north through spectacular coastal scenery, taking in missions, railroad museums, and Hearst Castle, the palatial mansion of newspaper tycoon William Randolph Hearst, near San Simeon. The drive ends at the Monterey County Line, just south of Big Sur.

PLANNING: The 57-mile (92 km) route follows Hwy. 1. *www.byways.org*

Greenery surrounds a reconstructed thatched house and corn granary at the Grand Village of the Natchez Indians.

TENNESSEE/ALABAMA/MISSISSIPPI

Natchez Trace

Forged by bison, enlarged by Native Americans, and used by explorers, traders, bandits, missionaries, and soldiers traveling between the Cumberland and Mississippi Rivers, Natchez Trace Parkway is one of America's most famous frontier trails.

From Nashville, the state capital, follow Tenn. 100 southwest to Franklin, the site of a Civil War battle in 1864, then Tenn. 96 west to enter the Trace Parkway. Wooded curves give way to the open fields of Tennessee's horse and farm country. Pass Gordon House, one of the few structures remaining from the Old Trace, and a park dedicated to Meriwether Lewis, which contains his grave and a reconstruction of the old log inn (or "stand") where he died from gunshot wounds in 1809. Cross Buffalo River and turn left to loop along a scenic ridge on a section of the old road. You leave the woods for open farmland, before trees return at Sweetwater Branch, where wildflowers garnish the trail in spring. Oak and hickory forests give way to Alabama's flat red-clay plains and cotton fields. Cross the Tennessee River at Colbert Ferry, where Chickasaw Indian George Colbert once charged Andrew Jackson $75,000 to ferry his army across the river.

Entering Mississippi, you come to the Jamie L. Whitten Bridge over the Tennessee-Tombigbee waterway. Beyond here, look out for Pharr Mounds, eight great, dome-shaped burial mounds constructed by the so-called Mound Builder culture 2,000 years ago. Next you head through a boggy area that is home to great blue herons, and past fields of cotton, soybean, and milo. The Trace then sweeps through pastures and forests before traversing a bottomland of shrubs and swamps. At River Bend, you get panoramic views of the Pearl River, before the parkway follows Ross Barnett Reservoir and reaches Ridgeland's Mississippi Crafts Center, which sells Choctaw baskets, pottery, quilts, and other crafts. Explore Mississippi's gracious capital, Jackson, then cross miles of farmland and the cultivated floodplain at Big Bayou Pierre. The road rolls past farms and wetlands before climbing up a forested ridge, and terminating at an intersection with U.S. 61. Seven miles southwest is the city of Natchez.

FROM: Nashville, Tennessee
TO: Natchez, Mississippi
ROADS: Tenn. 100, 96, Natchez Trace Parkway
DISTANCE: 444 miles (715 km)
DRIVING TIME: 8.5 hours
WHEN: Year-round
PLANNING: There's only one gas station on the parkway, at mile 193. www.nps.gov/natr

LOUISIANA

Cajun Country

Down by the bayou in Louisiana's Cajun country sits the Old Spanish Trail, a 19th-century frontier pathway and trading route passing moss-draped oaks, alligator-filled swamps, sugarcane fields, and former slave plantations.

The city of Houma is known for its Cajun music, swamps, fishing, and food. Try a spicy étouffée dish, or a gumbo, before leaving town, then head west on U.S. 90 passing roadside signs advertising swamp tours of the Atchafalaya Basin, the continent's largest river basin swamp. The road cuts through sugarcane fields and soon reaches the turnoff for the alligator farm and trapper's cabin at Wildlife Gardens. Return to U.S. 90 and head past the heavy equipment used by the inshore oil industry before crossing the bridge into St. Mary Parish along Bayou Boeuf, a good place to spot bald eagles. Leaving behind the enormous McDermott shipyard, you enter the major port of Morgan City. Following signs for Berwick/La. 182, take the Long-Allen Bridge across Atchafalaya River and go through the tiny towns of Berwick and Patterson. The drive now passes Louisiana's "sugar bowl," where plantations—each with its own sugar mill—flourished before the Civil War. Soon, La. 182 feeds into U.S. 90 before veering off into cane fields. A couple of miles on is Centerville, a former sugar hub with many Victorian homes and antebellum planter's mansions. After the small town of Garden City, the road becomes a stately boulevard through the restored downtown and elegant historic district of Franklin. Continuing northwest, you'll arrive at Jeanerette, whose Bicentennial Museum has exhibits on the sugar industry and bayou life. The drive wanders through cane country to the attractive historic district of New Iberia. Turn right onto La. 31, crossing more sugarcane fields to St. Martinville, an elegant French-style town known as Petit Paris. Continue on to your final destination, the friendly town of Breaux Bridge.

FROM: Houma, Louisiana
TO: Breaux Bridge, Louisiana
ROADS: U.S. 90, La. 182, 31
DISTANCE: 108 miles (174 km)
DRIVING TIME: 2 hours
WHEN: Spring through fall
PLANNING: Breaux Bridge holds a crawfish festival on the first weekend of May every year. www.drivetheost.com

Hidden History Known as the "Capital of Cajun Country," **Lafayette** is a 20-mile (32 km) trip on La. 182 from New Iberia. The colorful city has a number of dance halls, restaurants, and music venues where you can enjoy local zydeco music. Find out about Cajun history in Vermilionville, a heritage and folk park, and visit the Acadian Cultural Center to learn about the lives of the French-speaking Acadians who settled in the area at the end of the 18th century.

Zydeco music has its roots in the rural, black, French-speaking communities of 19th-century Louisiana.

NORTH DAKOTA/SOUTH DAKOTA

Lewis and Clark

Following in the footsteps of explorers Lewis and Clark, this drive along the banks of the Missouri River passes sites commemorating Native American history, from early settlements 10,000 years ago to the Indian wars of the late 1800s.

A traditional sod house built from tough, thickly rooted prairie grass at Fort Abraham Lincoln State Park.

In the early days of the 19th century, the land beyond America's western frontier was unknown to the still infant nation. In 1804, President Thomas Jefferson commissioned a group of fearless explorers—led by Meriwether Lewis and William Clark—to explore the wilderness, sail to the end of the Missouri River, and reach the Pacific Coast. This drive follows part of the route taken by Lewis and Clark, flanking both sides of the Missouri. You start on the river's east bank, heading north from the state capital, Bismarck, on N. Dak. 1804 (named after the year of the expedition). You soon pass Double Ditch Indian Village State Historic Site, a former village of the Mandan tribe, who were among the first Native Americans encountered by Lewis and Clark on their journey. From here, proceed 30 miles (48 km) to Washburn and follow the signs to North Dakota Lewis and Clark Interpretative Center, which provides an overview of the expedition, with a special emphasis on the time they spent at Fort Mandan. There are also displays of Native American artifacts from every tribe the pair encountered on their journey. Nearby, visit the reconstructed Fort Mandan Overlook State Historic Site, not far downstream from the original headquarters of the expedition during the winter of 1804–05. It was at Fort Mandan that Lewis and Clark met the French-Canadian trader Toussaint Charbonneau, whose wife Sacagawea, a Shoshone Indian, became their invaluable guide.

> "The bluffs of the river which we passed today were upwards of a hundred feet high... Considerable quantities of pumice stone and lava... are broken and washed down by the rain and melting snow."
>
> -MERIWETHER LEWIS

To see one of the few remaining wild sections in the area, take a detour 15 miles (24 km) south of Washburn via N. Dak. 200A to Cross Ranch State Park and Cross Ranch Nature Preserve. Here you can see what the landscape was like 200 years ago, when the river flowed unhindered through native prairies. The park has hiking trails, campgrounds, and canoes to rent.

Double back to Washburn and continue north on U.S. 83, through the state's coal-mining heartlands, to Audubon National Wildlife Refuge, a complex of refuges that provides sanctuary for Canada geese, white pelicans, threatened piping plover, and sandhill cranes. From here, head west on N. Dak. 200 along the southern shore of Lake Sakakawea, crossing Garrison Dam, one of the world's largest earthen dams. At Pick City, continue south on N. Dak. 200 to Country Road 37, and follow signs to Knife River Indian Villages

The Mandan and Hidatsa Tribes

The Mandan and Hidatsa of North Dakota built their characteristic earth-lodge dwellings on a wooden frame covered with willow branches, grass, and sod. Each lodge housed up to 17 people, and was owned by the matriarch of the family. She was responsible for building and maintaining the lodge, as well as for farming, dressing skins, and sewing clothing. Mandan history relates that their people predated the Hidatsa in the region, and that they taught the wandering Hidatsa to build settled villages and grow corn and vegetables. The Mandan also created a major focal point of trade on the Missouri, and established strong, well-defended communities.

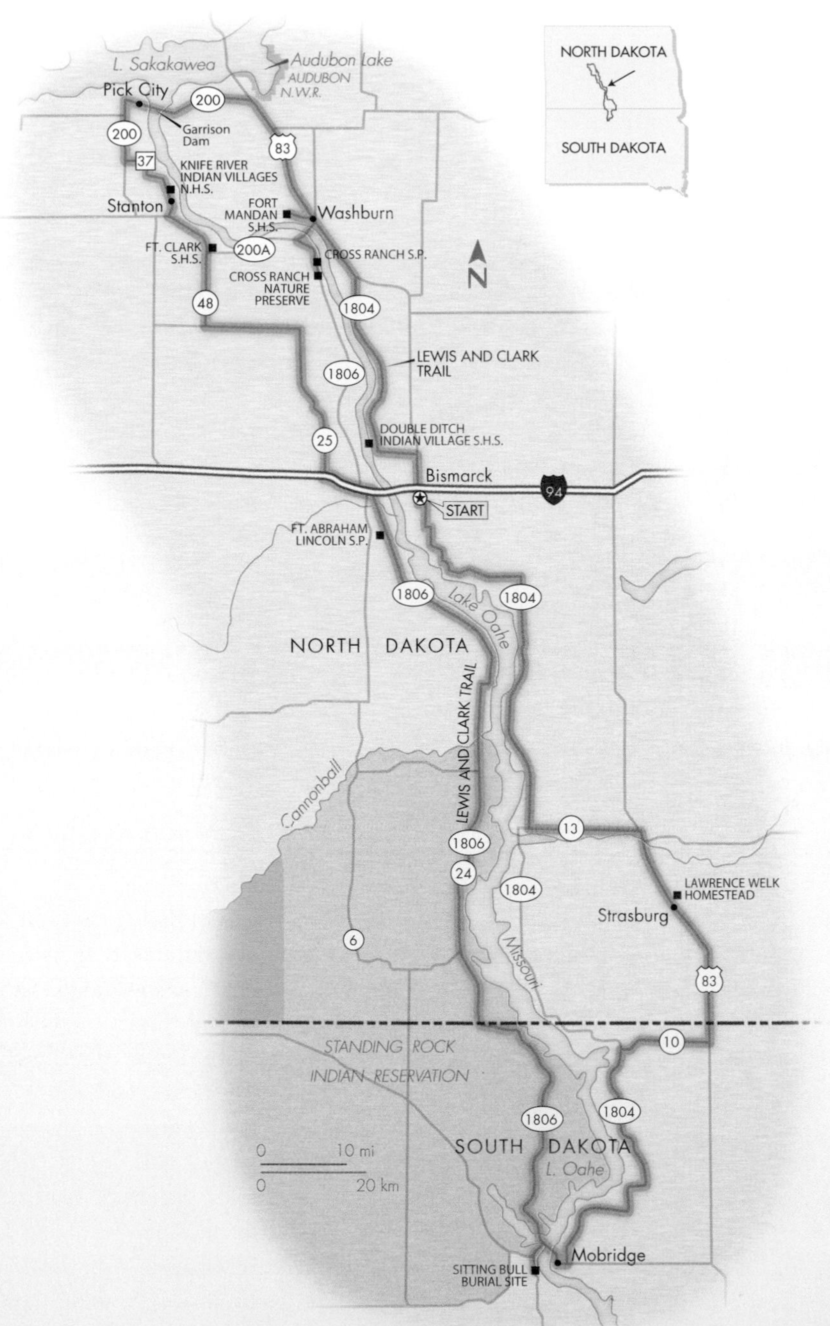

National Historic Site (see Highlights). Continue driving south, through the quiet town of Stanton, and then southeast on N. Dak. 200A to Fort Clark State Historic Site, where you can walk among the archaeological remains of a Mandan earth-lodge village and of the fort itself, a major fur-trading post built in 1831. From here, head south via N. Dak. 48 and N. Dak. 25 and then east on I-94, following signs to Fort Abraham Lincoln State Park (see Highlights). Lt. Colonel George Custer once lived here, and it was from Fort Abraham that he made his final journey to fight the Sioux and Cheyenne at the Battle of Little Big Horn. Drive south on N. Dak. 1806 (the year of the explorers' return journey from the Pacific) entering South Dakota. At Mobridge, you can see the grave of Sitting Bull, the victor of Little Big Horn who was shot and killed in 1890. Another marker here honors Sacagawea. Follow N. Dak. 1804 north, then cross back to North Dakota. Take U.S. 83 north through Strasburg, stopping off at the Lawrence Welk Homestead, the birthplace of the famous band leader, before returning to Bismarck.

FROM: Loop route from Bismarck, North Dakota
ROADS: N. Dak. 1804, 200A, U.S. 83, N. Dak. 200, Country Road 37, N. Dak. 48, 25, I-94, N. Dak. 1806
DISTANCE: 400 miles (644 km)
DRIVING TIME: 7 hours
WHEN: Spring through fall
PLANNING: www.lewisandclarktrail.com

A reconstructed and furnished earth lodge at Knife River Indian Villages National Historic Site.

Highlights

- For thousands of years, Native Americans lived, hunted, and gathered food in the region of **Knife River Indian Villages National Historic Site.** The visitor-center displays, traditional earth lodge, and walking tour to two Hidasta village sites are evocative of what their lives were like.

- Among the many attractions at **Fort Abraham Lincoln State Park** are the reconstructed Mandan Indian village of On-A-Slant, and, on Cavalry Square, the re-created Commanding Officer's Headquarters once inhabited by General Custer.

SOUTH DAKOTA

Black Hills

The high ridges and deep caverns of the isolated Black Hills are sacred to the Lakota, and have long been rich in gold and history. This drive takes in mines and gold-rush towns, living and prehistoric wildlife, stunning rock formations, and monumental carvings.

Crazy Horse Memorial in the Black Hills was begun in 1948 and is still to be completed.

In Rapid City, on the eastern edge of the Black Hills, visit the Museum of Geology to understand the ancient processes that shaped the mountain range. Then take I-90 (U.S. 14) northwest past the Black Hills National Cemetery to Sturgis—home to the Sturgis Motorcycle Museum & Hall of Fame. East of town, on S. Dak. 34, is Fort Meade Museum, established after the Battle of Little Big Horn as a frontier post. Double back and take I-90 to Spearfish for the D.C. Booth Historic National Fish Hatchery, built in 1896 to introduce trout to the area. Head south on U.S. Alt. 14—the colorful Spearfish Canyon Scenic Byway—to the goldrush town of Lead, where you can learn about the history of goldmining at Black Hills Mining Museum and the nearby Homestake Mine. Farther on is the casino town of Deadwood, whose Adams Museum tells the stories of the town's famous residents, including "Wild Bill" Hickok, who was killed in 1876 while playing poker at Saloon No. 10. Pan for gold at the Broken Boot Gold Mine in town before heading south on U.S. 385 to Crazy Horse Memorial, a work in progress that dwarfs the nearby faces on Mount Rushmore. Then take S. Dak. 89 south and U.S. 18 east to Hot Springs' Mammoth Site, where the skeletons of Columbian and woolly mammoths have been found. From here, head north on U.S. 385 to Wind Cave National Park, one of the world's most complex cave systems. Continue north on Needles Highway (S. Dak. 87) through needle-like granite formations and take U.S. Alt. 16 to the restaurants and curio shops of Keystone. Farther north, on U.S. 16, you reach Bear Country U.S.A., a drive-through wildlife park where you are restricted to your car as about 100 grizzly and black bears roam free. From here, return to Rapid City.

Excursion From Keystone, a short detour on S. Dak. 244 brings you to one of America's most famous monuments—the sculpted heads of **Mount Rushmore.** Between 1927 and 1941, the faces of Presidents Washington, Jefferson, Theodore Roosevelt, and Lincoln were blasted and carved out of the rockface—450,000 tons of rock were removed in the process. The mountain is lit up during summer evenings, and can be viewed complete with a talk, film, and singing of the national anthem.

OPPOSITE: Granite needle-like formations run alongside Needles Highway in Custer State Park, South Dakota.

Highlights

- Packed with spectacular formations of sparkling crystals, **Jewel Cave National Monument,** near Crazy Horse Memorial, is the second longest explored cave system in the U.S.
- In **Custer State Park,** adjacent to Wind Cave National Park, you can see free-roaming bison, deer, antelope, and mountain lions.
- **Reptile Gardens,** five minutes north of Bear Country U.S.A., is the perfect roadside attraction for kids, with a multitude of slithering creatures from alligators to boa constrictors.

FROM: Loop route from Rapid City, South Dakota

ROADS: I.-90 (U.S. 14), S. Dak. 34, U.S. Alt. 14, U.S. 385, S. Dak. 89, U.S. 18, S. Dak 87, U.S. Alt. 16, U.S. 16

DISTANCE: 258 miles (415 km)

DRIVING TIME: 6 hours

WHEN: Year-round

PLANNING: www.blackhillsbadlands.com

COLORADO/UTAH

Dinosaur Diamond Loop

Red-rock canyons, extraordinary geological formations, and cottonwood-lined rivers flowing through arid, high-plains terrain delight the eye at every turn on this drive. But the real stars are the dinosaur fossils and footprints you'll see in museums along the way.

The prehistoric "thunder lizards" give their name to the town of Dinosaur. Head west out of town on U.S. 40, stopping a few miles later in Jensen at Dinosaur Quarry to see thousands of dinosaur fossils, then drive on to Vernal to visit the Dinosaur Garden at the Utah Field House of Natural History State Park Museum, which has 18 life-size dinosaur models, including Utahraptor, a huge predator discovered in 1991. The route passes through Ashley National Forest, as U.S. 191 heads west and south into Indian Canyon. Cliffs rise steeply beside the conifer-flanked road as it climbs to the 9,100-foot (2772 m) Indian Creek Pass and then drops down to the small town of Helper. Follow the Price River to Price, stopping to visit the College of Eastern Utah Prehistoric Museum, then drive southeast for 60 miles (96 km) through rolling terrain to join I-70. Turn off south on U.S. 191 once more, toward Moab. After 16 miles (26 km), take a short detour right along a dirt road (impassable after rain) to explore the fossils of the Mill Canyon Dinosaur Trail. Just before Moab is the turning to Arches National Park. Leave your car for a few hours to view the rock formations that have made this region famous. Back on the road in Moab, pick up the Colorado River Scenic Byway (Utah 128) and after crossing the state line, stop in Fruita to visit the Dinosaur Journey Museum. From Fruita, detour into Colorado National Monument, famous for gorges and monoliths, and enjoy panoramic views from the overlooks on the 23-mile (37 km) Rim Rock Drive. Return to Dinosaur north along Colo. 139 and 64, climbing to the 8,240-foot (2510 m) Douglas Pass and through Canyon Pintado National Historic District—a "painted canyon" with at least 200 Native American pictographs and petroglyphs.

Excursion To visit the **Cleveland-Lloyd Dinosaur Quarry,** the world's richest collection of Jurassic-era dinosaur bones, leave Price and head south on Utah 10 for 12 miles (19 km) to Utah 155. Turn east to Elmo, then follow the signs. More than 12,000 bones and one dinosaur egg have been excavated so far, with more still in the ground. The visitor center has a complete skeleton of the carnivorous Allosaurus, one of the largest flesh-eaters of the Jurassic period, and a Stegosaur wall mount.

FROM: Loop route from Dinosaur, Colorado

ROADS: U.S. 40, 191, 6, I-70, Utah 128/Colorado River Scenic Byway, Colo. 139, 64

DISTANCE: 480 miles (770 km)

DRIVING TIME: 10 hours

WHEN: Spring through fall

PLANNING: Some side trips are on unpaved roads that can be impassable after rain or snow. www.dinosaurdiamond.org

Paleontologists carefully chip away rock, uncovering dinosaur fossils at Dinosaur Quarry.

Cacti and spring flowers flourish in the canyons of the Superstition Mountains.

Highlights

- **Goldfield** bills itself as a ghost town, but has found new life as a tourist attraction. Enjoy a narrated ride on the 1.5-mile (3.5 km) Superstition Scenic Railway, a replica of Mammoth Mine, two museums, horseback riding, restaurants, and saloons.
- Visit the **Roosevelt Dam Visitor Center** to learn how the area's four lakes were created in the early 20th century. The observation deck has excellent lake views.
- The Salado people lived in the well-protected caves about the Tonto Basin. The visitor center at **Tonto National Monument** tells their story; a hiking trail takes you up to the lower dwellings, where you can see 20 well-preserved rooms. The upper dwellings are even more spectacular. To take the 3-hour round-trip hike there, you'll need to book ahead.

ARIZONA

Apache Trail

Shadowing the ancient footpaths of the Apache Indians, this partly unpaved route gives dazzling views as it skirts the craggy Superstition Mountains just east of Phoenix, plunges into the sheer rock canyons of the Salt River, and encounters blue desert lakes.

To traverse the stunning Superstition Mountains in the footsteps of Native Americans and pioneers, begin in Apache Junction and take Ariz. 88 north past Goldfield Ghost Town (see Highlights) to begin the climb into the mountains. According to legend, Jacob "The Dutchman" Waltz discovered a mine and hid a cache of gold here in the 1870s. Gold-seekers can detour to the 4,553-foot (1,387 m) Weaver's Needle, a volcanic plug visible to the north. Inside the vast Tonto National Forest, the road curves past saguaro cacti up to a view of Canyon Lake, azure blue against a desertscape of steep, brown cliffs. The road winds around the lake for several miles, climbs again, and descends into Tortilla Flat, an old stagecoach stop and the trail's only town. The ramshackle stores are right out of a Hollywood set—the bar has saddles for seats and prickly pear ice cream. Beyond Mesquite Flat, the dirt road begins heading to Fish Creek Hill, the main attraction of the drive. A short trail leads cliffside for panoramic views of sheer-walled Fish Creek Canyon. From here, the road descends precipitously, dropping 800 feet (242 m) in the next mile (1.6 km) with sharp switchbacks barely wider than your car. Cross Fish Creek along a single-lane bridge, then follow the creek and other small streams until the road descends to views of Apache Lake and the desert rock face known as the Painted Cliffs of the Mazatzal Mountains. For the last 10 miles (14 km), the road snakes along Apache Lake, pushing between tall hills past the Burnt Corral Recreation Site to Theodore Roosevelt Dam (see Highlights). Continue to your journey's end at Tonto National Monument to see the cliff dwellings of the prehistoric Salado people (see Highlights).

FROM: Apache Junction, Arizona
TO: Tonto National Monument, Arizona
ROAD: Ariz. 88
DISTANCE: 46 miles (74 km)
DRIVING TIME: 3 hours
WHEN: Fall through spring
PLANNING: Best in dry weather as much of the road is unpaved.
www.arizonascenicroads.com

THE TOP

10 Ancient Drives

Beautiful, sacred, and historically significant, these drives encompass some of the most important Native American sites in the United States.

❶ Mohawk Trail, Massachusetts

Crossing northeastern Massachusetts, the Mohawk Trail (Rte. 2) was designated in 1914 as the country's first "scenic" drive. For hiking and whitewater rafting, stop at Mohawk Trail State Forest and the Deerfield River. Mohawk Park in West Charlemont is dedicated to regional natives, and Indian trading posts are located in Shelburne.

PLANNING: To reach the 38-mile (61 km) trail from Boston, take Hwy. 90 and Hwy. 91 north to the Hwy. 2 exit. *www.mohawktrail.com*

❷ Minnesota Scenic Byway, Minnesota

Wildlife is abundant along the byway, which passes vistas of hardwood forests, granite outcroppings, and expansive prairies. Visit Lower Sioux Agency Historic Site near Morton and Fort Ridgely State Park Historic Site to learn about the Dakota (Sioux) Indians who once held this land. Near Mankato, the Winter Warrior Sculpture marks the site where 39 captured Dakotas were hanged in 1862.

PLANNING: The 300-mile (483 km) drive follows the Minnesota River east from Minneapolis. *www.exploreminnesota.com*

❸ Native American Scenic Byway, South and North Dakota

The Native American Scenic Byway crosses four reservations of the Lakota Sioux, passing many sites that remain highly significant to the tribe. Sioux chief Sitting Bull is commemorated with a monument at Standing Rock, and at Cheyenne River, a memorial marks the site of the Massacre at Wounded Knee that marked the end of the Indian Wars.

PLANNING: The 300-mile (483 km) route begins in Pierre, South Dakota, and follows the Missouri River north. *www.byways.org*

❹ Peter Norbeck Scenic Byway, South Dakota

This 70-mile (113 km) loop route from Custer, the oldest city in the region, wends through the Black Hills—the spiritual center of the Sioux homeland—passing pine-covered peaks, rock spires, and clear lakes. Highlights include the Peter Norbeck Visitor Center and the Black Elk Wilderness.

PLANNING: Best in early summer and early fall. *www.byways.org*

❺ Geronimo Trail National Scenic Byway, New Mexico

The Apache chief Geronimo was one of the most sagacious of all the native opponents of the U.S. Army, and his home range has changed little since his time. Heavily forested mountains are interspersed with tremendous expanses of arid mesa lands, and sightings of elk and mule deer are common. Be sure to visit the historic district and museum in the town of Truth or Consequences. Chloride, a ghost town, is located near Winston.

PLANNING: The 154-mile (248 km) route forms a half-loop between San Lorenzo and Beaverhead. *www.geronimotrail.com*

❻ Taos Enchanted Circle Drive, New Mexico

The Taos region exhibits exhilarating natural beauty, and this 80-mile (129 km) drive affords an excellent one-day overview. Circling north and east of the town of Taos through the Carson National Forest, the drive skirts Wheeler Peak, New Mexico's highest mountain. Central to the tour is Taos Pueblo. The town has been continuously inhabited for more than 1,000 years and is the only Native American community that is designated as both a UNESCO World Heritage site and a National Historic Landmark.

PLANNING: Best from late spring through fall. *www.go-newmexico.com*

Opposite: The smooth-walled buildings of Taos Pueblo, New Mexico, are made entirely of adobe—a mixture of earth, water, and straw.

❼ Tuba City to Canyon de Chelly, Arizona

The past is present here, where Hopi families carry water to pueblo villages perched atop high mesas. The route passes Navajo National Monument—from where you can hike to the nearby 13th-century cliff dwellings of Keet Seel and Betatakin—and finishes up at Canyon de Chelly National Monument, with ruins dating from 2500 B.C.

PLANNING: The drive follows Hwy. 160, Ariz. 564, Reservation Route 59, Hwy. 191, Reservation Routes 12, 64, and South Rim Drive. *www.arizonaguide.com*

❽ Southeast Border Drive, Arizona

Southeast Arizona is one of the most biologically diverse areas in the continental U.S. and was once the home ground of the Apache. Both Cochise and Geronimo raided here. Stop off at Cochise's stronghold near Sunsites and the infamous Tombstone, known as the "town too tough to die."

PLANNING: Hwys. 10, 80, 82, and 19 form an irregular loop from Tucson of roughly 300 miles (483 km). *www.arizonaguide.com*

❾ Volcanic Legacy Scenic Byway, California and Oregon

Traversing the volcanic highlands of northern California and southern Oregon, this 500-mile (800 km) route passes active hot springs, expansive wildlife refuges, and spectacular waterfalls. Points of particular interest include Lava Beds National Monument, Mount Shasta, and Crater Lake.

PLANNING: From I-5 in California, take Hwy. 36 to Mineral and follow the byway north to Oregon. *www.volcaniclegacybyway.org*

❿ Bigfoot Scenic Byway, California

Hwy. 96 traces the Klamath River for 100 miles (160 km) through some of the wildest scenery in California. The area is notorious for supposed sightings of Bigfoot. The Yurok, Hupa, and Karok tribes continue to follow highly traditional lifestyles along the Klamath, and depend on subsistence salmon and steelhead trout fishing.

PLANNING: Take Hwy. 96 from Willow Creek. The road ends at Yreka on Hwy. 5. Winter can be cold and rainy. *www.byways.org*

NEW MEXICO/ARIZONA

Route 66

Running from Chicago, Illinois, to Santa Monica, California, Route 66 was inaugurated in 1926. On this stretch of the road, vintage diners and motels oozing fabulous fifties-era dazzle still lure today's motorists.

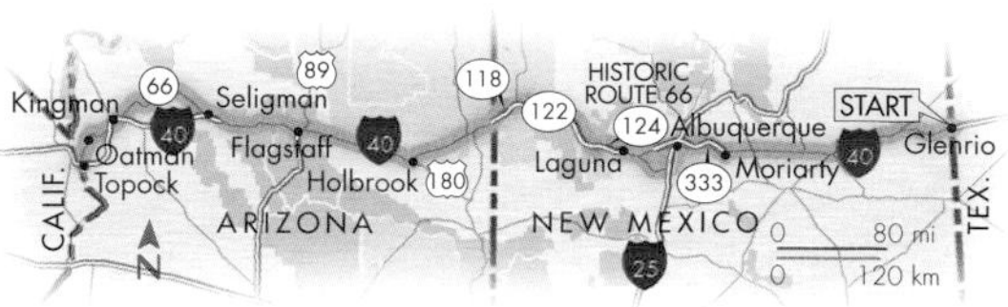

Immortalized in song and story, much of Route 66 has been replaced by other highways, but you can still drive parts of it. Begin at the almost abandoned town of Glenrio on the Texas/New Mexico state line, and follow the original Route 66 west along I-40. After 40 miles (64 km) of arid grassland, you reach Tucumcari, a fifties time capsule. Exit the interstate at the agricultural town of Moriarty, taking N. Mex. 333 west to Albuquerque, whose Central Avenue retains many buildings from Route 66's heyday, such as the 1927 Pueblo-style KiMo Theatre. From here, take I-40 west to the Native American pueblo of Laguna, and then follow N. Mex. 122 and 118 to Arizona. Rejoin I-40 at the state border, before detouring through the historic frontier town of Holbrook on I-40, to view the Wigwam Motel, with its 16 concrete "wigwam" rooms. Before Flagstaff, southern gateway to the Grand Canyon (see Excursion), leave I-40 and take U.S. 180/Historic Rte. 66 past vintage motels into the town. Rejoin the interstate and head west. The road drops through ponderosa pine forest into a drier landscape. Just beyond Ash Fork, leave the interstate for the longest remaining stretch of the original Route 66. The old railroad town of Seligman is the first of many small settlements that preserve the 1950s atmosphere with nostalgic motels, drive-ins, and shops. You'll then cross increasingly desert-like terrain on the way to Kingman, home of the Historic Route 66 Museum. From here, cross the Sitgreaves Pass to Western-themed Oatman, with mock-gunfights and semi-tame burros wandering the streets. It's real desert territory now as you wind down to rejoin I-40 and the Colorado River at Topock.

FROM: Glenrio, New Mexico
TO: Topock, Arizona
ROADS: I-40, N. Mex. 333, 122, 118, U.S. 180/Historic Rte. 66
DISTANCE: 733 miles (1,180 km)
DRIVING TIME: 10 hours
WHEN: Year-round
PLANNING: Old Route 66 does not appear on current road maps but is signposted off I-40. www.historic66.com

Excursion From Flagstaff, take U.S. 180 north to reach the **Grand Canyon's** South Rim, about two hours away. The 277-mile (466 km) long canyon is more than a mile (800 m) deep and was formed by the Colorado River cutting through the red rock. Like Route 66, the canyon is an American icon. Hike, stroll the path along the rim, or simply admire the spectacular view. The adventurous can ride a mule to the bottom. Seeing the canyon at dawn or sunset is an experience not to be missed.

Just another roadside attraction on Route 66, this diner's neon lights draw in drivers tempted by classic American food.

Small fishing boats bring an extra splash to the color of an iridescent river near Ocho Rios in Jamaica.

JAMAICA

Jamaica's Pirate Past

Follow in the footsteps of the real-life pirates of the Caribbean who sailed the seas in search of Spanish plunder. This route takes in old buccaneer sites, green savannas, sugarcane fields, and mountains, all with the azure Caribbean in the distance.

Begin in Port Royal, formerly known as the "wickedest city in Christendom" before it was destroyed by an earthquake in 1692, along with its thousands of resident pirates, prostitutes, and pieces of eight. What remains of Port Royal, now a quiet fishing town, lies at the tip of a 9-mile (14 km) breakwater road called the Palisadoes. Built in 1725, St. Peter's Church holds a silver Communion service said to have been donated by legendary pirate Captain Henry Morgan. Beyond the church, crenellated Fort Charles looks much as it did before the earthquake, despite having sunk 3 feet (1 m). From Port Royal, head along the Palisadoes to the modern-day capital city, Kingston. Heading west along highway A1, you pass Bob Marley's former home (now a museum) and come to Spanish Town, where the Georgian main square includes the remains of the 19th-century Old Courthouse. Continue west along A2 to reach the town of Negril, then head north and enjoy a drink in the exclusive Round Hill resort, with incredible views along the coast. From here, it's a stunning 63-mile (102 km) drive along the north coast on A1 through Montego Bay to Ocho Rios, where Dunn's River Falls drop 900 feet (274 m) through terraces and lagoons. On the same road, now called A3, just outside Port Maria stands Firefly, the estate of British playwright Noël Coward, near the "pirate cabin" once used as a lookout by Captain Morgan. Continue on the coastal road (now A4) past Port Antonio, skirting the Blue Mountains. Stop at the seaside village of Boston Bay for some authentic jerk pork. From here, head around the island's eastern tip and back toward Kingston.

FROM: Loop route from Port Royal, Jamaica, to nearby Kingston

ROADS: A1, A2, A3, A4

DISTANCE: 380 miles (612 km)

DRIVING TIME: 6 hours

WHEN: Year-round

PLANNING: Road conditions vary, so allow yourself plenty of time. www.visitjamaica.com

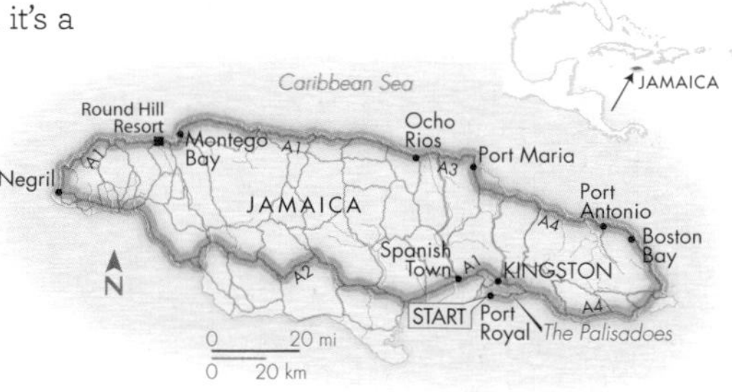

MARTINIQUE

In the Shadow of the Volcano

Beauty and the reminders of tragedy await on this drive through a Caribbean paradise. Martinique's tropical profusion is on display in the Jardin du Balata and in the untamed rain forest, while the grim but compelling story of St.-Pierre unfurls among century-old ruins.

The colorful Schoelcher Library was shipped from Paris after the 1889 World's Fair.

In May, 1902, Mont Pelée erupted for the first time in centuries, shaking the peaceful island of Martinique to its core and leaving only one survivor to tell the tale. Begin at Fort-de-France, whose inner-city ring road, boulevard du Général de Gaulle (Rte. N3), follows the Rivière Madame north toward Morne Rouge (see Hidden History) before climbing into the hillside suburbs. For a wonderful view over the capital, stop at the church of Sacré Coeur. The domed "Montmartre Martiniquais" was erected as a tribute to the dead of World War I. As the road winds its way upward past the Jardin de Balata (see Highlights), the air cools noticeably. Twist your way past the Pitons (peaks) flanked by 100-foot (30 m) high stands of bamboo, soft banks of fern, and rain forest. From the town of Deux Choux, take Rte. D1 west to St.-Pierre (see Highlights), passing banana plantations on the way to the Caribbean coast. Once known as the Paris of the Antilles, St.-Pierre was a thriving port until the volcano erupted, sending a pyroclastic flow with temperatures reaching more than 3,700°F (2,040°C) over the city and causing the sea to boil. You can wander around the shell of the old theater, stop at the cathedral that was rebuilt behind its surviving facade, and visit the underground cell where the cataclysm's only survivor, prisoner Louis Auguste Cyparis, was being held. The Cyparis Express tourist train makes a narrated circuit (in French) around the town's ruins. Take the coastal Rte. N2 south to Anse Turin, a town that once played host to celebrated French painter Paul Gauguin (see Highlights). The road continues along the coast back to Fort-de-France, passing the village of Le Carbet, where the founder of St.-Pierre, Pierre Belain d'Esnambuc, landed and claimed the island for France in 1635.

Hidden History Amateur volcanologists will be thrilled by a visit to **La Maison du Volcan** (closed on Sundays) in Morne Rouge. Take Rte. N2 north from St. Pierre to reach the small museum. As well as information on volcanism (in French), there is a 45-minute video compiled from footage of St.-Pierre before and after the 1902 eruption, vividly showcasing the destruction that befell the town; an English version is available on request.

OPPOSITE: Lush tropical greenery cloaks the hillsides of the hamlet of Morne Rouge.

Highlights

- The **Jardin de Balata** is a tropical garden paradise laid out in a Creole home above the coast. Paths meander through orchids, fruit trees, spice bushes, and red-and-pink torch ginger.
- St.-Pierre's **Musée Vulcanologique**, founded in 1932, has displays of photographs, melted glass bottles, fused nails, and other artifacts relating to the 1902 eruption.
- Painter Paul Gaugin stayed in Anse Turin for five months seeking the simple life. Visit the **Musée Gaugin** to see reproductions of his paintings, letters from the time he spent on the island, and exhibits of local artwork.

FROM: Loop route from Fort-de-France, Martinique
ROADS: Rtes. N3, D1, N2
DISTANCE: 40 miles (65 km)
TIME: 2 hours
WHEN: Year-round
PLANNING: www.martinique.org

The geometric patterning on the buildings at Mitla are characteristic of the Mixtec carving that superseded the figurative Zapotec styles.

MEXICO

A Pre-Columbian Trail

Smoky blue mountains form a perpetual backdrop to this drive east of the regional capital, Oaxaca, the original home of the Zapotec and Mixtec peoples. Along the way, 17th-century architecture mingles with pre-Columbian sites of great archaeological interest.

From sumptuous, baroque Oaxaca, head southeast on Hwy. 190 to tiny Santa María del Tule. The village's pride is its 2,000-year-old, 138-foot (42 m) wide cypress tree, which towers over the 17th-century church. After ten minutes or so, take a right toward Tlacochahuaya, a small Zapotec village with a picturesque plaza—the Dominican church and monastery are built on the site of a pre-Hispanic temple, which provided the building materials. Stylized vignettes of cherubs and flowers cover the interior, and its 1620 pipe organ has been meticulously restored. A little farther on, turn right onto a dirt road to Dainzú, a terraced Zapotec city that was inhabited circa 300 B.C. Stop to look at the bas-relief carvings of ball players on the remains of a step-platform structure. Next you come upon a left turn for Teotitlán del Valle, famous for its hand-loomed rugs, while in another ten minutes you are at the ruins of Lambityeco, a salt-mining center of circa A.D. 750. Very soon you reach Tlacolula de Matamoros—step inside the 17th-century Iglesia del Santo Cristo to see the stunning plasterwork. Farther along, and left off the highway, is Yagul, a fortified Zapotec city set on a hill where more than 30 tombs were discovered. Soon you reach Mitla (see In Focus), your final destination.

FROM: Oaxaca, Mexico
TO: Mitla, Mexico
ROAD: Hwy. 190
DISTANCE: 35 miles (56 km)
DRIVING TIME: 1 hour
WHEN: Year-round
PLANNING: Mitla ruins are closed on Mondays. www.advantagemexico.com

In Focus Lying 2.5 miles (4 km) east of Hwy. 190 are the impressive **ruins of Mitla.** The Zapotec called the place Lyobaa, meaning "place of rest" or "burial place," and built tombs above and below ground. The site was taken over from the Zapotec by the Mixtec around the 11th century. It consists of five groups of buildings, two of which have been excavated. The more exceptional is the Grupó de las Columnas, hewn from fine limestone and distinguished by geometric Mixtec decoration.

VIETNAM

Tour of the DMZ

To outsiders, Vietnam may still be more a war than a country. A guided tour through a small swathe that comprises the former demilitarized zone (DMZ) brings visitors face to face with resonant place names, landmarks, and memorials.

Dong Ha, the site of a U.S. Marine combat base during the war, is the starting point for this drive that first heads north along Hwy. 1. Outside town, you see U.S. tanks left to rot, their guns symbolically pointing downward, before reaching the Ben Hai River 9 miles (15 km) away. This was the former demarcation line between North and South Vietnam, with no-man's-land stretching for 3 miles (5 km) on either side. Memorials dot the river's edge, including the rebuilt Hien Luong Bridge, which U.S. bombers destroyed in 1967. You then backtrack to Dong Ha and turn west onto Rte. 9. Just before you reach Cam Lo—an American firebase during the war—a road veers right for Con Thien, 7.5 miles (12 km) away. In 1967, *Time* and *Life* magazines splashed images of besieged U.S. soldiers at Con Thien on their covers. Back on the main road west of Cam Lo, a trail leads to the summit of a 1,785-foot (544 m) hill known as Firebase Fuller, where U.S. artillery hurled shells as far as Khe Sanh, 25 miles (40 km) southwest. Continuing along Rte. 9, a short road to the left leads to a pepper plantation that was formerly Camp Carroll, the area's largest firebase with 22 artillery pieces. Farther on, Rte. 9 veers around a crag to the Rockpile, a 755-foot (230 m) hill that was a former observation post and artillery position. Continuing past farming villages toward the Dakrong Bridge, look out for the marker that memorializes the point where the Ho Chi Minh Trail intersected Rte. 9. Slightly to the west lies the largest U.S. combat base in the DMZ—Khe Sanh. From January through April 1968, it was the red-hot center of the war, and is now the site of a museum.

Hidden History North of the Ben Hai River are the **Vinh Moc Tunnels,** one of 14 tunnel systems in the region but the only one accessible today. The 1-mile (1.6 km) long complex, with family spaces, conference rooms, and even a maternity ward dug out of the sides of the central tunnel, was built over a 19-month period by refugees from a fishing village that had been destroyed by U.S. bombing. From December 1967 through January 1973, 90 families lived here, enduring a daily barrage of American bombing, yet not a single person lost their life, and 17 babies were born—a testament to the fortitude and resourcefulness of a besieged people. Today, a quarter mile (400 m) of the complex is open to tours.

FROM: Dong Ha, Vietnam
TO: Khe Sanh, Vietnam
ROADS: Hwy. 1, Rte. 9
DISTANCE: 63 miles (102 km)
DRIVING TIME: 2.5 hours
WHEN: Year-round
PLANNING: A guide is essential for this route. Some 7,000 people have been killed or maimed by unexploded ordnance since the end of the war, so do not venture off the main sites and tracks.
www.footprintsvietnam.com

Brilliant flags line the Hien Luong Bridge over the Ben Hai River—a memorial to Vietnamese leader Ho Chi Minh.

CAMBODIA

Around Angkor

Explore Cambodia's ancient Khmer civilization with a tour that leads from its most famous religious complex to quiet hilltop and jungle temples, and the sacred stones that sanctified Angkor's Kbal Spean River.

Angkor Wat, bathed in evening light, is reflected in the lavender-hued moat.

Siem Reap, once a quiet village, is today something of a tourist hotspot, but head north and you soon pass mighty Angkor Wat (see Highlights), and the step pyramid temple of Pre Rup, consecrated in 961. Continue east on Rte. 204 to Prasat Phnom Bok, sitting atop a 700-foot (212 m) mountain, 15 miles (24 km) northeast of Siem Reap. The temple was one of three built by Yasovarman I (ruled 889–910), founder of Angkor, and has well-preserved bas-reliefs, while the ruined towers are fun to scramble around. This is a perfect place to see the sunrise. Retrace your route to Preah Dak, paying a visit to the Cambodian Handicraft Association, where villagers sell craftwork and freshly cooked palm sugar. From ancient wonders, return to the modern world by heading north on Rte. 67 and visiting the Cambodian Landmine Museum to learn about the horrific impact of these weapons on the people during the war between the Khmer Rouge and Vietnamese in the late 1970s.

Continue north through Khnar Sanday to reach Prasat Banteay Srei, one of the most popular temples in Angkor. Its name means "citadel of the women," and its elegant construction of pink sandstone and elaborate bas-reliefs make it a masterpiece of Angkorian art and architecture. Just 11 miles (18 km) north is the Kbal Spean River, a tributary of the Siem Reap River. The Khmers of Angkor believed the water to be sacred and carved religious imagery onto the stones over which the river flowed. The carvings are found almost a mile (1.6 km) along a shady, moderately challenging trail—part of the Phnom Kulen National Park, home to 145 species of birds. Kulen Mountain was religiously important even before Angkor, and its prime attraction is the impressive waterfall, a favorite with the locals, but possibly not worthy of the entrance fee for foreigners. Retrace your route to Siem Reap.

Stay a While Lying 5 miles (8 km) north of Siem Reap on Rte. 66A off Hwy. 6, **Angkor Thom,** or "The Great Capital City," centers on the state temple Bayon, built by Jayavarman VII (ruled circa 1181–1218) and dedicated to the Buddha. The temple is distinguished by its towers, into which large, smiling stone faces are carved, and bas-reliefs commemorating Jayavarman's victory over the Chams in 1181. It also offers insights into everyday Angkorian life.

OPPOSITE: Intricately carved Prasat Banteay Srei is especially appealing because of its diminutive size.

Highlights

- One of the most spectacular and best-preserved Khmer temples, 12th-century **Angkor Wat** (literally, "city temple") is famed for its grandiosity and ornate decoration, most of which cannot be seen in less than three–four hours. Many people make return visits to appreciate the site in full.
- Just outside Phnom Kulen National Park, **Angkor Centre for Conservation of Biodiversity** is a wildlife rescue center and nature conservation area. There are free guided tours of its facility, and you may see pangolins, eagles, and porcupines.

FROM: Siem Reap, Cambodia
TO: Kbal Spean River, Cambodia
ROADS: Rtes. 204, 67
DISTANCE: 40 miles (65 km)
DRIVING TIME: 2 hours
WHEN: Year-round
PLANNING: Buy passes to Angkor Archaeological Park at least the day before. www.tourismcambodia.org

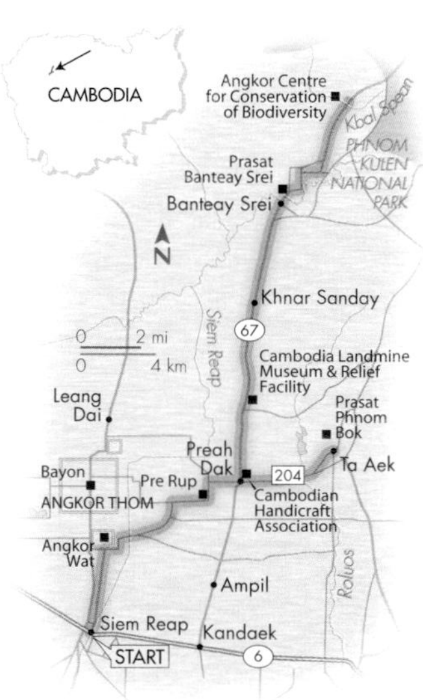

INDIA

A Slice of Goa

A short drive through Goa's lush coastal strip brings a juxtaposition of spiced, colored Hindu India with the baroque colonial style of its Portuguese past, as rich temples alternate with dazzling Catholic churches and monasteries.

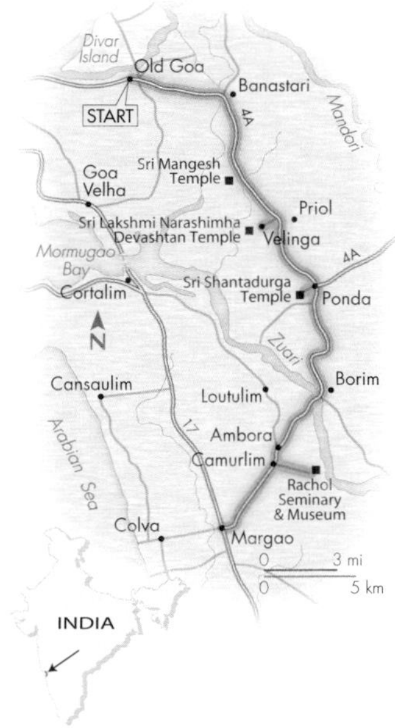

The city of Old Goa was the capital of Portugal's Indian empire until 1843, when the administration was moved to Goa's current capital, Panaji. Before you set off, wander Old Goa's main square overlooked by the Cathedral of St. Catherine, the Basilica of Bom Jesus, and the beautifully painted Convent and Church of St. Francis of Assisi. The last houses Goa's best museum, with a collection of sculptures and portraits of old Portuguese governors. From the now silent docks—where once more than 1,000 ships were loaded each year—drive up Holy Hill, dominated by the soaring 152-foot (46 m) high tower of the Church and Monastery of St. Augustine. Leaving Old Goa, head south on NH 4A, a road that twists and climbs into the hills, past cashew and jackfruit trees. In around 30 minutes you reach the village of Priol and nearby Ponda, where Hindu priests fled when Portuguese missionaries spearheaded the destruction of many temples. But Hinduism survived, so today there are three major temples to visit. Before Priol, Sri Mangesh Temple, with a yellow and white dome, is Goa's most richly adorned, while Sri Lakshmi Narashimha Devashtan Temple, set in the idyllic woodland of Velinga, is perhaps the most beautiful. The most popular is Sri Shantadurga Temple near Queula, always busy with people buying flowers before the main *puja* (worship) at 1 p.m. From here, the road goes through Borim before crossing the Zuari River. After the village of Camurlim, a left detour leads to Rachol Seminary, founded in 1574. Its Museum of Christian Art has some exquisite pieces. Nearing Margao, you pass Catholic churches standing alongside paddy fields. You will find southern Goa's bustling yet rural main town still strongly Portuguese in feel, with plenty to explore.

FROM: Old Goa, India
TO: Margao, India
ROADS: NH 4A, local roads
DISTANCE: 20 miles (32 km)
DRIVING TIME: 1 hour
WHEN: Year-round
PLANNING: www.goa-tourism.com

Excursion Drive another 8 miles (13 km) east of Margao and you reach the village of Chandor. It is dominated by the magnificent 16th-century **Menezes-Braganza Mansion,** an architectural jewel from Goa's colonial past. Its facade is the longest in Goa, and its interior a feast of antiques and objets d'art. The second-floor rooms are furnished with gilt mirrors, four-poster beds, and elegantly carved chairs. The ballroom has a blue-and-white painted zinc ceiling, Italian chandeliers, Belgian mirrors, and a portrait of the mansion's builder, Anton Francesco Santana Pereira. There is no entry fee to visit.

The 17th-century church of St. Cajetan in Old Goa was modeled on St. Peter's Basilica in Rome.

Neat fields with haystacks and woods in a vivid green valley epitomize the rural peace of northern Romania.

Highlights

- One of eight churches in the area deemed a UNESCO monument, **Biserica Sf. Arhangheli** is decorated inside with late 18th- or early 19th-century murals by an unknown hand. Ask for the key at the parish house beside the church gates.
- About a mile (1.6 km) before Budești, the road seems to go uphill when actually descending—an optical illusion that makes for an interesting driving experience.
- Budești's superb **Biserica Josani** of 1643 is one of two wooden churches in the village. Built for local *nemesi* (peasant nobles), it has four turrets around its tower's base, showing that the village once held judicial trials. The icons inside date from the 15th century, and the frescoes by Alexandru Ponehalschi from 1762.

ROMANIA

Rural Maramureș

On this gentle drive through rolling hills, you pass peaceful villages where rural traditions remain unchanged—women weave their own textiles from homespun yarn, and life revolves around haymaking, shepherding, and other activities of the agricultural year.

FROM: Baia Sprie, Romania
TO: Budești, Romania
ROADS: DJ184, local roads
DISTANCE: 25 miles (40 km)
DRIVING TIME: 1.5 hours
WHEN: Year-round
PLANNING: December brings numerous Christmas festivities in which people wear folk costume. www.visitmaramures.ro

From the center of Baia Sprie, once a gold-mining town, take the DJ184 south up a hill to Șișești and the Muzeul Memorial Vasile Lucaciu, which explains the life of Lucaciu, a Greco-Catholic priest known as the Lion of Șișești who fought for the rights of ethnic Romanians. The complex comprises a parish house, school and library, an 1890 church, and a much older wooden church covered with beautiful patterns. Continue southeast to Şurdeşti and turn right toward Copalnic-Mănăștur, following signs to *biserica* (church). At the end of a driveway flanked with walnut trees is the 18th-century Greco-Catholic Biserica Sf. Arhangheli, whose steeple is 177 feet (54 m) high, making it, until recently, Europe's tallest wooden church (see Highlights). Its bells ring out the start and finish of the day for haymakers working in the fields. Here, too, craftspeople make wooden hay rakes and forks, and finer pieces such as necklaces. Head back to the DJ184 and turn right for the winter resort of Cavnic, looking out for a cliff on the right with the Romanian flag painted on it. Legend has it that St. Peter turned haystacks underneath the cliff into the boulders (called Claile de Piatra) that stand here, to punish a farmer for working on a Sunday. Beyond Cavnic, the world opens up as the road winds through fir forests and over Neteda Pass. Admire the view on the other side of the pass, across velvet meadows dotted with haystacks toward where the Carpathian peaks enter Ukraine. Continue down the hill past myrtle groves and haystacks until you reach Budești (see Highlights), one of the largest villages in Maramureș.

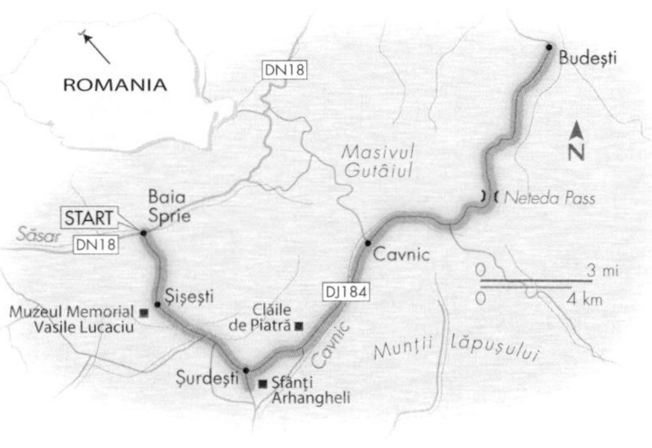

TURKEY

Azure Coast

It is worth taking the time for this lengthy drive that uncovers the story of empire-building in Asia Minor, now modern Turkey, and leads to some of antiquity's most celebrated towns and temples scattered along the shores of the sparkling Mediterranean.

The graceful columns of Didyma's Temple of Apollo soar skyward.

On the site of Smyrna, one of the most cosmopolitan cities in the Turkish Ottoman Empire, stands modern İzmir. Many traces of the city's long history survive, but it is richest in ancient sites, such as Alexander the Great's agora (market and meeting place), rebuilt by Roman Emperor Marcus Aurelius in A.D. 176. You can also visit Alexander's fortress on Kadifekale Hill, ideally at sunset. Savor the bazaar, the heart of the city, before leaving via the E881 west. Turn south onto Rte. 35-39 at Çamliçay to reach Seferihisar in around 45 minutes. A 3-mile (5 km) detour west brings you to the Greek ruins at Teos: city walls, theater, gymnasium, and a temple dedicated to Dionysos. Take the D515 south for around 50 miles (80 km) to the town of Selçuk and the ruins of Ephesus, once the second city in the Roman Empire (see Highlights). Pick up the D515 and D525 to Akköy and ancient Miletus (now Milet), most famous for its great theater, built by the Greeks and upgraded by the Romans. Other remains include baths, a temple to Serapis, and warehouses. Continue south for a couple of miles (3 km) to Didyma (now Didim). In ancient times, statues lined the road between Miletus and Didyma, signifying the sanctity of the route to one of ancient Greece's most sacred temples—Didyma's Temple of Apollo. Today, the sixth-century temple ruins retain much of their grandeur, with 8-foot (2.4 m) wide columns stretching 65 feet (20 m) to the sky. From here, take local roads east to Milas, and keep heading east through Muğla and Ortaca, a distance of 73 miles (118 km). At Ortaca, take local roads west for around 3 miles (5 km) through peaceful Dalyan to Kaunos, most famous for the temple tombs carved into the rocks. Head onto the D400 and turn right to Fethiye, an ancient Lycian city and present-day seaside hotspot with many sites to explore (see Highlights).

Stay a While About a 62-mile (100 km) trip north from Izmir on the D650 brings you to Bergama, the ancient city of **Pergamon,** a center of Hellenistic culture. In addition to a laid-back atmosphere, it offers a trove of archaeological treasures, including an exquisite temple to Dionysos and the Asklepion, an ancient medical center, where the great 2nd-century A.D. physician Galen worked and taught.

OPPOSITE: The Library of Celsus (at the top) is considered one of the most beautiful structures at Ephesus.

Highlights

- For many years, **Ephesus** was the Roman Empire's second city. The magnificent site includes a gymnasium, theater, temple of Hadrian, and grand terraced houses. The facade of the Library of Celsus has been carefully restored, and the area also includes the Basilica of St. John, believed to sit over the apostle's tomb.
- In Fethiye, visit the Ionic **Tomb of Amyntas,** carved into the rock face in 350 B.C. You can also take a boat ride along the coast to **Butterfly Valley,** a splendid Mediterranean fjord that is home to the Jersey Tiger butterfly.

FROM: İzmir, Turkey
TO: Fethiye, Turkey
ROADS: E881, Rte. 35-39, D515, D525, local roads, D400
DISTANCE: 325 miles (523 km)
DRIVING TIME: 8 hours
WHEN: Year-round
PLANNING: From mid-June to mid-July, the International İzmir Festival of music and dance takes place in Ephesus and İzmir. Selçuk has an oil wrestling festival in May and other festivals throughout the year. www.tourismturkey.org

THE TOP

10 Ancient Roads

Although not many of the famously straight Roman roads still exist, there are many ancient monuments waiting to be explored by car.

1 Damascus–Aleppo, Syria

Damascus's Via Recta (Straight Street) where St. Paul once walked, retains Roman colonnades and arches. The M1 heads north via the ancient cities of Hama and Homs, before reaching exquisite Aleppo. Tour the seven city gates, and, of course, the Citadel of Aleppo, which is still remarkable despite a turbulent history.

PLANNING: *www.syriagate.com*

2 Corinth–Mycenae–Epidavros, Greece

From Corinth, head southwest to reach the remarkable ruins of ancient Corinth, dominated by the Temple of Apollo. Backtrack and continue to Mycenae. Once home to Homer's King Agamemnon, the city was the setting of many of the great Classical tragedies. About an hour's drive east is Epidavros, where you'll see a remarkable ancient theater that has only recently been uncovered.

PLANNING: Bring a good translation of Homer to get in the mood. *www.gnto.gr*

3 Pula–Split, Croatia

About six hours north from Pula and its giant colosseum (with room for 20,000 gladiator fans), you enter seaside Dalmatia—"the heart of Croatia." Outside Split there are two of Dalmatia's best-preserved archaeological sites, Greek Issa and Roman Salona. At Split's very center is Diocletian's palace, built for the third-century Roman emperor.

PLANNING: To see more excavated wonders, visit the Museum of Croatian Archaeological Monuments in Split. *www.istria-pula.com*

4 Pompeii–Herculaneum–Paestum, Italy

In A.D. 79, ash from Mount Vesuvius' eruption turned a city to stone. There is a lot to see at the site, just 40 minutes from Naples, but it's also worth visiting the archaeological museum in Herculaneum, which stores more fragile artifacts. From here, take the A3 to the coastal ruins at Paestum, where a basilica, forum, and the Temple of Neptune are well preserved.

PLANNING: If you need a snack, close to Paestum is Battipaglia, a region famed for its buffalo mozzarella. *www.pompeiistites.org*

5 Agrigento–Selinunte, Italy

Agrigento in Sicily is one of the ancient world's most beautiful cities and retains much of its old splendor. From east to west along Via Sacra you'll pass the Temples of Juno, Concordia, and Olympian Zeus. From here, the ocean frames the two-hour drive north along the SS115 to Selinunte's numerous Greek temples.

PLANNING: *www.regione.sicilia.it*

6 Nîmes–Arles, France

From Nîmes' remarkable first-century Roman gladiator ring of Les Arènes, head 12 miles (19 km) northeast to the Roman aqueduct of Pont du Gard and, to the west, Via Domita—the original Roman road—which passes through vineyards. Continue southwest to Arles to visit the amphitheater and the Roman necropolis of Les Alyscamps.

PLANNING: *www.tourisme.ville-arles.fr*

7 Merida–Cadiz, Spain

Many ancient artifacts from Merida are now in the town's National Museum of Roman Art, yet the Temple of Diana and the Arch of Trajan still mark the city's edge. From here, take a three-hour drive south toward Cadiz to reach Prado del Rey and the ancient Roman site of Ocuri, which includes a theater from 45 B.C.

PLANNING: *www.cadiztourismo.com*

OPPOSITE: Arles' Roman amphitheater was once the site of chariot races and gladiator fights, but it is now used for bullfighting.

8 Hadrian's Wall, England

Hadrian's wall is 73 miles (117 km), or 80 Roman miles, measured in "milecastles" —small garrisons along the wall. Begun in A.D. 122, this vast barrier, which is the largest ancient monument in northern Europe, held more than 30 forts and lasted through many years of change as a frontier of the Roman Empire. Start from Newcastle-upon-Tyne in the east and head west along the wall's mammoth length all the way to Bowness-on-Solway, along the A69 and B6318.

PLANNING: Hadrian's Wall has a website that offers itinerary ideas—you can pick a title, such as Forts and Ports, and then use their interactive map to make plans. *www.hadrians-wall.org*

9 Tripoli–Leptis Magna–Cyrene, Libya

Libya's natural harbor capital, Tripoli, has always been an important city, and bears the marks of various historical cultures, such as the well-preserved Roman Arch of Marcus Aurelius. Around 81 miles (130 km) to the east, the famous first-century Roman city of Leptis Magna has some of Africa's best ruins, such as the beautifully decorated baths. Also along the Mediterranean coast, 14 hours' driving from Leptis Magna, is the Greek and Roman city of Cyrene, its ruins sprawling through the Green Mountains.

PLANNING: To visit Libya you must be part of an organized tour. *www.libyan-tourism.org*

10 Carthage–Bulla Regia–Douga, Tunisia

After the Romans destroyed Carthage in 146 B.C., they built from its leveled ruins great buildings, theaters, and the impressive Antionine Thermal Baths to make the city a suitably grand administrative capital for Africa. Drive from Carthage back through Tunis and 105 miles (107 km) west to visit Bulla Regia, which has impressive mosaics in cool underground caves. Head into the mountains to see one of ancient Rome's best-preserved African towns at Douga.

PLANNING: Visit the Bardo Museum in Tunis, which holds original pieces removed from each of the ruins. *www.tourismtunisia.com*

SLOVENIA

In the Julian Alps

A winding road in northwestern Slovenia combines the magnificent scenery of the Triglav National Park with the memory of some of the deadliest battles of World War I. Along the way, there is ample opportunity for exploration and water sports.

Starting in the tourist town of Kranjska Gora, on the northern foothills of the Julian Alps, follow Rte. 206 as it winds along 24 numbered switchbacks to the highest mountain pass in Slovenia, Vršič (5,285 feet/1,611 m), whose history is paved with Russian blood. The Russian Chapel (hidden in the forest off the eighth switchback) commemorates hundreds of prisoners of war who died in 1915–16 while forced to construct the road by the Austrian army. Take a break at Vršič, surrounded by the highest Slovenian mountains, including Mt. Triglav (9,396 feet/2,864 m). The road snakes for 7 miles (11 km) down the mountainside toward the village of Trenta. It was one of the bases for the writer Julius Kugy, who in the mid-20th century wrote several books about the Julian Alps. Today, Trenta is the gateway for exploring the spectacular upper valley of the Soča River.

After Trenta, don't miss the opportunities for a stop along the Soča for a stroll or even rafting and white-water kayaking. In Bovec, turn left on Rte. 203. Now the year-round recreational outdoor center of the Soča Valley, the mountains around Bovec marked the beginning of the Isonzo Front, extending 55 miles (88 km) along the mountain ridge to the Adriatic Sea. In World War I, the armies of Austria-Hungary and Italy fought along the Isonzo River in what is considered the biggest mountain battle in history, with an estimated of 1.2 million lives lost. The 12 successive battles are well documented at the award-winning museum in Kobarid, 14 miles (23 km) south of Bovec. Here you will also find the 3-mile (5 km) Kobarid Historic Trail, with a World War I museum, Roman settlement, and other historic sites. From Kobarid, take Rte. 102 and continue about 13 miles (21 km) to Most na Soči, where you can take a well-deserved ride in a boat on the artificial lake on the Soča, set under towering peaks.

Unexpected Pleasure Some 8 miles (13 km) west of Kobarid, you can swim in the **Nadiža River.** Virtually in the middle of a forest, the water is unexpectedly warm for this high, rugged environment. To reach it, take the 102/602/601, pass Podbela and continue for about a mile (1.6 km). You will not be alone, but likewise won't encounter crowds.

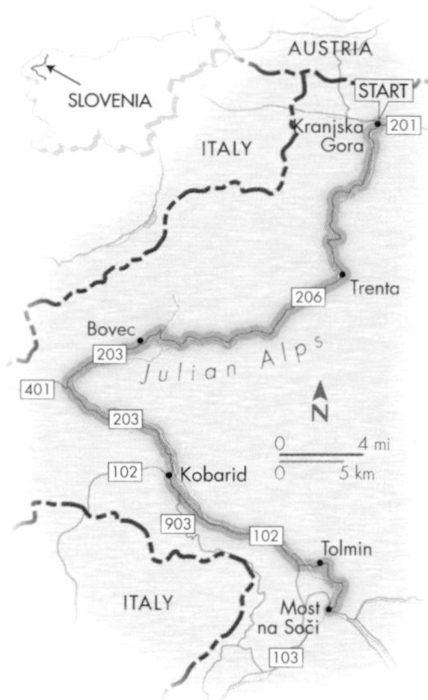

FROM: Kranjska Gora, Slovenia
TO: Most na Soči, Slovenia
ROADS: Rtes. 206, 203, 102
DISTANCE: 54 miles (87 km)
DRIVING TIME: 2 hours
WHEN TO GO: April through October
PLANNING: Avoid driving on Sundays and during holidays when traffic is heavy. There is likely to be snow on Vršič even in late spring and early fall.
www.slovenia.info

Kranjska Gora lies in an alpine valley overlooked by Mount Prisank in the Julian Alps.

No expense was spared in revamping the castle of Hluboká nad Vltavou in rampant neo-Gothic style.

CZECH REPUBLIC

Land of Castles

Castles of all shapes and sizes are scattered over southern Bohemia: strongholds guarding small towns; fortresses buried in the countryside watching over crucial trade routes; and rural aristocratic retreats, expressions of wealth, taste, and power.

From České Budějovice, a delightful town of baroque, Gothic, and Renaissance architecture, head north on Rte. 105 for about 5 miles (8 km) to the lofty castle of Hluboká nad Vltavou (see Highlights). This fantasy home of the Schwarzenberg family has many attractions, not least an excellent picture collection. Continue north for 15 miles (24 km) to Týn nad Vltavou, then take Rte. 159 toward Albrechtice nad Vltavou. Minor roads bring you 21 miles (34 km) to Zvíkov, a remote 13th-century castle set on a wooded bluff above the Vltava and Otava Rivers (see Highlights). Follow the Vltava north to Orlik Castle, another Schwarzenberg neo-Gothic confection in a serene setting by a reservoir. Return south, then go west through Mirotice to Blatná, which has a splendid moated castle with a bizarre set of furniture made from antlers. Head east on Rte. 20, then take Rte. 4 south for 33 miles (52 km) to Vimperk, where a restyled 13th-century castle sits on a crag towering over the landscape. It can only be reached by a steep path up from the main square but offers inspiring views. Head east toward České Budějovice for 22 miles (35 km) to Kratochvíle, a charming Renaissance chateau, then turn south on Rtes. 122/166/30 to Český Krumlov and continue on Rte. 160 to the village and castle of Rožmberk nad Vltavou, overlooking the winding River Vltava. The building resembles a succession of fortresses on a ridge—the finest room is the banqueting hall, covered in 16th-century frescoes. Return to Český Krumlov and take Rte. 39 northeast to Česke Budějovice. Leave town on Rte. 3, turning right at Dráchov onto Rte 23, then north at Kardašova Řečice toward Deštná. Watch for signs to Červená Lhota (see Highlights), an aristocratic retreat and the end of the drive.

Highlights

- An architectural romp, **Hluboká nad Vltavou,** built in 1662 and extensively refurbished two centuries later, is packed with crenellated towers and fearsome defenses to protect the Schwarzenberg owners from—no one. It has a sumptuously furnished interior and a handsome park.
- Medieval in origin, **Zvíkov Castle** was partly rebuilt after being damaged during the Thirty Years War. Yet it retains a formidable 13th-century round tower, Gothic cloisters, and lovely—though restored—16th-century frescoes.
- Most exquisite of all the castles is **Červená Lhota,** a 16th-century rust-red manor house sitting on an islet in a lake and reached by a cobbled causeway. It is all the more impressive for its lack of pretension or flamboyance.

FROM: České Budějovice, Czech Republic
TO: Červená Lhota, Czech Republic
ROADS: Rtes. 105, 159, 20, 4, 122, 166, 30, 160, 39, 3, 23
DISTANCE: 233 miles (375 km)
DRIVING TIME: 7 hours
WHEN: Year-round, although the castles are often closed during the winter months.
PLANNING: www.czechtourism.com

THE TOP

10 Castles in Europe

The warlike character of Europe's castles and other fortified buildings has mellowed with time, making them a perfect destination for driving tours.

❶ Transylvania, Romania

With battlements, towers, and drawbridges, Romania's fortified churches are as impressive as any castle. A good route starts in the city of Sibiu, then loops north and east to Braşov, taking in the churches at Valea Viilor, Biertan, Saschiz, Dârjiu, Viscri, Prejmer, and Cristian. Near Braşov stands the more traditional fortification of Bran Castle, associated with the fearsome 15th-century prince, Vlad the Impaler.

PLANNING: *www.romaniatourism.com*

❷ Zagorje, Croatia

Castles dot northern Croatia from the coast up into winelands of the Zagorje mountains and east to the Danube. The Habsburgs used much of this region as a military buffer zone between their empire and the Ottoman Turks. Base yourself in the baroque town of Varaždin, with a fortified Stari Grad (Old Town). From here, head west to Trakošćan and Veliki Tabor, two of the country's showcase castles.

PLANNING: *www.croatia.hr*

❸ Puglia, Italy

The first Gothic horror story ever written was Horace Walpole's *The Castle of Otranto*, published in 1764. But he had never visited the fortress, which is far from spooky. There are many other castles on Italy's heel, most notably those of the Holy Roman Emperor Frederick II. Starting in Otranto, head northeast to visit castles the emperor built or restored at Monopoli, Trani, Manfredonia, Monte Sant'Angelo, Lucera, and finally Castel Fiorentino (Torremaggiore), where he died in 1250.

PLANNING: The baroque city of Lecce makes an excellent base. *www.viaggiareinpuglia.it*

❹ Lake Geneva, Switzerland

The Château de Chillon at the east end of Lac Léman (Lake Geneva) is Switzerland's most visited monument. All around the lake are castles with museums and long histories. From Chillon, follow the northern (Swiss) shore westward via the châteaus at Morges, which has a large pewter collection; Prangins (the Swiss National Museum); Nyon; and Coppet.

PLANNING: *www.lake-geneva-region.ch*

❺ Castle Road, Germany/ Czech Republic

This road, mapped out in the 1950s, wanders 750 miles (1,207 km) from Mannheim, Germany, to Prague in the Czech Republic, taking in some 90 sites, including palaces and manors. En route is the dramatic castle of Heidelberg, from which the road continues east through the historic region of Franconia—including the city of Bayreuth, famous for its associations with the opera composer Richard Wagner—and into the Czech Republic. It ends just outside Prague, at the fairytale castle of Karlštejn, dating from the 14th century.

PLANNING: *www.burgenstrasse.de*

❻ Teutonic Castles, Poland/ Lithuania

The Teutonic Order of Knights—founded in the 12th century, originally to look after Christian pilgrims on their way to the Holy Land—created the world's largest brick-built fortress at Malbork (Marienburg) in northern Poland. It covers 52 acres (21 ha) and could house 3,000 people. Start your tour with the Teutonic fort of Bytów, then head east for Malbork and the castle at Reszel. Cross the border into Lithuania to take in the order's red-brick and stone castles at Kaunas and Trakai.

PLANNING: In summer, there can be delays at the E67 Via Baltica crossing from Poland into Lithuania. *www.imperialteutonicorder.com*

Opposite: Overshadowed by Alpine peaks on the shore of Lake Geneva, Switzerland's Château de Chillon is a romantic's paradise.

❼ Island Castles, Denmark

Kronborg Castle near Helsingør on the island of Sjælland (Zealand) is the Elsinore of Shakespeare's *Hamlet*. Nearby are the marble halls of Frederiksborg, a former royal palace. Head west to Fyn (Funen) Island for moated Egeskov, still occupied but open to the public in summer, and Holckenhavn, a Renaissance highlight where you can freely stroll the grounds.

PLANNING: All the castles are within easy reach of Copenhagen. *www.visitdenmark.com*

❽ Loire Valley, France

A fantasy of fairytale châteaus, pretty towns, and glowing vineyards make the valleys of the Loire and its tributaries a perfect touring ground. From east to west, visit Chambord, Chaumont, Chenonceau, Amboise (burial place of Leonardo da Vinci), Villandry, and Saumur—any one of which could be a whole day out.

PLANNING: Many châteaus have son-et-lumière performances in summer. *www.loirevalleytourism.com*

❾ Cashel to Killarney, Ireland

You have to kiss the Blarney Stone, of course, but Blarney is just one of dozens of castles in southern Ireland. Start with the spectacular Rock of Cashel, home to the kings of Munster, in South Tipperary. Continue south to Cahir, then to Blarney and Blackrock near Cork, finishing at Ross Castle in Killarney National Park, where you can go boating on a lake.

PLANNING: Spend a night in a castle hotel to make your journey truly historic. *www.discoverireland.ie*

❿ South to the Algarve, Portugal

Begin in the lovely town of Évora, east of Lisbon. Head southeast to the castle towns of Valonga and Monsaraz, where bullfights are held within the battlements. Next along are the castles at Beja and Mértola before you reach Silves, once the capital of a Moorish emirate in the Algarve (*al-Gharb* in Arabic), with the remains of a splendid Moorish castle. Nearby is a smaller version at Paderne.

PLANNING: After Silves, head on to Sagres Point, an evocative extremity of Europe, with a 16th-century fort. *www.visitportugal.com*

GERMANY

The Romantic Road

Enter a fairytale world of ancient palaces and castles, walled towns and cities, and natural wonders as you follow the fabled Romantische Strasse (Romantic Road) through the southern German states of Bavaria and Baden-Württemberg.

Romantic writers and artists in the 19th century loved the age-old charm of Rothenburg ob der Tauber.

The baroque splendors of Würzburg's Residenz—the palace of the prince-bishops who ruled the city until 1808—offer a lavish starting point for the tour. Let your jaw drop as you stand on the grand central staircase and look upward at the world's largest ceiling painting, created by the 18th-century Venetian artist Giovanni Battista Tiepolo. After that, it's time to head southwest out of the city, taking the signposted route to the medieval wine village of Tauberbischofsheim. From here, follow the Tauber River upstream to the spa town of Bad Mergentheim, whose attractions include the Renaissance palace of the Grand Masters of the Order of Teutonic Knights. Next comes Weikersheim, with a moated castle, then Creglingen, whose Herrgottskirche (Lord God's Church) is famous for its altarpiece of the Virgin Mary carved in linden wood. Rothenburg ob der Tauber's ring of medieval ramparts shelters a medieval townscape of near perfection. Farther south, Feuchtwangen has a fine old marketplace and Romanesque cloisters. South of that is the walled city of Dinkelsbühl (see Highlights), after which the route passes through the strange, bare landscape of the Ries, a crater, 15.5 miles (25 km) across, formed by a giant meteorite strike about 15 million years ago. A good place from which to survey the area is the tower of St. George's Church in Nördlingen (see Highlights)—yet another medieval gem of a town, protected by a ring of ramparts, with 16 towers and five gateways. From here, cross the Danube at Donauwörth and skirt the city of Augsburg, south of which Lechfeld is the site of one of Europe's most decisive battles in 955, when Otto the Great, Duke of Saxony, drove the pagan Hungarians back east. The foothills of the Alps begin beyond the town of Landsberg am Lech, as you approach the end of the Romantic Road at Füssen.

Unexpected Pleasure Perched on a crag amid forests and waterfalls, 2.8 miles (4.5 km) east of Füssen, King Ludwig II of Bavaria's wildly romantic castle of **Neuschwanstein,** started in 1869, forms the final, crowning glory of the Romantische Strasse. The best way to view it is from the Marienbrücke, a footbridge 300 feet (90 m) above a raging torrent. The castle's interior decor was inspired by the operas of Wagner and Ludwig's idealized view of the Middle Ages.

OPPOSITE: Cobbled streets zigzag up a hillside in Rothenburg ob der Tauber ("Red Fortress above the Tauber").

Highlights

- You can still only enter Dinkelsbühl through one of its four gates. Inside the walls are grand merchant houses and the 15th-century **St. George's Minster,** one of southern Germany's finest churches, whose lofty interior creates a wonderful feeling of calm.
- A display of 6,000 tin soldiers in Nördlingen's **Municipal Museum** depicts the battle of Nördlingen (1634) during the Thirty Years War.

FROM: Würzburg, Germany
TO: Füssen, Germany
ROADS: Romantic Road (Romantische Strasse)/local roads, B25, B17
DISTANCE: 220 miles (350 km)
DRIVING TIME: 6 hours
WHEN: Year-round
PLANNING: Try out the excellent local dry white Franconian wines, bottled in flask-shaped *Bocksbeutel*. www.romantischestrasse.de

ITALY

Historic Puglia

Still relatively undiscovered, Puglia is a magical region of plains and low limestone hills that includes the heel of Italy. Among its glories are beautiful Romanesque cathedrals and churches, dating from the early Middle Ages.

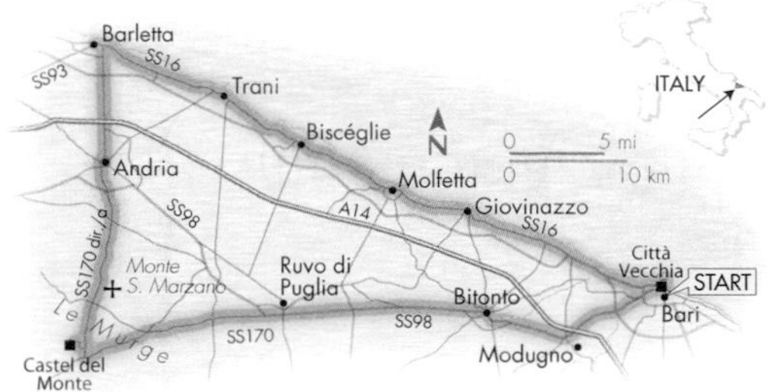

Begin in the city of Bari, whose modern port and suburbs crowd in on the Città Vecchia (Old City), a labyrinth of streets and alleys that includes most of the city's monuments. Chief among them are the 12th-century Basilica di San Nicola and Cattedrale di San Sabino, both supreme examples of Puglia's Romanesque architectural heritage. From here, follow the SS16 northwest along the Adriatic coast to Trani, another busy port with whitewashed buildings and an outstanding Romanesque cathedral, famed for its bronze portals. Farther along the coast, sights in the town of Barletta include the Romanesque Chiesa del Santo Sepolcro and the Colosso di Barletta, a massive 16-foot (5 m) high bronze statue of an unknown late Roman emperor. Head south on the SS170 through the town of Andria and follow signs for one of southern Italy's most memorable and mysterious sights, the Holy Roman Emperor Frederick II's great fortress at Castel del Monte. Built in 1229–40, the castle betrays an obsession with the number eight—octagonal in plan, with an octagonal courtyard, and eight octagonal towers, each of which contains two stories of eight rooms each. No one knows the significance, but the number eight clearly had some special meaning: Castel del Monte was the only octagonal fortress among some 200 quadrilateral castles commissioned by Frederick II on his return from the Crusades. After enjoying these tantalizing mysteries and the spectacular hilltop position, make your way back east on the SS170 to Ruvo di Puglia, with another Romanesque cathedral. Farther east, the tour's last cathedral, again Romanesque, is at Bitonto, surrounded by olive groves. From here, it's an easy 12.5-mile (20 km) drive back on the SS98 to Bari.

FROM: Loop route from Bari, Italy
ROADS: SS16, SS170, SS98
DISTANCE: 89 miles (143 km)
DRIVING TIME: 2.5 hours
WHEN: Year-round
PLANNING: Be sure to sample the delicious and much-prized local ewes'-milk cheese, Canestrato Pugliese. This hard cheese with a strong flavor is typically served grated over other dishes. www.viaggiareinpuglia.it

Excursion The city of **Matera,** some 40 miles (65 km) southeast of Bari, is known for its ancient cave dwellings. The Strada Panoramica (Panoramic Road) gives a good view of the caves, but the best way to explore the honeycomb of dwellings is on foot. Visit some of the 120 or so *chiese rupestri* (cave churches), carved out by monks in the 8th–13th centuries.

Enjoy a promenade along Bari's elegant *lungomare* (seafront drive).

The hilltop site of Peyrepertuse is so cramped that the fortifications are only a few feet wide in places.

FRANCE

The Cathar Trail

When Catharism swept across southern France in the early 12th century, the Catholic Church launched a crusade against the heretics. This troubled history forms the constant context for a tour of spectacularly located castles in the wild Pyrenean foothills.

The 13th-century castle keep outside the village of Arques makes a gentle pastoral starting point for a drive through "Cathar country." Enjoy the valley setting, and in the village visit the House of Déodat Roché, a noted 20th-century historian of the Cathars. Head east along the D613, then north to the dramatic hilltop ruins of the Château de Termes, built on the site of an earlier Cathar stronghold, which fell to forces led by the Anglo-French nobleman, Simon de Montfort, in 1210. Back on the D613, head east to the village of Villerouge-Termenès, whose imposing castle dates from the 13th century. An audiovisual guided tour tells the story of the last Cathar leader, or Perfecti, Guilhem Bélibaste, burned at the stake in Villerouge-Termenès in 1321. Double back on the D613 for 2 miles (3 km), then head south through a rocky gorge of the Torgan River to the village of Padern (see Highlights), set in a fertile valley among rocky peaks. From here, head 8 miles (13 km) west for the Château de Peyrepertuse, parts of which date to Cathar times. Be prepared for a long, winding drive up to the castle—it takes at least half an hour. Inside is a chapel, and stairs lead to a final inner refuge. The views to the sea and the peaks of the Pyrenees are breathtaking. The next stop, 7 miles (11 km) to the southeast, is the Château de Quéribus, whose keep and chapel look out over the Roussillon plain. From here, head south, then west along the D117 for the awe-inspiring crag-top castle at Puilaurens. The D117 carries on to Puivert, whose château, despite its sturdy defenses, is more a palace than a castle. Your last stop is the great rock (or *pog*) of Montségur (see Highlights).

Highlights

- Built at the foot of another castle-topped crag, **Padern** lies at the heart of a wine-growing area. To sample the local vintages, visit Les Terroirs du Vertige, a wine cooperative with a shop in the village, open year-round. **Cucugnan,** near Quéribus, also has a cooperative and some private caves that you can visit.

- The **Pog de Montségur,** a 3,000-foot (1,207 m) outcrop of volcanic rock looming above the small village of Montségur, evokes the bitter dying struggles of the Cathars. A challenging climb to the summit brings the reward of superb views and a chance to visit the ruins of the 13th-century castle, built over an earlier fortification. In 1244, this was the last major Cathar stronghold to fall to French royal forces. Just behind the castle are the foundations of buildings that have been confirmed as authentically Cathar.

FROM: Arques, France
TO: Montségur, France
ROADS: D613, D117, local roads
DISTANCE: 113 miles (182 km)
DRIVING TIME: 3.5 hours
WHEN: Year-round
PLANNING: The spectacular walled, hilltop city of Carcassonne, a World Heritage site, is a good place to base yourself.
www.languedoc-france.info

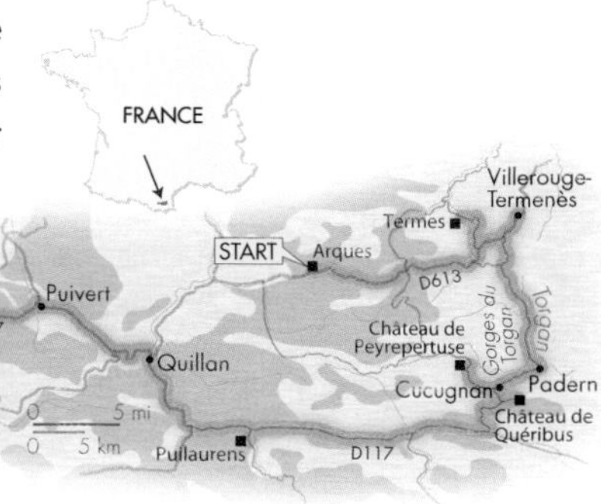

FRANCE

Le Val de l'Indre

A tributary of the Loire, the Indre rivals the more famous river and its valley for exquisite châteaux and a rolling sylvan landscape. Follow the river upstream from its junction with the Loire to the ancient walled town of Loches, one of the most beautiful in central France.

The Château de Montrésor's treasures include its richly furnished Renaissance interiors.

Outside the village of Rigny-Ussé, the romantic turrets of the Château d'Ussé have a fairytale look against a backdrop of dark forest. Not surprisingly, perhaps, the 17th-century writer of fairy tales, Charles Perrault, is said to have based Sleeping Beauty's castle on Ussé. After touring the château, head east on the D7, flanked by the Indre on one side and the Forest of Chinon on the other, with enticing detours leading south to woodland hamlets. Beyond the town of Azay-le-Rideau (see Highlights), you reach the village of Saché, whose 16th-century manor house, set among chestnut trees, was the country home of the 19th-century novelist Honoré de Balzac. The house is now a museum with first editions of Balzac's works and some well-annotated publishers' proofs. The D17 continues through a gentle landscape of orchards, châteaux, mills, wooded valleys, and waterside villages. In Montbazon, be sure to climb the 11th-century castle keep for magnificent views. The little town of Cormery has the remains of a medieval Benedictine abbey and a 12th-century parish church with interesting frescoes, statues, and carvings; it is also well known for its macaroons. Continue on the D143 and D17 to Azay-sur-Indre (see Excursion), from where you head via Chambourg-sur-Indre to Loches on the D17 and D25. Its old town center built high on a rock overlooking the Indre, Loches will keep you busy for a couple of hours at least. Explore streets lined with Renaissance buildings and visit the château, whose 12th-century central keep was built by King Henry II of England. In the 15th century, Charles VII of France gave the château to his mistress Agnès Sorel, who lived here in great luxury and is buried here.

Excursion A 16th-century residence enclosed in the walls of an 11th-century fortress, the **Château de Montrésor,** 15 miles (24 km) east of Azay-sur-Indre, is another must-see. To get there, follow the D10 along the valley of the Indrois, a tributary of the Indre. When you've explored the château and its English-style park, stroll through the village, which has an impressive 16th-century church, or along the riverside.

OPPOSITE: A mingling of late Gothic and early Renaissance styles gives the Château d'Ussé its storybook aspect.

Highlights

- The 16th-century **Château d'Azay-le-Rideau** is built on an island in the Indre, with its foundations rising sheer out of the water. One of France's earliest Renaissance châteaux, it has been completely restored and furnished with Renaissance furniture.
- A short detour southeast from Azay-le-Rideau leads to the village of **Villaines-les-Rochers**, famous for basket-making (*vannerie*) using river rushes. Visit the shop run by the Coopérative de Vannerie de Villaines for an array of every kind of basketware product imaginable. Also, keep an eye out for some of the village's semi-troglodytic homes built into the hillsides.

FROM: Rigny-Ussé, France
TO: Loches, France
ROADS: D7, D17, N143, D25, local roads
DISTANCE: 44 miles (70 km)
DRIVING TIME: 2 hours
WHEN: Year-round
PLANNING: Numerous hiking trails crisscross the Indre Valley. You can buy maps from the Office de Tourisme du Val de l'Indre in Montbazon. www.ot-valdelindre.com

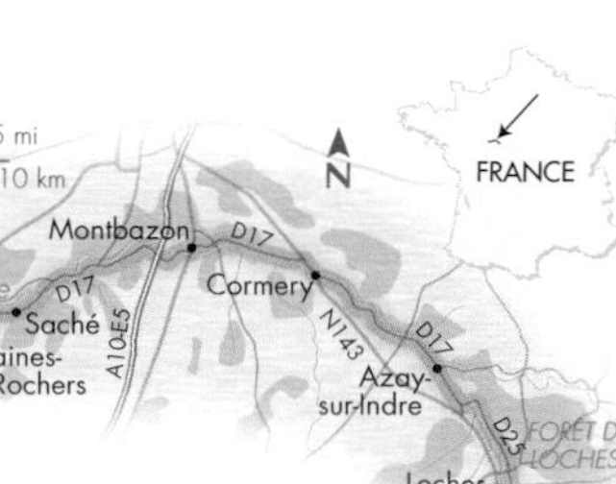

A burly kilted contender takes part in the caber-tossing event at the Braemar Gathering.

SCOTLAND

Royal Deeside

Queen Victoria and her consort, Prince Albert, were so captivated by the valley of the River Dee that they built Balmoral Castle, their summer home, there. A drive west along the valley from Aberdeen takes you past alluring woodlands, mountains, and romantic castles.

The port city of Aberdeen has plenty to detain you at the start of your jaunt. Don't miss the 16th-century Provost Skene's House, the Art Gallery (with a good collection of paintings by the early 20th-century Scottish Colorist school), and the Maritime Museum. Watch out for the effect of the northern sunlight on the pale local granite—giving the Granite City its nickname—which can sparkle magically on a summer's day. Once out of the city, head west along the A93, turning right beyond the village of Peterculter to Drum Castle and Garden, an impressive 13th-century keep with a 17th-century Jacobean mansion attached. Back on the A93, pick up signs to another castle and garden at Crathes—a turreted 16th-century tower house. In the town of Banchory, turn left on the High Street for a short detour to the Bridge of Feugh, where from May through September you can enjoy the entrancing sight of salmon leaping the Falls of Feugh on their way upstream to their spawning grounds. The A93 continues west through Aboyne to the town of Ballater, once a popular spa resort. After Ballater, the road hugs the wooded banks of the Dee as far as Crathie, whose simple parish church is the one attended by Queen Elizabeth and the Royal Family when they are staying at Balmoral in summer. You catch glimpses of Balmoral through the trees on the south side of the road. The town of Braemar, with the peaks of the Cairngorm Mountains rising to the north, is famous for the annual Braemar Gathering, whose events include caber-tossing and hammer throwing. On weekends, you can visit the imposing Braemar Castle, owned and run by the local community. From Braemar, follow signs for Linn of Dee, one of Queen Victoria's favorite viewpoints, where the River Dee foams dramatically through a narrow, rocky channel.

FROM: Aberdeen, Scotland
TO: Linn of Dee, Scotland
ROADS: A93, minor roads
DISTANCE: 68 miles (109 km)
DRIVING TIME: 2.5 hours
WHEN: Year-round
PLANNING: Royal Deeside and the Cairngorms are a wildlife paradise. Keep an eye out for red squirrels, pine martens, and ospreys. www.discoverroyaldeeside.com

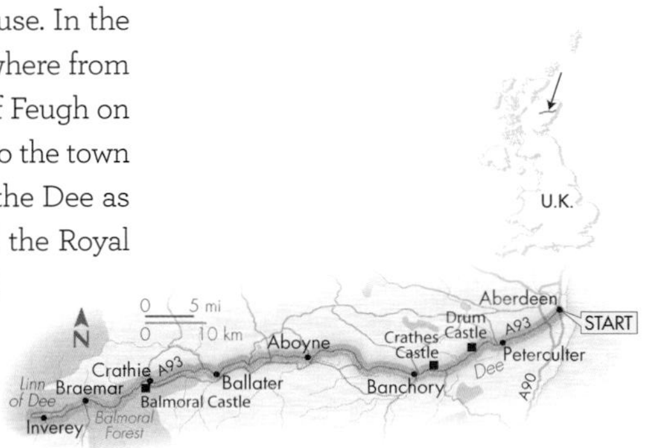

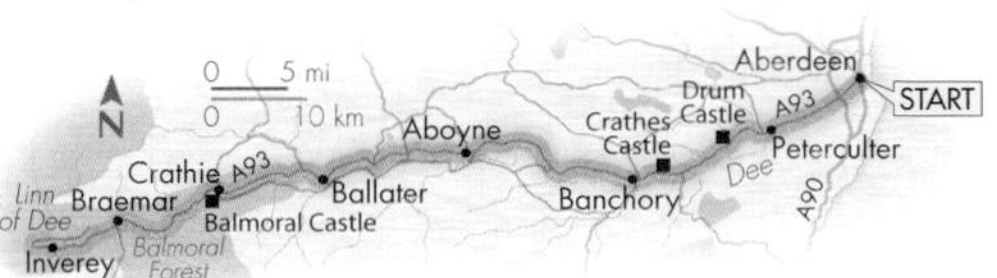

Also Recommended

❶ Lakes to Locks Passage, Adirondacks, New York

Military history abounds on this 234-mile (377 km) drive from Waterford to Rouses Point, passing Saratoga National Historic Park, which reverberated with the sounds of revolutionary gunfire in 1777, and the 18th-century Fort Ticonderoga, which has a museum and costumed re-enactors.

www.byways.org/explore/byways/2479

❷ Discovery Route, South Carolina

Begin in Charleston and head northwest on I-26, following the course of the old South Carolina Railroad. Pass through old plantations and mill towns on your way to Walhalla, 136 miles (219 km) away on the edge of the Appalachians.

www.sc-heritagecorridor.org

❸ Historic National Road, West Virginia

This 16-mile (26 km) drive from Wheeling to Oglebay Park and Resort, passes two National Historic Monuments—the elegant 1849 Wheeling Suspension Bridge across the mighty Ohio River, and Independence Hall and Museum, where West Virginia declared statehood in 1863.

www.historicwvnationalroad.org

❹ Copper Country Trail, Michigan

During the 1840s, copper prospectors swarmed into the Keweenaw Peninsula, sparking the U.S.'s first mining boom. Popular with birders, this 47-mile (76 km) drive from Hancock to Copper Harbour provides insight into the mining legacy and expansive views of Lake Superior.

www.coppercountrytrail.org

❺ Enchanted Circle, New Mexico

From Eagle Nest, take N. Mex 38 east to the ruins of the 1860s gold boom site, Elizabethtown. Past Questa, head north on N. Mex 378 to the D. H. Lawrence Ranch and Memorial, the author's 1920s home. End the drive at the Native American Taos Pueblo site, following signs off N. Mex. 522.

www.enchantedcircle.org

❻ Steinbeck Country, California

Some of John Steinbeck's most famous novels are set on this 65-mile (105 km) drive. In Steinbeck's hometown, Salinas, visit the National Steinbeck Center and drop by Roosevelt School (East of Eden's West End School). Farther on U.S. 101 is Soledad *(Of Mice and Men)*, King City on County Rd. G13 *(The Red Pony)* and Jolon on County Rd. G14 *(To a God Unknown)*.

www.steinbeck.org

❼ Archaeology on the Gold Coast, Hawaii

This 122-mile (196 km) loop from Waimea passes national parks, mountain and ocean views, and important archaeological sites. Stop off to see the Puako petroglyphs, the hundreds of archaeological sites at Kaloko-Honokohau National Historical Park and the ancient temple and other remains at Pu'ukohola Heiau National Historic Site. The drive follows Hawaii 250, 270, 19, 190, Hawaii Belt Road, and local roads.

www.gohawaii.com

❽ Arrival of the Conquerors, Mexico

In the 16th century, Hernán Cortés's expedition led to the downfall of the Aztec Empire. The marks of conquest and of pre-Spanish history are revealed on this 50-mile (80 km) drive from ancient Quiahuiztlán south on Hwy. 180 to the 400-year-old seaport of Veracruz, such as Cortés's first garrison at Villa Rica de la Vera Cruz, and the ruined city of Cempoala.

www.visitmexico.com

❾ Bangkok to Ayutthaya and Old Sukhothai, Thailand

Just 40 miles (64 km) north of Bangkok, is the historic capital, Ayutthaya. The 15th-century city has three palaces and 400 temples, holding such wonders as the huge pagoda, Wat Yai Chai Mongkhon. Another 5 hours north along Rtes. 23 and 117 is an even older center of power, Sukhothai. The 13th-century capital city has 193 well-preserved ruins covering 27 square miles (70 km^2), including the Mahathat Temple.

www.sacred-destinations.com/thailand

❿ The Golden Triangle, India

Camels and cows share the road with cars on this route. From Delhi's Red Fort, drive south on the NH 2 to Agra, and the resplendent Taj Mahal, then head west to Jaipur's Amber Fort and summer palace.

www.incredibleindia.org

⓫ Route of the Saints, Poland

Krakow's Route of Saints, connects 16 beautiful churches. Also visit the 14th-century Wawel Hill cathedral, which has an incredible 18 chapels and is the burial ground for most of Poland's royalty. Here you can climb the Sigismund Tower and see its famously enormous bell.

www.krakow-info.com

⓬ Medieval villages, Germany

Running for around 750 miles (1,207 km) from Mannheim to Prague, the Castle Road (see also p. 271) leads travelers from one medieval gem to the next. Mixed into the landscape are rustic historic villages, such as Mosbach, Bad Wimpfen, Schwäbisch Hall and Rothenburg, all with picturesque half-timbered buildings.

www.cometogermany.com

⓭ Castles and Eyries, Spain

This 77-mile (124 km) drive from Huesca to Jaca showcases Spain's mixed Islamic and Christian heritage. On the way, visit the Colegiata, a Renaissance church built on ruins of an Arab castle in the hill village of Bolea; Castilo de Loarre, a walled-and-turreted 11th-century castle built on Roman walls; and the partly ruined 18th-century Monasterio de San Juan de la Peña.

www.turismodearagon.com

⓮ Historic Graves, Ireland

Glencolmcille was settled by farmers at least 5,000 years ago, and their well-preserved tombs can be seen at Mainnéar na Mortlaidh and An Clochán Mór. At Málainn Mhóir, less elaborate tombs date from as early as 2000 B.C. Drive southwest toward Siglio to arrive at Carrowmore's 30 megalithic tombs in "dolmen circles"—small dolmens circled by boulders.

www.irish-tourism.com

5,5t
Motta
Motta
Glaces
Motta
MIKO
Glaces

CHAPTER 8

Gourmet Road Trips

For those who love good food and wine, all roads lead to dinner—or to a glassful of something delicious. Such travelers savor journeys involving vineyard-covered slopes, orchards radiant with ripe fruit, street markets crammed with spicy delicacies, freshly harvested greens for sale at a farm gate, fishing boats landing their silvery catch, and country inns whose kitchens make the most of the local bounty. The routes on these pages lead not only to fabulous food and drink but into fascinating landscapes—feasts for the eye and nourishment for the soul. A meander through rural Michigan in August finds the state's legendary cherries at their juicy peak. Adventurous coffee-lovers on a quest for the perfect cup will discover it on a road through the Costa Rican rain forest, not far from a town named Paradise. A loop through the wide-open spaces of Australia's Hunter Valley showcases the vineyards of a region celebrated for its production of some of the finest New World wines. In Sicily, archaeology meets gastronomy in a haunting landscape of ancient temples and epicurean delights—honey, wild herbs, handmade ravioli with pistachio nuts, aromatic olive oils pressed from the fruit of centuries-old groves.

Like many Mediterranean communities, the town of Cotignac in the Var region of Provence boasts a buzzing outdoor café culture, the perfect way to sample indigenous specialties and escape from the midday heat.

KENTUCKY

Kentucky Bourbon Trail

Spend a leisurely day or two touring the rolling hills of central Kentucky—where distilleries are situated no more than an hour's drive apart—and sampling the legendary caramel-color bourbons that have been produced here for centuries.

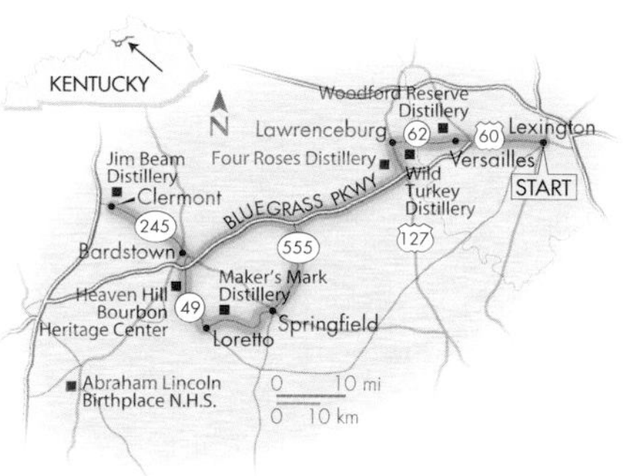

Begin in Lexington and head west on U.S. 60 to Versailles, following signs to Woodford Reserve, the first distillery on the route. You will pass open fields filled with majestic thoroughbred horses—an added attraction, especially on Kentucky Derby weekend. Drive a short way out of Versailles on U.S. 62 toward Lawrenceburg, making a stop on the outskirts of Lawrenceburg at Wild Turkey Distillery, where production techniques have remained unchanged for generations. From Lawrenceburg, head south on U.S. 127 for 4 miles (6 km) until you arrive at Four Roses Distillery. An extensive tour is offered here, which includes sampling "white dog," pure corn liquor fresh off the still and ready for putting in barrels for aging. Less than a mile (1.6 km) farther south on U.S. 127 you reach the Bluegrass Parkway, which runs through the Bluegrass Hills of central Kentucky. Drive west to Bardstown, the Bourbon Capital of the World, and stop off at The Old Talbott Tavern, which has been serving America's Native Spirit for 200 years. A short detour along Ky. 245 brings you to Jim Beam Distillery, the largest distillery in the area, run by the seventh generation of the Beam family. The next stop on the route is the Heaven Hill Bourbon Heritage Center, founded as Prohibition ended in the 1930s. Warehouses dot the verdant landscape as you continue on Ky. 49 through Loretto to Maker's Mark. Don't miss out on this final distillery, where the bright red and black buildings contrast beautifully with the surrounding emerald green hills. The picture-postcard setting is further enhanced by the perfectly manicured grounds, ideal for a stroll. To return to Lexington, drive west to Springfield, head north on Ky. 555, and take the Bluegrass Parkway.

FROM: Loop route from Lexington, Kentucky
ROADS: U.S. 60, 62, 127, Bluegrass Pkwy, Ky. 245, 49, 555, local roads
DISTANCE: 197 miles (317 km)
DRIVING TIME: 5 hours
WHEN TO GO: Year-round
PLANNING: Check with individual distilleries for their visiting hours. www.kybourbontrail.com

Stay a While After the third or fourth distillery, take a short break to rest your palate. Drive southwest 25 miles (40 km) on U.S. 31 from the center of Bardstown to reach Hodgenville and the **Abraham Lincoln Birthplace National Historic Site.** Here you can tour the Lincoln museum and see Lincoln's boyhood home at Knob Creek Farm, where his family rented a portion of the land for five years. Knob Creek is also the name of a famous bourbon brand.

These copper stills represent one stage of the historic distillation process used to create Kentucky bourbon.

The harvesting of grapes in vineyards across California usually takes place in October.

CALIFORNIA

Napa Valley Wines

The wine country of Sonoma and Napa Valleys lies within easy reach of San Francisco, and this drive takes in many wonders of northern California along the way—redwood forests, remote seashores, and charming rural towns.

Leave San Francisco north on U.S. 101, crossing the Golden Gate Bridge. Beyond the tunnel, pretty Sausalito—with stunning views back across the bay to San Francisco—overlooks the harbor. Once you reach Victorian Petaluma, turn east on Calif. 116 toward the Sonoma Valley, which claims to be the birthplace of the California wine industry; premium wineries have been making wine here since the mid-19th century. Stop off in the town of Sonoma on Calif. 12, visiting the Sonoma State Historic Park with its 1823 mission and other attractions. Wind through backcountry on Calif. 12 and, on the outskirts of Santa Rosa, turn right onto Calistoga Road. At the intersection with Petrified Forest Road, turn right again. About 4 miles (6 km) before Calistoga, you reach the Petrified Forest, a preserve of redwoods felled by a volcanic eruption 3.4 million years ago and turned to stone over centuries. You now enter the Napa Valley, home to many famous vineyards, including Krug, Beaulieu, and Beringer. Calistoga's thermal springs and geyser, Old Faithful, have also been attracting visitors since 1859. To return to San Francisco, head south, passing the towns of St. Helena and Napa on Calif. 29 before turning west along San Pablo Bay on Calif. 37 and rejoining U.S. 101.

In Focus One of the most widely planted grape varieties in California, **Zinfandel** can be used to make red or white wines, although it is most commonly used for red. These reds emphasize flavors like spicy pepper, raspberry, or cherry, with tannins that give a kind of texture or thickness. The founder of the historic Buena Vista Carneros winery, Count Agoston Haraszthy, was also the first to introduce Zinfandel grapes to California wine, and there are still daily tastings in the original 1862 cellar.

FROM: Loop route from San Francisco, California
ROADS: U.S. 101, Calif. 116, 12, Calistoga Road, Petrified Forest Road, Calif. 29, 37
DISTANCE: 170 miles (274 km)
DRIVING TIME: 4.5 hours
WHEN TO GO: Year-round
PLANNING: www.napavalley.com

10 Wayside Bounty

In countless corners of the U.S., gastronomists can search out their favorite foods and ingredients, often in staggering quantities.

1 Cheese, Vermont

In winter, when artisanal cheeses are ripe, follow Vt. 22a, over the hills and pastures of the "Cheese Trail," north from Bennington to Middlebury (with seven cheesemakers in the vicinity), then to Burlington. Aside from famous aged Vermont cheddar, artisans are now extending the range of choices to include feta, goat's milk cheese, and ewe's milk cheese.

PLANNING: The Vermont Cheesemakers Festival is held each July. *www.vtcheese.com*

2 Blueberries, Rhode Island

As you journey along R.I. 77 from historic Tiverton Four Corners to Sakonnet Point, watch as the landscape changes from stone-fenced pastures and woodlands to vineyards. After a wine tasting, stop to enjoy the cooling sea breezes of Sakonnet. Return to Tiverton for blueberry ice cream at Gray's Ice Cream Shop.

PLANNING: Visit in August, when the produce on roadside stalls runs from blueberries to fresh corn. *www.gonewport.com*

3 Pumpkins and chocolate, Pennsylvania

From Philadelphia, head west on U.S. 30 through Amish farm country to Lancaster, where the Landis Valley Museum hosts Pumpkin Patch Harvest Days in October. The same weekend, a "Chocolate Walk" in nearby Lititz invites you to visit more than 20 chocolate-tasting sites. Take the slow lane in an Amish buggy ride in Bird-in-Hand or Ronks, down roads lined with amber fall color.

PLANNING: For all things chocolate, plus a theme park and spa, visit Hershey, northwest of Lititz. *www.padutchcountry.com*

4 Peaches, Georgia

Start a tour of the Peach State at Macon, and head south to Byron. In the warmth of June, peaches are at their peak, weighing down farm stalls. They are celebrated at the Peach Festival in Fort Valley. This is a chance to see—and taste—the world's largest peach cobbler at 11 feet (3.5 m) wide. It's so big that its sweet cookie topping has to be stirred with canoe paddles.

PLANNING: Ga. 49 south of Byron is known as Peach Parkway. *www.gapeachfestival.com*

5 Cherry Orchard Drive, Michigan

Early in July, just as cherries ripen all across Michigan and are ready for picking, Traverse City hosts the National Cherry Festival, first held in 1926. Here you will find cherries used in everything from distilleries to cheesecakes, pies, and soups, showcased in numerous events. Then drive northwest—stopping to sample cherry wine en route—past orchards, vineyards, and forests to Glen Arbor, where all sorts of cherry-themed treats can be found at the Cherry Republic Shop.

PLANNING: You will need to buy tickets in advance for many events during the National Cherry Festival. *www.absolutemichigan.com*

6 Valley Wine Country, Missouri

In the 19th century, German immigrants founded wineries west of St. Louis. Visit Hermann, 80 miles (129 km) from St. Louis on U.S. 44 and Mo. 19, a quiet riverside town playing the part of a Rhineland settlement. The Hermann Wine Trail meanders some 20 miles (32 km) east from here along the banks of the Missouri River on Mo. 100 to Berger, another small, wine-making community. Several wineries along the route open their cellar doors to the public for tours and tastings.

PLANNING: Both Hermann and Berger are at their most lively during the annual Oktoberfest. *hermannwinetrail.com*

Opposite: Pumpkin stalls spring up in Pennsylvania during harvest time in September and October.

7 Pick-your-own fruit, Idaho

From summer onward, potatoes, apples, and even rosy apricots roll in from Idaho's fields and mountain orchards. For a pick-your-own fruit tour, drive northwest from Boise on Idaho 44 through Eagle, then on to Emmett in Gem County, passing orchards and woodlands. In early August, look out for the Tilton variety of apricots with their sweet-tart taste. By September, a wide range of apples are ready for picking from farms that line the roadside.

PLANNING: Visit during summer, when roadside stalls overflow with fresh fruit. *www.rockypointorchard.com*

8 Shellfish, Mississippi

Take U.S. 90 along the spectacular Mississippi Gulf Coast. Shrimp boats dock at Biloxi's small craft harbor and the Pass Christian harbor, loaded with shellfish bounty. Whether you buy pink, white, or brown shrimp, bring a cooler. In early May, witness the Blessing of the Fleet, a colorful custom initiated in 1929 by fishermen of Croatian descent.

PLANNING: The gulf's seafood industry has been severely impacted by the 2010 oil spill. Check *www.gulfcoast.org* for updates.

9 Citrus fruits, Arizona

In the Mesa area of Arizona, during March and April, roll down your windows to soak up the aroma of orange blossom. Turn off Ariz. 202 onto Reebs Road, which leads south to Val Vista Drive and East Brown Road. After April, stalls and stores close until October, but along some roads you'll find everything from tamales to tangerines being sold from car trunks and pickups.

PLANNING: The Mesa region is a short drive southeast of Phoenix. *www.mesa-goodlife.com*

10 Shellfish, Washington

Crab season in Puget Sound begins in June and is the perfect time to explore the northwest's culinary treasures. Drive north from Tacoma on I-5 to Bellingham at a leisurely pace, skirting Seattle and lunching on juicy crab claws along the way. Allow time for a detour to Whidbey Island, which you can reach by ferry from Mukilteo.

PLANNING: Allow at least a week to tour this beautiful area. *www.experiencewa.com*

COSTA RICA

Coffee in Costa Rica

This loop drive takes you southeast of Paraíso into Costa Rica's premier coffee-growing region, through a Shangri-La canyon edged by the thickly forested flanks of the Talamanca Mountains and along the shore of tranquil Lago de Cachí.

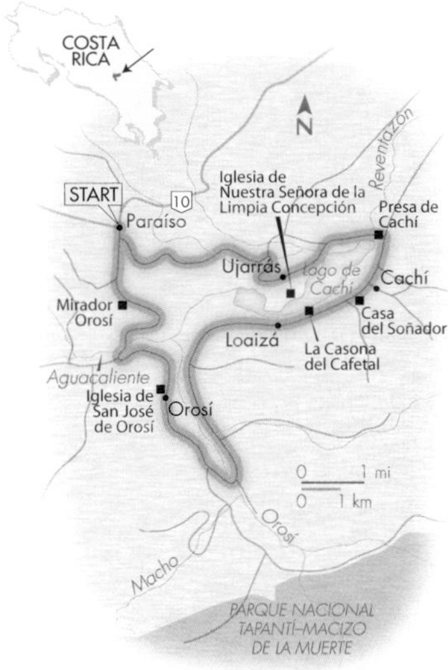

Paraíso means "paradise" in Spanish, and the town, south off Hwy. 10, brims with the fruits of the fertile surrounding landscape, especially at its famous farmers' market in the center of town. Follow a winding road for 1.5 miles (2.4 km) to the Mirador Orosí, with views over the valley. Soon the road descends steeply into the canyon, and you wend your way beyond the Río Aguacaliente, past fields of shiny-leaved coffee bushes, to the village of Orosí, backed by forested hills. On your right, you pass the charming Iglesia de San José de Orosí, whose thick adobe walls and beamed roof have withstood many earthquakes. Visit the hillside thermal baths on the edge of the village. Just south of Orosí, the Beneficio Orlich coffee-producing plant sits at the junction to Parque Nacional Tapanti Macizo de la Muerte, a rain forest with rich vegetation and countless waterfalls. The park attracts dedicated bird-watchers, for whom it opens at 6 a.m. Stay on the main road, which crosses the Río Grande de Orosí via a narrow suspension bridge. Immediately beyond the river, turn left and trace its course along a deteriorated section of road. After 4 miles (6 km), rejoin the paved road along the southern shore of Lago de Cachí. The lake, now a haunt of waterfowl, was created in the 1960s when the Río Reventazón was dammed for hydroelectricity. Try the fishing and boating from La Casona del Cafetal, a lakeside coffee farm and restaurant, from where you can also go hiking and horseback riding. Continue east to the Casa del Soñador, the former home of sculptor Macedonia Quesada, whose children continue his tradition of making and selling wood carvings over hospitable cups of coffee. Soon the road turns west and crosses the Presa de Cachí; 5 miles (8 km) farther on, you'll see signs for Ujarrás, renowned for its ruined church (see Hidden History). Continue west to return to Paraíso.

Hidden History The ruins at **Ujarrás** stand on the fringe of Lago de Cachí. The church, Iglesia de Nuestra Señora de la Limpia Concepción, dates from 1681 but was abandoned in 1833 when the valley flooded. Due to recurring floods and earthquakes, it remains in ruins. Sitting on lawns fronted by bright flowers, it is a popular picnic spot.

FROM: A loop route from Paraíso, Costa Rica
ROADS: Hwy. 10, mountain roads
DISTANCE: 19 miles (30 km)
DRIVING TIME: 1 hour
WHEN TO GO: Dry season is from December to April.
PLANNING: This drive can be done in a day from San José. www.govisitcostarica.com

Coffee beans in the Orosí Valley are harvested between September and February.

Cloudy Bay, more than any other winery in the area, made Marlborough's Sauvignon Blanc famous.

Highlights

- Each February, the **Marlborough Wine Festival** showcases the finest wines, matched with delicious locally sourced produce.
- Southeast of Blenheim, **Montana Brancott**—a pioneer of the New Zealand wine industry—offers winery tours and has a restaurant and children's playground.
- Enjoy the freshest seafood and many watersports amid the dramatic scenery of **Marlborough Sounds,** which is bordered by forests down to the water's edge.

NEW ZEALAND

Marlborough Wine Trail

Marlborough is New Zealand's premier wine-growing district, and the sun-drenched plain of the Wairau Valley produces more than 70 percent of the area's wine. Famous for its Sauvignon Blanc, the region also produces Riesling, Chardonnay, and Pinot Noir.

At the northern tip of New Zealand's South Island, a short drive from the coast, the small town of Blenheim is the main base from which to explore this region, with dozens of wineries an easy drive away. Wander through the town, sampling the local cuisine offered in cafés and restaurants around the center. From here, drive south toward Fairhall on New Renwick Road, stopping at Wither Hills, which has one of the valley's largest and most impressive cellars. Farther along the New Renwick Road lies Matua, one of New Zealand's biggest wineries, famous for its Shingle Peak brand. Ask a staff member to point out its namesake—Shingle Peak Mountain—from the garden. Cross Renwick Road to reach Renwick, a peaceful place to stay the night in the heart of this prolific wine district. Head west through Fenwick and then drive north on Terrace Road to meet Rapaura Road, known locally as the "Golden Mile" because of the abundance of wineries and vineyards in the area, most of which are open to visitors. The family-run Wairau River Winery offers lunch at the cellar door, with specialties such as blue cod caught in the Marlborough Sounds (see Highlights). Alternatively, Domaine Georges Michel is south on Vintage Lane, with a restaurant nestled among the vines. To reach another popular dining spot in the valley, head north onto Jefferies Road to Herzog's pretty cottage wine cellar, which serves Mediterranean-influenced food. Back on Rapaura Road, turn south on Jackson Road to Cloudy Bay, where you can sample some of the finest wines of the area. Nearby Gibb's Restaurant serves consistently good food in a peaceful garden setting. As you head back to Blenheim on Hammerichs Road, you have a choice of wineries to visit along the way.

FROM: Loop route from Blenheim, New Zealand

ROADS: New Renwick Rd., Terrace Rd., Rapaura Rd., Jefferies Rd., Jackson Rd., Hammerichs Rd.

DISTANCE: 26 miles (42 km)

DRIVING TIME: 1 hour

WHEN TO GO: Year-round

PLANNING: Herzog's restaurant is only open during the summer. www.destinationmarlborough.com

हरी ओम
चना मसाल
Sp.CHANA Rs. 7.
SADHA chana Rs 5.
BUTTER FRY chana 10

MAST MAST है! चना मसाला
हरी ॐ
AMUL BUTTER
FRY CHANA MASALA

INDIA

Mumbai

As you travel through the colonial heart of Mumbai, visit the bustling markets where brightly colored spices are piled perilously high, and sample the legendary Indian fast food sold on every street corner. Forget hamburgers; food here is hot, cheap, and very spicy.

The High Court building in Mumbai, designed in Victorian Gothic style, was completed in 1878.

Apollo Pier, on the waterfront in southern Mumbai, is the site of the Gateway of India (1924), a majestic archway built to commemorate the visit of the King-Emperor George V and his consort Queen Mary in 1911. A prime example of colonial architecture, it is now a major city attraction. The area is brought to life by street vendors tempting tourists to try corn sizzling on white-hot charcoal and fishermen returning with their catch (see Highlights). Opposite stands the century-old Taj Mahal Hotel with its iconic red dome. Drive north on Mayo Road past Mumbai's finest High Victorian Gothic architecture, including Colonel Fuller's High Court and several imposing university buildings with views over the open park, where informal cricket matches often take place. Turn right onto Veer Nariman Road to the brightly colored Flora Fountain. Beyond the fountain lies Horniman Circle, on the edge of the old Fort Area, which was the heart of the 18th-century city and still retains some of its old charm. You will find numerous small eateries in this part of town specializing in thick, coconut-based Mangalorean curries, often made with caviar or spiced baby shark.

Take Frere Road (P. D. Mello Road) past old fort bastions to explore the vast Victoria Terminus, an impressive Gothic structure modeled on St. Pancras Station in London. Outside the station, various carts and hawkers are always on hand to sell their wares to hurried travelers. Just north of the station, on Dr. D. N. Road, is Crawford Market, where the fragrance of fresh fruit and vegetables piled high inside carries for quite a distance. Several of the friezes and the fountain in this medieval complex were designed by Lockwood Kipling, father of the novelist Rudyard. Cruise along Lokmanya Tilak Road (Carnac Road), diverting to the streets north if you wish, where stores selling exotic foods, clothing, and jewelery cluster together by type. Once you reach Marine Drive, head north along the coast until you reach Chowpatty Beach, a highlight of a visit to Mumbai. At night, makeshift stalls appear, crowds arrive, and hot and cold *chaat* (snacks) are peddled with gusto (see Highlights). Take a moment to look back at the view along Marine Drive, fondly known as the Queen's Necklace because of the glittering lights that shine out over the bay.

OPPOSITE: Often deserted during the midday heat, Mumbai's beaches come to life in the evening.

Highlights

- Next to the Gateway to India, visit the frenzied **Colaba Fish Market** at dawn, when colorfully clad Koli fisherwomen sort the catch.
- **Chowpatty Beach** takes on a carnival atmosphere at night, with sand sculptors, musicians, and fairground rides entertaining the crowds.
- One of many specialties, **Kulfi** is a delicately flavored Indian version of ice cream—the perfect after-dinner treat for soothing the tastebuds.

FROM: Gateway of India, Mumbai, India
TO: Chowpatty Beach, India
ROADS: Mayo Rd., Veer Nariman Rd., Frere Rd., Dr. D. N. Rd., Lokmanya Tilak Rd., Marine Drive
DISTANCE: 6 miles (13 km)
DRIVING TIME: 30 minutes
WHEN TO GO: October to February
PLANNING: Standards of culinary hygiene are variable, so exercise caution. www.mumbai.org.uk

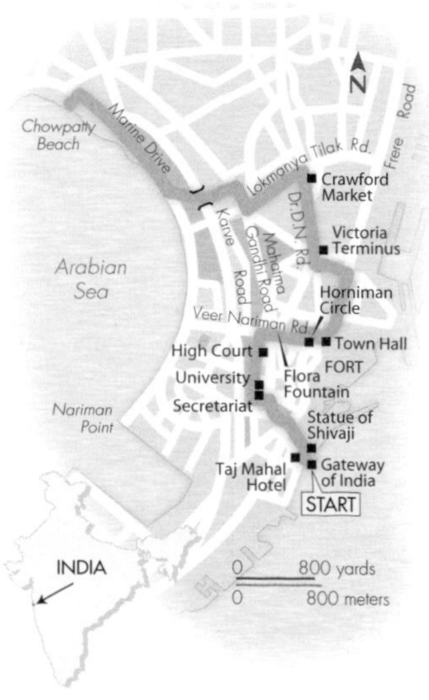

AUSTRALIA

Hunter Valley Wines

Drive through the Lower Hunter Valley, where vines flourish in the rich volcanic soil and the area is littered with wineries both big and small. Don't hesitate to make detours—there are 40 or more wineries to visit off the main route.

Drive north on the Allandale Road from Cessnock to the Hunter Valley Wine Society, which represents 80 wine producers throughout the region and provides an introduction to wine making and tasting. Behind the Society, Petersons Champagne House specializes in sparkling wines, which you can savor with oysters on the deck as you enjoy the view over a lake. Go west along Broke Road, turning left onto Halls Road for Pepper Tree Wines, a large winery and restaurant where an old nunnery set in lovely gardens is now the Pepper's Convent Guesthouse. Continue west to Blaxlands Restaurant and Wine Centre, where you can relax in front of a campfire with a glass of local wine or dine under the stars on specialties such as lobster wasabi. When Broke Road reaches the intersection with McDonalds Road, follow the signs to McGuigan Cellars and the Hunter Valley Cheese Company, which run joint tours. The strongly flavored cheeses make a superb accompaniment to the local wines. Just next door is the Smelly Cheese Shop, an eccentric delicatessen that stocks a huge range of foodie treats, including cheeses, meats, and olives from all over the world. Travel south on McDonalds Road to Tamburlaine Wines, where staff passionately promote their organic wine-making philosophy during excellent group tours and tastings. Overlooking Lindemans Winery, a stalwart of the area established in 1843, is the best picnic spot in the Hunter Valley atop a small hill. If you're lucky, live music may drift up from events at the winery below. Just off nearby Marrowbone Road is McWilliams Mount Pleasant Estate, an established name with an enviable reputation for wine-making. To return to Cessnock, head east for 5 miles (8 km) on Marrowbone and Mount View Roads.

Stay a While Whether you have sated your thirst for bold Australian wines or are looking for more to sample, a short drive north on the New England Hwy. from Cessnock to the **Upper Hunter Valley** is worth the effort. Another 27 wineries operate here, but many tourists are drawn by the magnificent scenery: the Hunter River has carved a labyrinth of ridges and creeks into the landscape. Climb rocky outcrops to see the river plunging down the valley and view remnants of Aborginal culture.

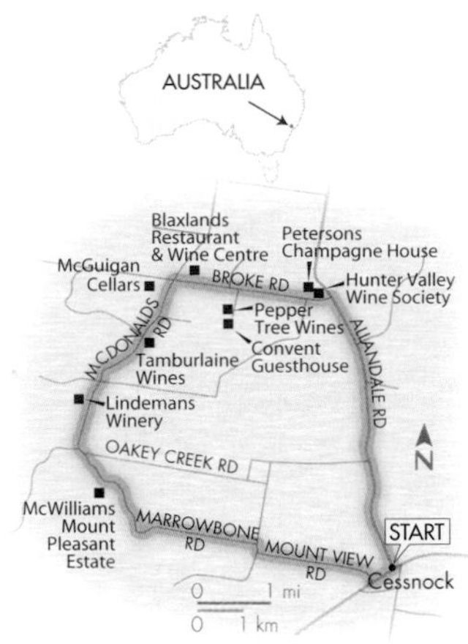

FROM: Loop route from Cessnock, Australia

ROADS: Allandale Rd., Broke Rd., Halls Rd., McDonalds Rd., Marrowbone Rd., Mount View Rd.

DISTANCE: 16 miles (26 km)

DRIVING TIME: 30 minutes

WHEN TO GO: Year-round

PLANNING: Not all roads off the main route are paved. www.winecountry.com.au

Kangaroos can sometimes be spotted amidst the Hunter Valley vines—it is best to keep your distance.

The outstanding Deidesheimer Hof restaurant is a favorite of Germany's ex-Chancellor Helmut Kohl.

GERMANY

German Wine Route

Running along the eastern edge of the vast Palatinate Forest beside the sandstone Haardt hills, this route visits a succession of wine villages and small towns where history and gastronomy dominate the culture and vineyards are a constant backdrop.

A monumental gateway, built in the 1930s, marks the southern starting point of the Weinstrasse (Wine Route) at Schweigen-Rechtenbach, on the border with Alsace. Head north, passing wine taverns along the roadside to Rhodt, an enchanting village where historic part-timber houses line the narrow streets. The easily navigable Weinstrasse, marked by yellow signs with bunches of black grapes, leads north past stretches of vineyards, mostly growing Riesling grapes. Kiwis, figs, and lemons also thrive here in the shade of wooded hills. As you approach Neustadt, you see the 11th-century Hambacher Schloss on the hillside. This stronghold, where 30,000 patriots demonstrated for German unity in 1832, is a symbol of German democracy. In March, the countryside north of Neustadt is ablaze with the pink and white blossom of thousands of almond trees (see In Focus). Deidesheim is home to some fine restaurants, many situated inside stately mansions. The small town of Bad Dürkheim has a pretty marketplace and several outstanding restaurants. It is also the venue for the Würstmarkt und Weinfest (see In Focus). Finally, you arrive in Bockenheim, where a church dedicated to Our Lady of the Grapes pays homage to the region's livelihood.

In Focus From March to October, festivals take place along this route almost continually. The **Almond Blossom Festival** in the small town of Gimmeldingen starts the season as the surrounding countryside bursts into bloom. Bakeries sell flower-shaped cookies and fruity Riesling is available to sample. Bad Dürkheim is home to the **Würstmarkt und Weinfest** each September—this wine festival claims to be the largest in the world and has been running in some form for 600 years.

FROM: Schweigen-Rechtenbach, Germany
TO: Bockenheim, Germany
ROADS: Weinstrasse (Rtes. 38, 271)
DISTANCE: 53 miles (85 km)
DRIVING TIME: 2.5 hours
WHEN TO GO: Year-round
PLANNING: www.cometogermany.com

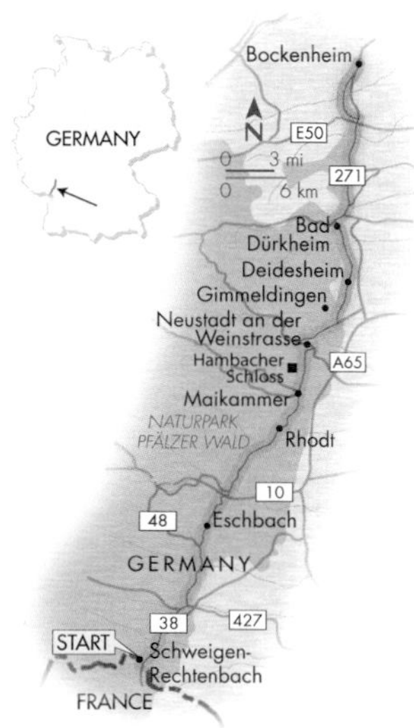

FRANCE

Through the Haut-Médoc

This tour of the Haut-Médoc (actually the southern part of the Médoc, nearer Bordeaux) stars some of the most celebrated vineyards in the world, in an area that has some 4,000 named, single-vineyard (or château) wines.

At Château Margaux, wine is aged in oak barrels for about two years before bottling.

For this tour of the crème de la crème, take the D2—the Route des Châteaux—north out of Bordeaux through row upon row of vines, planted in the gravelly ground flanking the Gironde estuary between the river and the forest of the Landes. Stop first at lovely Château Siran (see Highlights), producing the superlative refined, silky wine of the Margaux appellation. Nearby, Château Margaux (see Highlights), dubbed the Versailles of the Médoc, has been famous since the Middle Ages for its claret, quaffed by Richard I, King of England. Almost as historic is the vast and beautiful Château Beychevelle, where you can drop in to tour the cellars—tastings are by appointment. Take a deep breath as you approach the river port of Pauillac, where signs point you to some of the most hallowed names in wine. At Château Mouton Rothschild (see Highlights), part of the cellar is now a museum, with paintings, sculpture, tapestries, ceramics, and old glass, all faithful to the vinous theme. Château Lafite Rothschild, set in a grand park, has belonged to a different branch of the Rothschild dynasty since 1868. The wine was popularized at Louis XV's court by the Duke of Richelieu, and it became known as the "King's Wine," while Thomas Jefferson, the U.S. ambassador to France in 1787, also became a connoisseur. Head onward to Château Cos d'Estournel, founded in the 19th century by Louis-Gaspard d'Estournel, who exported his exceptional wines as far as India, for which he was nicknamed the Maharajah of Estournel. He therefore turned his château into a bizarre quasi-Oriental palace, which produces one of the five *crus classés* (wines of exceptional quality) from St.-Estèphe—this little river port has one of the oldest vineyards of the Haut-Médoc. From here on down the estuary, the land becomes simply the Médoc and the wines are classified accordingly as Médoc (but still very distinguished). Retrace your steps or take the fast route back to Bordeaux on the N215 and D1.

In Focus Skip the town of Margaux and take a detour on the D5 to Château Maucaillou and the **Musée des Arts et des Métiers de la Vigne et du Vin.** From Vauban's star-shaped fortress, the 17th-century Fort Médoc, there is an all-encompassing view of the Gironde estuary and the vineyards of the Blaye beyond.

OPPOSITE: Eastern-style pagodas adorn the cellars at Château Cos d'Estournel.

Highlights

- Once home to forebears of the artist Henri de Toulouse-Lautrec, **Château Siran** is splendidly furnished.
- A rare example of the neo-Palladian style in France, **Château Margaux** is more village than château, with a grand avenue of trees leading up to the colonnaded facade.
- At **Château Mouton Rothschild,** you may visit the reception rooms and banqueting hall, and view wine labels designed by some of the greatest modern artists, such as Pablo Picasso, Salvador Dalí, and Henry Moore.

FROM: Bordeaux, France
TO: Château Cos d'Estournel, France
ROADS: D2, N215, D1
DISTANCE: 65 miles (105 km)
DRIVING TIME: 2.5 hours
WHEN TO GO: Mid-September, just before the grapes are harvested.
PLANNING: You must make an appointment to visit most of the estates—some need a month's notice in summer. Some do not accept visits from the public at all. www.bordeaux-tourisme.com

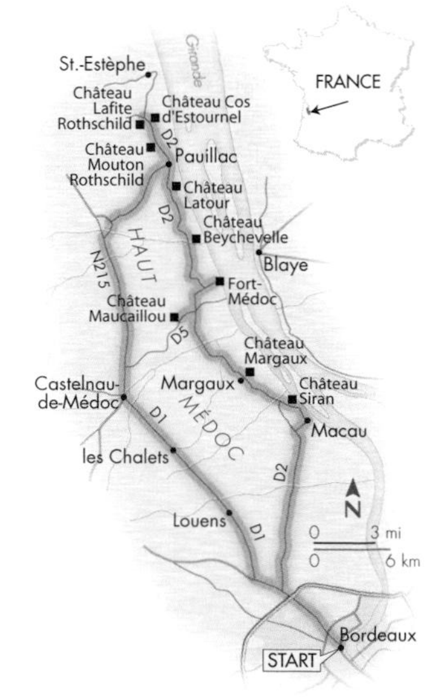

The classic village shops found throughout the South of France are ideal places to buy local wine and products.

FRANCE

Provence Wine Estates

Medieval villages, forests, vine-covered hillsides, and tastings of world-famous Provençal rosé await on this valley drive deep in the huge, non-contiguous wine region of Côtes de Provence AOC—Appellation d'Origine Contrôlée, a strict French wine classification.

Begin in Les Arcs sur Argens, with its medieval core and Villeneuve castle, and take the N7 southwest past the Maison des Vins—an excellent introduction to Côtes de Provence wines. After Vidauban, turn onto the D84 toward Le Thoronet and wind through woodsy hills interspersed with vines and hamlets for about 20 minutes. The D17 and D79 bring you to the Cistercian abbey of Notre-Dame-du-Thoronet, built of vivid rose stone in Romanesque style. Follow the tiny D279 then the D13 to picturesque Carcès, perhaps stopping for a tasting at one of the domaines along the way. Medieval Cotignac lies 5 miles (8 km) away on the D13, tucked up against a hillside. Above, tufa cliffs hold caves once hollowed out for wine cellars and even dwellings. The D50 leads on to Entrecasteaux, another picturesque medieval town. Vineyards alternate with pine-clad hills along the D31 until you reach Salernes, famous since the 18th century for its *tomettes*—red, hexagonal floor tiles. Follow the D51 for 3 miles (5 km) to Villecroze, whose ancient pastel-shuttered houses brim with flowers. It is set against tufa cliffs full of troglodyte caves, which you can visit. Take the D557 back onto the D51 for a twisty climb up to Tourtour, from where the views are stupendous. Descend via the D77, D557, and D10 through ecru cliffs and pine trees. Passing the Orthodox monastery of St.-Michel du Var (1985), open to visitors, you reach the lovely medieval town of Lorgues, replete with châteaus and chances to sample more wine. Return to Les Arcs via the D10 and D57.

In Focus From Les Arcs, follow the D91 for 4.5 miles (7 km) to **Château Sainte Roseline,** an ancient abbey converted into a castle, with a vineyard setting where you can taste a *cru classé* produced since the 14th century. St. Roseline was the pious daughter of the Marquis de Villeneuve, and mother superior of the abbey 1300–29. Her body lies in the chapel.

FROM: Loop route from Les Arcs sur Argens, France

ROADS: N7, D84, D17, D79, D279, D13, D50, D31, D51, D557, D77, D10, D57

DISTANCE: 60 miles (90 km)

DRIVING TIME: 2.5 hours

WHEN TO GO: June through September

PLANNING: The Maison des Vins in Les Arcs has free wine tastings daily and an excellent restaurant. www.provencebeyond.com

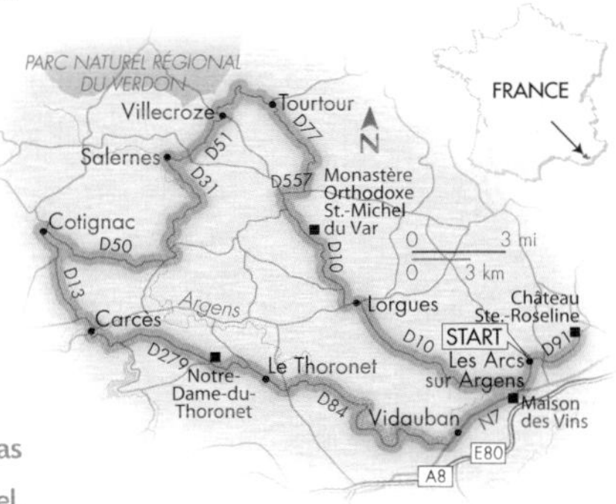

SCOTLAND

Speyside Whisky

Soft water from the burns, local peat, and highland barley are just some of the ingredients of Scotland's trademark single malt whiskies, each one subtly unique. This tour around the River Spey brings you to famed distilleries that ply their artful trade in surprising quietude.

Tiny Dufftown, set on the rivers Fiddich and Dullan and surrounded by heather-covered hills, has six working distilleries, whose productions include the world-famous Glenfiddich, winner of the most awards. As Scotland's foremost whisky town, Dufftown is an ideal place to enjoy tutored nosings. Connoisseurs can also visit the whisky museum, with its small collection of historical artifacts, as well as the celebrated Whisky Shop. After enough sniffs and sips, travel north along the A941 through ancient woodlands to Rothes, which has four working distilleries. Tour Glen Grant distillery, whose pale golden whisky is prized for its crisp, clean taste, and explore the magnificent Victorian garden. The town is also well known for its fishing and is a popular base for hikes through the surrounding hills. Back on the A941 continue north to the elegant town of Elgin to shop at Gordon & Macphail, a legendary specialist whisky shop, and to visit the cobbled medieval marketplace and ruined 13th-century cathedral. Glen Moray, one of seven distilleries in town, has a visitor center, tours, and tastings. Take the A96 west for around 10 miles (16 km) to the old town of Forres, famous for its gardens and floral sculptures, for Findhorn Bay, where you can spot seals and dolphins, and for Dallas Dhu, preserved as a historic working distillery. Here you can also enjoy a tour of Speyside's smallest distillery, Benromach. Head south on the A940 and A939, passing through Grantown-on-Spey, and take the A95 east to rural Ballindalloch. The magnificent castle is home to the MacPherson-Grant family, who also run the Glenfarclas distillery. The town's other distillery, Cragganmore, offers tours of its facilities, where makers still use traditional wooden worm-tubs for aging the whisky. Farther northeast lies Aberlour (officially Charlestown of Aberlour) in a beautiful setting, a must-visit for any whisky connoisseur—you can even fill up your own bottle here. Return to Dufftown on the A941.

In Focus About 15 miles (24 km) northeast of Dufftown is the town of Keith, home to the **Strathisla** distillery, where the Chivas Regal blends are made. It has been in operation since 1786, which makes it the oldest working distillery in the Highlands—it is also the prettiest, with a cobbled courtyard and a drying kiln housed in twin pagoda-style buildings.

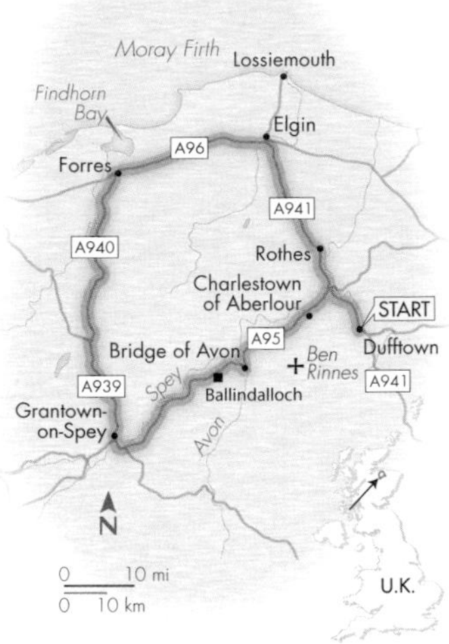

FROM: Loop route from Dufftown, Scotland

ROADS: A941, A96, A940, A939, A95

DISTANCE: 90 miles

DRIVING TIME: 2.5 hours

WHEN TO GO: Spring through fall

PLANNING: Dufftown has excellent restaurants and Findhorn wonderful seafood, while Aberlour offers spectacular scenery and quality places to stay. www.maltwhiskytrail.com

At Strathisla distillery, the malt is smoked over smoldering peat in the pointed buildings on the right.

FRANCE

The Alsace Wine Route

The Alsace vineyards (home to 50 *grands crus*) stretch for more than 130 miles (200 km) across the foothills of the wooded Vosges Mountains. You could spend days here exploring the vineyards and eating like a king, but this section makes a fine day trip.

The vineyards surrounding Niedermorschwihr are threaded with walking trails.

The white wines of Alsace range from dry Rieslings to sweet dessert *grands crus* that are harvested late. Made from a single grape variety, they are identified by grape and maker's name. To pick up the wine route, take the D417 west from Colmar to Wintzenheim and turn north onto the minor road that crosses the River Fecht to Turckheim, with its three medieval gateways. From here, follow the Route du Vin signposts along mountain roads, climbing through vineyards to tiny, flower-decked Niedermorschwihr, where Grand Cru Sommerberg is produced. Follow the road in an east-west loop to Katzenthal, known for its Rieslings, and north to the village of Ammerschwihr, which has 50 wineries, including ones that use organic production and make the latest *grand cru*, Kaefferkopf. Follow the N415 north to Kaysersberg—birthplace of the missionary doctor Albert Schweitzer—set in the woods. Turn east through vineyards along the D28 and then left onto the D1B. A detour takes you to Riquewihr (see In Focus), then follow the D1B north to medieval Ribeauvillé, set on a south-facing slope dotted with castles and offering excellent restaurants and classic wines.

On the D1B, continue to Begheim, where a Wednesday market is held in the cobbled square, and then to St.-Hippolyte, whose medieval ramparts are overlooked by the spectacular towers of Château du Haut-Kœnigsbourg (see Highlights). In 1899 the castle was given to the German kaiser, Wilhelm II, when Alsace was a German possession; it was returned to the French after World War I. From St.-Hippolyte, the D35 meanders north through a string of wine villages—Orschwiller, with a small wine museum; Riesling-producing Scherwiller (see Highlights); the old commune of Dambach-la-Ville; Ottrott, which makes red wine from its Pinot Noir grapes; and Rosheim, whose Maison Païenne (Pagan House), dating from 1170, may be the oldest domestic dwelling in Alsace.

In Focus A detour off the D1B along the D3 leads to the walled town of **Riquewihr**, a 16th-century gem. Colorful timbered houses line its streets, and a stroll around the narrow, cobbled alleyways reveals a profusion of charming architectural detail. The aroma of wine-making fills the air, and you can taste the results in one of the many *winstubs*.

OPPOSITE: A stone house and bell tower in Turckheim typify Alsatian architecture.

Highlights

- At St.-Hippolyte, visit the **Château du Haut Kœnigsbourg,** which commands the most magnficent views across Alsace to the Rhine River. From 1900 to 1908, Kaiser Wilhelm II had it rebuilt from ruin in 15th-century style.
- In Scherwiller, the **Sentier Gourmand** (Gourmet Path), a 4-mile (6 km) walk with stop-offs for food and tastings, takes place every September. Book early to participate in this gourmet experience with local producers.

FROM: Colmar, France
TO: Rosheim, France
ROADS: D417, N415, D28, D1B, D35 (Route du Vin)
DISTANCE: 52 miles (85 km)
DRIVING TIME: 1.5 hours
WHEN TO GO: April through October
PLANNING: Independent growers offer wine tastings and vineyard tours, and are signposted along the way. Wine fairs and festivals are held from April onward. www.vinsalsace.com

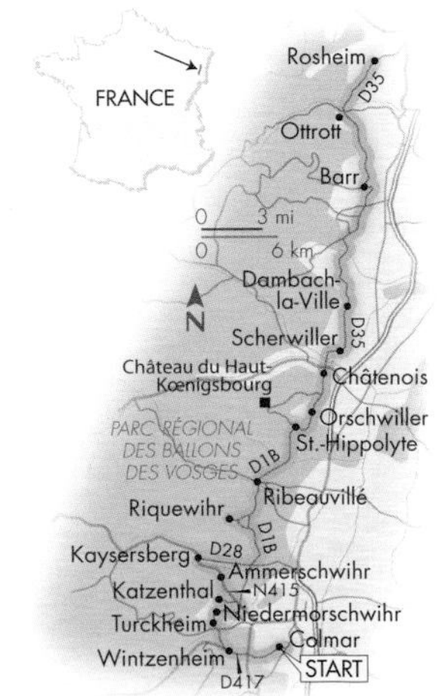

ITALY

The Langhe Valley

Robust Barolo and the world's finest truffles make Piedmont a gourmet's paradise. This drive runs through the fertile heart of the Langhe, a region of single-estate vineyards and pretty villages, including red-roofed Alba and Barolo.

Vine-covered hills bask in the sun, with the castle of Serralunga d'Alba visible on the horizon.

The noble red wines of the Langhe have the classification Denominazione di Origine Controllata e Garantita (DOCG), a strict standard of quality like the French appellations, and are produced in artisanal, mostly family-run wineries. This itinerary through the area's central and western parts takes in many such estates, and you can branch off en route.

Leave Alba on Corso Enotria, heading south on the S29. After a few minutes, turn right on the winding road that climbs to Diano d'Alba, home to a decent Dolcetto red wine. The 16th-century church of San Giovanni Battista affords sweeping views over the hills. Farther west, at Grinzane Cavour, the beautiful 11th-century Castello Cavour houses a food and wine museum and the Enoteca Regionale Cavour, where you can taste and buy local wines, grappas, and foods, all rigorously selected.

Continue southwest via Gallo d'Alba to La Morra, which commands breezy views and preserves a charming medieval center—more than 2,000 years ago, Julius Caesar recorded sampling the local wine here. You can follow suit at the Cantina Communale, which represents 50 local producers. From La Morra, drive south to Barolo (see Highlights), which gives its name to the most famous of Piedmont's red wines, typically clear and light-colored, full-bodied and aromatic. In about 10 minutes you reach Monforte d'Alba, another center of Barolo production, including the outstanding wines of Gianfranco Alessandria, Aldo Conterno, and Domenico Clerico. Drive north 6 miles (10 km) over hills etched with vineyards via Castiglione Falletto, and then turn right before Gallo d'Alba to Serralunga d'Alba. The majestic Castello Falletti makes it one of the Langhe's most striking villages—and a good place to stop for wine and snacks.

> "Peaceful roads crisscross the Langhe Valley's pastoral countryside, winding through a patchwork of celebrated vineyards and climbing to medieval hilltop villages."
>
> -TIM JEPSON
> NATIONAL GEOGRAPHIC WRITER

Follow more pretty roads south via Roddino and Serravalle Langhe to Bossolasco, which has a locally renowned cake shop. Farther south, Murazzano is another lovely hilltop village, known for its eponymous cheese, which is available in local shops. From here, head to Viglierchi and north along the ridgetop road, with magnificent valley views, via Mombarcaro and Niella Belbo as far as Cravanzana.

A short way beyond Cravanzana, turn right down to the Bormida Valley and Cortèmilia, a village dating back to pre-Roman times but now the light-industrial capital of the Langhe—it preserves some medieval pockets among modern buildings

The Magic of Truffles

Piedmont is home to the fabled white truffle—*Tuber magnatum*—one of the world's rarest and costliest foodstuffs. Truffles were enjoyed by the Babylonians, the Greeks, and the Romans, who consumed them as much for their reputed aphrodisiacal qualities as their gastronomic allure. These curious but delicate fungi grow underground among the roots of trees, particularly oak, hazel, beech, and lime. When ripe, usually in November, they exude a highly charged perfume redolent of undergrowth, and for a few brief days are sniffed out by specially trained dogs. This is the time to savor them in local restaurants and at the truffle fairs in Alba and other towns.

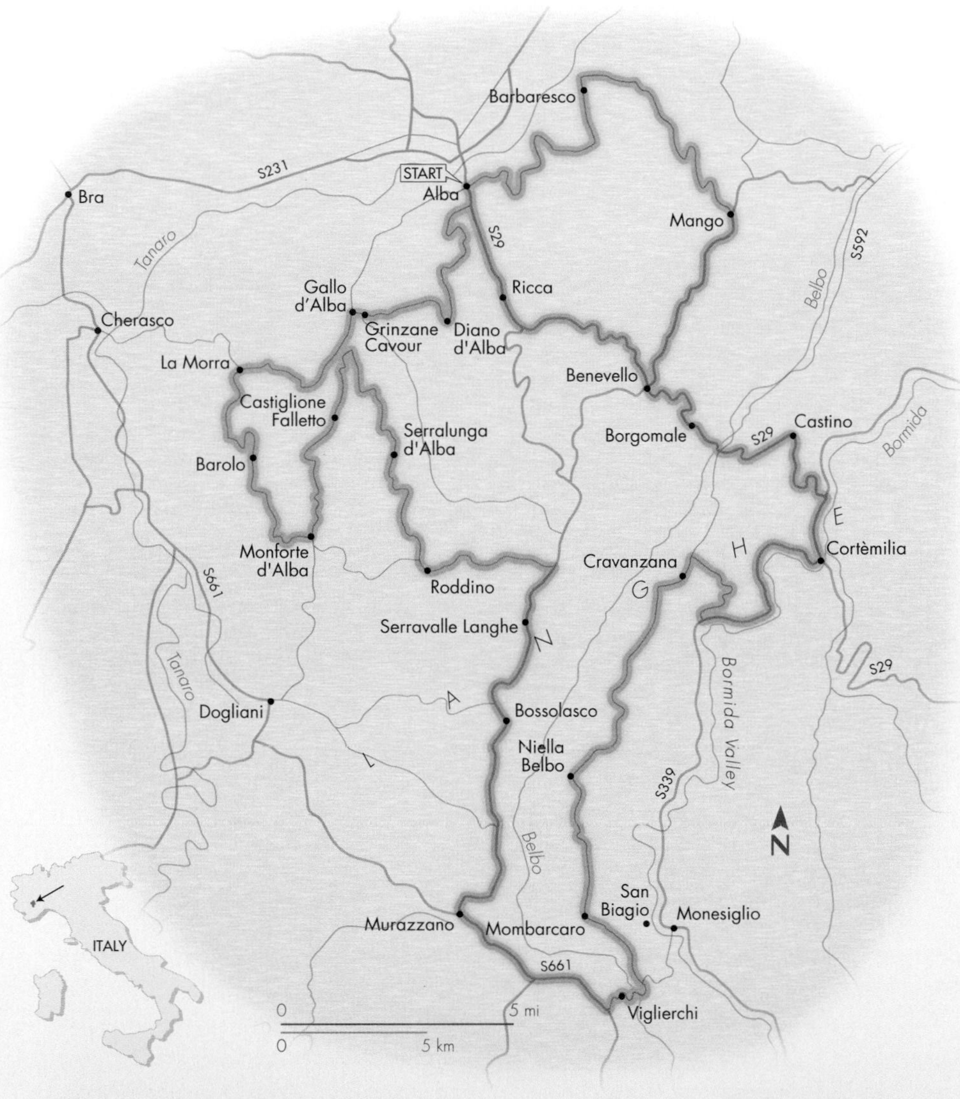

In Grinzane Cavour, the 13th-century castle houses a regional *enoteca* for tasting and buying wine.

on both sides of the river. From here, you can head northwest back to Alba, taking the scenic S29 20 miles (31 km) through still more lovely countryside, climbing to Castino and dipping and winding between hills and valleys to Borgomale, with its 13th-century castle. Slightly farther on, at Benevello, you can either head straight on, via Ricca to Alba, or detour northeast via Mango, where the Castello dei Marchesi di Busca is home to the Enoteca Regionale Colline del Moscato. Here you can buy sweeter Moscato and Asti wines, and dine in the Ristorante Castel di Mango.

Continue on to Barbaresco, which gives its name to the second of the region's great red wines. Visit the Enoteca Regionale and the premises of Angelo Gaja, one of Italy's most celebrated wine producers. The winding return to Alba lies ahead. If time allows, you can make a 10-mile (16 km) trip from Alba west to Bra, the center of the Slow Food movement that promotes authentic tastes and dishes using produce grown by sustainable methods.

FROM: Loop route from Alba, Italy
ROADS: S29, local roads
DISTANCE: 83 miles (134 km); 95 miles (152 km) via Mango and Barbaresco
DRIVING TIME: 3.5 hours
WHEN TO GO: May through mid-October
PLANNING: Most of the region's roads are unnumbered and follow north-to-south running valleys and ridges. There are few lateral links crossing the hills west to east. In fall, delicate mists give the hills an ethereal beauty. www.piemonteitalia.eu

Highlights

- In Barolo, at the Enoteca Regionale in the **Castello Comunale Falletti di Barolo,** you can sample and buy about a hundred different Barolos and other wines. There is also a visitor center, museum of viticulture, and the cantina of the Marchesi di Barolo, a historic wine estate.

- From Vigliierchi, make a detour on the road that strikes east to Monesiglio, following it as far as the hamlet of San Biagio. The tiny Romanesque **Santuario di Santa Maria dell'Acqua Dolce** has rare early frescoes of Christ and the saints.

ITALY

Monti Iblei

A trip around this wild, rugged limestone plateau in southeast Sicily mixes the culinary delights of specialty olive oil, honey, and local dishes with the aesthetics of lovely baroque buildings and major archaeological sites.

Set off from Syracuse (Siracusa), once a powerful Greek city, and head west on the local road toward Belvedere. Pass under the autostrada and turn right, then left after 3 miles (5 km) to the Anapo River. At Ponte Diddino, turn right on the high scenic road to Sortino, which stages a honey festival in October—the Greeks thought the herbs and flowers of Monti Iblei produced the nectar of the gods. Another delicious specialty here is *pizzolo*, a garnished pizza that is split and stuffed with cheese, meat, or vegetables—there are even sweet versions for dessert. From Sortino, head west toward Buccheri on a minor road that dips and climbs past Monte Santa Venere. After 10 miles (16 km), turn left to Ferla, where another left turn takes you 5.5 miles (9 km) above the Anapo Valley to spectacular Pantalica, where the rock is honeycombed with more than 5,000 prehistoric tombs. Retrace your steps and head west for the mountain hamlet of Buccheri. From here, the S124 ridgetop road runs northwest to Vizzini, famous as the birthplace of the author Giovanni Verga and the hub of ricotta cheese-making. Drive south to Giarratana (see In Focus), where gigantic sweet onions, weighing up to 5 lb (2 kg) apiece, are grown and celebrated in a summer festival where you can savor onion focaccia and cheese with onion jam. Head east toward Palazzolo Acreide, which has baroque buildings and a good museum of rural life, but is better known for the ruins at Akrai, Greek Syracuse's first inland colony in the 7th century B.C. The village's gastronomic treats include local porcini and ovoli mushrooms, sausage, ravioli with pistachio, and carob-flavored custard. Another 50 minutes along the S124 brings you back to Syracuse, where you can enjoy a well-earned dish of *pasta fritta alla siracusana* (spaghetti dusted with breadcrumbs and fried with anchovy until crispy), grilled tuna, or octopus salad washed down with Nero di Avola.

FROM: Loop route from Syracuse, Italy
ROADS: Local roads, S124
DISTANCE: 95 miles (153 km)
DRIVING TIME: 3.5 hours
WHEN TO GO: April through October
PLANNING: In spring, the area is covered in wildflowers, summer is very hot, and fall brings harvests and gentler temperatures. www.bestofsicily.com

In Focus **Chiaramonte Gulfi,** a center of production for the famed olive oil of Monti Iblei, lies about a 25-minute drive due southwest of Giarratana on the S194. At the family estate of Frantoi Cutrera, only the early green harvest of the Tonda Iblea olives is used with the cold extraction method, producing a spicy and sweet oil.

A stallholder at the local food market at Palazzolo Acreide purveys cheese, oil, and other local products.

The road through the Priorat wine region curves alongside terraced vineyards in the hills of Catalonia.

Highlights

- In **Falset,** the wine-cooperative was designed by modernist Cesar Martinell, a follower of Antoni Gaudí. Also visit the castle, baroque church, and arcaded Plaça Quartera.

- Half a mile (0.8 km) outside the little stone village of **Escaladei** lies the 12th-century monastery of **La Cartoixa,** now picturesquely ruined. It was here that monks introduced the techniques of vine cultivation and wine-aging to the area. Escaladei has a well-organized winery, where you can taste and buy wine and exquisite Siurana olive oil.

- The forbidding **Castell de Miravet,** a former castle of the Knights Templar—a medieval order of soldier-monks—is one of the best examples of military architecture of the period. The panoramic views are enchanting.

SPAIN

Priorat Vineyards

This route through rugged Catalonian *serra* (sierra) takes you to a remote wine-producing region and an impressive stronghold of the medieval Knights Templar. Along the way, you discover tiny, steep villages and the monastic origins of viticulture in this area.

Take the N420 from Tarragona to Reus, and turn right onto the beltway (Rondes), following signs to Montblanc and then Falset. You pass vineyards set against the Serra de la Mussar as you climb 1,800 feet (548 m) then descend through pine-clad hills to Falset, a pretty, medieval town and wine-producing center (see Highlights). Follow the T710 to scale the remote hills of the Priorat wine region. At Gratallops, you can taste and buy wine and olive oil at any of three cooperatives—the Celler Cecilio uses time-honored methods. Leave on the T710, then turn right onto the narrower T711, twisting through semiarid landscapes to tiny, hilltop Torroja del Priorat. After admiring its tiled roofs and cobbled streets, return to the T711 and turn right for lovely Escaladei (see Highlights). From here, a 3-mile (5 km) detour brings the village of La Morera de Montsant, perched below the 3,660-foot (1,115 m) Seyales peak. Back at Escaladei, turn right onto the T702 to drive beside the serra to La Vilella Baixa. Rejoin the T710 back to Falset, from where you follow signs to Móra d'Ebre on the N420 that crosses the agricultural plain. Over the Ebre River, take the T324 for Miravet and follow the signs uphill to Castell de Miravet (see Highlights). After exploring the old town, drive along the river to Pas de Barca and take the tiny ferry across the river. Join the C230 for 20 miles (32 km) through forested serra, meandering by the river and passing through extensive orange groves to reach the heritage town of Tortosa, with its Gothic cathedral and impressive hilltop castle of La Zuda, now a parador.

FROM: Tarragona, Spain
TO: Tortosa, Spain
ROADS: N420, beltway (Rondes), T710, T711, T702, N420, T324, C230
DISTANCE: 90 miles (145 km)
DRIVING TIME: 2.5 hours
WHEN TO GO: April through October
PLANNING: The ferry at Pas de Barca is closed 1–3 p.m. and in bad weather. Roads are of varying quality, often poor around the hilltop villages.
www.cellartours.com

THE TOP

10 European Food Drives

From Hungarian paprika to sun-ripened Provençal melons, food and fresh local produce are the inspiration for these glorious theme tours.

1 Cretan seafood, Greece

Follow Crete's rolling north coast road, E75/90, from the capital, Heraklion, to Chania. An overnight stop and stroll in the old Venetian port of Rethymnio is perfect for a *psarotaverna* (fish tavern) supper of crisp calamari and grilled fish. Leave early for Chania, set on a bay against the shining White Mountains (Lefka ori). In Chania's market hall, select Greek olive oil and almond pastries—and look for packets of fragrant wild oregano.

PLANNING: *www.travel-to-crete.com*

2 Paprika, Hungary

Rte. 51 from Budapest sweeps south across the Puszta, Hungary's great plains, to the town of Kaloçsa. In September, orange-red peppers from the surrounding fields are brought in to be ground, packed, and celebrated at the Kaloçsa Paprika Festival. Visit the Paprika Museum, packed with details of this capsicum's virtues. Learn that its flavor is enhanced by stirring it into hot oil before adding to a stew.

PLANNING: *www.1hungary.com/info/kaloçsa*

3 Cornelian cherries, Austria

From St. Pölten, 80 miles (130 km) south of Vienna, follow the B39 through the Pielach Valley to catch the Cornelian bush cherry harvest in late August. For six weeks, in the Kirschberg region, the cherries are picked and processed for jams, jellies, and the famed Dirndl Schnapps. Cornelian cherries, sold from farms and markets, pack a high dose of vitamin C. They aren't botanically related to tree cherries, which ripen earlier.

PLANNING: *www.lower-austria.info*

4 Truffles in Umbria, Italy

Enjoy Umbria's hearty cuisine in late February, when Norcia's black truffles are in the spotlight. Turn off the SS3 at Spoleto and drive through Vallo di Nera and Cerreto di Spoleto to the Nero Norcia festival, held during two weekends. Tuck into wild boar stew, local Castellucio lentils, and earthy black truffles while sipping the region's fine Ascoli Piceno wines. Winter driving in Umbria's rugged mountains may require snow chains, so be prepared.

PLANNING: *www.neronorcia.it*

5 Baltic herrings, Sweden

In the fall, the drive on E20/E6 along Sweden's southwestern coast from Malmö to Gothenburg (Göteborg) is herring heaven. Find your way to Gothenburg's Rosenlunds Canal and step inside the Feskekôrka (fish church) market to be greeted by a dazzling spread of freshly caught and smoked fish. Then lunch upstairs in the Gabriel Restaurant on dense, thinly sliced rye bread with different kinds of herring, such as spicy, cured *glasmästar sill* (literally, glassmakers' herring) or *sotare* (char-grilled herring). The market is open Tuesday through Saturday, from 9 a.m. to 5 p.m.

PLANNING: *www.goteborg.com*

6 Dutch cheese, The Netherlands

Start in Gouda, the hub of traditional Dutch cheese. Near the Gouda City Hall, visit the Waag, the 18th-century cheese-weighing house. Lunch in a restaurant may feature a *kaasdoop*—cheese fondue for dipping boiled potatoes or black bread. Try Gouda seasoned with cumin seeds, caraway, or nettles, especially good when covered in black wax and aged 12–18 months. Continue the cheese theme by driving north, via Haarlem, to the city of Alkmaar, famous for its Friday market, where cheese has been traded for 600 years.

PLANNING: *www.zuid-holland.com*

Opposite: In Alkmaar, a member of the Dutch cheese-carriers' guild wears its uniform of white shirt and trousers with a straw hat.

7 Atlantic oysters, France

The D25 from Royan follows the stunning Atlantic coast to Marennes, on the north side of the Seudre estuary. Tons of oysters are grown in beds spread across the estuary between here and La Tremblade on the south side. From Marennes, take the toll bridge to the Île d'Oléron, then follow the Route des Huîtres (oyster route) northwest from Château d'Oléron. In summer, sample a delicate Bouquet d'Oléron—pink and gray shrimp—with a glass of white wine from the nearby Île de Ré.

PLANNING: *www.huitres-courdavault-alain.com*

8 Melons in Provence, France

Just 30 minutes' drive from Avignon on the D973, Cavaillon in Provence annually hosts a festive Foire aux Melons. Early in July, roll past fields where neat stacks of melons lie ready for this special market. Vendors line shady boulevards, sliced melons scent the air, and samples of artisanal melon jams and *calissons*, sweets made using candied melon, are on offer. It's a good idea to arrive a day or two in advance, as streets are blocked for the fair.

PLANNING: *www.avignon-et-provence.com*

9 Cornish seafood, England

For a fish-lover's lunch, take the A389 to Padstow on the Camel River estuary, then follow the breathtaking north Cornish coast southwest. Get out for an invigorating walk along the beach at Watergate Bay. On the way back, stop in the village of Rock for Cornish specialties on the waterfront at Mariners Rock or French twists on the seafood theme at L'Estuaire. May into June is prime time to enjoy this rugged coast.

PLANNING: *www.cornwall-calling.co.uk*

10 Isle of Wight garlic, England

The Portsmouth to Fishbourne ferry whisks you to the Isle of Wight, where the climate is perfect for growing garlic. From Ryde, follow the A3055 south to Sandowne, then turn inland on the garlic route to Newchurch, where a garlic festival takes place in August. On this island of new taste sensations, try garlic mussels, garlic fudge, or garlic jelly beans.

PLANNING: *www.isleofwight.com*

SPAIN

Seafood and Wine in Galicia

A tour through the seafood paradise of Galicia, in Spain's northwest corner, winds alongside the fjord-like Rías Baixas, revealing superb land- and seascapes, rustic architecture, and taverns where maritime morsels are served with local Albariño white wine.

A carved stone cross in Pontevedra is typical of *cruceiros* found in town and village squares all across Galicia.

What could be more evocative than to start a drive at Fisterra (Finisterre, "land's end"), once the end of the known world? Today, the town of Fisterra has handsome stone houses and the imposing Romanesque church of Santa María das Areas. Drive 2 miles (3 km) south and you reach Cabo Fisterra (Cape Finisterre), whose lighthouse presides over the dramatic Costa da Morte (Coast of Death), famous for shipwrecks. Head back into Fisterra for some nourishment, then drive east to the town of Corcubión and southeast on the A.C.-445/550 to Muros, standing on the shore of the *ría* (tidal river inlet) named after the town: Ría de Muros y Noia. Known for its granite houses with cozy glassed-in galleries overlooking the fishing port, Muros is a good place to find a tavern serving *pulpo a feira* (octopus on potato slices), a Galician favorite, washed down with Albariño wine. Carry on around the ría to Noia for a stop to wander through its medieval town center. Continuing south along the A.C.-550 coast road brings you to Ribeira on the Ría de Arousa, after which you head northeast on the A.G.-11 to the ancient town of Padrón, famous for its *pimientos de Padrón*, small green chili peppers. Take the P.O.-548/549 coastal route to Cambados, whose stylish parador (state-run hotel) is a perfect place for a drink or meal or to spend the night. Also worth investigating are Cambados' elegant Plaza de Fefiñanes and the Michelin-starred Yayo Daporta restaurant. From Cambados, a coastal route continues to O Grove, south to Sanxenxo, then east along the Ría de Pontevedra to San Salvador de Poio, where Pepe Solla serves pristine seafood and baby vegetables at his family restaurant. Across the ría, Pontevedra, with its parador, its medieval old quarter, and its Santa María la Mayor church, welcomes you with open arms—and restaurants.

Unexpected Pleasure Vigo, southeast of Pontevedra, is the gateway to one of Spain's best-preserved natural parks—the **Cíes Islands,** 21 miles (35 km) out in the Atlantic. The archipelago consists of three main islands—Monteagudo, Montefaro, and San Martiño. Ferries connect them with Vigo eight times daily. For hiking, beaches, and bird- and butterfly-watching, the Cíes are an ideal day trip, or you can stay overnight in the campground.

OPPOSITE: Statues of the Apostles adorn the 15th-century church of San Martino in Noia.

Highlights

- Miradors, or lookout points, abound along this coastline. The **Mirador de la Curota,** in the Sierra de Barbanza, north of Ribeira, is famous for its sweeping vistas of the Ría de Arousa.
- Cambados, at the heart of the **Val de O Salnés** winegrowing region, is the best base for visiting wineries (bodegas) making fresh and fruity white wines from the Albariño grape. Among the best known is **Bodegas Martín Códax** in the nearby village of **Vilariño.** Named for a 13th-century Galician poet and troubadour, the winery prints extracts from his music and verse on its corks.

FROM: Fisterra, Spain
TO: Pontevedra, Spain
ROADS: A.C.-445, A.C.-550, A.G.-11, P.O.-548, P.O.-549
DISTANCE: 162 miles (260 km)
DRIVING TIME: 6 hours
WHEN TO GO: May–June and September–October offer good weather and not too many tourists.
PLANNING: If you want to visit wineries, call in advance. The local tourist offices can help with this. www.riasbaixas.org

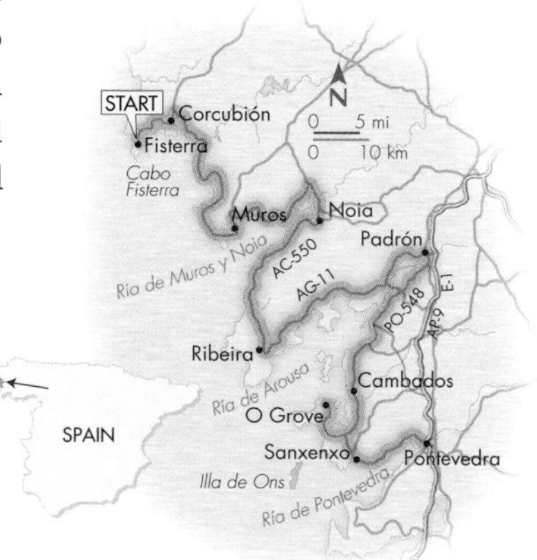

SPAIN

Vineyards of Penedès

A glorious mix of fine wines and fine architecture makes this drive through Catalonia special. You'll take in wineries with buildings designed by famous Catalan modernist architects, as well as ancient monasteries and castles.

The best introduction to this tour of the Penedès and neighboring wine regions is the Vinseum (wine museum) in the town of Vilafranca del Penedès. Housed in a medieval palace on the central square, this is where you will learn about the region's long wine-making history, dating back to the 6th century B.C. From here, head northwest toward Sant Martí Sarroca, turning left after about 5 miles (8 km) to visit the family-owned Romagosa Torné bodega (winery), whose offerings include an organic cava (sparkling wine). Carry on into the town of Sant Martí Sarrocca, which has a lovely Romanesque church and castle. Then continue 19 miles (30 km) west to the village of Santes Creus (Holy Cross), dominated by its austere but magnificent *reial monestir* (royal monastery), founded by Cistercian monks in the 12th century. Vila-rodona, to the south, offers a different kind of architectural treat—the warehouse of its wine cooperative. Sample the wines, but also admire the building: one of a number of bodegas across the region designed in the early 20th century by a well-known modernist architect—in this case, Cèsar Martinell. A scenic drive northwest leads you to the town of Sarral, with another modernist bodega, designed by Pere Domènech. Continue northeast to Vallbona de Les Monges, one of those dusty, neglected towns that signals to you that you are far from the beaten tourist trail. This is doubtless how the nuns who still live in the town's reial monestir—another glorious example of Cistercian Gothic architecture—prefer it. Wind your way south to the imposing castle of Riudabella, set among rolling acres of vines, then east to Santa Maria de Poblet for a third reial monestir, whose walled precinct conveys a wonderful sense of Cistercian purity. The tour ends via the N240 in the town of Montblanc, surrounded by 15th-century walls with 17 of the original 28 towers still standing.

FROM: Vilafranca del Penedès, Spain
TO: Montblanc, Spain
ROADS: Local roads and N240
DISTANCE: 85 miles (137 km)
DRIVING TIME: 3 hours
WHEN TO GO: Year-round
PLANNING: The Castell de Riudabella is one of a number of vineyards and wineries that also offer luxurious places to stay in a stunning rural setting. www.altpenedes.net

In Focus Eight miles (13 km) northeast of Vilafranca del Penedès, **Sant Sadurní d'Anoia** is an emblem of the wine trade. Here you'll find the bodegas of Codorníu and Freixenet, the two biggest names in cava production, amid 20 or so other wineries. Don't miss the Codorníu bodega, completed in 1915 and designed by the modernist architect, Josep Puig i Cadafalch.

All is order in the vast underground cellars of the Codorníu bodega in Sant Sadurní d'Anoia.

Rabelos are the traditional boats that were once used to carry port downriver for export.

PORTUGAL

Douro Valley

A drive along the Douro Valley in northern Portugal offers glorious views of terraced vineyards and olive groves perched on the steep valleysides. This is the wild and beautiful home of port, where you can sample the fortified wine on remote *quintas* (wine estates).

Allow yourself time to linger in the town of Peso da Régua, situated on a bend in the Douro River, with a maze of narrow streets and small shops, cafés, and restaurants. Why not prepare yourself for the drive ahead with a visit to Régua's Museu do Douro, dedicated to the wines, history, and culture of the Douro Valley? Sample the wines at the Solar do Vinho do Porto, run by the Port and Douro Wines Institute on Rua da Ferreirinha. Thus fortified, head east on the N222, which runs along the south bank of the Douro, giving great views of the valley's sunlit northern side. The farther east you travel, the more beautiful the valley appears as the hills fall steeply to the river and the landscape becomes ever more sparsely populated and wild. Keep an eye open for quintas to visit, such as the Quinta do Panascal, which offers fascinating vineyard tours. After 17 miles (27 km), the town of Pinhão stands where the Pinhão River joins the Douro, a perfect place for lunch. Backtrack south to the point where the N222 turns eastward, diverging from the Douro and taking you on a spectacular mountain route toward the town of Vila Nova de Foz Côa. In the hamlet of Touça, take a detour north to Freixo de Numão, where you can relish award-winning olive oil made by a local cooperative, not to mention its wines and grape spirit. The village also has a baroque palace and remarkable Roman remains, including the stones of a Roman road where you can see the ruts made by carts. Back on the N222, you soon reach Vila Nova de Foz Côa, built high above the Côa River, another tributary of the Douro, amid olive and almond groves.

FROM: Peso da Régua, Portugal
TO: Vila Nova de Foz Côa, Portugal
ROADS: N222, local roads
DISTANCE: 58 miles (94 km)
DRIVING TIME: 2 hours
WHEN TO GO: Visit in spring for the almond blossom, late summer for the wine harvest, and fall for leaf color.
PLANNING: You can extend your tour after Vila Nova de Foz Côa by pressing on eastward with a two- or three-day trip into the rugged Tras-os-Montes region. www.ivdp.pt

1834 J VDS

SOUTH AFRICA

The Cape Winelands

The historic charms of Stellenbosch—South Africa's second-oldest European-founded city after Cape Town—make a perfect starting point for a tour of neatly staked vineyards set among the green valleys and dramatic mountain ranges of the Western Cape.

Fall colors tinge the vineyards of the Franschhoek Valley, with rocky peaks rising in the background.

Highlights

- Near Lanzerac in the Jonkershoek Valley, the **Assegaaibosch Nature Reserve** lies wedged between the Eerste River and Stellenbosch Mountain and is well worth a short detour. Enjoy the wildflower garden and numerous walking trails. You are likely to see brightly colored agama lizards bobbing their heads as they sun themselves on warm rocks.

- On your return journey, pause a while outside **Groot Drakenstein** correctional facility near Simondium in the northern Franschhoek Valley. This was where former South African president, Nelson Mandela, made his "short walk to freedom" in February 1990 after 27 years of imprisonment by the apartheid regime.

Stellenbosch's oak-lined streets and picturesque setting on the Eertse River give it a storybook aspect, while students from the university add a youthful tempo. You don't have to travel far for your first wine tasting: The partly subterranean Bergkelder Wine Centre occupies a spectacular position on the slopes of Papegaaiberg (Parrot Mountain) in the heart of the small city. From here, make for the eastern outskirts, where Lanzerac (see Highlights) in the Jonkershoek Valley is among the Cape's oldest wine estates. Sample the famous Lanzerac Pinotage vintages and admire the manor house, one of the finest examples of early Cape Dutch architecture.

Leave Stellenbosch on the R310, which loops its way northeast through the glorious Helshoogte Pass, with the 4,590-foot (1,399 m) peak of Simonsberg rising to the north. Beyond the pass, Boschendal estate has been producing wines since 1685. Visit its wine-tasting center and gabled manor house, built by the de Villiers family in 1812. After Boschendal, turn right onto the R45, which follows the course of the Franschhoek Valley. La Motte is another historic wine estate, with an 18th-century manor house, which also cultivates flowers and produces essential (or ethereal) oils, obtained from plants such as lavender and rose geranium. Vineyards cover the valleysides around the pretty village of Franschhoek, where you can browse in arts, crafts, and antiques shops. The village's name means "French corner" in Afrikaans, and it was settled in the late 17th century by French Huguenots (Protestants), celebrated in the Huguenot Monument near the top end of the main street. Among the many wineries you can visit, the family-run Stony Brook vineyard is a great stop, 2.5 miles (4 km) beyond the Huguenot Monument.

Backtrack on the R45, then head north on the R301 to the town of Paarl, where the K.W.V. Wine Emporium offers a large selection of wines and brandies. Just west of Paarl, the Fairview estate produces delicious goat's milk cheeses as well as wine. Returning on the R45/310 will take you down the northern end of the Franschhoek Valley and back over the Helshoogte Pass to Stellenbosch.

FROM: Loop route from Stellenbosch, South Africa
ROADS: R310, R45, R301
DISTANCE: 100 miles (160 km)
DRIVING TIME: 2 hours
WHEN TO GO: September through April
PLANNING: Keen walkers should go to the Stellenbosch Tourism Information Bureau for a map of vineyard hiking trails around the city. www.sa-venues.com

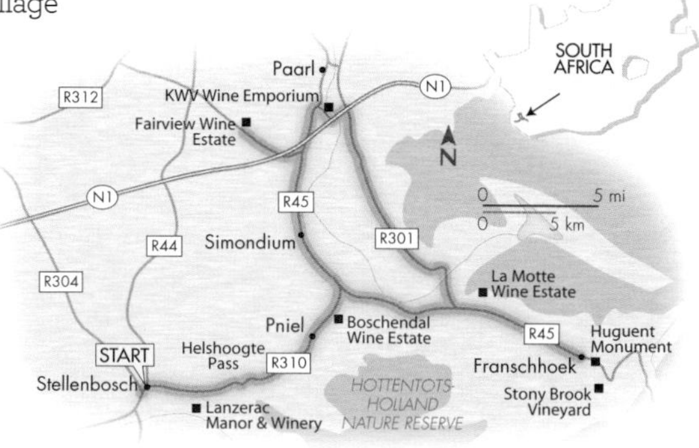

OPPOSITE: The spirit of the European pioneers survives in a Cape Dutch cottage in Stellenbosch.

Workers sort the harvested grapes at a vineyard near Malmesbury.

SOUTH AFRICA

Swartland Wine Route

Enjoy a leisurely tour through wheat fields and vineyards cradled among glorious mountains. Here, all is fertility and brilliant color, despite the region's name—the Swartland, or Black Country, after the indigenous *renosterbos,* a shrub that turns black in winter.

Start in the town of Darling, whose quiet streets are lined with Cape Dutch and Victorian-era cottages. From here, the R315 takes you east through golden wheat fields and undulating Shiraz-producing vineyards toward Malmesbury in the heart of the Swartland. In the vineyards, notice the bush vines that thrive in the dry soil—bush vines produce smaller grapes with a more concentrated flavor than conventional trellised ones. Just beyond Malmesbury, off the R45, your first stop is the Swartland Winery, with a white-gabled estate house and acres of vines set against the backdrop of the Perdeberg Mountains. Return to the R45, then turn east onto the R46, with the ridge of Kasteelberg ahead of you. Turn off for Meerhof estate, whose beautifully crafted wines are fermented in open-top oak fermentation tanks. Farther along the R46 is Kloovenburg, described by its owners as "hanging like a swallow's nest below Kasteel Mountain." The estate grows olives as well as grapes.

Turning north onto the R311, you see the white church steeples of Riebeek-Kasteel and Riebeek-West. In Riebeek-Kasteel, watch out for the castlelike structure that marks the entrance to the Het Vlock Casteel estate, which produces olives, fruit, and wines. In season, you can buy peaches, grapes, and oranges, along with a large range of preserved products. Pause in Riebeek-Kasteel's town square, surrounded by artists' galleries, restaurants, and cafés. Just south of Riebeek-West, Allesverloren's name translates to "all is lost." This relates to the estate's early history, when the settler family returned from an outing to Stellenbosch—a long trip by wagon—to find their house burned to the ground and the farmland devastated. In spite of this setback, the family rebuilt the farm, and today the estate celebrates more than 200 years of wine making.

FROM: Darling, South Africa
TO: Riebeek-West, South Africa
ROADS: R315, R45, R46, R311
DISTANCE: 39 miles (63 km)
DRIVING TIME: 1 hour
WHEN TO GO: September through April are the best months.
PLANNING: www.swartlandwineroute.co.za

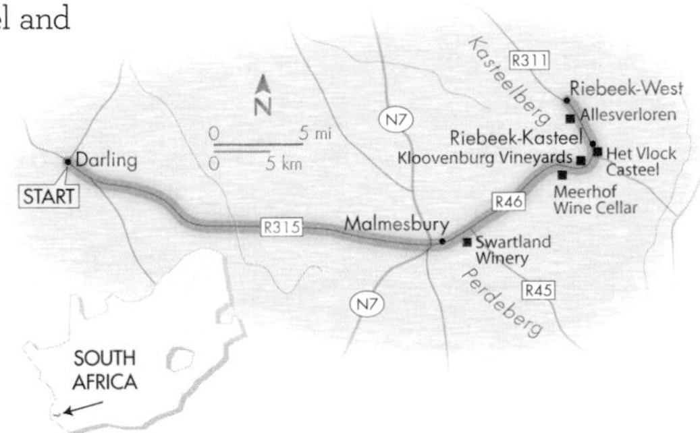

Also Recommended

❶ Prince Edward County "Taste Trail," Ontario

Pick from a list of 31 wineries, restaurants, breweries, creameries, and bistros scattered around the roughly 12-mile (19 km) Taste Trail—County Road 33, linking Wellington, Bloomfield, and Picton. Try the "best bread in the county" at Bloomfield Carriage house. Also in Bloomfield, Slickers County Ice Cream serves vanilla mixed with apple pie, and down the road in Picton is Buddha Dog for "Canada's Best Hotdog."

www.tastetrail.ca

❷ Maple syrup, Vermont

To taste the terroir varieties of maple syrup, visit Sugarhouses along 110 miles (177 km) of Vermont's Rtes. 7 and 100, starting near Burlington and winding through Woodstock and Ladlow. Dakin Farm, Sugarbush Farm, and Green Mountain Sugar House also offer maple fudge, cream, and candy; and at Dakin there is a weekend pancake breakfast.

www.vermontmaple.org

❸ Clams of Cape Cod, Massachusetts

Begin this 160-mile (256 km) circuit at Cape Cod Canal, stopping in Sandwich for Sam's crunchy battered clams. Farther north at Provincetown, visit "The Pot"—the Lobster Pot restaurant famous for its historic harbor view. Then drive to Chatham for the ultimate cape pub, Chatham Squire, and its ultimate clam chowder.

www.visitcapecod.com

❹ Beer trail, Oregon

Portland has more microbreweries than any other U.S. city. Visit Widmer Brothers Gasthaus and Racoon Lodge & Brewpub, then head off to the coast for McMenamins Lighthouse Brewpub. A stunning drive south on Hwy. 101 leads to the 50 beers on tap at Rogue Brewery in Newport.

www.traveloregon.com

❺ Taco trail, Texas

In sprawling San Antonio, begin at about 9 a.m. on East Hildebrand with Taco Taco's giant tortillas overflowing with cheese, chorizo, egg, potato, or refried beans. Stop on San Pedro for a lunch of Teka Molena's deep-fried "puffy" tacos. Arturo's Barbacoa has unusual meat versions, while for purists, the best fish tacos are at Rosario's in King William.

www.visitsanantonio.com

❻ Tequila trail, Mexico

To learn about the Aztec origins of tequila, drive the 30 minutes from Puerta Vallarta to Bucerias. Here the new highway meets the old two-lane highway at the town of Tequila. After visiting a few original distilleries, head back to Puerto for some nighttime tasting at the famous bar, La Casa de Tequila (Morelos 589).

www.visitmexico.com

❼ Two wine routes, Chile

Visit the Aconcagua Valley, about an hour's drive north from Santiago, known for the Cabernet Sauvignon, Syrah, and Carmenere grapes, the latter virtually exclusive to Chile. Southward lies Maipo, the oldest wine region in Chile, where prestigious classics mingle with new boutique labels partnered with French, American, and Italian wine makers.

www.winesofchile.org

❽ Tea plantations, India

From Kochi, the NH 49 travels 68 miles (110 km) into the cool green hills of Munnar, covered in tea plantations. The air is filled with the aroma of tea and spices: pepper, cinnamon, cloves, and cardamom all grow locally. Investigate Munnar's tea museum, then climb 15 miles (25 km) by 4WD up to Kolukkamulai Estate, at 7,873 feet (2,400 m) India's highest plantation.

www.munnar.com

❾ Balsamic vinegar tour, Italy

In Modena, *aceto balsamico* (balsamic vinegar) is made from local grapes and aged in wooden barrels. Taste at an *acetaia* (vinegar-maker) and then take the A1 to nearby Parma to savor local cured meats and pasta topped by nonpareil Parmigiano-Reggiano—Parmesan cheese.

www.lebaccanti.com

❿ Iberian ham route, Spain

Montánchez in the Extremadura is a center for superlative *jamón Iberíco*, Iberian ham, sold in tiny bodegas and bars. Hence you can have a glass of local pitarra wine with your ham sampling. Continue tasting in Monesterio to the south, moving westward for Calera de León and Cabeza la Vaca.

www.spain.info

⓫ Cake treats, Portugal

The most famous place to taste the *pastel de nata*, a small but perfect custard tart, is Antiga Confeitaria de Belém, just 15 minutes from downtown Lisbon, right outside the Monastery of Jerónimos. Here almost 10,000 pastries are sold every day, fresh from the oven. Back in Lisbon, visit the sumptuous 1920s Pastelaria Versailles.

www.pasteisdebelem.pt

⓬ Cider route, France

In May, Cambremer in Normandy hosts the A.O.C. Festival of cider, cheeses, and other local products made to strict standards (Appellation d'Origine Controlée). The village is also the starting point for the 25-mile (40 km) *route du cidre* (cider route). The domaines en route are open for tours and tastes of cider, calvados (apple brandy), and pommeau (a cider/calvados mix).

www.cambremer.com

⓭ Black Forest route, Germany

Loop into the Black Forest region from Villingen-Schwennigen along local roads to Waldkirch and Titisee. Between swathes of meadow and dark green forest, you can sample local specialties—fruit schnapps, rye bread baked over wood, Black Forest ham, and genuine Black Forest gâteau.

www.germany-tourism.de

⓮ Gourmet trails, England

Gourmet Yorkshire offers four self-drive trails focused on local beef, game, cheese, and markets, starting and ending in York. Visit a water buffalo farm in Brompton, eat a "Celebrated" pork pie in Skipton, and have a comforting lavender and brown bread ice cream at Ryelands of Helmsley.

www.gourmetyorkshire.co.uk

INDEX

The following abbreviations are used: NHS = National Historic Site; NM = National Monument; NP = National Park

Index entries for the United States will be found under names of individual states.

Q

R

S

Authors

Rita Ariyoshi
Ian Armitage
Kathy Arnold
Katherine Ashenburg
Jackie Attwood-Dupont
Rosemary Bailey
Christopher P. Baker
Sandra Bardwell
Michael Bright
Steven Brook
Christopher Catling
Marolyn Charpentier
Peter Clubb
Roberta Cosi
Greg Critser
Antonia Cunningham
Bob Devine
Carole Douglis
Fiona Dunlop
Jerry Carmarillo Dunn, Jr.
Gary Ferguson
Mike Gerrard
Nick Hanna
Michael Ivory
Tim Jepson
Ann Jones
Caroline Juler
Alison Kahn
Michael Lewis
Glen Martin
Antony Mason
Mark Miller
Haas H. Mroue
Jenny Myddleton
Dean A. Nadalin
Louise Nicholson
Barbara A. Noe
Geoffrey O'Gara
Donald S. Olsen
Jane Onstott
Bob Rachoweicki
Samantha Reinders
John F. Ross
Katrina Grigg Saito
Victoria Savage
Kay Scheller
William G. Scheller
Jeremy Schmidt
Thomas Schmidt
George Semler
Damien Simonis
Roff Martin Smith
Christopher Somerville
Emma Stanford
Barbara A. Szerlip
John M. Thompson
David St Vincent
Paul Wade
Roger Williams
Dan Whipples
Richard Whitaker
Joe Yogerst

Toucan Books would like to thank:
Brittany R. Brown
Ashley Mathieu
Sally Younger

Picture Credits

Abbreviation: PL (www.photolibrary.com)

2–3 Giovanni Simeone/SIME/4Corners Images; **4** Sylvain Grandadam/age fotostock/PL; **5** Alan Majchrowicz/age fotostock/PL (1); Justin Foulkes/The Travel Library/PL (2); John Warburton-Lee/PL (3); picturegarden/Getty Images (4); Joe Cornish/Britain on View/PL (5); Santiago Fdez Fuentes/age fotostock/PL (6); Witold Skrypczak/Lonely Planet Images (7); niceartphoto/Alamy (8); **8–9** Alan Majchrowicz/age fotostock/PL; **10** Radius Images/PL; **11** Jeremy Woodhouse/Getty Images; **12** Eric Horan/Alamy; **13** Kordcom/age fotostock/PL; **14** Arkansas Department of Parks & Tourism; **15** Greg Ryan & Sally Beyer/PL; **16** Superstock/PL; **17** Visions LLC/PL; **18** James Frank/PL; **19** Macduff Everton/Corbis; **20** Jeff Vanuga/Flirt Collection/PL; **21** Willard Clay/Oxford Scientific/PL; **22** Douglas Cox/Imagestate/PL; **23** Andre Jenny/Alamy; **24–25** StockShot/Alamy; **26** White/PL; **27** David L.Brown/Design Pics Inc/PL; **28** Zach Holmes/Alamy; **29** Robert Shantz/Alamy; **30–31** Ghiotti/Photographer's Choice/Getty; **32** Jim Brandenburg/Minden Pictures/National Geographic Stock; **33** Dan Sherwood/Design Pics Inc/PL; **34** Thomas Hallstein/Ambient Images/PL; **35** John Warden/Superstock/PL; **36** Eric Martin/Iconotec/PL; **37** Riccardo Lombardo/Cuboimages/PL; **38** Jerry Alexander/Lonely Planet Images; **39** Glenn Bartley/All Canada Photos/PL; **40** Robert Francis/South American Pictures; **42** Christian Kober/John Warburton-Lee Photography; **43** Best View Stock/PL; **44** C.Novara/De Agostini Editore; **45** Guenter Fischer/imagebroker.net/PL; **46** FB-Rose/imagebroker.net/PL; **47** Picture Finders/age fotostock/PL; **48** casinozack/Shutterstock; **49** CuboImages srl/Alamy; **50–51** Brian Lawrence/Imagestate/PL; **52** Riccardo Lombardo/Cuboimages/PL; **53** Steve Lewis/Britain on View/PL; **54** Davidmarty/Dreamstime.com; **55** Chris Brink/View Pictures/PL; **56** Nina Korhonen/Nordic Photos/PL; **57** Monica Gumm/White Star/imagebroker.net/PL; **58** O.Alamany & E.Vicens/Corbis; **60–61** Justin Foulkes/The Travel Library/PL; **62** Rolf Hicker/All Canada Photos/PL; **63** Barrett & MacKay/All Canada Photos/PL; **64** Jerry and Marcy Monkman/EcoPhotography.com; **65** Vittorio Sciosia/Cuboimages/PL; **66** Michael Townsend/Getty Images; **67** Mike Briner/Alamy; **68** Michael Gadomski/Animals Animals/PL; **69** Stuart Westmorland/Corbis; **70** Alaska Stock Images/National Geographic Stock; **71** Craig Tuttle/Corbis; **72** Michele Wassell/age fotostock/PL; **73** Visions LLC/PL; **74** Darrell Gulin/Corbis; **75** Ron Dahlquist/Pacific Stock/PL; **76–77** Wojtek Buss/age fotostock/PL; **78** World Pictures/Photoshot; **79** Panoramic Images/Getty Images; **80** Pablo Corral Vega/Corbis; **81** Gavin Hellier/Robert Harding Travel/PL; **82** David Clapp/Oxford Scientific/PL; **83** John Warburton-Lee Photography/Alamy; **84** J & C Sohns/ Picture Press/PL; **85** Doug Pearson/JAI/Corbis; **86** Manfred Gottschalk/Lonely Planet Images; **87** Don Bartell/Alamy; **88–89** Manfred Gottschalk/Lonely Planet Images; **90** Steven Lam/Getty Images; **91** Guenter Fischer/imagebroker.net/PL; **92** Oleg Nikishin/Epsilon/Getty Images; **93** Manfred Gottschalk/Lonely Planet Images; **94–95** Art Kowalsky/Alamy; **96** Werner Otto/age fotostock/PL; **97** Carola Koserowsky/age fotostock/PL; **98** Gerhard Zwerger-Schoner/imagebroker/PL; **99** Giuseppe Masci/Tips Italia/PL; **100** Charles Bowman/age fotostock/PL; **101** Jose Fuste Raga/age fotostock/PL; **102** Jim and Mary Whitmer/Digital Light Source/PL; **103** Isidoro Ruiz Haro/age fotostock/PL; **104** Gerald Hoberman/Hoberman Collection UK/PL; **106–107** John Warburton-Lee/PL; **108** Walter Bibikow/age fotostock/PL; **109** Eryk Jaegermann/Design Pics Inc/PL; **110** Stephen Saks Photography/Alamy; **111** David Muench/Corbis; **112–113** Ronald M.Maratea/Superstock/PL; **114** Gavin Hellier/JAI/Corbis; **115** Don Smetzer/Alamy; **116** Jason Lindsey/Alamy; **117** Richard Cummins/Superstock/PL; **118** David R.Frazier Photolibrary, Inc/Alamy; **119** Stephen Saks/Lonely Planet Images; **120** Gerhard Zwerger-Schoner/imagebroker.net/PL; **121** Rolf Nussbaumer/naturepl.com; **122** Scott T.Smith/Corbis; **123** Richard Broadwell/Beateworks/Corbis; **124** Julie Buehler/Shutterstock; 125 Charlie Munsey/Corbis; **126** William Helsel/age fotostock/PL; **127** Witold Skrypczak/Lonely Planet Images; **128** Stockage/Dreamstime.com; **129** Tristan Deschamps/Photononstop/PL; **130** Andrew Watson/John Warburton-Lee Photography; **131** ©Nagano Prefecture/©JNTO; **132** Martin Rugner/age fotostock/PL; **133** Jochen Knobloch/Picture Press/PL; **134** Michael Nitzschke/PL; **135** Gilles Rigoulet/Hemis/PL; **136** A Demotes/Photononstop/PL; **137** Nicholas Thibaut/Photononstop/PL; **138** Luis Castaneda/age fotostock/PL; **140–141** picturegarden/Getty Images; **142** Alexandra Kobalenko/All Canada Photos/PL; **143** Jerry and Marcy Monkman/EcoPhotography.com/Alamy; **144** Jack Dykinga/Getty Images; **145** Riccardo Savi/Getty Images; **146** Layne Kennedy/Corbis; **147–150** Danita Delimont/Alamy; **151** Radius Images/PL; **152** Michael Routh/Ambient Images/PL; **153** Ian Dagnall/Alamy; **154** Peter M. Wilson/Corbis; **155** Jon Arnold Images Ltd/Alamy; **156–157** Doug Priebe/Alamy; **158** Robert Weight/Ecoscene/Corbis; **159** Robin Smith/PL; **160** Christian Kapteyn/imagebroker/PL; **161** Steven Vidler/Eurasia Press/Corbis; **162–163** George Steinmetz/Corbis; **164** Michele Falzone/JAI/Corbis; **165** blickwinkel/Alamy; **166** Sheila Terry/Robert Harding Travel/PL; **167** Laurence Simon/Tips Italia/PL; **168** Tony Eveling/Alamy; **169** Alberto Nardi/Tips Italia/PL; **170** John Short/Design Pics Inc/PL; **171** Robert Cousins/Robert Harding Travel/PL; **172** Jan Wlodarczyk/The Travel Library/PL; **173** Hoffmann Photography/age fotostock/PL; **174** Upperhall Ltd/Robert Harding Travel/PL; **175** Nigel Pavitt/John Warburton-Lee Photography/PL; **176** Christian Heinrich/imagebroker/PL; **178–179** Joe Cornish/Britain on View/PL; **180** Barrett & MacKay/All Canada Photos/PL; **181** Bilderbuch/Design Pics Inc/PL; **182** Alan Copson/The Travel Library/PL; **183** Craig Brewer/White/PL; **184** Jeff Greenberg/Alamy; **185** Philip Scalia/Alamy; **186** Walter Bibikow/JAI/Corbis; **187** Walter Bibikow/age fotostock/PL, **188** Alan Majchrowicz/age fotostock/PL; **189** Richard Cummins/Superstock; **190** Sylvia Cordaiy Photo Library Ltd/Alamy; **191** Ross Barnett/Lonely Planet Images; **192** Diana Mayfield/Lonely Planet Images; **193** Craig Pershouse/Lonely Planet Images; **194** Rene Mattes/Mauritius/PL; **195** Pixtal Images/PL; **196–197** John Arnold Images/PL; **198** Steve Vidler/Imagestate/PL; **199** J.Boyer/Getty Images; **200** Glenn Beanland/Lonely Planet Images; **201** White/PL; **202** Richard Watson/Britain on View/PL; **203** Renaud Visage/age fotostock/PL; **204** Ken Welsh/Design Pics Inc/PL; **205** imagebroker/Alamy; **206** Bob Krist/Corbis; **208–209** Santiago Fdez Fuentes/age fotostock/PL; **210** Megapress/Alamy; **211** Darwin Wiggett/All Canada Photos/PL; **212–213** Bill Heinsohn.Getty Images; **214** James Lemass/Index Stock Imagery/PL; **215** Richard Cummins/Corbis; **216** Bruce Heinemann/age fotostock/PL; **217** D.Hurst/Alamy; **218** PCL/Alamy; **219** Panoramic Images/Getty Images; **220** Alfredo Maiquez/Lonely Planet Images; **221** Walter Bibikow/age fotostock/PL; **222–223** Mark Eveleigh/Alamy; **224** Terrance Klassen/age fotostock/PL; **225** Almor67/Dreamstime.com; **226** Paul C.Pet/Corbis; **227** Sam DCruz/Shutterstock; **228** Paul Harris/John Warburton-Lee Photography/PL; **229** Brian Lawrence/Imagestate/PL; **230–231** Daniel Hurst/PL; **232** Angelo Cavalli/Superstock/PL; **233** The Travel Library/PL; **234** Adam Jones/Getty Images; **235** Erfgoedhuis Zuid-Holland; **236** David Robertson/The Travel Library/PL; **238–239** Witold Skrypczak/Lonely Planet Images; **240** Barrett & MacKay/All Canada Photos/PL; **241** Brian Jannsen/Alamy; **242–243** Jose Fuste Raga/age fotostock/PL; **244** Danny Lehman/Corbis; **245** Kulla Owaki/ Flirt Collection/PL; **246** Tom Bean/Corbis; **247** Macduff Everton/Corbis; **248** Glen Allison/White/PL; **249** Sergio Pitamitz/Robert Harding Travel/PL; **250** James L.Amos/Peter Arnold Images/PL; **251** Les David Manevitz/Superstock/PL; **252–253** Yoshio Tomil Photo Studio/Aflo Foto Agency/PL; **254** Steve Vidler/Imagestate/PL; **255** Bill Bachmann/Alamy; **256** Walter Bibikow/Jon Arnold Travel/PL; **257** Robert Harding/PL; **258** age fotostock/PL; **259** David R. Frazier Photolibrary, Inc./Alamy; **260** Radius Images/PL; **261** Japan Travel Bureau/PL; **262** Peter Giovannini/imagebroker.net/PL; **263** Russell Young/Jon Arnold Travel/PL; **264** Francisco Gonzalez/age fotostock/PL; **265** Japan Travel Bureau/PL; **266–267** Guido Alberto Rossi/Tips Italia/PL; **268** David Robertson/Alamy; **269** Egmont Strigl/imagebroker.net/PL; **270–271** Jose Fuste Raga/age fotostock/PL; **272** Walter Bibikow/Jon Arnold Travel/PL; **273** Rene Mattes/Hemis/PL; **274** Ghigo Roli/Cubo Images/Robert Harding; **275** Joel Damase/Photononstop/PL; **276** Gerrit Buntrock/Fresh Food Images/PL; **277** Hervé Gyssels/Photononstop/PL; **278** Andrew Stuart/Stringer/Getty Images; **280–281** niceartphoto/Alamy; **282** Bob Krist/Corbis; **283** Jim Sugar/Corbis; **284–285** Donald C. & Priscilla Alexander Eastman; **286** Fredrik Naumann/Panos Pictures; **287** Ian Shaw/Cephas; **288** David Collins/Lonely Planet Images; **289** Mick Elmore/Lonely Planet Images; **290** Owen Lexington/Getty Images; **291** Deidesheimer Hof; **292** Christian Braud/Photononstop/PL; **293** Mick Rock/Cephas; **294** John James/Shutterstock; **295** David Woods/Shutterstock; **296** Yves Talensac/Photononstop/PL; **297** SGM/age fotostock/PL; **298** Heinz Wohner/LOOK-foto/PL; **299** Targa/age fotostock/PL; **300** PhotoStock-Israel/Alamy; **301** Per Karlsson, BKWine 2/Alamy; **302–303** Glow Images/PL; **304** Tono Labra/age fotostock/PL; **305** Alan Copson/JAI/Corbis; **306** Juergen Richter/LOOK-foto/PL; **307** Alan Copson/Jon Arnold Travel/PL; **308** Fraser Hall/Robert Harding Travel/PL; **309** Hoberman Collection/PL; **310** Alain Proust/Cephas.

COVER PICTURES

Front cover: Gavin Hellier/JAI/Corbis.
Back cover: Yuriy Davats/Shutterstock.
Spine: Tom Morrison/Getty Images.

Drives of a Lifetime

Published by the National Geographic Society
John M. Fahey, Jr., President and Chief Executive Officer
Gilbert M. Grosvenor, Chairman of the Board
Tim T. Kelly, President, Global Media Group
John Q. Griffin, Executive Vice President;
President, Publishing
Nina D. Hoffman, Executive Vice President;
President, Book Publishing Group

Prepared by the Book Division
Barbara Brownell Grogan, Vice President and Editor in Chief
Marianne R. Koszorus, Director of Design
Barbara A. Noe, Senior Editor
Carl Mehler, Director of Maps
Lawrence M. Porges, Project Editor
Olivia Garnett, Mary Stephanos, Contributors
R. Gary Colbert, Production Director
Jennifer A. Thornton, Managing Editor
Meredith C. Wilcox, Administrative Director, Illustrations

Manufacturing and Quality Management
Christopher A. Liedel, Chief Financial Officer
Phillip L. Schlosser, Vice President
Chris Brown, Technical Director
Nicole Elliott, Manager
Rachel Faulise, Manager

Created by Toucan Books Ltd
Ellen Dupont, Editorial Director
Helen Douglas-Cooper, Senior Editor
Peter Clubb, Andrew Kerr-Jarrett, Alice Peebles,
Victoria Savage, Amy Smith, Editors
Jackie Attwood-Dupont, Editorial Assistant
Leah Germann, Designer
Christine Vincent, Picture Manager
Sharon Southren with Mia Stewart-Wilson, Picture Researchers
Caroline Hunt, Proofreader
Marie Lorimer, Indexer

The National Geographic Society is one of the world's largest nonprofit scientific and educational organizations. Founded in 1888 to "increase and diffuse geographic knowledge," the Society works to inspire people to care about the planet. It reaches more than 325 million people worldwide each month through its official journal, *National Geographic*, and other magazines; National Geographic Channel; television documentaries; music; radio; films; books; DVDs; maps; exhibitions; school publishing programs; interactive media; and merchandise. National Geographic has funded more than 9,000 scientific research, conservation and exploration projects and supports an education program combating geographic illiteracy. For more information, visit nationalgeographic.com.

For more information, please call 1-800-NGS LINE (647-5463) or write to the following address:

National Geographic Society
1145 17th Street N.W.
Washington, D.C. 20036-4688 U.S.A.

Visit us online at www.nationalgeographic.com

For information about special discounts for bulk purchases, please contact National Geographic Books Special Sales: ngspecsales@ngs.org

For rights or permissions inquiries, please contact National Geographic Books Subsidiary Rights: ngbookrights@ngs.org

ISBN 978-1-4262-0677-1
ISBN 978-1-4262-0773-0 (deluxe edition)

Library of Congress Cataloging-in-Publication Data
Drives of a lifetime : 500 of the world's most spectacular trips / introduction by Keith Bellows.
p. cm.
Includes index.
ISBN 978-1-4262-0677-1 (hardcover)
1. Automobile travel--Guidebooks.
GV1024.D75 2010
796.7--dc22

2010026609

Printed in the United States of America

10/RRDW/1

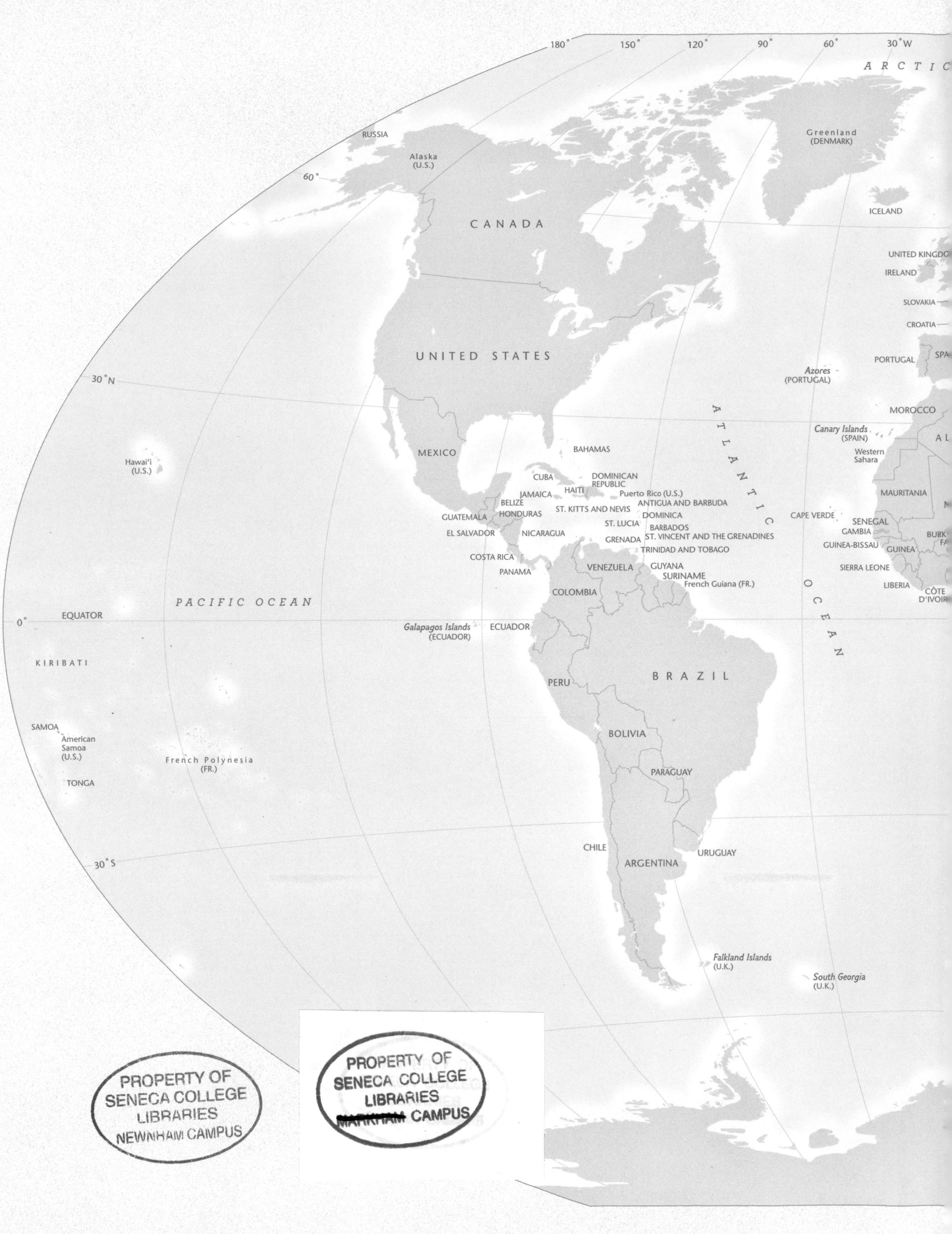
180°
150°
120°
90°
60°
30°W
ARCTIC
RUSSIA
Alaska (U.S.)
60°
Greenland (DENMARK)
ICELAND
CANADA
UNITED KINGDO
IRELAND
SLOVAKIA
CROATIA
UNITED STATES
PORTUGAL
SPA
Azores (PORTUGAL)
30°N
MOROCCO
ATLANTIC
Canary Islands (SPAIN)
MEXICO
BAHAMAS
Western Sahara
Hawai'i (U.S.)
CUBA
DOMINICAN REPUBLIC
HAITI
JAMAICA
Puerto Rico (U.S.)
BELIZE
ANTIGUA AND BARBUDA
MAURITANIA
GUATEMALA
HONDURAS
ST. KITTS AND NEVIS
DOMINICA
CAPE VERDE
SENEGAL
GAMBIA
EL SALVADOR
NICARAGUA
ST. LUCIA
BARBADOS
ST. VINCENT AND THE GRENADINES
GRENADA
GUINEA-BISSAU
GUINEA
TRINIDAD AND TOBAGO
COSTA RICA
VENEZUELA
GUYANA
SIERRA LEONE
PANAMA
SURINAME
French Guiana (FR.)
LIBERIA
CÔTE D'IVOIR
COLOMBIA
PACIFIC OCEAN
OCEAN
0°
EQUATOR
Galapagos Islands (ECUADOR)
ECUADOR
KIRIBATI
PERU
BRAZIL
SAMOA
American Samoa (U.S.)
BOLIVIA
French Polynesia (FR.)
PARAGUAY
TONGA
CHILE
URUGUAY
30°S
ARGENTINA
Falkland Islands (U.K.)
South Georgia (U.K.)